After Servitude

After Servitude

ELUSIVE PROPERTY AND THE ETHICS OF KINSHIP
IN BOLIVIA

Mareike Winchell

UNIVERSITY OF CALIFORNIA PRESS

University of California Press
Oakland, California

© 2022 by Mareike Winchell

Library of Congress Cataloging-in-Publication Data
Names: Winchell, Mareike, author.
Title: After servitude : elusive property and the ethics of kinship in Bolivia /
    Mareike Winchell.
Description: Oakland, California : University of California Press, [2022] |
    Includes bibliographical references and index.
Identifiers: LCCN 2021052485 (print) | LCCN 2021052486 (ebook) |
    ISBN 9780520386433 (hardback) | ISBN 9780520386440 (paperback) |
    ISBN 9780520386457 (ebook)
Subjects: LCSH: Social movements—Bolivia—Ayopaya (Province) | Land
    tenure—Bolivia—Ayopaya (Province) | Social classes—Bolivia—Ayopaya
    (Province) | Ayopaya (Bolivia : Province)—History.
Classification: LCC HN273.5 .W56 2022 (print) | LCC HN273.5 (ebook) |
    DDC 306.0984/23—dc23/eng/20211209
LC record available at https://lccn.loc.gov/2021052485
LC ebook record available at https://lccn.loc.gov/2021052486

Manufactured in the United States of America

28 27 26 25 24 23 22
10 9 8 7 6 5 4 3 2 1

For Palca

CONTENTS

ILLUSTRATIONS

PREFACE

Gregorio Condorí pointed toward a pile of sunken adobe and wood fragments overgrown by grass shoots and tender eucalyptus stalks. "The master's house," he remarked. It was drizzling lightly that morning as I joined several Quechua farmers, children of former hacienda laborers, to harvest peaches near the rubble.[1] Afterward, we sat on a hill and devoured the crisp, almost-ripe fruit, gazing out over a sea of vibrant green potato plots below. Gregorio, an Indigenous Quechua farmer and trained agronomist, had planted the peaches when his parents died some years before. His elder sister, whose dry goods store I often frequented in town, had sorrowfully recalled the violent treatment their parents endured when they worked without pay growing corn and potatoes for the hacienda master, but on this day the orchard felt oddly serene.

After eating, we stored the remaining peaches in grain bags to bring back to town, where they would be dehydrated to make *mocochinchi* juice. Then we wandered through the orchard. I asked Gregorio whether he planned to pursue a land title through a new Bolivian government program. He shrugged dismissively. "For what? It's half gone anyway." Erosion had eaten away at his land, with a meter of soil falling into the Sacambaya River during the previous rainy season. I persisted: "But how do people distinguish their land or know whose is whose if they don't have a title?" Gregorio laughed at my naïve question. "People know their land like they know how to play a guitar. They just know [*sabenps*]," he replied firmly, his Spanish inflected by a Quechua dialect.[2] Although the land lacked a property title, Gregorio's long familiarity with place and neighbors made paper regimes unnecessary. Moreover, while the state's new land titling program promised to formalize property rights, for many Ayopayan farmers it also risked splintering existing land use traditions. This was especially true in cases, like Gregorio's, in which contemporary land use had been established by patterns of labor and residence under an earlier system of bonded labor or *pongueaje*.[3]

I first met Gregorio Condorí in April 2011, while I was carrying out ethnographic fieldwork in the town of Independencia, located in the rural province of Ayopaya.[4] As I rested beside a bright turquoise fountain in the town square, he approached and offered to rent me a cabin. Seven months later, we sat together with peach nectar dripping from our hands and faces while Gregorio described how he had inherited this plot. As hacienda workers, his parents had qualified for property through the state's formal land redistribution program, which began in 1953. While haciendas originated in colonial land grants (encomiendas) that were first formalized in 1645, in Ayopaya this labor system persisted until the mid-twentieth century.[5] Residents, including Gregorio's sister, recalled how their parents had been forced to "serve" the hacienda masters as domestic servants, tenant farmers, sheep and cattle herders, and producers of cheese and fermented corn beer. Gregorio's family was not alone in shouldering this burdensome past. In Ayopaya many Quechua farmers with whom I spoke recounted how relatives, siblings, parents, and grandparents had been whipped, beaten, and subjected to the sexual whims of hacienda masters. Those who fought back, either through labor strikes or organized ambushes on haciendas, were frequently tortured and imprisoned.[6]

The state's formal abolition of forced labor in 1952 promised to change these conditions. Yet like many other Ayopayan farmers, Gregorio's parents had found state promises of titled property elusive. His father had belonged to an organized group of hacienda workers who struggled for land titles, petitioning state agencies and ultimately pursuing a lawsuit. When that proved unsuccessful, they organized labor strikes and ambushes on hacienda estates to chase out recalcitrant landlords. But through a legal loophole in how the property was defined, the master had avoided the estate's liquidation in full. As a result, a title, and its accompanying assurance of legitimate ownership, never materialized. Thus, while the hacienda building now lay in ruins, both strife with its earlier master and the sense of doubt such strife produced in the present could not be relegated to a distant past.

Gregorio's peach orchard points to the ways that histories of violence are compressed and materialized in contemporary land and social relations.[7] Ayopaya's foggy mountain crags are dotted with elderberry trees where servant relatives were tied and whipped; they also house the rubble of old adobe walls and barbed wire fencing, testaments to the violent enclosures and dispossessions that defined the hacienda system. As we finished lunch later that day, Gregorio spoke in hushed Quechua to one of his friends about an ongoing land dispute with the late master's son, who owned the green potato plots next to Gregorio's orchard. The dispute went back to 1957, yet in 2012 it still remained unresolved. Yet when I suggested to Gregorio that officials at Bolivia's Instituto Nacional de Reforma Agraria (National Institute for Agrarian Reform, INRA), could help resolve this dispute, he bristled: "They are the ones who gave [his Mestizo neighbors] land titles in the first place!" With this, Gregorio summarily dismissed the notions both that Morales-era government agencies were natural allies of rural Indigenous people and that firmer property rights offered essential routes to indigenous empowerment.

Such deep-seated pessimism toward institutional projects of Indigenous and peasant justice has long defined rural Quechua perceptions of the state in Ayopaya. In a 1957 letter, Teofilo Garcia, the union leader representing former laborers of the very same hacienda where Gregorio's mother had worked, called on state agencies to confer the promised titles or risk further demoralization: "Será justicia" (This would be justice), he wrote. Justice, in Teofilo's formulation, remains slippery, speculative, and ever-elusive: its contingencies constrain it to the conditional tense.[8]

In the months that followed, I learned more about the Bolivian government's furtive efforts to address this conditional nature of justice. The causes of impediments to Indigenous land rights encountered renewed scrutiny under President Morales (2006–19), whose party promised to redistribute land to Indigenous farmers and peasants across former hacienda and plantation regions, including Ayopaya.[9] Not only in state ministries but also in the crowded corridors of government institutions like INRA, I became familiar with the work entailed in revolutionary efforts to produce, affirm, and distribute property. Property, in such efforts, exceeded the problem of titled land; rather, it connoted a broader understanding of historical repair. That is, property would allow the living kin of indentured servants to reclaim ownership over land but also, with it, their very selves. As Gregorio's rebuke of my suggestion of land titling showed, however, this process faced significant opposition, including by the very subjects the reform promised to aid.

I had been living in Cochabamba city for the preceding five months before moving to Independencia. As an avid reader of national newspapers and through volunteer work with two Bolivian pro-Indigenous agrarian organizations, I had been closely following contemporary policy efforts aimed at decolonizing Bolivian society, including Agrarian Reform Law (3525), a 2010 revision to the 1996 Agrarian Reform law, which focused on securing firmer land rights as well as eliminating labor oppression and "servitude." Recalling Fausto Reinaga's powerful and highly influential critique of hacienda labor and sexual abuses in *Tesis India* (1971), these policy efforts treated rural land and labor relations as charged microcosms of broader projects of revolutionary change—namely, of how to forge Indigenous justice against Bolivia's entrenched racial hierarchy. For urban activists and state reformers, rural labor practices in which Indigenous farmers and peasants worked for Mestizo bosses pointed to uninterrupted legacies of colonial agriculture, ones synthesized in the figure of the hacienda estate. In the aftermath of massive Indigenous and peasant labor movements that rocked the nation between 1999 and 2005, demanding the decolonization of a neoliberal, colonial order, eventually toppling President Sánchez de Lozada in 2006, and bringing President Evo Morales Ayma to power, rural practices of labor, alliance, and kinship that are deeply familiar to people like Gregorio Condorí came to be recast as vicious obstructions to a more just, more egalitarian, future.

I returned to Cochabamba in 2012, this time to conduct archival research and interviews with government officials at INRA. There I encountered what I would come to think of as an origin story about land titling, one that cast Bolivia's hinterlands as backward spaces still tenaciously gripped by a colonial labor past. This narrative acted to legitimize further government interventions, including land titling but also social and educational efforts to change historical perceptions and political behaviors. Yet as farmers like Gregorio taught me, Ayopayans did not always take kindly to these governmental aid programs. The month I arrived, unionized Quechua and Aymara farmers voted to reject a proposal to convert the region into native community land. In a place where Indigenous and Mestizo residents lived and worked side by side (and where land had often been granted through informal land gifts), titled property carried notable risks. In fact, I never dared ask him directly, but I suspected that Gregorio's land claims stemmed from his mother's work as a servant on a nearby hacienda.[10] Hence, while many Bolivians welcomed land titling, in Ayopaya it seemed this initiative was double-edged.[11] For farmers who had benefited from earlier land gifts and labor exchanges, these property titling programs carried with them threats of further Indigenous land dispossession as well as assimilation within nationalist paradigms of ownership and repair.

Gregorio's disillusion with land titles offers a key jumping-off point from which to rethink the common yoking of legally-defined property to liberty. It invites us to attend to the relations to land and history that property regimes try to supplant but which also persist despite property titling initiatives. In fact, Gregorio's elusive property title did not prevent him from fostering other attachments to land and people and, with them, to the region's bonded past. He planted peach trees in the fertile pockets of land between crumbling hacienda ruins, and pine trees at its peripheries. These efforts drew from his training as an agronomist, which he completed with financial help from his godfather, a member of the province's Mestizo elite.[12] As a schoolchild, Gregorio lived with his godfather, a hacienda-owning priest, where he had worked unpaid in exchange for food and a place to sleep. His orchard also gained support through Gregorio's auspicious ties to more-than-humans. Each month he hosted an offering (*q'oa*) for the Pachamama, an earth-being associated with fertility.[13] On those occasions I joined him and his employees around a small fire, where we chewed coca, smoked hand-rolled cigarettes, and drank *trago* (cane liquor) and corn beer (*chicha*), dripping some on the soil *Pachamamapaq* (for the Pachamama). Like the peach trees, these projects sprung forth from the depths of intimate violence, on land where parents had toiled unpaid and suffered the whip for any infraction.

What does it mean to refuse state gifts of property? What remains of justice in property's wake? For farmers like Gregorio, land was central even as property remained elusive and insufficient. In Ayopaya this widespread uncertainty about normative promises of liberty through property lent support to alternate engagements with racialized dispossession through grounded, if deeply fraught, relations among former servant and master families. While urban activists and state reformers whom I met frequently cast these informal land use practices and arrangements of Quechua alliance with Mestizos as the dead weights of a pernicious colonial tradition, for rural farmers like Gregorio these practices also marked important lines of attachment and obligation across a divisive past. Through such practices, rural farmers strove to seek redress for deeply injurious pasts, sustaining attachments to places and among people who were variously entangled in the hacienda's debris. By insisting upon accountability as a problem of abiding connections both to landscapes and across families, Ayopayans sought historical redress in ways that opposed the spatial and temporal abstractions that have long defined institutional paradigms of property.

Introduction

This book focuses on ethical disagreements about how to remedy violent labor pasts. In Bolivia the past thirty years have seen a dramatic upsurge in organized struggles and institutional reforms aimed at securing Indigenous rights to land, resources, and sovereignty. Yet even while these efforts have sought to dispense with all aspects of a deeply oppressive earlier hacienda system, Quechua farmers in the rural Bolivian province where I carried out research inhabit a milieu defined by ambiguous ownership regimes and abiding ties to Mestizo families who violently mistreated their kin. The practices that Quechua farmers, gold miners, peasant unionists, and relatives of indentured hacienda servants and Mestizo masters use to navigate this space are distinct from organized struggles for rights, but they share a concern with clarifying the terms of historical accountability: the debts and obligations attached to long-run histories of colonial dispossession and violence. This raises several key questions: How are injurious pasts redeployed by the dispossessed? What are the relational possibilities of history where land rights appear both elusive and insufficient as mechanisms of historical redress?

After Servitude offers the first ethnographic study of Indigenous land politics in Ayopaya, a center of antihacienda militancy since the 1940s.[1] It analyzes competing orientations to Bolivia's earlier hacienda system to demonstrate how they shape present-day mining and agrarian relations as well as Quechua land struggles in Ayopaya. During seventeen months of fieldwork carried out with former militants, Quechua farmers, Indigenous miners and domestic laborers, peasant unionists, and municipal officials in Ayopaya, as well as pro-Indigenous activists, agronomical volunteers, and agrarian officials in Cochabamba, I learned about the Movimiento Al Socialismo (Movement toward Socialism, MAS) Party's (2006–19) revolutionary land titling program.[2] Like its Republican and colonial predecessors, the program was premised on faith in titled property as a way to clarify land use, upend unpaid labor, and thereby craft modern citizens. Committed to bureaucratic transparency, viable agricultural subsidy programs, greater gender equity in ownership, and supporting Indigenous sovereignty, especially through collective land rights, agrarian reformers with whom I worked saw land titling as foundational to a nationalist, decolonial project of political change.

The urgency of land titling within MAS's decolonial agenda followed from broader demands for resource sovereignty and Indigenous rights that accompanied nationwide protests and political organizing against neoliberal austerity measures since the 1980s, and which self-consciously drew both from mid-twentieth-century peasant struggles for land rights and from a long history of Indigenous rebellion since the early colonial period.[3] From 2006 to 2019, the MAS party sought to make good on these promises through a nationwide reform program, El Proceso de Cambio. The program installed new gender quotas, increases in minimum wage, dramatic advances in maternal and child health, new funding for rural infrastructure and resource development, particularly hydrocarbons and gas, and revisions to Bolivia's 1996 Agrarian Reform Law. Through a revived land titling property, agrarian officials promised to improve Indigenous livelihoods, conferring stable, legally defensible land rights upon rural people whom reformers saw as especially vulnerable to land grabs and labor abuses.[4] Members of the MAS party often cast this project as one of revolutionizing Bolivia by way of overcoming "slavery"—a term used to connote the racialized inequalities that derive from colonial labor regimes and are reproduced by neoliberal economic policies and Mestizo governance regimes.

In Ayopaya these state programs of Indigenous uplift were perceived as double-edged: Indigenous land titling promised to secure property rights but it also absorbed rural people into national bureaucracies and in many cases turned resource rights over to the Bolivian state. Collective land titling, too, retained governmental control over subterranean resources while frequently marginalizing families who, because of relatives' work as servants, had weaker land claims. Moreover, Quechua residents were also disturbed to find that this program could be manipulated by Mestizo residents to cement hierarchical ownership regimes. Their formalization in turn allowed elites to withdraw from older aid relations with former servants and workers.[5] In response, many Ayopayans whom I met disputed the normative premises of property not only as titled land but also as a broader orientation to the region's labor past, and to the families of former hacienda masters in particular.

Gregorio Condorí, for instance, dispensed with titles but also privileged existing attachments to land, earth-beings, and to former masters; a godparenting arrangement with a local parish priest allowed him to pursue an education and, later, to found a successful agroecological organization. Other Quechua farmers insisted that Mestizo elites supply money to their school-age godchildren (and the kin of parents' and grandparents' servants), that the son of the hacienda master buy a coffin for his childhood servant, and that *hacendado* heirs should adopt children and half-kin who were abandoned by their father, the master. Failure to acquiesce to these demands could have dramatic consequences for Mestizo mining bosses, fueling legal challenges and labor strikes and eliciting bankruptcy or forced retreat to the city.

For Quechua farmers and mine workers with whom I carried out this research, abiding structures of racial hierarchy in the Bolivian countryside revealed the false optimism of property: the idea that power relations had been equalized by the legal transfer of ownership. To navigate these hierarchical entrenchments, Ayopayan workers undertook actions that insisted upon wealth as an artifact of earlier racial violence that carried with it necessary debts to the people on whose labor, sweat, tears, and bloodshed those hierarchies were built. Those debts could not be left to institutional programs of resource redistribution but instead required Quechua farmers' unending vigilance in putting pressure on Mestizo elites through legal actions, labor organizing, and road blockades. In their insistence that reparation take shape as *action*—and as Mestizos' concrete responsiveness to workers and neighboring villagers—Indigenous Ayopayans contested the passivity enabled by justice as an institutional project.[6]

These demands reveal property's elusiveness as a model of restorative mastery, but they also show how such absences are creatively inhabited to pursue other pathways of historical redress. In fact, despite their overlap with state-based programs of colonial reparation and repair, the practices I describe relied upon an ethical rubric that is fundamentally at odds with the insistence on temporal and spatial alienability that underpins land titling. In insisting upon answerability to an ongoing history of racial labor violence, Quechua farmers cut through Mestizos' efforts to diffuse responsibility by evoking distant government bodies and abstract citizenship logics. This allowed for a clarity about the continued grip of racial inequalities stemming from hacienda servitude. Hence, Ayopayans' repurposing of inherited intimacies and obligations enabled demands for accountability from Mestizo bosses in ways that pushed back against the closures sanctioned by institutional paradigms of property. That justice might be sought through the creative reworking of inherited ties poses key challenges to normative ideals of historical rupture that guide rights-based approaches to Indigenous dispossession in twenty-first century Bolivia, and elsewhere.

KNOTTING AS THE REPURPOSING OF RUINS

For Ayopayan interlocuters and government agrarian officials alike, the nation's twentieth-century history of labor subjection remained productively open: more than a conclusive record of past events, history instead constituted an *ongoing* site of care, political struggle, and ethical claim-making. To attend to these active engagements with Ayopaya's violent labor past, *After Servitude* undertakes an ethnography of history. Subsequent chapters focus on the range of ways that Bolivians sought to address a divisive past, including through relations of informal land gifting, adoption, and the circulation of money, resources, and aid from the families of former hacienda masters to servants. I name this condition of life "after servitude"—*after* simultaneously connoting sequential ordering, pursuit, a continual following, in the style or imitation of, commemorative naming and in accordance with the nature or desires of another thing.[7] Such practices point to the *multiple lives of afterness*, in which intimate ties and affects emerged as crucial devices for negotiating vulnerabilities stemming from earlier colonial labor regimes.[8] Through relations among people and to spirits, more-than-humans, and land as a site of temporal accretion, Ayopayans navigated history less as a series of epochs to be overcome but rather as a collection of cross-cutting and interwoven threads that could be cultivated in order to transform the present.

My analysis focuses on illuminating the messy relational knots through which Bolivian histories of sexual and labor violence are inherited, challenged, and remade.[9] These knots are analytic devices, but they spring from people's varying efforts to direct and redirect attachments across time and space.[10] For instance, Gregorio's peach orchard was dotted by the ruins of earlier hacienda buildings, with adobe and wood fragments testifying to a recent, oppressive past. However, this did not foreclose his effort to remake the place into something new, both by planting young fruit trees and by allowing time to weather and break down the old adobe foundation. Where the old structure once stood, young eucalyptus trees slowly grew over the adobe. Here, I develop the figure of such knotting to make sense of the various ways that Quechua Ayopayans imagined but also demanded attachment, insisting that Mestizo people remain bound to and beholden by history in ways that they did not necessarily want.[11] These knots, unlike more common ideas of historical ruins, were not just things ordinary people found or were left with; they were a *doing* and an active binding.[12] Recalling the English language phrase "to be tied down," knotting draws together a range of practices of historical claim-making.[13] Using such a knot conferred local people both with possibilities for building and renewing lines of attachment and obligation across landscapes but also for critically assessing people in positions of (often racialized) economic and political power.

This book concentrates, in particular, on three such processes of knotting, which also constitute paradigms of historical redress: kinship, property, and exchange. First, I examine how Quechua groups in Ayopaya mobilized kinship as a model of authority and a relational structure for demanding accountability after violence. Practices of making kin through godparenting, adoption, and religious sponsorship offered former hacienda families a means to convert stigmatized forms of intimacy into socially valued if precarious arrangements of aid centered on the figure of a generous, devout mother. Next, I trace property as an aspirational object that is contingent on its continued enactment but also liable to failure and reinscription. This became especially clear in the range of technical, bureaucratic, relational, and physical practices by which agrarian officials sought to produce property both as a naturalized object and a future promise. Finally, I consider how kinship- and property-based understandings of historical redress intertwined to give way to a conjunctural understanding of wealth as historical accretion. By insisting that authority remain tethered to history, Ayopayans pushed back against ideals of alienability and detachment that traverse revolutionary land titling efforts and new arrangements of gold, sodalite, and antimony mining.

Ayopayans' insistence on this binding of past and present critically reframes scholarly debates about time and the political, cutting through the tendency to narrate the lives of vulnerable people as sites of *potential* awakening and critique. Instead, the ethnographic material presented in this book demonstrates the *actualities* of claim-making that occur through the critical refashioning of inherited affective ties and labor and kinship relations.[14] This is a crucial shift of analysis, especially in light of how languages of victimization and impeded modernity have been used to deny agency and political reason to the formerly colonized.

In Bolivia late colonial debates focused on the problem of Indigenous groups' readiness for full political rights. That Indigenous populations were often victimized by Criollo agrarian and mining bosses, colonial administrators argued, was evidence that they were not yet ready to be granted citizenship. Late colonial concerns with racial hierarchy and inherited dependencies haunted twenty-first-century agrarian reform efforts. Agrarian reform officials with whom I spoke frequently cast Ayopaya as a lawless, backward place that was problematically bogged down by its labor past. While the province was a center of anticolonial revolutionary activity leading up to Bolivian Independence in 1825 and a heart of antihacienda militancy in the mid-twentieth century, many officials described Ayopaya as a place defined by earlier conditions of hacienda servitude.[15] For the state to secure the uplift of Indigenous residents, such residents themselves would have to adopt more critical, mature political outlooks that appreciated that "the hacienda is past."[16]

Around the world, promises of a sovereign future have been used to defend extreme acts of violence against Indigenous populations, including bodily harms as well as cultural assimilation programs, denials of land rights, forced sterilizations, and the deculturation (and in some cases, deaths) of children in settler-run boarding schools.[17] Despite President Evo Morales's emphasis on forging a revolutionary break from the nation's colonial and neocolonial pasts, land titling programs carried out under his government preserved this faith in property as a belated means to secure Indigenous liberty.[18] The agrarian reform program that I examine reproduced aspects of racial formations defined by an insistence that Indigenous subjects be improved and integrated through their exposure to modern systems of contract law.[19] This reveals rights-based ideals of emancipation through contract as belonging firmly within, rather than outside of, enduring imperial formations.[20] Contemporary Bolivia further clarifies how efforts at political repair rooted in this emancipatory model conjoin with ongoing projects of assimilative subject-making and possessive extractivism.[21] Indeed, Bolivian laws conferring Indigenous recognition since the 1990s have gone hand-in-hand with juridical efforts to constrain and invalidate Indigenous claims to resources and land.[22]

Perhaps for this reason, many of the Ayopayans I met decoupled their struggles for historical redress from institutional arcs of property both as a program for redistributing land and of revived cultural identity related to national frameworks of unified ethnicity. Alongside governmental land titling projects, Ayopayans rearticulated the flow of goods, money, labor, and aid from Mestizo elites to Indigenous families as modes of historical redress. Such practices allowed them to made claims upon one another and upon the past in situations where hierarchies remain durable, even constitutive, features of shared relational life. Perceived through the prism of these contending practices of historical claim-making, Bolivian agrarian reform measures appear both elusive but also nonabsolute as an arena for addressing the long shadow cast by earlier hacienda violence and Indigenous land dispossession.

My account attends to the moral and political trappings of property, but it also excavates the practices of historical redress that a contract-based formation of sovereignty (as self-possession and land ownership) disallows. Indigenous farmers' demands for ongoing relations with Mestizo families in Ayopaya complicate familiar paradigms of postcolonial sovereignty that insist dispossessed groups must achieve a degree of autonomy from the past, thereby reclaiming their own mastery over land, resources, and their own labor. While I found these hierarchical entanglements that defined rural life among Mestizo and Indigenous people deeply disturbing, Ayopayan interlocuters invited me to reassess the idea that such entanglements only work negatively or as constraints.[23] Against reformers' insistence that rural people leave history and one another behind, the people I came to know strove to reshape the terms of such entanglements to assert a different vision of human flourishing. Their efforts followed from an awareness of the injuries perpetrated in the name of sovereign citizenship but also from a view of lived sociality as shot through with mutual dependencies, willed and unwilled. This insistence on the binding of past to present illustrates a more capacious approach to justice beyond property, but it also raises broader questions about the obligations that history places upon us as varied, if unequal, heirs of colonial violence in other parts of the world.

KNOT I. KINSHIP AS HISTORICAL ETHICS

Kinship is often viewed as ahistorical—as occurring outside of, and prior to, modern economic relations.[24] This presumption guides modern legal regimes of multicultural recognition, which frequently cast as authentic only those Indigenous relations that adhere to expectations of a continuity of kinship over time.[25] Although this assumption of the separation of economy from kinship has been readily challenged by scholars in a range of disciplines, it has continued to define the ways that contemporary state officials (and many labor scholars) have come to narrate Bolivia's servitude past—namely, the hacienda system was conceived principally as a matter of economic and labor abuses that dispossessed laborers of land and agricultural fruits.[26] The remedy to that dispossession lay in granting Indigenous laborers secure land rights. This characterization of the problem overlooks how practices of concubinage, forced adoption, sexual violence, and honorific languages of parentage supported Ayopaya's hacienda system. Agrarian estates there have relied on forms of sexual labor and family ties that spill over neat boundaries between the domains of paid labor ("economy") and sexual relations and family ties ("kinship").

This book explores the centrality of family and sexual relations to hacienda bondage and asks what this immersion of ostensibly discrete spheres of kinship and economy means not only for understanding earlier servitude but also for contemporary efforts to seek redress for this violent past (Hartman 1997: 79; Moten 2003: 18).[27] My fieldwork with Quechua farmers, Mestizo bosses, rural municipal staff, and city-based agrarian officials in Cochabamba suggested that contemporary Bolivian reform efforts centered upon property as a method of historical repair also had dramatic consequences for existing evaluations of kinship, specifically of godparenting ties, adoptive relations, and practices of gift-giving and patronal aid among relatives of Mestizo masters and Indigenous servants. The occlusion of kinship from modern economy, in this instance, was not an accident so much as a matter of design: policymakers hoped that property (here in the form of titled land) would install firmer divisions around economic activity, thereby allowing rural Indigenous people to extricate themselves from labor-based and kinship dependencies rooted in earlier agrarian servitude.

The liberating connotations of modern property were first spelled out by Adam Smith, whose moral philosophy ([1776] 1977) sought natural laws of economics premised on an ostensibly universal proclivity for contractual exchange.[28] Utilitarianism, or a theory of exchange based on use-value, promised to displace what classical economists cast as the dead weight of tradition and its obstruction of progress.[29] Peasant families, community values, and an emphasis on subsistence had to be replaced by individual self-interest, economic calculus, and the search for "equilibrium" as an ostensibly natural state of the economy. This would make it possible to cast off feudal bonds and the chains of monarchic and church authority as well as religious superstition. Orientations to land and resources that did not meet the criteria of utilitarian exchange were deemed "premodern," "uncivilized," and "savage." The notion of self-interested exchange (as a natural proclivity that would find equilibrium outside culture, kinship, or society) operated not only as a historical accompaniment but also a key accomplice to colonial slavery and Indigenous dispossession.[30] Following Bhandar (2018: 30), Smith's human (a subject imbued with a natural proclivity for self-interested exchange against the bonds of family, church, or community) here arises as a thoroughly *racialized* paragon of subjectivity.[31]

In the Andes and elsewhere these "natural" laws were deployed not just as philosophical reflections but as policy guides that facilitated and legitimated sixteenth- and seventeenth-century mercantile expansion and then imperial trade.[32] Colonial jurists, building from Smith, defended Indigenous land dispossession and Black enslavement by arguing that such groups were unfamiliar with or incapable of cultivating property, thus forfeiting their rights to others who were. Spanish imperialists sought to upend precolonial traditions of kinship-based alliance and communal landholding, both through divine possession (as *dominio*) and then secularized property.[33] Colonial kinship and gender relations were constrained not only by Victorian and Catholic ideals of modesty and virtue but also by colonists' need to secure Mestizo property institutions through gender normativity.[34]

Blood-based definitions of kinship had long served as key mechanisms for the legal transfer of wealth in European inheritance systems (Levi-Strauss 1955). Such transfers faced new instabilities in colonial settings, where racial superiority and ownership had to be cleaved apart from the slippery intimacies of family life and domestic labor bondage.[35] Legal definitions of legitimate kinship (e.g., genealogical models of *limpieze de sangre* in Latin America and institutions of the Christian White family in the United States and Canada) here became crucial for colonial administrators' efforts to police bloodlines and, with them, to secure economic privileges rooted in what they took to be the supremacy of Whiteness and the illegitimacy of Indigenous landholding (Collins 1998; TallBear 2018: 146).[36] In the Andes alienable landholding was first imposed when colonists constricted sprawling kinship-based networks into towns whose male heads of (nuclear) households owed the colonial state tribute, requiring new paid labor economies in agriculture and mining.[37] Indigenous women's "unruly" sexualities arose as crucial sites of discipline and containment given early colonial economic and spiritual interests in securing property through languages of divine ownership and racial genealogy (Burns 1999: 1–15). Later, the installing of modern kinship ties in nuclear households went hand-in-hand with the colonial production of cheap (and bonded) labor and the shoring up of racial hierarchy.[38]

Conversely, the fragmentation of Indigenous kinship relations (which rarely ascribed to European ideals of the genealogical family)—through forced adoption, sterilization, boarding schools, and the depriving of land and membership to the Indigenous wives and children of nonreservation spouses—served as a key mechanism within colonial efforts to assimilate and deculturate Indigenous populations.[39] In colonial Peru (a portion of which is today Bolivia), Spanish women were called upon to raise Mestizo children whose Spanish fathers did not want them inculturated by Indian mothers (Burns 1999: 16).[40] Similarly, Indigenous children born to elite men out of wedlock were characterized as orphans or as "abandoned" in order to avoid humiliating the family. Others were reincorporated into Mestizo and Criollo families as adoptees or servants.[41] These practices bear early traces of *mestizaje*, a narrative of national cultural assimilation through racial admixture.[42] In this context, property (meaning the ownership of goods, and the sexual "conquest" of Indigenous women) was not only an outcome but also a *means* of producing Mestizo masculinity as racialized ownership and as an enduring vision of nationhood that traversed the colonial and Republican eras.[43]

Slippages of the purportedly separate domains of domestic and public—kinship and economy—became especially urgent matters after Republican independence, as nascent nationhood demanded that governments grant full legal rights to the formerly colonized.[44] Rights-based reforms throughout Latin America focused on reshaping domestic labor and nonconjugal sexual relations in light of a nascent ideal of the "Mestizo family."[45] Bolivian reformers sought to root out "loose women," prostitutes, and concubinage in general: modern citizenship was to be forged by establishing and constricting the Mestizo family within firmer boundaries, both spatial and economic.[46] Domestic labor, for instance, was cast by progressive reformers as a "feudal enclave" that blocks a nation's progress toward democratic modernity.[47] Into the late twentieth century, emerging civilizational discourses of authentic love, individual self-fulfillment, and gender equity came to restrict the forms of Indigenous life that could be legally recognized or celebrated within liberal governance.[48]

However, in the Andes relational practices guided by expectations of attachment and mutuality both across hierarchies and to places make the region paradigmatic of the limits to a modern ethos centered upon the alienability of land and labor and, with it, the requisite that kinship be divided off from economy.[49] Incan arrangements of child loaning in the northern Andes often preceded material transactions and military alliances.[50] Similarly, in Incan child integration practices, çapçi churikuna or "sons of the community" were raised by women whose own children had died.[51] Moreover, John Murra's (1968) ethnohistorical study of the "vertical archipelago" traced the exchange of goods (grain, tubers, textiles, coca, fruit) across geographic islands of the Andes among kinship-based descent groups or ayllus. Colonized groups' reliance and repurposing of exchange traditions and precolonial kinship ties supplied dramatic obstructions to the smooth expansion of colonial capital.[52]

Liberalizing efforts to produce modern citizens through legal interventions in family life have been deeply contested. Alongside practices of legal petitioning and armed uprising, such contestations have taken shape in Indigenous Andeans refusals to dispense with practices of adoption, child circulation, and kinship forms that do not ascribe to nuclear ideas of spatial containment or blood-based genealogy.[53] Quechua ideals of *ayni* (or reciprocity) continue to shape contemporary Indigenous movements as well as legal disputes about adoption and the circulation of children. Their evocation as an ethical paradigm has opened up new routes to economic mobility as well as shaping alternate forms of dispute resolution among urban Indigenous people.[54] For instance, arrangements of material care and accountability respond to a distinctly Quechua kinship imaginary of child-rearing (*prohijamiento*) through informal adoption (Leinaweaver 2008).[55] In addition, counternationalist discourses of Aymara revivalism and anticolonial struggle often have drawn upon kinship-based ideals of racialized consanguinity: an Aymara brotherhood that can recover earlier territorial rule through kinship-based ayllu structures.[56] Against the masculinist bias of organized politics, Indigenous feminists in Latin America and elsewhere emphasize the desirability of kinship attachments at odds with the models of freedom elaborated both in settler governance and White feminism, which tend to focus on autonomy and individual choice.[57]

The violent imposition of modern citizenship through the constricting of Indigenous relations within the shape of the Mestizo, nuclear family and the subsequent repurposing of this model as a method of colonial redress imbue non-normative kinship practices with great importance for decolonial political and ethical projects, particularly for Indigenous people.[58] In Bolivia specifically, the earlier targeting of kinship practices within modernizing reforms has politicized intimacy as a crucial site for recasting and refusing hegemonic institutions of family and property historically so central to assimilative *mestizaje*. Moreover, Indigenous peoples' elaborations of land, and attachments to place over time, coarticulate material and spiritual worlds in ways that subvert modern expectations that objects can be both absolutely possessed by, and hence also separated from, human inhabitants or from longer arcs of exchange and residence.[59] Insistence on the inalienable quality of Indigenous attachments to place (and of places as kin) has generated new forms of legal experimentation with the rights of nature, on the one hand, and the need to protect ecologies as sites of Indigenous heritage, on the other.[60]

Nonetheless, in Bolivia property—as alienable land rights and self-possessed subjectivity—has remained nearly ubiquitous as a model of historical redress for earlier hacienda labor violence. Agrarian reformers employed by the MAS party shared eighteenth-century reformers' concern with modernizing the nation through the clarifying of land ownership and the narrowing of kinship relations that are not transparent to legal formations of genealogical inheritance and legitimate paternity.[61] While they emerge out of a parallel history of peasant and Indigenous struggles, in twenty-first-century Bolivia collective land titling initiatives, too, replicated many of the presumptions that underlie modern property regimes. To gain state approval, Indigenous territories must align with existing municipal and regional borders and demonstrate continuities of land use despite earlier hacienda incursions.[62] Like property, such territory must comprise a bounded, discrete unit, one at odds with practices of labor mobility and fluid land transfers. This casts in a new light the popular disaffection with land titling that I encountered in Ayopaya, as well as some Quechua farmers' abiding insistence on sustaining asymmetrical alliances and aid relations with Mestizo residents.

Throughout this book I explore how Ayopayans of diverse backgrounds summoned kinship as an idiom and a relational structure for demanding Mestizo accountability to a violent labor past and the structures of racial hierarchy it left in its wake. This occurred through the repurposing of ties established within hacienda households. During the hacienda period and after, master families adopted and raised out-of-wedlock children, acted as godparents and religious sponsors, and supplied material (and, in the case of godparenting, spiritual) assistance to servants. My conversations with adults who had been gifted to hacienda masters as children, adopted by half-siblings, or worked as longtime servants even after abolition revealed hacienda households as defined by mutual dependencies among masters and servants. In their spanning of labor, kinship, and affective relations, these alliances implode formalist definitions of economy based on holding apart private and public, family and capital, reproduction and production.[63] In doing so, they also muddy Bolivian cultural revivalist projects that inherit from mid-twentieth reforms an assumption that true Andean Indigeneity—particularly the expansive highland community form or ayllu—is that which has been untouched or has survived intact despite earlier hacienda labor economies.[64]

Relational ties across Mestizo and Indigenous groups in Ayopaya raise new questions about how people refashion colonial intimacies and kinship patterns not only as mystifications but also as mechanisms of historical redress.[65] Rather than only being uprooted or fractured through contract-based arrangements of law and marriage, we might ask how more expansive Indigenous kinship relations—what Kim TallBear (2019: 37) calls "making kin"—persist and can be demanded of non-Indigenous people in ways that open up new possibilities for care and accountability against settler mythologies. Attending to such improvised forms, "the critical remixing of nonconvergent tracks" (Moten 2003: 11), challenges both a theory of passive capital and the mode of subjectivity that narratives of commodification subsume, silence, and promise to resuscitate. I call this remaking the creative duration of kinship. My account strives to show that while kin-making practices among Mestizo and Indigenous subjects upheld disturbing racial hierarchies, for interlocutors they also offered a key relational structure for demanding Mestizo accountability for earlier labor and sexual violence.[66] This is the *after* as a contiguity of relational ties in which elements of those ties—including double-edged intimacies and inherited obligations—are reelaborated and thereby put to new political and ethical ends.

KNOT 2. ELUSIVE PROPERTY

The second theme that this book addresses is property, specifically its workings as a technology of colonial modernity and of postservitude justice. In the Andes and elsewhere, late colonial modernity hinged on securing a bounded sphere of ostensibly natural economic activity apart from religious traditions, kinship ties, or prescientific superstitions: the mechanism for doing so was *property*. But property is notoriously hard to define.[67] Most broadly, modern property emerged within broader efforts to topple European feudalism and landed monarchic and ecclesiastic church hierarchies. But, as is particularly clear in John Locke's writing about tolerance, for instance, this operated less as a displacement of mastery that its reinsertion at the level of the individual.[68] In classic economic theory property came to connote both ownership but also self-mastery: the capacity to act as master over one's body, thoughts, and acts.[69]

This model of self-possession paved the way for juridical notions of the willing transfer of one's sovereignty to the state. Where the proclivity for exchange in these modern terms was found lacking, such as when Indigenous Andeans cultivated multiple, dispersed agricultural islands, land and people could be claimed as the property of others.[70] Because natives did not hold private property (nor "improve" it in ways that colonists could recognize), colonizers argued, their land and labor could be rightfully appropriated.[71] Hence, modern legal ideas of property promised new liberties, but they also facilitated the alienability and transfer of liberty to another subject, such as through regimes of slavery and labor servitude.[72]

This demonstrates how colonial institutions of racialized bondage, enslavement, and subjection were mediated and enabled by logics of consent and contract.[73] If property historically served as a paragon of exemplary ownership over self and land, this logic of alienability also made chattel slavery defensible, sanctioned by the idea that a subject could "forfeit" his or her liberty.[74] In her work, Cheryl Harris showed how the making of slaves into property worked historically to shore up and consolidate the idea of Whiteness as property and as status—that is, entitlement to goods.[75] This challenges the tendency to collapse property with "real property," especially land.[76] Instead, it requires we pose the materiality or object life of property itself as an ethnographic and historical problem, one that requires scrutiny of the fusing together of ownership and racial subjectivity through legal stipulations of land use and improvement as well as of unevenly dispersed expectations of benefit.[77]

After the abolition of slavery, governments made property the pinnacle of efforts to reverse dispossession; land rights, labor contracts, and marriage rights supplied a key legal means for the formerly enslaved to reclaim ownership and thereby become "masters" of their own bodies and labor.[78] Hence, the formerly enslaved were expected to achieve liberty and overcome subjection through the extension and refashioning of colonial logics of property and contract, rather than their dismantling.[79] In the postbellum

United States and elsewhere, a restorative model of property also grounded new disciplinary regimes organized around the requirement of self-mastery and presumptions of racialized blameworthiness.[80] This double-edged quality of property raises questions about the transformations entailed by the spread of rights-based ideals of liberty as secured by contractual exchange.[81] Rather than only *giving* liberty to the formerly enslaved, processes of affording rights through labor contracts and then citizenship also imposed new ideals of political subjectivity that made other understandings of personhood and ethics unthinkable.[82]

Property hereby arises as both poison and remedy, illness and cure. Alongside land titling and contractual labor, property also took hold as a powerful model for imagining self-sovereignty.[83] In some cases—for instance, in the Caribbean—this new imaginary eliminated alternatives to property that slaves had carved out of the plantation system, including their use of provision grounds that grew out of maroon traditions.[84] Nonetheless, as scholars of reparation point out, it is equally simplistic to characterize all such legal conversions of claims into rights-based languages as *only* inhibiting. In the case of reparations for slavery, property-based ideas of repayment for debt supply a crucial legal mechanism for addressing illicit land seizures and labor violence.[85] Reparation processes challenge the long-standing insistence, defining of neo/classical theories of exchange, on dividing apart economics and ethics.[86] As a framework of justice, property remains at once indispensable and insufficient.

In the Andean region in particular, private ownership arose as both a means of national progress and of colonial redress, ones at odds with precolonial and contemporary Indigenous exchange traditions.[87] Latin America was colonized predominately by Spain and Portugal, so the forms of ownership elaborated there do not follow the trappings of English common law (as they did in British colonies such as the United States, Australia, and Canada).[88] Instead, the *repartimiento* or partitioning of land in the seventeenth century implemented Spanish-style town squares constructed around churches and displaced Indigenous people from their ancestral lands. As such, the use of the term "property" may seem misplaced.[89] Spanish colonists framed their efforts instead in the language of *dominio* (dominion), or claiming possession both through demonstrated transformations to a place and through Christian conceptions of manifest destiny. *Dominio* was not just imposed—it coexisted with, and was elaborated through, conflicts with colonized groups and preexisting institutions of political authority and land use.[90] However, while the Spanish colonial project was initially driven by Christian imaginaries of dominion, property subsequently arose as the key means to displace what Republican reformers framed as backward, feudal imperial designs. This model articulated the legal subject of rights as a temporally bound, proprietorial agent who "owns" his body and his actions.[91] This imposition of property as a model of landholding and modern political subjectivity was crucial to the spread of racial institutions of alienable landholding.[92]

However, unlike less densely populated regions of the Americas, the Andes was home to a firmly established agricultural tradition that precluded facile arguments about "wild" or vacant lands that could be seized by the Spanish crown. The region was marked by interethnic land negotiations among Incaic lords and Quechua field hands for several hundred years before the Spanish arrived.[93] This mountainous landscape could not be defined either in terms of human absence (*tierras baldías*) or of a timeless communal land tradition to be fractured absolutely by colonial ownership. As a result, colonial juridical law in the Andes unfolded by integrating key elements of Inca political systems, including honoring usufruct land rights for valley populations who could demonstrate a continuity of land use and loyalty to earlier Incan overlords.[94] For instance, in the Cochabamba valleys of present-day Bolivia, Spanish administrators borrowed from Incan political traditions, honoring land allotments Incas made to migrant Quechua laborers who divided their time between home communities or ayllus, distant farm outcroppings (*mitmaqs*), and rotating field labor to fulfill tribute obligations to Inca overlords.[95]

If property assumed moral force as a powerful colonial discourse of historical improvement that required the alienation of land, labor, and, at times, (Inca) tradition as mediated through a paradigm of the benefits of contract, it was also crucial to subsequent efforts at rectifying earlier injustice and Indigenous dispossession.[96] After Bolivian Independence from Spain in 1825, Republican reformers were faced with the challenges of breaking up landed monopolies, including churches and haciendas. This is evident above all in the 1874 Ley de Exvinculación, which dismantled the "tributary apparatus, establishing universal property tax [*catastro*] to be paid in the new devalued currency of bolivianos," which effectively raised Indian taxes by 20 percent (Larson 2004: 220).

Resistance to the racial abstractions underlying modern legal and commodity forms, with their disavowal of other frameworks of landholding and authority, took specific shape in the Andes. In Upper Peru, a region that today encompasses Bolivia and Peru, colonial attempts to consolidate Spanish authority and appropriate and possess native lands were repeatedly challenged in massive anticolonial rebellions that swept the Andean region. The largest of these was the 1780–81 insurrection led by Aymara peasant leader Túpaj Katari, a partial outgrowth of the 1780 insurgencies led by Túpac Amaru in Peru. Insurgents spread across the countryside from estate to estate, destroying hacienda buildings and mills, burning crops, and slaughtering landlords' animals. These insurgencies point to widespread Indigenous opposition to new political and legal structures premised on private landholding as well as unmarked citizenship, specifically a universal property tax.

Such movements refashioned European-inspired ideals of emancipation, but they also creatively reworked the social and juridical claims linked to "Indio" status as a distinctly colonial achievement.[97] The incursions of private property created new routes of legal contestation and labor militancy that often reinscribed the benefits associated with earlier colonial juridical categories.[98] The early juridical recognition of the ayllu community form—as a kinship-based political and relational order centered on reciprocal exchange and redistributive authority—remained crucial to later Indigenous efforts to contest private property through collective ownership and the semiautonomy of political systems. Likewise, the category of *Indio* was initially developed to secure a malleable labor force through tribute, but it also afforded Indigenous Andeans a relative degree of autonomy over communal political and economic orders and, after the Bourbon Reform period, protection from severe colonial taxation practices associated with a universal property tax or *catastro*.[99]

Private property (and its early colonial expressions as chattel slavery and indentured Indigenous labor on encomiendas) did not absolutely displace alternate systems of landholding and Indigenous collectivity. This is apparent in early Republican census data about ayllu membership. In 1846, Bolivia's first official census showed 138,104 families as members of an ayllu and Quechua as the primary language spoken.[100] This suggests that enormous tracts of land remained under the control of semiautonomous communities. In 1877, the last year an official tribute was recorded, the vast majority of Bolivia's *indios tributarios* continued to claim membership in communal villages, with peasant communities holding half the land and half the population. Likewise, 1869 reforms bent on destroying the juridical basis of Indian communities led to a violent backlash and a peasant insurgency. In these ways, the imposition and experience of liberal value systems was uneven throughout the Andes (Larson 2004: 226). Divestitures, protests, and legal struggles elicited dramatic transformations to intra-ayllu practices of political succession, local justice practices, and allocations of land, taxes, and ritual responsibilities, yet these interventions also politicized the ayllu form as an institution by which to contest neocolonial modernizing efforts. The imposition of titled land was supposed to detach Indigenous people from communal traditions; instead, it politicized and revitalized highland organizing around communal life and Aymara political and religious systems.[101]

Mid-twentieth-century projects of socialist land collectivization again imagined land rights as key antidotes to Indigenous and peasant dispossession.[102] In the 1950s, Bolivia's Movimiento Nacionalista Revolucionario (MNR) government initiated but did not follow through with promises of land redistribution and collective land rights for rural peasants.[103] Indigenous communities and peasant unions comprised of former hacienda workers took action to secure the hacienda's demise. This bottom-up process often challenged governmental paradigms of "land for those who work it" to instead agitate for "land to the original owners."[104] In the former hacienda stronghold of Ayopaya, this generated intense conflict among hacienda workers (tenant farmers and servants) and with members of neighboring ayllu communities. Community land rights could undermine the claims of former hacienda workers; conversely, privately titled land offered a crucial route of redress for hacienda servants while reproducing gendered labor hierarchies and leaving intact broader histories of Indigenous land loss.

The promise of collective land rights assumed new significance in the twenty-first century, as *Indianista* activists and some government officials sought to revive the ayllu community model as a premise for an anticolonial, neo-Incan vision of pan-Indigenous governance rooted in Quechua and Aymara traditions of reciprocity and exchange. In the 1990s lowland activists and labor organizers also reworked the community model as a path to Indigenous sovereignty and land redistribution. Present-day Aymara activists continue to draw from a long history of ayllu movements in their calls for an ayllu-based revivalism that could challenge entrenched structures of Mestizo governance and displace them by a supranational struggle against racial subordination.[105] Ayllu-based visions of Indigenous justice have also entered institutional spheres. After Morales took office, his MAS government introduced new legal mechanisms for Indigenous recognition that drew from this earlier concern with Indigenous community, now cast within the framework of territorial "autonomy."[106] This model weakened Indigenous sovereignty as it uncoupled land rights from resource rights. This was related to the fact that the Morales government institutionalized a restricted definition of territory that reserved the state's control over nonrenewable natural resources as "national property."

While distinct in their efforts to support collective landholding as a path to Indigenous sovereignty, revolutionary agrarian efforts under Morales (2006–19) in many regards mimicked the colonial logics of self-possessed property discussed earlier. For agrarian reformers working under President Morales's government, property constituted both a path to political liberty and an externalization of that liberty: access to a land title marked a person's arrival as an owner-citizen who had both land rights and self-possession.[107] Bolivia's 2006 governmental agrarian reform required the establishment of private property as well as the drawing of firmer spatial lines around legitimate forms of Indigenous collectivity.[108] For instance, Penelope Anthias (2019) has shown how lowland groups have used Indigenous autonomy programs to negotiate private mining contracts with multinational corporations. In this regard, legalistic approaches to Indigenous territory in Bolivia often do not vary as substantially from private property regimes as might be expected. Moreover, here the fixing of property seems to have also been accompanied by the shoring up more reified understandings of race, namely, of Indigenous citizenship.[109]

Suspending the tendency to treat property as coterminous either with land or with self-possessed liberty, *After Servitude* traces the spatial, material, and conceptual processes by which property comes to be produced as a set of transferable objects and resources, and the benefits associated with that entification.[110] My fieldwork with Bolivian agrarian officials showed me their painstaking efforts to produce property as titled land and as normalized expectations of the benefits of modern citizenship for rural Indigenous people. This involved their attempts to draw absolute property lines, binding land to titles and subjects to state in ways that officials deemed necessary to Indigenous groups' liberty.[111] At the same time, however, I found that even as INRA approaches to property sought to dispense with the racialized trappings of hacienda servitude, the labor arrangements that defined that system served as a precedent for distinguishing rightful land claims in the present. INRA staff's efforts to wrest with the entailments of earlier bonded labor as defining of legitimate ownership (and titled land) offer a key point of insight into the instabilities, but also remaking, of property as a naturalized paradigm or a priori ontology.[112] They also complicate fantasies of historical detachment associated with the cartographic production of space and, in this case, titled property.[113]

INRA staff taught me that about the processes of material transformation, spatial fixing, and slippage at play in their efforts to integrate land and people into a bureaucratic formation centered upon titled property.[114] Such efforts assumed noteworthy characteristics related to the MAS government's focus on protecting rural farmers. Property could be secured through installing titled landholding, but its design also implied racialized benefits that had to be newly extended to communities of formerly indentured laborers. Reformers strove to translate land into property but also to remake rural farmers—particularly the Quechua relatives of indentured hacienda servants—into something much like property: modern citizens awakened to the integrity and force of their cultural and racial heritage.[115] This effort carried weighty connotations in former hacienda zones like Ayopaya, where the 1953 Agrarian Reform had not thoroughly transformed landed racial hierarchies and where many rural farmers retained ambivalent attachments both to Indigenous communities and the families of former *hacendados*.[116] In fact, as I discuss at greater length in chapter 2, Quechua farmers with whom I spoke recounted that unpaid labor upon one regional hacienda persisted until 1983.

Beginning from the premise that property is rarely fixed, this book considers both how agrarian officials at INRA repurposed hacienda labor systems to establish legitimate property through the alignment of paper titles and land, and how those frameworks of titled ownership were contested by Quechua farmers like Gregorio.[117] To him, property had failed when the paper slips reformers promised were never delivered or did not correspond with any existing parcels. Moreover, faith in property was shaken when farmers experienced famine, hunger, and dire poverty as endemic to rural life well after hacienda abolition, and promises of peasant justice, in 1953. People waited in vain for titles but also gave up on property as an ideal. Still others, such as unionized farmers, contested property as a retainer model for enclosing land and attaining Indigenous sovereignty, one that solidified the labor hierarchies that defined earlier subjection. Faced with the inadequacy of state efforts to install property, Ayopayans pursued and demanded historical redress in other ways, including through practices of asymmetrical aid and exchange that grew out of the region's history of Mestizo-Indigenous hostility and violence.

Exchange is an arena that overlaps economy and kinship but also, I argue, mediates the values associated with each sphere. In approaching exchange in this way, I depart from more common uses of the term that equate it with economy as such. This reflects a commitment, shared with Karl Marx ([1844] 1978: 70, 81), to denaturalize entities by attending to the *activity* that is concealed when they are treated as a state or condition.[118] If economy, when stripped to its most simplistic definition, consists of the exchange of goods as commodities, then kinship (in the Western tradition at least) is similarly built upon the circulation of women as wives and the exchange of gifts and money (dowries) between men that this circulation enables.[119] While commonly treated as distinct, then, the fact that the exchange of women through kinship secures property (for men) blurs these two spheres. Despite this slippage, modernity was frequently cast by liberal economists like Adam Smith as the evolution of "exchange" from its primitive (that is, kinship-based) form to its modern property-based one.[120] Historical change is herein often framed as contingent on progressive shifts in exchange relations.

For proponents and opponents alike, this progressive transformation of exchange relations (from "primitive" to "modern," gift to commodity) reveals the possibilities and risks of modern contract-based systems. In this vein, anthropologists have frequently yoked primitive exchange to the social form of "the gift," taken to depart from the commodity form in its focus on durative sociality.[121] If a commodity sale is fast, a gift relation is extensive and ongoing. Obligations can span generations, but in a liberal juridical tradition centered on individuated responsibility, legal culpability cannot.[122] Different exchange regimes give way to distinctive possibilities for imagining how people should relate to objects, and to one another, over time. Exchange regimes not only persist or not but are also called upon by people to do certain kinds of political work, addressing injustices related to the commodification of people and things as well as the inequalities sanctioned by new systems of legal abstraction and racialized status. For this reason, rethinking this telos—the shift from kinship to property, from inalienability to alienated capital—has been crucial for efforts to contest gendered and racialized forms of subject-making and subjection associated with modern liberalism.[123]

As discussed earlier, in the Cochabamba valleys to which Ayopaya belongs, competing expectations about exchange (whether tribute should be individual or ayllu-based, and whether land rights should follow from legal contract or Incan labor practices) operated as key sites in which Indigenous Andeans contested and sought to reshape colonial and then liberal systems of racialized abstraction. These included their opposition to the imposition of alienated landholding as well as cultural evolutionist visions of democratic futurity based on the inevitable assimilation of Indigenous people as citizens. Quechua and Aymara practices of armed rebellion sought to defend the benefits associated with *Indio* status, and more recently, populist and Katarista organizing has centered upon calls to revive the highland ayllu community as a basis both of Indigenous collectivity and modern political orders. In this way, the juridical recognition of ayllus as spatially constrained community entities reshaped religious, political, and economic traditions, but it also offered a vital tool in ongoing struggles for Indigenous land rights and political sovereignty.

The analysis offered in this book highlights how, given Ayopayans' disillusionment with MAS efforts to settle colonial accounts through land allotments, alternate exchange relations remained paramount for continued efforts to check the power of a landed Mestizo elite. As I discussed earlier, their doubts about institutional programs of Indigenous land rights stemmed both from historical experiences of the state's sluggishness in distributing titles, and from the fact that they inhabited a broader milieu of Mestizo-Indigenous negotiation that complicated more straightforward claims to Indigenous community or being "in-ayllu."[124] In this province, hacienda institutions of labor exploitation kept a tight grip on rural life into the late twentieth century, producing Indigenous community institutions, kinship relations, and exchange practices at odds with paradigms of exploitative or reparative property.[125] Practices of Indigenous labor mobility, overlapping systems of land use across municipal boundaries and with multiple owners, and asymmetrical aid relations with Mestizo elites spilled over the spatial and ethnic enclosures implied by governmental programs of individual property and Indigenous autonomous territory.

Ayopaya's long history of antihacienda labor militancy, combined with what many villagers perceived as the inadequacy of institutional solutions to racial hierarchy, led to broad disaffection with formal processes of land titling, both individual and collective. Contemporary Quechua and Aymara farmers and mine workers sough to navigate relations to Mestizo bosses and landowning families by reformulating a competing tradition of claim-making premised upon expectations of asymmetrical exchange and aid. Suspending the promise of property as a normalized division or "cutting" between here and there, then and now, Ayopayans demanded that Mestizos uphold a more relational orientation to wealth as carrying unwilled obligations to workers and villagers.[126] They did so at times by refusing their own labor and challenging mine owners' legitimacy in the countryside, and in other cases by reaffirming alliances with powerful Mestizos that had been rendered suspect by new languages of territorial autonomy and Indigenous rights.[127]

Exchange here emerged as a zone of renewed claim-making by which Ayopayans sought to navigate a deeply inegalitarian present, in which property and kinship supplied opposing routes for addressing the ethical quandaries of life after servitude.[128] Against state promises of property, Indigenous Ayopayans evoked a set of durative obligations to navigate what they interpreted as their marginality from national politics and new vulnerabilities that emerged out of illicit mining activities in the region. This involved a broader insistence that debts for earlier arrangements of forced labor were tethered in place in ways that could not be willed away by a property title or the death of a father or grandfather.[129] In linking earlier hacienda economies to contemporary mining infrastructures, Ayopayans denaturalized a more discrete orientation to wealth and reframed it in terms of a personal ethical failing that must be contested.[130] This stance did not interrupt global flows of capital or supersede racialized hierarchies, yet it subversively refused *distance* as a key normative presumption underlying the reproduction of capital.[131]

Hence while such aid relations across racial hierarchies were deeply unsettling to reformist paradigms of equality and historical displacement, for participants they were key in allowing a more durative engagement with wealth as an outcome of still operative systems of labor violence and land dispossession.[132] This raises broader questions about the normative work that analytic categories of economy do, both for anthropologists and ethnographic interlocuters. In this case, Ayopayans' efforts to delineate desirable from pernicious exchange practices (exploitative if "free" capital from patronage aid, sexual violence from exemplary kin-making) served not only to reproduce commodity systems but also to contest and redefine their very terms. My analysis demonstrates how, in this context, the existing alternative to a property-based reparation scheme did not lay in unchanging kinship traditions; instead, it emerged in a paradigm of exemplary exchange that was itself conjunctural and that reflected purposeful efforts to contest the violence sanctioned by programs of land titling and Indigenous awakening from which many Ayopayans were doubly marginalized.

By bringing kinship vocabularies and practices to bear upon non-normative intimacies, Ayopayans whose relatives had labored on haciendas evaded requirements—both anthropological and legal—that Indigenous people be made legible through blood quantum, family and property inheritance, or revivalist framings of culturalist collectivity (e.g., ayllus).[133] Their practices reveal interrelatedness as a key condition of the present in regard to Indigenous legal recognition and for quotidian, settler-Indigenous engagements with history.[134] Like kinship, here exchange was not the singular purview of Western or non-Western societies, but rather a domain where conflicting paradigms of value are purposely brought into play (Strathern 2005: 6–7). Demands that Mestizo bosses uphold an alternate exchange relation were not sealed off from colonial histories of capital; rather, they followed from residents' earlier and ongoing efforts to contend with tenacious histories of racial violence and loss.[135] As Snelgrove, Dhamoon, and Corntassel (2014) point out, the ability to *not* confront history is a key aspect of settler consciousness. In yoking contemporary money relations to older traditions of asymmetrical exchange, Quechua Ayopayans denied Mestizo residents the luxuries of property as the privilege to seek profit without accountability, capital without kinship.

THREADING LABOR PASTS IN AYOPAYA

Between March 2011 and March 2012, I lived in the rural town and municipal center of Independencia, in the province of Ayopaya, an eight-hour bus ride from the city of Cochabamba. The municipal center (which includes the town and surrounding villages) has a population of almost five thousand people, among them merchants, farmers, shopkeepers, pastoralists, and a small Mestizo elite. About 75 percent of the municipality's residents speak Quechua, making it one of the most heavily Quechua areas of Bolivia.[136] Agriculture (which accounts for 92.6 percent of the region's economy), mining, and manufacturing constitute the dominant sources of employment. Farmers mainly cultivate potatoes, corn, wheat, broad beans (*haba verde*), oats, oca (a tuber, *Oxalis tuberosa*), and alfalfa. Coca and coffee are grown in the tropical *yungas* (jungle) areas of Ayopaya that border the La Paz region; tubers, *oca*, and *tarwi* are produced in highland parts, and *chirimoya*, apples, and peaches in the temperate inter-Andean valleys around Independencia.

In Independencia, I attended union meetings, spent time in people's farmlands and orchards, attended monthly *ch'alla* rituals, accompanied municipal officials to survey roads, celebrated holidays and patron saint festivals, and gathered with villagers and townsfolk for two much anticipated visits from President Morales.[137] I also visited former hacienda buildings and agricultural lands, gold, antimony, and sodalite mines, abandoned mills, churches, and a distillery that was in disuse. This was augmented by archival research at the National Institute of Agrarian Reform (INRA) in Cochabamba in 2012, where I collected case files for 125 land redistribution cases initiated since 1953 and also carried out interviews and oral histories with select staff. I also accompanied staff for a three-day retreat and annual soccer tournament in the Bolivian city of Sucre in 2012, where teams comprised of city-based INRA offices competed against one another.

Bolivia's haciendas grew out of colonial encomiendas first founded in 1645, providing land and tribute to Spanish administrators, merchants, and imperial elites. Unlike plantations in Bolivia's eastern lowlands, haciendas in the Cochabamba region were smaller farms owned by Mestizo landlords or, in other cases, former tenant farmers or small bosses (*juch'uy patrones*) who bought their way out of servitude. During rotating shifts of forced *mitani* labor "service," Quechua women recounted to me, they had prepared food, cleaned, wove, brewed *chicha*, fed animals, and cared for children—including the master's children, servant children, and adoptees. The ubiquity of "unnatural" (sexual) abuses combined with tight control over labor conditions contributed to widespread antihacienda uprisings in Ayopaya in 1947—the only twentieth-century armed rebellion in Cochabamba preceding the National Revolution of 1952.[138] Following hacienda abolition in 1953, most estate land in Ayopaya was redistributed or abandoned. However, racial inequalities did not disappear from the region. Many relatives of former landlords still live and work in the region, with agriculture supplemented by small-scale mining operations in search of gold, antimony, and sodalite.

The research trajectory that brought me to Ayopaya was far from determinate. During preliminary research in the Bolivian city of Cochabamba in 2007, 2008, and 2009, I was gripped by interlocuters' invocations of what was at that time a counternationalist discourse of revolutionary struggle and historical transformation. The urban, pro-Indigenous activists I came to know privileged a revolutionary narrative of Bolivian history centered around what they framed as recurrent rhythms of popular Indigenous rebellion, including uprisings led by Túpaj Katari, Bartolina Sisa, Pablo Zárate Willca, and Che Guevara; events like Bolivia's 2000 Water War constituted recent iterations of this deep revolutionary past. Activists carried worn copies of books by and about these historic figures in their leather satchels, and also sold them on a card table next to a "radical news bulletin" composed of newspaper clippings annotated with red pen, which they (and I, on some days) lugged to the central Plaza 14 de Septiembre in Cochabamba each weekday morning. These same texts formed the basis for weekly Thursday night "popular history lessons" led by activists in that same plaza. Alongside this emphasis on disseminating an occluded history of Indigenous political struggle, activists also sought to recuperate traditional practices that had been squeezed out of public life. They spent time at outdoor markets sipping *api* (a warm corn drink), in *chicha* (brewed corn beer) halls to booming performances of *música folklórica*, and at memorials for revolutionary martyrs Túpac Katari and Bartolina Sisa.

Bolivia's history of hacienda violence was notably absent from activists' narratives of "popular history" that I encountered during preliminary research and again in 2010 when I began long-term fieldwork.[139] While bonded agrarian labor was a target of post-2006 MAS agrarian reform and had been central to earlier waves of antihacienda militancy in the 1940s, activists' accounts of Bolivia's rebellious past focused instead on ethnically Aymara highland histories of Indigenous uprising, centered on the defense of collective landholding on rural ayllus. The fact that activists made little mention of a more recent labor past—especially as Cochabamba was the heart of hacienda grain production—struck me as odd. Moreover, I was disturbed to find that well-meaning activists at times disparaged Quechua and Aymara peasants whom they saw as failing to reclaim their Indigeneity. This was most apparent in a *chicha* hall one evening, when activist interlocuters insisted that an elderly man speak Quechua in order to join our table. When he did not, one activist leader lamented, "They are like dogs: they understand but don't speak." I wondered how revolutionary processes of political change were experienced by people on the outskirts of urban activism, including those whose relatives had labored on haciendas. How did this occlusion from popular narratives of Indigenous uplift—and indeed humanity—condition rural people's orientations to the MAS party's decolonial agenda?

I learned more when I went to live in Ayopaya permanently in March 2011. In these fertile farming villages nestled in the inter-Andean mountains between the city of Cochabamba and La Paz, the children and grandchildren of *hacendados*, tenant farmers, and servants continued to live, and often work, side by side. Evo Morales's election in 2005, combined with Bolivia's booming economy from 2008 on, led many urban Mestizos (especially men) to leave the city, undertaking new economic ventures in rural regions where they had inherited land from *hacendado* relatives. According to residents with whom I spoke, in 2008 the children of many former *hacendados* had returned to the countryside to start cultivating fruit trees, produce honey, and mine for antimony and gold on land bordering parcels owned by their relatives' former workers. Their sources of employment ranged from apiaries to gold mining to the making of specialty fruit beverages from *chirimoya*, pear, apple, and peach. This repopulation of the countryside, combined with new land titling mechanisms, created new pressure on land and led many migrant landholders to return from seasonal work in the lowland coca fields of Chapare hoping to secure their property claims.

These land pressures stemmed from new institutional projects of hacienda reparation and decolonial reform centered on property titling. Starting in 2006, agrarian officials at INRA initiated a state-wide land titling program. In 2011 widespread disagreements over the Ayopaya province's potential conversion into Native Community Land (Tierra Comunitaria de Origen, TCO) led the peasant union to eject all persons affiliated with INRA from the province. By 2012 titling projects were being reinitiated in the region, and by the end of my fieldwork there, INRA officials were a steady presence in neighboring villages, identifiable by green vests adorned with a *wiphala* flag signaling Bolivia's "plurinational" composition. In monthly meetings of the Central Sindical Única de Trabajadores Campesinos Originarios de Ayopaya (Central Union of Campesino Workers of Ayopaya, CSUTCOA)—the subregional branch of Central Obrera Boliviana (COB)—that I attended, MAS officials gave presentations on recently passed laws and participants debated the merits of proposed aid projects.[140] Bouncing between the INRA archive and Ayopaya allowed me to retroactively retrace land conflicts that were too sensitive to discuss openly with interlocutors as they unfolded. Despite the delicate nature of land titling initiatives at that time, the municipal government and representatives of CSUTCOA authorized my research project. Upon completing oral history interviews with monolingual Quechua elders, I provided them with printed copies of our interviews. At the conclusion of my fieldwork, I also presented this research to the pro-Indigenous activists in Cochabamba mentioned earlier.

Contrary to standard "arrival" narratives that punctuate the introductory pages of classic ethnographic monographs, my foreignness was nothing new in Ayopaya. In Independencia, villagers are familiar with White foreigners as the town is home to a Quechua girls school founded by a German Catholic nun who first visited the region while completing social work there thirty years ago. Since then, the school has annually hosted two or three German student volunteers who thereby fulfill that country's foreign service requirements. In addition, Dutch researchers, including A. Tekelenburg (2001), collaborated with agronomists and farmers like Gregorio in the 1980s in cultural ecology projects aimed at reintroducing native cochineal and cactus pear species. As a researcher, I was entering an already permeable world with ties to many other foreign individuals and nations—a province defined by other White foreigners' humanitarian and research presence in Independencia, locals' weekly bus commutes to Bolivian cities like Cochabamba, Oruro, Potosí, and La Paz, and their seasonal and permanent emigration abroad to sites in Argentina, Brazil, Chile, Spain, and Portugal. There, residents pursued jobs in construction and domestic service, as well as commercial and arts ventures; for instance, the local folklore band Ayopayamanta has toured Switzerland and Germany three times.

Nonetheless, Bolivians' perceptions of my Whiteness, gender, and economic privilege unavoidably shaped this research, positioning me socially alongside the relatives of former *hacendados*.[141] Despite my Quechua fluency, which signaled support for Indigenous knowledges and narratives, I found fieldwork to be an uncanny experience marked by a sense of my own inadequacy and lack of practical (especially medical) knowledge. Visiting a former hacienda distillery with a hired Quechua driver, an elderly man approached us and began weeping, showing us an infected wound on his arm and explaining that his son had abandoned him. He needed medicine. Later that day, we gave him a ride to the medical center some two hours away. On other days, meeting elderly folk with no food and no transportation, I returned to deliver vegetables and dry goods, and to offer rides. Thus, during fieldwork I was at times drawn into hierarchical aid relations I had imagined I would only learn about second-hand. Initially I experienced these demands for assistance as uncomfortable, awkward, and even distressing, foreclosing as they did my ability to hide behind presumptions of human similarity in order to obscure the obvious privileges conferred by my perceived Whiteness, foreignness, education, and class positioning. Over time, this discomfort shifted into an awareness of the need to inhabit my privilege in a way that aligned with villagers' expectations of me, thereby honoring my historical and racialized situatedness in the field.[142]

For these reasons, in this book I necessarily position myself within, not outside, the nascent zones of creative, fraught sociality that I describe. My ethnographic method relied on a *threading* in which I, too, was a line of attachment. My participation in this threading responded to a raw awareness of anthropology's own culpability in histories of racialized subjection. During fieldwork, I often assumed a position as a student or apprentice. In addition to my own humility about the limits to my understanding of local events as a White outsider, my research was defined by an awareness of the *contingency* of my presence in Ayopaya. In a region known for militant ejection of unwelcome outsiders, the fact that I was able to complete this work owed not only to my interlocuters' goodwill but also to their unwavering support for this project. This support, in turn, was related to local assessments of the significance of studying the region's labor past. By stepping back from a sense of singular ownership over these ideas, I distance myself also from a model of research grounded in property. This allows other entanglements to emerge related to how my own positioning conditioned the ethnographic enterprise and, in turn, how Ayopayans' concerns regarding history and colonial debts shaped the research process and the key theoretical stakes of this written work.

ORGANIZATION OF THE BOOK

This book consists of three parts. The first part ("Kinship") considers Ayopaya's bonded past and its reshaping of rural landscapes and affects; it argues that this has produced an enduring sense of doubt about the promises of state-led decolonial change. Chapter 1, "Claiming Kinship," outlines the ways rural villagers and farmers redeploy kinship as an idiom of exemplary care and historical accountability after labor servitude. I propose kinship as a flexible idiom that people use to organize land, labor, and people whose connections do not align with heteropatriarchal ideals of biological consanguinity and inheritance that have guided Mestizo citizenship projects since the early twentieth century. Chapter 2, "Gifting Land," examines the historical antecedents of present-day kinship-based aid, particularly land gifting, from the late precolonial era and draws on first-hand oral history accounts of twentieth-century labor bondage and antihacienda organizing. I approach these kinship forms as outcomes of choices that, while constrained, afforded different possibilities for proximity and alliance with hacienda masters and other Spanish-descended elites.

The second part of the book ("Property") turns away from Ayopaya to examine titled property as a model of spatialized mastery over land motivating INRA reform approaches to untitled individual properties as well as frameworks of recognized Indigenous territory. Chapter 3, "Producing Property," outlines the formal dimensions of the MAS agrarian reform program, which began in 2006 but refurbished existing legal frameworks of individual and collective land titling initiated in 1996. For INRA reformers, the kinship-based exchange practices traced in early chapters obstruct ideals of bounded property and must therefore be resolved by disconnecting relational pasts, including histories of land gifting and labor servitude. Chapter 4, "Grounding Indigeneity," tracks the ways Indigeneity was retethered to rural histories of labor, political struggle, and Quechua collectivity through the refusal of state resources and recognition, and through positive elaborations of spatially fluid belonging. In unionists' widespread opposition to a land collectivization plan, they took issue with MAS party officials' invocation of reified, romantic ideals of national Indigeneity and their use of these models as guides for land titling. The chapter describes how Quechua groups contested property as the racialized reification of Indigeneity and instead reclaimed a distinct mode of Quechua belonging as necessarily bound in place and to history.

The third part of the book ("Exchange") explores Indigenous claims that emerge alongside administrative approaches to the nation's divisive hacienda past. Chapter 5, "Demanding Return," looks at a case in which Indigenous mineworkers in Ayopaya appropriated and critically redeployed older idioms of agrarian obligation to demand resources and aid from new mining elites. I argue that workers' withdrawal of labor was effective because it tapped into older patterns of hacienda worker mobility in Ayopaya. By defining the role of this older exchange tradition in animating labor conflicts in rural gold mines, the chapter advances debates concerning the challenges facing a telos of alienated capital. Chapter 6, "Reviving Exchange," extends the earlier discussion about exchange to consider how these older paradigms of agrarian authority worked to shore up yet also unseat MAS party political legitimacy in Ayopaya. I examine President Evo Morales's visits to the Ayopaya region, during which he hosted feasts with municipal leaders and peasant unionists, fulfilling the criteria for older figures of authority including hacienda masters and, before them, priests and encomienda lords. My account of these events highlights the aspects of contemporary Ayopayan dynamics that conflict with the dualistic understanding of Indigeneity and governance circulated within Bolivia's revivalist project, which cast Indigeneity as pure and the state as innocent of its earlier and ongoing role in delimiting the scope and content of legitimate alterity.

The conclusion, "Property's Afterlives," reflects on what we may learn from Quechua groups' refusals of property as a model of mastery over space and self that underpins land-based reparation programs. The Bolivian case reveals the extent of property's shadow not only over economic life but also rights-based movements for racial justice. Refusing these restrictions, as Ayopayans did, in turn elicits broader questions about how to approach justice beyond an ethos of spatial and temporal alienability. By tracing Ayopayans' ethical negotiations of their past through the refashioning of inherited intimacies, *After Servitude* illuminates a zone of Indigenous claim-making that challenged unequal access to resources and rights but also the broader relational terms by which justice could be sought. In this regard, Indigenous Ayopayans' demands that elites atone for racialized regimes of labor violence expand existing frameworks for addressing colonial debt and repayment. Their insistence that ordinary people be *affected* by history and answer to its debts through action powerfully pushes back against White disavowals of histories of subjection and slavery in Bolivia but also closer to home.

PART ONE

Kinship

ONE

Claiming Kinship

Ramón Colque and I sat on a ledge outside the former hacienda building, letting the sun warm us before the raw night air encroached. In his nineties, Ramón was bent over from many years of farm work on the hacienda—now converted into a smaller family farm with an adjacent gold mine—nestled on the fertile plateaus of Ayopaya's Sacambaya River valley. As we sat there sleepily, Ramón recalled his work as an unpaid servant (*pongo*) on the hacienda, where he had been adopted as a godchild and servant at age eight. He still lived on the property, in the same house where he had worked all those years. But the house had recently been sold by the former master's nephew, Fabio, to his grandson Martín. This affected the security of Ramón's current arrangement, distancing him from his original host family and their now-grown children. In the hacienda days, by contrast, Ramón would walk these dirt roads with the master's nephew Fabio, then a toddler, perched on his shoulders. Fabio visited Ramón regularly into his adult years, driving him to the village market to buy food and stock up on supplies. This changed when the house was sold in 2010. When we visited in 2011, Ramón lamented that Fabio had stopped coming by. We asked whether Martín provided any help, but Ramón shook his head. "No. He does not give to me."

Over subsequent months Ramón's health worsened. With his injured back, he could no longer carry food home from the village produce market, located some three miles away. Fabio and his wife claimed they would send food to their former servants, including Ramón, yet none had arrived. Ramón's desperation during our 2011 visit had been so palpable that an acquaintance and I sent along a box of food with one of Martín's miners. When Ramón's condition further declined that spring, Martín hired the wife of one of his mine workers to bring Ramón food and keep up the house.

Ramón died the following December. The owner of an adjacent gold mine discovered the body, and Martín phoned Fabio to make funeral arrangements. After a day passed, Fabio had still not returned his call, so Martín bought a casket in town that Sunday and began to prepare for the burial. The miners' wives and women maids employed by Martín had helped wash the body and prepare it to be buried. The funeral was sparsely attended. Martín and several farm workers gathered in a field to drink beer before the casket was lowered into the ground.

Many of Ramón's neighbors and even some of his kin saw him as having been unduly attached to the hacienda. Ramón's wife had not wanted to stay and had moved to the city of Cochabamba alone. But Ramón would not part ways with the former hacienda, even after his children arranged for him to come live with them in nearby Independencia. When I met him, Ramón resided in one of the former hacienda structures, earning a modest daily wage (forty-five bolivianos, about five US dollars) to care for the building and adjacent grounds. Doña Julia Yupanqui, one of his neighbors, had reproached Ramón for this arrangement when we spoke. Seated on a woven blanket (lliqlla) in the shade of her patio one morning, she described how she and her sister "served" the master as rotating mitani servants. She suggested we visit "Ramón, in Don Fabio's home, who remains a slave." Doña Julia explained: "He has accustomed himself to it. He doesn't know anything else." Yet no one demanded this labor. In fact, Martín was not keen on it. It had been the elderly Ramón, whom Martín recognized from childhood vacations, who approached Martín to complain that he had not been "entrusted" with any work. Privately, Martín wryly noted that he "bought the house and Ramón with it." But his account was misleading, for it was Ramón who had insisted on staying, expecting Fabio to look after him with wages, food, and board. This "arrangement" was rooted in an agreement between Ramón's father and the master, an arrangement that Ramón felt should be honored even after others deemed it anachronous and grotesque.

What made this arrangement problematic to many people was not only Ramón's continued monetary dependency on former masters but also his abiding affective attachments to these masters. In her account Doña Julia emphasized the intimacy of Fabio and Ramón's relationship, noting that they had been "very close" over the years, "like father and son." Fabio's younger cousin even implied that the men had been lovers, an idea mediated by the figure of the maricón. In Ayopaya this homophobic slur was leveled at men who did not meet the criteria of heteropatriarchal, Mestizo masculinity.

This ideal could accommodate lovers, Indigenous and Mestiza, but was premised on the ideal that those relations be subordinated to residence and emotional attachments with members of one's nuclear family. In Ramón's case his attachment to the former hacienda—to its sprawling potato plots, the dilapidated house he called home, and the former master's son Fabio—outweighed his felt ties to biological kin or his wife. Ramón's ties to former hacienda lands and masters went against twentieth-century reformist and unionist efforts to replace hacienda dependencies with more liberated orientations to land as property and to work as wage labor.[1] This positioned him as sexually and socially transgressive: a *maricón,* a man whose gender is not affirmed through sexual relations with women, a slave.

This chapter attends to the ways Ayopayans reworked kinship ties to negotiate what they took to be problematic intimacies between Mestizo masters and Indigenous servants. In their descriptions of godparenting, adoption, and aid to former servants, participants bound sentiments of love, care, and affection to earlier economic relations on agrarian estates.[2] Approaching "after" less as epochal displacement than as a sort of continuity of design, I elaborate three figures of posthacienda kinship: *the mother (mamitay* or *madrina*), the *huérfano* (orphan or illegitimate child), and the *maricón* (man who engages in nonregularized sexual relations). While aid relations like these might have allowed Mestizos to stave off violent conflicts in the hacienda era, in the present they were decoupled from land conflicts in ways that suggested their significance in a more than instrumentalist way. In some cases, Mestizo elites found themselves indebted to former servants even where they took issue with the premise of that burden.[3] Yet precisely what made these relations so offensive to some people like Doña Julia was also what imbued them with affective force. As I would learn, as an idiom of historical obligation, kinship held the promise to bind people together across a violent past, reconfiguring oppressive kinds of intimacy as ethical grounds for Indigenous demands for accountability in the present. In this regard, these kin-making practices could be activated to insist upon Mestizos' answerability to rural Indigenous farmers in ways that were deeply disturbing to twentieth-century projects of Indigenous and peasant justice oriented toward free labor and atomistic property.[4]

Indeed, not all villagers and townsfolk saw Ramón's reliance on Mestizo families as problematic. Rather, Ramón's death also supplied an occasion for people to reflect on and discuss what they took to be proper relations between former servant and master groups. When Martín next encountered

Fabio at the Sunday market in Independencia, he asked Fabio to repay him for the cost of the casket. When Fabio berated Martín for buying such an expensive one, Martín answered that there had only been one model and so that was the cost. In the end, according to Martín, Fabio did not contribute "even a cent." This lapse was greatly commented on by villagers and townsfolk. As Fabio's neighbor sharply noted: "Fabio has no shame." Fabio's godson, in turn, conjectured that Fabio's attitude was due to his own declining health. Others reasoned that it was because Fabio's wife had cancer and the cost of her chemotherapy had left him penniless. Martín, however, rejected these explanations. "It's that it doesn't awaken anything in him," Martín bluntly declared. "He isn't affected." To his mind, to be responsive to the needs of former servants followed from a selective capacity to be "affected"; it was this quality of being touched by a sense of duty to others and to a shared past, and not just money, that Fabio had shown himself to lack.

Martín was not alone in harboring this view. During my visits to Fabio's home in Ayopaya, his wife Lola outlined what she saw as appropriate treatment of *los viejos* (the elderly, here used as shorthand for former servants).[5] Over lunch, Lola noted that she continued to send food to her childhood servants, including the *mitani* cook who had worked for her parents and, before them, her grandparents. She recounted a conversation she had with a young man hired to deliver the food to her family's aging servants twice a week. The man complained to Lola that it was unnecessary to send along food, that she should not bother with this arrangement anymore. In response, Lola admonished him: "Someday you will be old and need help, and others will care for you in the same way." Although her account emphasized age, such practices also followed the relational lines of earlier labor hierarchies: among a host of elderly villagers, only former servants qualified for Lola's aid. Even where such duties were shirked, people agreed that *hacendado* families should care for their former servants.

During Evo Morales's presidency (2006–19), informal arrangements of labor, land gifting, and asymmetrical aid like these became newly suspect in their affronts to rights-based projects of installing Indigenous land ownership, paid labor, and gender equity.[6] Yet despite this stigmatization in a national climate defined by reformist and activist efforts to secure Indigenous autonomy and independence from Mestizo groups, for many interlocutors in Ayopaya these kinship-based aid relations offered vital alternatives to masters' earlier repudiation of illegitimate children. Of course, most former hacienda masters and servants had died long ago; with a few exceptions the people undertaking these aid relations had not experienced servitude first-hand. Making strangers into kin—for instance, by adopting an abandoned servant as a godchild or sibling—entailed relational, material, and emotional labors.[7] Children slept in bedrooms with elite Mestizos' own children; they needed money for education, at times earning degrees in specialty fields like medicine or law. In converting a friend into a coparent, a half-sibling into a godchild, these practices produced families but also new lines of accountability to a violent past. Even among those who were imagined to "share blood" or biological ties, kinship had to be constantly made in ways that attached new possibilities to older practices.[8]

Aid relations like these highlight the centrality of kinship ties to contemporary efforts to navigate violent labor histories and their dynamic afterlives. Sponsors like Martín and Lola invoked sentiments of tenderness, love, care, and affection (*cariño*) for former servants. Female sponsors in particular often assumed positions of maternal beneficence, addressed by recipients of aid as *mamitay* (my little mother, also what people called female saints) and *madrina* (godmother). Naming practices like these belong to broader patterns of religious authority within haciendas, with masters' accompanying demands for worker "respect" as an affective disposition.[9] Ramón's insistence that former *hacendado* families continue to "give" to him or that *hacendado* kin be "affected" by former servant claims points to the force of shared emotions in generating feelings of compelled action.[10] Rather than treating such practices only as recursive cultural residues of feudal agriculture, I argue that such practices depended upon subjects' ability to foster a vulnerability or openness to history's debts, one captured in Martín's allusion to being "affected" or "awakened" by others' plight. For recipients of Mestizo aid, this mobilization of kinship languages provided a mechanism to negotiate material vulnerabilities but also to purposefully navigate earlier labor and sexual violence. Ayopayans' recrafting of these inherited kinship languages sheds new light on the creative ways that institutions associated with oppressive histories are inhabited, and reworked, to transform the present.

MOTHER, ORPHAN, *MARICÓN*: DOUBLE-EDGED INTIMACIES

In the Andes, as elsewhere, the parameters of domestic servitude and its significance to family life have been key sites of legal refashioning as well as ethical disagreement. As Raka Ray and Seemin Qayum (2009: 99, 103) have discussed, in many parts of the world, including India, the twentieth century shift from an older "family retainer" model based on predominantly male live-in servants who labored exclusively for a single family to a liberal, contract-based wage labor model, rendered earlier kinship-based idioms of care newly problematic. This family retainer model was common in colonial settings where the European "big house" model was recombined with native labor institutions such as the Indian *jajmani* caste model or, in Chile and Columbia, *latifundio* social relations in hacienda estates.[11]

Across these settings former employers likened servants to family members or children and emphasized the "love" and affection binding employers to servants.[12] Where bonded labor was legally displaced by ostensibly "free" (or at least paid) labor, these sentiments became anachronous and offensive. Within "modern" wage labor economies, by contrast, domestic servants are to be paid rather than sustained by employers' aid, including help in cases of workers' illness or family difficulties. As Laura Gotkowitz (2007: 192) and Marcia Stephenson (1999) have discussed, in Bolivia early twentieth-century women's rights groups and labor organizers held up institutions of *mitanaje* and *pongueaje* (domestic servitude) as examples of lingering "feudalism" at odds with rights-based citizenship, wage labor, and the modern (nuclear) Mestizo family.[13]

Households have long been sustained by various kinds of affective labor, by women and mothers but also by nonfamily members such as nannies, cooks, wet nurses, and other live-in servants.[14] In many industries paid work and formal kinship blur, such as when hostesses become brides or when home health workers frame their own labor practices in terms of kinship obligations.[15] As I learned from carrying out oral histories with former servants, in Ayopayan haciendas unmarried women and the daughters of tenant farmers were required to "serve" in shifting rotations each year in practices that blurred household labor with sexual relations that ranged from rape to concubinage to marriage. While these intimate relations were often concealed, kinship-based idioms also organized labor and social hierarchies. Servants addressed masters using the respectful titles "my mother" (*mamay*) and "my father" (*taytay*), and servants called employers' children "my child" (*niñoy*). Alongside gendered household labor (cleaning, cooking, sewing, weaving blankets, or producing fermented corn beer), *mitani* laborers were also required to care for and "raise" (*criar*) employer's children.

This suggests that haciendas were agricultural but also *affective* economies; for those forced "to serve," labor was provided as a service rather than a material good. Although this service labor was summarily dismissed by Karl Marx and downplayed by scholars who have privileged haciendas as agrarian institutions, it was crucial to hacienda economies and, in turn, continued to define Indigenous orientations to former master families in Ayopaya.[16] Like other domestic labor institutions, haciendas confused the categories of home and work, family and contract, affection and duty, making them what Raka Ray and Seemin Qayum (2008: 2) have called a "dense site" for viewing social constitution and reconstitution over time (Figure 1).

The importance of placing kinship alongside economic formations was a central point elaborated in Lewis Henry Morgan's ([1868] 1997) classic study of marriage. In that work he showed how kinship is not outside of but rather a conduit for the traffic in money and property. Gayle Rubin (1975: 45) further clarified that anthropologists should look for the oppression of women not only in the exchange of merchandise but also in the traffic of women *as women*. Hence, rather than existing outside of economy, kinship too arises as a form of production. This blurs the line between property as rights to things and in people.[17] Moreover, as Ann Stoler (2002) and Audra Simpson (2014) have demonstrated, controlling these money flows via heteropatriarchal marriage institutions has historically been crucial to colonial and settler-colonial efforts to shore up White superiority. Hence, while property is often painted in neo/classical accounts as a universal object of exchange outside of sociality, this scholarship recasts property—as racialized ownership but also as masculine desire and expectation of benefit—as contingent on its shaping of institutions of marriage and kinship. Instead of existing forthright outside of history, property as ownership also entails knotty configurations that span material, affective, and sexual dimensions. Property, like kinship, is produced and maintained through the control of objects as well as bodies and desires.

In Latin America specifically, anxieties about the slippage between economic interests and affective ties, including kinship hierarchies, has been most evident in scholarship concerning agrarian patronage. Eric Wolf and Sidney Mintz (1957) examined aid relations in agrarian settings mainly as "patronage" or as client-patron ties which, they argued, were inherited from earlier "feudal" institutions of debt peonage that arrived with Spanish colonialism. In accord with this argument, clientelist ties to masters can constrain people by making them dependent on elites for work and aid, but they also enable Indigenous and peasant workers to make claims on authorities that would not be possible in their absence. These studies reveal liberalism

FIGURE 1. Hacienda estate master and servant in Ayopaya province, circa 1930. Mendizabel-Crespo family archive. Photo by author.

as double-edged: a juridical model of private property eradicates earlier "customs" of aid on agrarian estates without installing anything in their place.[18] At the same time, as Marc Edelman (2018) argues, this tendency to emphasize the economic and labor dimensions of haciendas led many classic works to neglect the question of why such institutions proved so tenacious and so obdurate to rights-based reform. Answering that question requires renewed attention to the affective dimensions of the exchange systems that upheld servitude.

In his influential analyses of Malaysian peasant relations, James Scott (1971, 1976) drew from historian E. P. Thomson to argue that feudal customs did not just disappear from modern agriculture but rather continued to organize a moral economy premised upon the exchange of labor for favors and prestige. Questions of "premodern" custom have been especially urgent in the central Andes, given the well-documented longevity of an asymmetrical authority complex in which economic power was contingent on gift relations. In the precolonial Andes, and specifically the Cochabamba valleys where Ayopaya is located, political authority was linked to the exchange of gifts and services to lords and with place-based deities, both of which responded to an understanding of power as dependent on redistributive acts.[19] Legitimacy stemmed from redistributive capacities and was guided not simply by materialist concerns but also by religious authority in which local chiefs mediated relations with unruly local deities who were thought to control rain and drought and thus had to be appeased through gifts and sacrifice (Harris 1989; Parry and Bloch 1989). Despite the broader historical transformations elicited by colonialism and the imposition of encomiendas, this formation retained relevance both in highland ayllu communities and in Andean haciendas into the late twentieth century, and arguably the present.[20]

While a "moral economy" approach has raised crucial questions about how modern economies remain inflected by older customs of agrarian exchange that also supply points of resistance and opposition for workers, in this work I reassess both the transactional instrumentalism and material (resource-based) emphasis of a framework of microresistance. I draw in particular from more recent studies of godparenting that foreground the centrality of kinship idioms to patronage relations. Classic studies highlight what they characterize as the unlikely emotional or affective grip of a sentiment of obligation or duty to uphold kinship ties.[21] Recent ethnographic approaches ask more explicitly about the ethical traditions guiding such sentiments. In her study of Peruvian child circulation, for instance, Jessica Leinaweaver (2008: 11) showed how practices of godparenting fit into Quechua traditions of child circulation that participants mobilize "to build the layers of kinship and connectedness" across racialized and economic hierarchies.[22]

Sian Lazar (2008) further demonstrated how kinship claims inform modes of political collectivity in La Paz, Bolivia, leading among other factors to the revival of community organizing after Bolivia's Popular Participation Law of 1992.[23] In this context, kinship-based paradigms of authority shaped expectations of redistribution and political responsibility in ways that held dramatic consequences for Indigenous engagements with state political leaders. Susan Ellison (2018: 15), also centering her study in La Paz, examined how paradigms of reciprocal care and obligation came to be reworked within Bolivian conflict resolution programs, remapping the bounds both of domestic life and citizenship in the process. Rather than seeing private life as naturally constrained to the family, she illuminates how *domestication* arose as a key mechanism by which alternate conflict resolution workers depoliticized militant Indigenous (especially urban Aymara) labor struggles by converting unwieldy sentiments into a civil society model centered around nuclear kinship and heterosexual coupledom.

I build upon these classical and contemporary approaches to draw new attention to the purposeful labor of producing and reproducing kinship relations—including so-called "fictive" kinship ties elaborated in godparenting and adoption—as key for Indigenous and Mestizo efforts to navigate historically entrenched racial hierarchies. This was a pressing problem in a place where the relatives of servants and masters continue to reside side by side. I approach aid relations like these as a point of insight into the creative remaking of earlier hacienda intimacies related to the dynamics of domestic labor and kinship within haciendas. As I described in the preface, in Ayopaya the material ruins of haciendas are evident in the surrounding landscape (Figure 2), yet ruins also take physical shape in abiding attachments across families and in the objects, money, and sentiments that circulate among them. Rather than focusing on strategic efforts to redirect resources as a practice of microresistance, however, I inquire into the ethical ideals of authority and obligation guiding these relations.[24]

In Ayopaya these ideals cannot be traced back *either* to highland ayllu traditions or national projects of *mestizaje* as racial assimilation.[25] To understand the present-day underpinnings for this approach to wealth, it is important to keep in mind that former servants like Ramón had experienced the loosening of aid ties following hacienda abolition as deeply wounding. For Ramón, pay had problematically displaced earlier employer-servant relations framed in kinship terms and accompanied by aid. Recalling Quechua notions of the *waqcha* (orphan) as a pitiful, cast-off, and absolutely isolated subject with no affective ties, for subjects like Ramón autonomy was not desirable; it meant social abandonment.[26] That people pursued and even tried to extend these claims was clear in Ramón's implicit suggestion that not only Fabio but also Martín *should* give to him. Unexpectedly, notions of economic responsibility did not diverge notably between master and servant groups—with

FIGURE 2. Former hacienda estate building in the village of Sailapata, Ayopaya province, 2011. Photo by author.

former servants striving to subvert dominant languages, for instance—but often formed a shared framework centered upon wealth as a retainer or end-effect of earlier labor violence that introduced ethical burdens in the present.

In Ayopaya, kinship-based languages of debt, repayment, and accountability emerged as crucial mechanisms by which residents sought to thread money to history, wealth to violence. Against classical understandings of money as a contentless form, or a sort of empty mediator that links people through exchange, they insisted that profits and fortunes carved out of the soils and mines of former haciendas necessarily retained debts to former systems of labor servitude. Rather than deriving from the seemingly global structure of class relations, these ties were interpreted along the lines of the grounded experiences of Indigenous workers to economically influential bosses.

Many Ayopayans sought to address the continued debts accrued through earlier hacienda bondage by creatively repurposing, rather than cutting off, lines of attachment linking former master and servant families. Kinship here offered a grammar for contesting more abstract, isolated understandings of money as essentially decoupled from Ayopaya's violent hacienda past. Relations of godparenting, adoption, and sponsorship worked to bind Mestizo subjects to their earlier hacienda kin and ancestors, and to the debts these Mestizos had inherited from relatives. In this way kinship emerged as a knot that could be mobilized to demand historical redress, binding Mestizo families to Indigenous villagers and to genealogies of hacienda violence, at times even against their will.

ILLICIT INTIMACIES:
THE *MARICÓN* AS PROPERTY RISK

We sat at a blue sodalite table under a thatch hut in the former hacienda buildings' courtyard. Martín Rodriguez, the *hacendado*'s grandson and the property's sole heir, was drinking with his uncle, godson, and cousin. His cousin had brought Martín a bottle of Jack Daniels whiskey, hoping to convince him to help repair a damaged road: they needed Martín's tractor. For my part, I was seated awkwardly at a distance with my tape recorder, trying to assess what all this drink would mean for my ride back to Independencia with Martín's godson later that evening. The conversation turned to Martín's great-grandfather, the earlier hacienda *patrón* (master), and his five sons and five daughters. Martín's godson Edgar playfully interjected: "Those are the ten *that we know of*." Martín turned to me: "You see, I'm the only son my father had, and he was his father's only son, but when I go to town and say this, people laugh and say, 'Here, this is your aunt, this is your uncle.'"

Later, Martín explained that his grandfather had four brothers "and that one whose name I can never remember." A pause. "Hugo, the eldest. My great-grandfather disowned him, stripping him of his name and fortune." Hugo had eloped with a Quechua woman, angering his father. When the Chaco War started, Hugo refused to fulfill his military duty and so his father threw him out for "being a *maricón*, for mixing himself up with an old lady, with a peasant." Martín continued: "So my grandfather disowned him, and he left." Edgar interjected: "Your grandfather also had lots of children, right?" Martín nodded. "Supposedly yes, but the only one who was recognized was my father. What luck for me! But then it had always been like that. People had children everywhere, but it was frowned upon to recognize them." I asked whether Martín knew any of them. "I know one," he told me, "but it's messy. My father recognized him as a brother and continues to help him, but he doesn't share our name."

As they sipped whiskey in the interior patio of the former hacienda estate, these men described a familial past interspersed with illicit liaisons, including sexual relations between hacienda masters and Quechua women. Where they concerned *hacendados'* long-term relations to Quechua women and servants, such relations were viewed as perversions of Mestizo masculinity. This was a kind of masculinity crafted through military service and heterosexual marriage within perceived racial and class categories.[27]

This history was etched into their memories, but also the surrounding landscape. Visiting Martín's gold mine one day, his cousin looked around and commented to Martín: "Uncle Rafael's house was around here, right?" Martín gestured toward a dry hill. "Yes, up over there," he said. Shifting my gaze up the hill, I saw the crumbling remains of a house structure and an old stone wall. Martín filled me in: "My uncle turned *campesino*, or worse. He stopped bathing and just chewed coca. There were two of them. Now they moved to Santa Cruz." Such liaisons were part of a range of practices identified with the children of Mestizo *hacendados* "going peasant," abandoning bourgeois sensibilities and assuming lives as *campesinos*, often by eloping with Indigenous (*campesina* or *chola*) women.

Such sexual relations with Indigenous or peasant (*campesina*) women threatened racialized ideals of Mestizo heteropatriarchy. Participation in this ideal produced legitimate masculinity but also secured family-based property ownership in accordance with sanctioned procreative relations organized around heterosexual marriage. In twentieth-century Bolivia, securing Mestizo property ownership required securing sexuality but also a broader flow of affects and sentiments. Fears about sexual perversion and improper desires assumed special weight in a region where *hacendados* rarely fulfilled nationalist ideals of urban Mestizo status, and where many landowners belonged to a lower-income class of Quechua *juch'uy patrones* (little masters).

Later that evening, Martín disappeared into his grandfather's old library—a dark room off the main courtyard filled with dusty books and an unused desk. He reemerged with a newspaper clipping, a 1992 article from the Bolivian newspaper *Los Tiempos*. The clipping outlined how one "Indio Rodriguez" had gained land in the region through a Jesuit land grant in the eighteenth century. Martín had also retrieved a worn document, an original property title dating back to the 1770s. It outlined a land grant made from Jesuit missionaries to the Rodriguez family to which he belongs. After Martín read from the newspaper clipping, his godson Edgar looked over at him, notably disturbed. "But why do they describe him in such a derogatory way," he said, "as an *Indio*?" Edgar paused, then as if to convince himself, added: "He was *Mestizo*." Martín shrugged dismissively. "We're all a little bit Indian," he said. Eloping with local Indigenous women was particularly problematic given their *hacendado* progenitors' already tenuous racial status. This tenuousness stemmed from the specificities of Sarahuayto's hacienda, whose master fell short of the racial and class criteria for inclusion in a Mestizo elite. Masters' abilities to uphold racial status as Mestizo sat uneasily alongside actual hacienda lives wherein *hacendado* children grew up alongside Quechua servants, "orphans," and adoptees who had been integrated into the household.

Concerns with the relational entailments of wealth were especially pointed in Ayopaya, a region characterized by dramatic Indigenous social mobility as well as violence. Confronted with mounting antihacienda rebellions beginning around 1938, culminating in a 1947 uprising in which haciendas were sacked or burned and several landlords killed, hacienda lords were forced to depart quickly on mule or horseback.[28] Many landlords were rumored to have left gold behind, hiding riches in kitchen cupboards, grain pots, and flour tins, and burying gold and silver in the gray sands of the winding Sacambaya River.[29] For poor peasants who had only just made the jump from hacienda workers to "little masters," new wealth also elicited new questions of duty to those who had been less fortunate.[30]

In fact, in the era of the hacienda's violent undoing in the late 1940s, landlords' upholding of exchange relations often determined their fate; as Quechua farmers commonly explained, there "the bad masters were killed." Cruel and greedy masters perished in armed conflicts with *colonos* or by more indeterminate means, whether illness or bewitching. Such accounts framed Mestizos' ability to live in the countryside as contingent on upholding duties to peasant workers, neighbors, and kin—an expectation that imbued seemingly banal practices with a potent, militant underside.

In Independencia, elderly Mestizo townsfolk held childhood memories of these earlier events, when hacienda workers, peasant unionists, and *comuneros* (members of Indigenous communities) ambushed homes, eventually toppling the oppressive hacienda system. The post-2006 period again brought out related feelings of fear and uncertainty for Mestizos residing in the countryside. Like the period of antihacienda uprising preceding the 1952 Socialist Revolution, the mass mobilization, road blockades, and at times fatal clashes between peasant unionists, conservative anti-Indigenous protestors, and state police and military in the early 2000s turned an existing order on its head.[31] Morales's 2005 election, coupled with the subsequent 2008 global economic crisis, led many *hacendado* children to migrate back to the countryside, finding urban bureaucracies and traditional sources of employment less welcoming than before. In 2010, as I began fieldwork, older hierarchies and Mestizo-Indigenous relations were in flux, imbuing rural relationships with new kinds of uncertainty. Given this broader climate of racialized uncertainty and risk, I was surprised to find people involved in a broad set of exchange practices I had associated with the earlier hacienda era. In aid relations like Ramón's, money was aligned not only with risky, punishable greed but could also work as a redemptive form, especially when distributed in ways that participants understood as ethical.[32]

Alongside sheer questions of racialized inequality, the living kin of Ayopayan *hacendados* also reckoned with a set of intimate ties that could potentially disrupt racialized regimes of property. Securing property here required controlling sexuality, and heteropatriarchal inheritance along family lines promised to stave off incursions from Indigenous claimants. For instance, in the case of Martín's wayward uncle *maricón*, unsanctioned sexual relations threatened existing structures of family land ownership and authority that secured hacienda estates as the sole property of former hacienda masters, their Mestizo wives, and their recognized Mestizo children as future heirs. Yet life in Ayopaya has long been defined by intimacies at odds with this exemplary kinship frame, including nonregularized sexual relations in which *hacendado* sons eloped with *campesinas* (Quechua peasant women): that at issue in what Fabio and his friends characterized as their uncle, the *maricón*. *Hacendado* families looked to regularize these relations by newly incorporating unrecognized children (*huérfanos* or orphans) into families as legitimate kin: godchildren. Regularizing property required regularizing sexuality, a process that hinged on converting illicit bonds into sanctioned godparent and adoptive kinship ties.

BECOMING MOTHER: ABSORBING WAYWARD KIN

On a temperate afternoon in February 2012, I ascended the slippery cobblestones off the main street in Independencia, the municipal center in Ayopaya province. Continuing along a muddy road, I arrived at the lush croplands of Flora Soliz, the daughter of the former hacienda master. I had been invited to her annual *ch'alla de terrenos,* a ritual sacrifice centering on offerings of fermented corn beer and llama or sheep blood that was typically performed in the fecund, rainy months following Carnival.[33]

By late morning, Flora and her sons, municipal and union officials, villagers, and townsfolk had gathered together on a green hillside amid fields of corn, peas, and squash. Earlier that morning they had sacrificed a sheep, distributing its blood across agrarian plots and storage buildings as an offering to the Pachamama, who is understood to determine crop fertility and family health in the year to come. The sheep meat was baked with corn and potatoes in *pampakuy* (earth-oven) style in which buried embers are covered with stones. A small fire was prepared, and a *q'oa* offering consisting of coca leaves, confetti, incense, and the heart of the sacrificed sheep was carefully placed in its middle. As the *q'oa* burned, Flora's sons distributed coca, chicha beer, and cigarettes, and guests stood around solemnly chewing coca and dripping *chicha* on the *q'oa*. Later, women guests aided Flora as she doled out steaming plates of mutton, potatoes, and corn and then a bonfire was built up. Flora's sons retrieved their guitars and *charangos*, serenading guests in Quechua and Spanish. At sundown, a group of men carried cornstalks down to Flora's *chicha*-brewery, where guests drank to the lively tune of *cueca* song until dawn.

Each year, during the spring *ch'allas*, the kin of former landlords, servants, and tenant farmers gather to drink *chicha* and to consume meat baked in *pampakuy* ovens. According to elderly villagers in Ayopaya, hacienda masters had forced workers there to attend patron saints' day celebrations, imposed heavy fiesta obligations, and in turn allowed workers to congregate in the chapel, yards, and surrounding mountains for several days of feasting and rest. *Hacendados'* distribution of food and drink was ritually reciprocated by workers who brought farm produce to the master's home, a practice recalled in the present when villagers carried cornstalks to Flora's *chicharia*.[34]

In 2012 this event was attended by townsfolk and by Quechua villagers, relatives of unpaid *colonos* or tenant farmers who had worked for Flora's father. The guests included Flora's half-sister. As I discuss below, Flora had adopted and integrated this child into her own household as a godchild after the girl was born to one of the unwed servants in Flora's father's hacienda. Along with hosting *ch'allas*, Flora acted as a godparent, adopted children, funded local municipal projects, and distributed food, clothing, and money to former servant families from the tables of her rundown *chicharia*. Thus, while elsewhere hacienda-based systems of sponsorship and patronage seem to have broken down after agrarian reform, in Ayopaya elements of this system persisted, constituting what Flora termed a "custom."

Several days after attending Flora's *ch'alla de terrenos*, we met at her *chicharia* to discuss her position in town. We sat side-by-side on a long wooden bench in the covered outdoor patio as Flora recalled her childhood memories of the region's tumultuous period of antihacienda uprising. Flora's grandparents had owned humble parcels of land outside of town. Then, in 1953, the agrarian reform occurred. "It was a severe time," she said. "I remember there were *searches* for property owners. Yes, *searches* (*buscas*). They took the lands of my grandparents and all his family. Everything was taken." Flora recounted how she and her siblings had hidden, huddled up at home and afraid that militants would enter and kill them. "I remember those days of 1952, during the revolution," she said. "The *Indios* rose up. They were cruel. In Tiquirpaya they killed three people. They came with their concha shells and they made us suffer. We hid ourselves. 'They are coming to kill us,' people said. 'They are going to slit our throats,' said the children. They had killed a professor, an officer, and another one too. Did you know?" I nodded.

To Flora, this turbulence persisted. The year before, her great-nephew had visited land that he had inherited from Flora's father. According to Flora, he was sleeping in his truck overnight when he awoke to these words: "Leave now, before something happens to you, before we enact community justice. We will kill you. Because this is not your land." These words are almost a verbatim repetition of Quechua phrase put to *hacendados* in the late 1940s and as recounted to me by former leaders of antihacienda militias (see chapter 2). According to Flora, her cousin then hastily departed. Turning to me for emphasis, Flora concluded, "These conflicts continue."

As this account demonstrates, Flora was deeply offended by calls for "community justice" to be achieved by lynching or ejecting Mestizo city-folk (and the unknown kin of former *hacendados*). For her, these conflicts stemmed from *campesinos'* problematic "lack of tenderness" toward their former masters. This went against her own efforts to cultivate spaces of patronal sharing and distribution. As Flora put it: "Peasants don't have even a little bit of tenderness for the person they loved so much before. Instead, they are always trying to damage the masters. But there aren't masters anymore."

Flora's account captured the ambiguous status of former hacienda masters in places like Ayopaya. In one breath she lamented the lack of "tenderness" of former servant groups toward masters; in the next she corrected herself to clarify that "there aren't masters anymore." This marked a tension between, on the one hand, a narrative emphasizing the continuity of racialized modes of authority and property rooted in the hacienda system and, on the other hand, a liberal discourse naming those forms of authority anachronous and irrelevant in the present.

Despite competing ways of narrating these practices, Flora's narrative reveals an abiding expectation on the part of Ayopayan Mestizos that Indigenous residents uphold relations of "respect" and deference toward former *hacendado* families and in return would continue to benefit from hierarchical aid relations rooted in hacienda labor economies. Where this did not occur, Flora narrated it as a matter of lacking affects (*cariño* or tenderness). Relatedly, she hoped that her position as a religious sponsor and a *Patrona* of ritual feasting events would protect her from otherwise ubiquitous kinds of racial violence.

According to Flora: "Last year my relatives went to the lands by truck and were told that they should leave before blood runs. They were told that the villagers do not want to see them there, because the lands do not belong to them and that now the local peasants are the owners. Upon telling me this, the peasants came and said to me, '*Mamitay*, the lands are yours. Why don't you come? If you visit, we will roast a sheep. We will make you grilled meat, *mamitay*, with corn too. Just come.' They came to the *chicharia* and suggested this to me." (In fact, during the spring *ch'alla* at Flora's *chicharia*, which I discuss below, I was introduced to several of the villagers from the Indigenous community that now lives where the former hacienda stood.)

Later that night, after the frigid mountain air drove us merrymakers back to town, I crowded into Doña Flora's *chicharia* with her guests where she served *chicha* to friends, municipal officials, farmers, and villagers, including the children of her father's former hacienda servants. Out of earshot from Flora, a young Quechua union leader supplied his account of the land conflict with Flora's cousin. This relative had laid claim to the land, citing the fact that he had bought it rather than inheriting it. In this way he strove to contest peasant challenges to his land ownership premised on the Instituto Nacional de Reforma Agrarian (INRA) stipulation that land not serving a "social or economic function" must be turned over to Indigenous communities and redistributed.[35] I learned that the man whose land claims were in dispute had been an unrecognized hacienda child—a child born out of wedlock after the coupling of the hacienda master and a Quechua *mitani* servant.[36] Villagers were unsympathetic to his claims. He was, to use a common slur in Ayopaya at that time, an *hijo del patrón* (son of a bitch) thought to be complicit with hacienda servitude despite his mother's victimization within it. As villagers and unionists opposed to this man's land claims crowded into Flora's *chicharia*, they cemented her position of authority in the region.

This case surprised me in the ways that Quechua villagers had backed the land claims of the master's daughter rather than those of local villagers, including hacienda servants who had come to inherit land through marriage. Instead, villagers aligned themselves with former *patrones* like Doña Flora who, while striving to inhabit the position of the exemplary patron and religious sponsor, ostensibly had no interest in reclaiming land. The land claims of other groups, including the aforementioned son of the *mitani* servant and hacienda master, constituted more immediate threats to land tenure.

Villagers negotiated these conflicts over land tenure by repurposing an older kinship-based patronage idiom. For villagers the networks of religious sponsorship and ritual feasting (including adoption of orphans as godchildren) were treated as legitimate, supplying valued lines of affiliation for villagers and former *hacendados*. Conversely, children born from nonregularized sexual relations occurring within haciendas (synthesized by the figure of the *hacendado* as *maricón*, as enacting desires at odds with Mestizo, heteropatriarchal family) continued to violate sanctioned lines of affiliation, descent, and property inheritance. Doña Flora's hosting of villagers at the *ch'alla* and villagers' reciprocal invitation to her to visit her father's ancestral lands consolidated Flora's position as *Patrona*, an exemplary boss and sponsor. Yet this position also allowed farmers to limit other land claims, particularly by the former *hacendado's* estranged *campesina* wife and children.

In the age of Evo Morales and given continued INRA land titling initiatives centered on dismantling inherited structures of economic and social power in the countryside, Flora's case struck me as counterintuitive and disturbing. It attested to the importance of enduring kinship attachments for shared perceptions of legitimate authority in the posthacienda countryside. At the same time, however, Flora's position also demonstrated that these networks supplied villagers with different possibilities for affiliation and support based on their efforts to position themselves alongside a particular Mestizo personage. As apparent in the aforementioned case, for Quechua villagers maintaining ties to people like Flora opened up possibilities for negotiating a tense rural climate marked by unresolved land disputes.

Villagers' preference for Doña Flora over and above the claims of the *mitani*-turned-*hacendado* wife point to the continued legitimacy of older masters who violently mistreated laborers in the past but who continued to offer material support, acknowledge abiding relations, and who were not in any immediate sense trying to exploit them or take their land. By contrast, people harbored doubts about new land claimants, however more Indigenous or peasant they seemed. Here, hierarchical attachments centered on the figure of the Mother—as *Patrona*, as godmother, and as adoptive mother— shored up protection for the kin of hacienda masters but could also be creatively deployed by villagers to refute the claims of estranged *campesina* wives and out-of-wedlock hacienda children.

It would be easy to frame these configurations of motherly patronage principally as instrumental mechanisms for retaining land access. Yet, for Flora personally, these exchanges were not about property, or at least not in the sense of a material resource: she had no interest in reclaiming that land.[37] Her grown sons had urban businesses in Oruro and Cochabamba, and she herself had suffered a stroke that limited her ability to work. While she retained control over a small parcel of land near the center of town, where the *ch'alla* had been hosted, most of this land was used for growing specialty fruits (especially peach and apple). I found it hard to imagine that she would be in pursuit of more distant agricultural lands where irrigation was difficult due to their remoteness from water sources, especially the Sacambaya River.

Instead, in Flora's view, these relations responded to a sense of duty to "help" (*ayudar*) the needy. "I have helped many people," she recounted. "As you saw yesterday, the way I provided a meal for all those people. Ours is the only hacienda that still has these customs, that attends to all the people who come. Here too in the *chicharia*, in the early mornings and for the poor I always bring clothes to distribute. I give to those in need, those who do not have food. Help arrives even to those who don't need it, sometimes." I asked when these "customs" began. "I've always done this," Flora explained, though it had been grander when her husband was alive. Back then, their *ch'allas* were attended by *campesinos* as well as fine townsfolk. "But," she added, her face brightening slightly, "yesterday many good people were introduced to us, no? Doctors, people from the municipal government, the mayor, and the architect sleeping." She lifted her arm and waved vaguely toward a man snoring loudly at the far end of the table. Turning away from him, Flora paused pensively. "These customs haven't been taken away," she said. "I've continued with them."

As if on cue, a man in rags stumbled in, leaning unsteadily on his cane. Calling out to him in Quechua, Flora waved him over to a table and then turned to me in a hushed voice: "He's half stupid. He's asking for food that one gifts. One must always gift it to them. He always comes like this, asking for food." She nodded at a woman employee, who promptly carried out a bowl of soup from a small kitchen situated under an overhang of corrugated metal roofing.

For Flora, acts like these constituted material expressions of godly devotion. Of her half-siblings, she noted: "I give them a lot. For His wishes, one must give every day. Food, clothes, a bed, I give a lot. What can I do? I simply have to give." This explanation, combined with Flora's position in town, suggests the importance of Mestizo relations of aid as both reproducing economic and racial hierarchies but also drawing diverse groups together across a divisive past. Flora's positioning as *mother* here belongs to a shared idiom of authority that contrasts with, and promises to resolve, excessive intimacies related to masters' earlier rape of Indigenous servants and the out-of-wedlock "orphans" those unions had produced.

But while Flora expected those relations to uphold and confirm her status, this was not always the case. Speaking about her half-siblings turned godchildren, Flora said, "I helped Hasintu Soliz, who is now a lawyer, [and] his sisters since they were young. For this reason, they will never forget me. When I am there, these girls bring me to their homes or call me over and give me gifts. Only Hasintu is proud." She described how, one day, he drove past her door with a new Toyota truck. Flora perceived this as an affront to her economic status, an effort to say, "Look how I am now." Braking, Hasintu had leaned his head out the window: "Flora," he called. "What?" she had replied. Pausing in her story, she turned to me. "I've told him," she said. "I am the godmother of your marriage, and you should call me *madrina*. But he doesn't anymore." She returned to narrating: "'Flora!' 'What?' His wife sat beside him and behind her their maid. 'This is our new automobile. Now I don't have any reason to suffer.' He is overly proud."

In recounting this event, Flora expressed her sadness that her godson seemed unappreciative of her earlier help in his childhood, now being unduly "proud." This shift in demeanor was especially disturbing to Doña Flora as her own business had not fared terribly well. If the once-impoverished child of a Quechua kitchen servant had risen to the status of a prominent municipal government official who owned a shiny Ford truck and could afford a maid, Flora instead spent afternoons with the flies and drunks in her run-down *chicharia*.

Ayopayan gift relations drew upon kinship models of care and authority to navigate entrenched hierarchies related to earlier hacienda servitude, relations that assumed noteworthy weight in the context of broader decolonial struggles aimed at stamping out Indigenous dependencies on Mestizo elites. Despite its indeterminacy and risk, mothering here aspired to resolve forms of sexual and social transgression synthesized in the figure of the *maricón* as incestuous lover. But it also relied upon deeply racialized connotations that positioned the *patrón* as superior. Of her half-siblings, fathered by the master with the daughter of a Quechua *mitani* servant, Flora noted: "These are Indian hicks with their same faces. They are the children of *campesinos*, and their mother has the same face. They did not come out our color, because I have two other brothers from my father with another concubine, but they have my eyes."

Flora here displayed a disturbing sense of racialized superiority, one that implicitly excused earlier sexual violence in haciendas as a mechanism for "Whitening" the nation. Given the authority that such relations conferred upon former *hacendados*, people like Hasintu understandably refused to uphold the racialized deference that Mestizos like Flora expected, and which in turn reproduced the racial hierarchies that defined hacienda subjection. These relations were open to contrasting narratives, however. In Ramón's case, for instance, the aid relations enabled by abiding attachments to former master families outweighed the experiences of social isolation and stigma he faced on the part of neighbors and relatives who insisted he dispense with outmoded hacienda ways. Likewise, members of former masters were not in agreement about how best to ethically address this violent past.[38] While many Mestizo families left the region or dropped their second names marking descent from abusive *hacendados*, Flora and her family strove to uphold aid relations as ethical orientations to earlier sexual and labor violence.

OBLIGATIONS TO ORPHANS: THE GIFT AS REPAYMENT

By late February the Carnival celebrations were well under way in the municipal town of Independencia. Sustained by a case of beer left over from the government's festivities, a group of men and women continued their merrymaking at one municipal official's home. Seated around a long table, people played a dice game called *cacho*. Flora's son Raul, a Quechua and Spanish-speaking agronomist, told me about his family. His grandmother, I learned, had owned a hacienda nearby. When she separated from her husband, she moved to the town and took her children with her, including Raul's mother

Flora. Her ex-husband had continued to live on the hacienda and this, Raul noted ambiguously, "was the situation in which the *campesinos* offered someone to the hacienda. They brought a woman called a *mitani* to the house in order to serve. This ended with children being born there, my mother's siblings."

As if anticipating my question of what this arrangement might have looked like, Raul added: "It's not that there was a rape or anything like that. [The woman] ended up living with my grandfather, but she was incredibly young." They lived together until the man died. Such arrangements were common, Raul explained, among women sent to work as unpaid servants in regional haciendas. While he denied the presence of "rape," Raul used the term "service" to also connote sexual labor acts. "If at some time the landowner wanted something," Raul explained, "he had the service of the *mitani*. And so...children were born."

Servicio, the root of the word "servitude" (*servidumbre*), here carried multiple valences, including that of fulfilling another's sexual needs. Mestizo townsfolk posited these sexual relations as indeterminate. Don René Vasquez, the son of a particularly violent hacienda master, put it bluntly: "To what degree was it rape, and to what degree was it *not*?" In some cases, Don René explained, women also sought out *hacendados* as desirable fathers for their children and subsequently lived with and married hacienda masters. Many Mestizo elites problematically attributed this birth of out-of-wedlock children to servant women's aims of getting pregnant to "get something out of" masters. According to this narrative, women servants tried to subvert hacienda labor hierarchies through making themselves available sexually to masters.[39]

By contrast, servants' adult children to whom I spoke instead described these practices as part of a tragic and painful history of *violación* (rape) committed by *patrones* against unmarried girls and women servants in haciendas. The brothers and sons of Indigenous Quechua *mitanis*, for instance, spoke about having to "deliver" sisters and daughters to the *hacendado*. Gregorio, whose mother had labored as a *mitani*, spoke guardedly about this history. When we returned from the peach orchard one day (as I wrote in the preface), our discussion turned to what the *hacendados* did with their female servants. "What would they have done? Gregorio asked. "Who knows." This question allowed him to avoid getting into details. On another occasion, two aging daughters of a *mitani* who had children with the hacienda master did not address the nature of that sexual relationship but recalled a difficult childhood walking for miles to get water from a well and awaking at dawn to start their work at a grain mill. Archival materials from this time allude to sexual violence. Hacienda worker petitions brought before the national agrarian court in 1942 list abiding *hacendado* abuses, among them the whipping of workers and *estupro* (rape).[40]

In their guarded talk about this practice, *hacendado* children and servants alike emphasized the opacity of earlier sexual relations in the present. This opacity—specifically the uncertainty about who fathered children with whom and whether that relation was consensual or not—did not shield people from accountability but rather generated a more distributed orientation to history as a site of present-day obligation and duty. For the descendants of hacienda masters, demands for aid came from former servant families who might also include blood relatives: nieces, nephews, cousins, aunts, uncles. Systems of godparenting and sponsorship in part resolved this uncertainty by making the question of biological descent irrelevant. Former servant families and their children, however conceived, constituted appropriate recipients of Mestizo aid from town personages like Flora.

Despite this, however, the birth of out-of-wedlock children within haciendas was disturbing to many of the living relatives of *hacendados*. According to Raul, in the case of his own family, his mother Flora and her brother "felt bad" for the innocent children, their younger half-siblings. Raul recalled his uncle remarking, "My father did this and it is not the children's fault." The two siblings decided to integrate these children, their half-siblings, into their own families as children. Raul's uncle informally adopted his half-brother, and Raul's mother Flora adopted two girls, her half-sisters. Eventually, as the children got older and following the death of Flora's brother, all three children came to lean heavily on Flora not only for room-and-board but also for broader assistance such as money for schooling and education, as Flora recalled.

Raul's narration of these earlier events confirmed what I had heard from Flora: there had been a young Indigenous girl working in the hacienda who ended up sexually involved with the *patrón*. However, his account diverged in its emphasis on the affective impetus for this arrangement. Raul framed his mother's deeds as exemplary in her effort to confront rather than deny the violence so endemic to hacienda servitude. Describing his mother and uncle, Raul said: "They did not deny [*rechazar*] the situation, though that would have been normal. Most [*hacendado* families] denied it." Raul explained such failed accountability in terms of Mestizos' efforts to refuse or deny (*rechazar*) the hacienda past.[41] By contrast, his family's willingness to aid the children responded to his mother's feelings of sadness and guilt about her own father's sexual improprieties. As Raul put it: "There was a lot of tenderness [*cariño*]. My mother felt very sad about what had happened with my grandfather, so she ended up being a mother to them [her half-siblings]. She raised them. Hasintu was her eldest son, more or less, although he was actually her brother. That is, she assumed the responsibility of her father. There was a moral, familial obligation."

I was struck by how Raul made sense of his mother's aid to these out-of-wedlock children as a question of kinship. In his language his mother Doña Flora had been "a mother to them." Affection (*cariño*) here promised to undo lingering guilt and sadness, guiding his mother's raising (*criar*) of children who, in biological descent terms, were her half-siblings. This willingness to provide care was motivated by a sense of culpability for the perceived lapse in duty on the part of *hacendado* men—in Flora's case, her father. By taking in the children, Flora "assumed the responsibility of her father," fulfilling duties her father had shirked. Raul narrated this practice not as product of her biological ties to the children as her half-siblings; rather, the sense of duty was derived from a responsibility Flora had as her father's daughter to support former servants.

According to Raul, this had been a difficult, atypical response to the situation that reflected the specificities of their family's place as hacienda owners. "All of the masters committed errors with their female servants," he explained. "Those few [children] who were recognized belonged to my family."[42] When I asked why his family had been willing to recognize them, Raul replied quickly: "Because my grandfather was not from here. He was from Cochabamba, a *forastero* [landless Indigenous migrant]. He, too, was other."

Instead of describing these ties in terms of abiding master relations, Raul framed his mother's adoption of her half-kin as an exceptional practice of historical duty. In particular, Raul saw his mother's willingness to take responsibility for the past as an ethical response to the lessons learned by her father's position as a *juch'uy patrón* (small master) who had been estranged from both the category of Mestizo elites and Indigenous peasants. His family's position of marginality within regional systems of racial classification, he implied, underlay Flora's sense of "moral, familial obligation" to the children born to Quechua servants at her father's estate. While Flora had emphasized her position as a sort of perennial *Patrona*, Raul instead underlined the precarity of his family's place in the countryside; one apparent in their position as

Quechua owners of a meager expanse of land that had been bought through manumission, when his grandfather was able to buy himself out of his seasonal work as an hacienda worker—a typical source of employment for landless *forasteros*.[43]

In this case, stated sentiments of guilt and efforts to resume shirked responsibility could not be read only instrumentally. After all, as discussed earlier, Flora's case was interesting because these aid relations were not coupled with active pursuit of land. Rather, it was the master's *campesina* wife who maintained formal land rights to what remained of the property. In addition to Flora's sense of inherited shame or guilt from her own father, her generosity toward the children of former servants was more broadly inspired by an intimate experience of economic precarity rooted in the family's origins as landless peasants or *forasteros*. As Quechua "small masters" (*juch'uy patrones*), members of the family knew very well what it meant to be "other," to be socially stigmatized vis-à-vis broader cultural logics of esteemed masculinity and Indigenous personhood rooted in land ownership. Less than recursive traditions, Raul narrated aid practices as outcomes of ethical awareness and reflection in which family histories of suffering and social estrangement conditioned an exemplary willingness to respond to, or to be "affected" by, history's burdens in the present.

Raul emphasized that his speaking of these family secrets constituted a politics, one rooted in a commitment to answer for colonial and hacienda pasts even though others sought to refuse or deny that history. After this uncle's death several years before, Raul felt at greater liberty to talk about the family's past. He explained: "My uncle died and I am not afraid to tell this history, because in the end it is the history of my family." But for Raul these events held significance beyond the particularities of his family. Still seated at the table, the game of *cacho* now abandoned, Raul noted thoughtfully: "It seems that history depends on what passes, one goes forgetting or one goes improving it, I don't know. This is the true history." For Raul this "history" was not a dead record; it was alive and vital, open to reelaboration or even "improvement," depending on how one carried it. In contrast to a more familiar engagement with hacienda violence that aspired to displace dependencies, Raul emphasized the need not only to remember but also to transform the past. History was burdensome, but it also held ethical promise for responding to debts incurred by *hacendado* kin.

These relations of exchange and aid among differentially situated hacienda families can be understood as points of insight into the double-edged nature of tenacious hacienda intimacies both as inheritances and potential routes of repair. For people like Raul, reflection on this history cemented particular notions of accountability to Quechua neighbors, whether they were former servants, kin circulating as adopted children, or peasant villagers (*campesinos*) with whom one might share *chicha*. Part of this expansive duty emerged precisely out of the indeterminacy of this past: the impossibility of knowing, with certainty, the nature of earlier sexual relationships and the children who today arise as tangible testaments to that shrouded past.

The aid relations described earlier proceeded from lines of racialized authority and dependency elaborated in earlier agricultural economies, yet they also arose as mechanisms by which to answer to the ethical debts generated by hacienda labor and sexual violence. More than just the continuity of these older forms, here old forms were working in new ways. This was clear in Raul's narration of inherited practices that supplied a way for elites to "improve upon" history—namely by behaving better than their *hacendado* parents.[44]

Such engagements with historical redress challenge the idea, shared by Bolivian reformers and some scholars, that a legitimate subaltern or Indigenous politics must inhabit a position outside or exterior to liberal, settler-colonial modernity.[45] This expectation was inscribed in the spatial requirements imposed by new reparation measures through collective land titling, which saw the remedy for an unjust past in the creation of delimited, homogenous communities of Indigenous residents.[46] In Ayopaya particularly, and as I discuss further in chapter 4, efforts to secure a spatially bounded, autonomous form of Indigenous community risked reproducing gendered and racialized hierarchies rooted in earlier hacienda labor structures and land tenure patterns. In this regard, Flora's position in Independencia and her family's history as landless Quechua migrants as well as the land disputes among Indigenous community members and the children of Quechua servants and Mestizo masters point to the muddying of more monolithic racial categories such as Mestizo masters and Indigenous farmers.

Surely, these aid relations were not bereft of racialized power dynamics: gifts and hosting practices here buttressed Flora's position as a long-suffering *Patrona* in the posthacienda countryside.[47] But rather than being outgrowths only of her structural position, they might rather be understood as evidence of the material and affective work by which legitimate authority comes into being and is reproduced.[48] After all, for participants these aid relations were ethical insofar that they were not merely recursive or given by a predetermined historical status; they were rather understood as pointed individual responses to Ayopaya's violent past that required a given subject's vulnerability or affectability to others' plight. Challenging the notion that relationships are always freely chosen, participants in these practices insisted on the importance of upholding relationships and fulfilling obligations, even where unwilled.

Likewise, that former servants like Ramón made claims from a position of enduring dependency on *hacendado* families requires a subtler understanding of dependency at large. Dependencies, in this frame, are not the opposite of independence but are necessarily mutual. These conceptions of mutual vulnerability made history an intimate affair that linked families and held the capacity to transform even the most fragmenting, divisive past into a possible line of redress. This burden was experienced less as an effect of volition or choice than as a visceral, compelled condition. For, as Flora put it: "What can I do? I simply have to give."

Flora's adoption of her biological half-siblings as godchildren and her broader position as *madrina* (godmother, sponsor) to former servant groups highlight the importance of kinship as an idiom of obligation to a divisive, tenacious past. The relations that cohered around this position of familial authority evoked an expansive sense of obligation at odds with a juridical framework of family that opposes the interests of child and adult. As Marilyn Strathern (2005: 116) has argued, what legal talk of tradition and modernity misses is "any need to determine the kind of *obligations*" in which subjects might find themselves. More precisely, the Euro-American idiom of family posits "relationships [as] realized in the activation of ownership," one that cuts people off from one another through a division at once spatial but also temporal (Strathern 2005: 127).

To clarify, I do not mean to imply that Ayopayans were somehow engaged in an alternate, more relationally oriented kinship tradition at odds with "Western" legal models of individual choice. Legal approaches, including Bolivia's new paternity law, centrally emphasize the obligations of family members to their kin. For instance, according to Bolivia's 2014 Family Code, parents' obligations toward their children include the fulfillment of needs in health, education, housing, and recreation.[49] However, in a national atmosphere wherein Bolivia's bonded hacienda past had become deeply politicized, this expansive framework of obligation challenged legal ideas of individual responsibility, instead affirming continued practices of accountability and care among former master and former servant groups.

The *Patrona* "mother" held the power to remedy sexual anomalies, assimilating servants, illegitimate children, and workers into her extended family. Through practices of integrating out-of-wedlock children and servants as kin, of acting as a godparent and sponsor, Ayopayans worked to address—and also to regularize—what were framed as problematic kinds of cross-racial intimacy and labor bondage within earlier hacienda households. In the process, people strove to refashion hacienda-based labor ties into potential avenues for answering to past sexual violence. That people who never experienced servitude upheld these inherited networks casts doubt upon analyses of these relations in terms of a recursive institution, such as of agrarian patronage, for instance. They instead ask us to take seriously the agentive dimensions of positioning oneself as a dependent. Dependency here arose not as a one-sided orientation to authority but rather as a mutual condition of vulnerability. This positioning reframes hierarchy not only as a matter of dependents' dominance by masters but also of Mestizo residents' reliance on the support of villagers living near their inherited land. In Ayopaya these ties' persistence reflected everyday efforts to work on—and also transform—the past.

For interlocutors in Ayopaya, dependency thus entailed an active positioning that grounded ethical claims of those in positions of power and privilege.[50] Suspending the idea that these arrangements were merely symptoms of cultural inertia, whether of Indigenous exchange (*ayni*) or as feudal patronage, here the relational continuity from the hacienda to the postabolition era was also an intentional outcome of various kinds of relational and affective labor. When chastised by his *campesina* neighbors and by unionists whose families had struggled against hacienda servitude, Ramón nonetheless persisted in seeking out aid from people like Fabio.[51] Echoing Ramón, the kin of former masters spoke of "helping" (*ayudar*), "giving" (*dar*), or "gifting" (*regalar*) aid to poor Indigenous peasants (*campesinos*) and former servants. As in other postservitude settings, these practices were weighty matters for former servants like Ramón as well as for the relatives of former colonizing groups.

These aid practices and relational networks assumed new urgency within President Morales's rights-based reform program. If for reformers they arose as a synecdoche for the disturbing duration of a servile order, for rural Mestizos they offered an often-unwelcome reminder of the precarity of life on an overwhelmingly Indigenous frontier. As I discuss in later chapters, that fear was maneuvered by Quechua unionists and workers as a leverage point in rural disputes about resource extractivism, and Mestizos' entitlements to labor and profit, in the region.

CONCLUSION

This chapter has examined kin-making as a relational practice and an asymmetrical structure for making claims on people in positions of power. The possibilities of making kin—and of making "biological" kin into "fictive" kin as godchildren—assumed noteworthy ethical importance in light of the various kinds of sexual and labor violence that defined Ayopaya's haciendas. Children born out-of-wedlock marked the limits to the regularization of property through the controlling of heteropatriarchal sexuality, and thereby registered the fragility of the economic and racial hierarchies underlying hacienda servitude. In the indeterminacy about paternity and origins that this title marked, the figure of the orphan, whether as the out-of-wedlock child or parent-less servants, registered an outstanding debt for Mestizo families. This debt was addressed through a gendered idiom of responsibility synthesized by the figure of the mother as *patrona*, godparent, and saint. While historically master women also sustained earlier subjection, in the present women like Flora were looked favorably upon by many Indigenous villagers for whom she served as a joint reference for a set of binding debts.

In these circumstances it was the fragility of kinship processes that allowed people to attach new meanings and new ethical possibilities to older practices. While aid relations among these groups supported problematic forms of racial hierarchy, in Ayopaya former servant groups also activated kinship ties as a set of claims that sought to tether wealth to history and power to obligation at odds with ideals of discrete ownership and self-possession. Kinship here emerged as a flexible idiom to organize land, labor, and people whose connections did not align with heteropatriarchal ideals of biological consanguinity and inheritance that have guided Mestizo citizenship projects since the early twentieth century. By claiming intimacy with *hacendado* families, vulnerable subjects put forth their own vision centered on the relational debts incurred by domestic servitude. In the process, demands for aid from Mestizo bosses associated with an earlier "family retainer" were made to outlive the formal hacienda institution. That repayment followed the grooves of earlier structures of racialized authority and intimacy within haciendas but was imbued with new ethical resonances.[52] Such kin-making practices bound wealth to history to contest a more atomistic framings of rural Mestizos as bosses who owed only wages to the communities of former servants.

Mestizo townsfolk's distribution of material aid hereby operated as a sort of historical repayment—or, to use Marcel Mauss's earlier language, a return (*rendre*) of debts incurred through brutal hacienda violence, including sexual abuse and indentured labor.[53] The present-day opacities of earlier sexual violence left the terms of history's accounting productively open, spurring continued dialogue about Mestizo elites' debts to former workers. This asks us to reconsider what justice is or could be for subjects, like Ramón, who remain partly entangled in the relational and affective debris of racialized labor systems. While this chapter has highlighted the opposing perceptions of historical debt mainly among the relatives of hacienda masters, I now turn to rural disagreements among former servants and Quechua villagers about the entailments of undertaking such aid relations. The next chapter offers a genealogy of regional hierarchical exchange traditions and describes how they have shaped available routes for addressing historical violence and abiding racial hierarchies in rural Ayopaya.

TWO

Gifting Land

When we arrived in the village of Sarahuayto, Epifanio parked his truck near the old Jesuit chapel, used for weekly sermons during the hacienda era. We piled out of the truck, eager to stretch our legs after the two-hour drive from Independencia. Oscar Torrico, a Quechua municipal official in his forties who had grown up in the village, had invited Epifanio, his two adolescent daughters, and me to Sarahuayto for the Virgen de Candelaria saint's day celebrations, which were to begin later that day. We split up, and I followed Oscar down a muddy path through agricultural plots where maize stalks stretched tall and potato plants crowded together in rows of dark green. Pausing near an adobe wall, Oscar pointed to a rectangular potato plot: "This land belongs to my father, it was a gift from the master." Intrigued, I asked whether his father had received the land because he was a hacienda manager (*melga runa* or *hilacata*). "No," Oscar replied. "It's that my father's mother was raped by the master, and so he gifted her land." He paused. "But don't say anything to him about it. He has nearly no land here. When he was nine, he left for Chapare to make a life for himself, and only recently returned."

Sarahuayto is a village situated in the inter-Andean mountain province of Ayopaya and home to about seventy people. In 2011 it was home mainly to Quechua descendants of earlier hacienda workers, like Oscar's father. Many families had left the region over the years; the population was only about a quarter of what it had been before the 1953 agrarian reform.[1] Along with Indigenous farming families, several Mestizo farmers and mine owners lived in the area. Martín Rodriguez, the *hacendado*'s grandson, resided in the old estate building at the village's edge, and farmed some 200 square hectares of croplands, which the family still owned. In addition, the family had retained ownership over two nearby gold mines. Martín operated one, and his uncle had sold the second to urban mining entrepreneurs in 2002. I look at the difficulties generated by mining given the region's tenacious bonded past in chapter 5; here, I ask how, despite midcentury agrarian reform, divisions related to earlier hacienda hierarchies and reentrenched in state agrarian reform remained key to the spatial and relational layout of the area. These hierarchies positioned servants as the lowest tier of hacienda labor but also as privileged recipients of aid, including land gifts. For people like Oscar's father, this perceived alliance with earlier masters continued to elicit rebuke from fellow villagers.

In former villages like this one, hacienda masters often had children out of wedlock, leaving children land even where they did not legally recognize them as heirs. In this case, Oscar's father received a fertile plot of coveted farmland near to the central estate. Sarahuayto had been of the largest haciendas in the region, and land titling there had been a conflictive affair—in part because of a drawn-out legal case fueled by the master's opposition to the distribution of his estate to former workers and Quechua villagers. Following the state's 1953 agrarian reform, the hacienda estate was divided such that its former upper and lower halves each became a separate village. This division was a common outcome not only of this agrarian reform but also, since then, of municipal decentralization policies beginning in the 1990s. These policies were modeled on peasant unions and then rural municipalities that often retained crucial dimensions of ayllu political leadership and deliberation.[2] Rather than replacing haciendas with scattered households, mid-twentieth-century agrarian reform split estates into villages whose formal political orders subsequently came to approximate those of highland ayllus.

Sarapaya, the lower village, bordered the hacienda building and held more fertile land, formed of lush agricultural valleys next to irrigation sources (Figure 3). Sarahuayto, by contrast, stretched across more distant, dry, and eroding land with limited agricultural viability, much of which could be used only to pasture animals. Former hacienda managers, godchildren, and favored servants lived in the lower part, while tenant farming families who had been most active in antihacienda militias resided in the dryer plots closer to the *altiplano* or high plains. These inequities were particularly delicate matters in 2011, given that the MAS party government had laid out new opportunities to register the villages as a single peasant community and to process collective titles, a project that promised to dismantle land hierarchies related to earlier labor systems but also risked dispossessing marginalized Quechua villagers, servants' kin most of all.

FIGURE 3. Agricultural plots situated upon former hacienda parcels in Ayopaya province, 2012. Photo by author.

This chapter looks at gifts of land and circulations of laboring bodies as part of a regional tradition of asymmetrical aid that continues to shape contemporary practices of authority and claim-making in former hacienda villages like Sarahuayto. Ayopaya as a province is defined by a specific history of exchange not only as racialized labor extraction in the encomienda era and since, but also as abiding understandings of money as a mechanism of historical compression and claim-making bound up with itineraries of labor circulation since the precolonial era. Methodologically, I follow Paul Carter's call for a "spatial history" based on an effort to "put bodies back into the historical picture."[3] By holding together historical studies of agricultural change in the Cochabamba valleys and firsthand accounts and oral histories that Sarahuayto villagers shared with me during my fieldwork there, I endeavor to illustrate how Ayopaya has been shaped by a distinct land-labor nexus that coarticulates people and labor, authority and wealth, one that persists as a possibility for navigating relations with non-Indigenous outsiders.

In Bolivia these labor-based claims to land and gift-based productions of authority have been deeply problematic for modernizing projects geared to producing alienable property, projects that span the initial period of liberalizing reform in the 1780s and the twentieth century. As a system that treated people and place, labor and land, as analytically intertwined, the arrangements of asymmetrical aid that I describe have also enabled vulnerable Indigenous subjects to make claims on those in racialized positions of power. Such claims were subject to contending normative assessments. For instance, while the land gift that Oscar's father received was seen by some villagers as an offensive betrayal of the peasant cause, for others it was a legitimate outcome of servants' demands for retribution given the violence and dispossession they suffered under the hacienda system. Recalling the historical precedents for networks of gift-giving in the Cochabamba region, and Ayopaya specifically, raises crucial questions about orientations to power as historically and culturally variable.

My account begins with the precolonial period, which highlights the unique positions of Quechua field hands in an Incan agricultural order. It then looks at the creation of a deeply servile regional political culture and economy in colonial-era Ayopaya—a development that is at odds with the crumbling of haciendas in Cochabamba's central valleys. Finally, we turn to Ayopaya's twentieth-century history of peasant activism and unrest, including the modes of transformational agency that this labor organizing produced. Ayopaya's history offers a longue durée perspective on land titling as overdetermined by a series of earlier conjunctures in which anxieties over labor conditions also supplied opportunities for state centralization and the regularization of land and labor relations. Placing Ayopaya in this transregional, historical context illuminates the distinctiveness of a provincial configuration of authority and its ordering of land, people, and labor. Positioned alongside the discussion of the claims of former servants like Ramón (whom I discussed in chapter 1), this configuration has posed important challenges to the smooth expansion of alienable property in the region. More broadly, this configuration of authority underscores how alternate traditions of money and land exchange can be remade into key sites of ethical engagement with hierarchy.

The Sarahuayto case provides an opportunity to rethink a historical typology based on yoking specific institutions to delimited historical epochs and geographies. While Bolivian reformers and INRA officials tended to associate reciprocity-based exchange relations in ayllus (dual-moiety communities) with precolonial Aymara life in the highlands, they explained labor hierarchies and asymmetrical aid practices as outcomes of Spanish colonial life, particularly lowland encomiendas and haciendas. Analytically, my argument here departs from this geographic and epochal imaginary to illuminate how a kinship-based system of asymmetrical aid has operated as a knot or a mechanism of Indigenous claim-making on Mestizo elites. That this authority complex continued to define money's relational content in Ayopaya complicates presumptions of a defining break in rural orientations to power across Bolivia's precolonial, colonial, and postcolonial eras.

This movement across periods and geographic spaces requires scholars to treat the colonial as less straightforward or self-contained than is usually assumed; in many cases, colonial institutions were also reshaped by relations of power that preceded them. Rethinking this periodization is crucial for anthropologists who, in Bolivia as elsewhere, are frequently called upon to differentiate authentic from inauthentic traditions.[4] In Ayopaya land relations have been marked by a more fluid mode of belonging related to the ubiquity of itinerant Quechua labor. In this context, alliances with Mestizo elites have proffered a key mechanism for navigating institutions of racialized power and labor violence. This raises questions about the tenacity of an exchange tradition rooted in Ayopaya's distinctive labor past, one that has proved unexpectedly resistant to the telos of modern property.

SHIFTING TOPOGRAPHIES OF EXCHANGE

Prior to the arrival of the Incas, Aymara tribes in the central Andes made use of the diverse landscape of high plains, fertile valleys, and tropical lowlands for a range of pastoral and agricultural practices.[5] Local chiefdoms were strongly stratified, with chiefs having multiple wives, servants, and access to the labor of the community at large. Labor was reciprocated in the generous and festive distribution of food and drink.[6] Abundant maize harvests were stored for communal use in silos used to mitigate food shortages from drought or disease. According to John Murra's (1968) influential account of the "archipelago system," at this time various ecological zones were controlled by single communities that created "peripheral islands" of kinsfolk in the eastern *kichwa* regions, enabling access to varied produce and protecting groups from famine in cases of crop failure in one region. Unlike nucleated settlements, systems of reciprocity-based control were premised on "nested groups" including ayllus (dual moiety communities), lineages, community, tribe, and ethnic lordship linked by a shared ancestor-god and divided into dual moieties and satellite *mitmae* settlements. Political authority was expressed in exchanges of gifts and services both to native lords and place-based deities.

Mid-fifteenth-century Aymara systems of political rule and agriculture were transformed by Inca expansion under emperor Pachacuti (1438–1471). Under the Incas tribute was paid in young male Aymara warriors whose efforts were rewarded by the generosity of the Inca state in elaborate feasts where maize beer, quinoa flour, meat, and other valuable items were distributed. In addition, they received land grants to valuable maize plots in the Cochabamba valley. Communities that provided warriors to the Incas were also absolved of other tribute burdens, including herding, serving in seasonal labor duties (*mit'a*), weaving cloth, or agricultural labor (Larson 1998, citing Soriano [1582] 1969: 21–24). Alongside these hosting relations, the Incas introduced the large-scale movement of migrant laborers from the highlands to the fertile valleys, as well as a system of forced labor tribute. In this way the Incas drew highland groups into new migratory flows in which labor was repaid in land access, the distribution of valuable dry goods, and broader arrangements of asymmetrical exchange premised on Inca rulers' positions as generous hosts and sponsors.

Regional labor flows and systems of political order changed dramatically under Spanish colonial rule. While encomiendas (grants that included land but also claims to the tribute payments and labor of its native inhabitants) were modeled on Inca systems, early colonial attempts to delimit types of tribute in 1550 elicited shifts in land use, splitting apart moieties and limiting access to earlier vertical archipelagos. Existing, fluid patterns of labor and land ownership posed problems for Spanish tribute collectors, limiting the colonial state's ability to secure a permanent labor force. The so-called archipelago model contrasted sharply with nucleated settlements familiar to Europeans and instituted as part of the later *reducción* of Andeans into villages, towns, and "Indian communities" during the Toledo program of forced resettlement in the sixteenth century.

By the mid-sixteenth century new tribute regulations were introduced. Caciques (native administrators) made Andean peasants pay tribute not only in labor, in accordance with Incaic customs, but via a mixture of labor, goods, and money. Monetizing tribute required peasants to turn from farming to wage-labor in encomiendas or mines.[7] These changes met resistance in the Cochabamba region, where agriculturalists and *mitmaq* laborers had cultivated deep patronage alliances with Inca overlords. Land conflicts in Cochabamba from the 1550s to the 1570s centered on whether land gifts made to highland caciques by the Incas constituted property rights. Administrators argued that Aymara groups had little exposure to private property and so did not deserve for their Inca land grants to be recognized. Conversely, Quechua highland migrants sought to paint themselves as loyal Incan and now Spanish subjects who were deserving of land.[8]

If these tribute-based hierarchies created new positions for Quechua valley groups to claim alliance and loyalty to Spanish elites, they also conditioned the terms of colonial agrarian authority. Concerned with the "unbridled greed" of encomenderos, Toledo introduced wide-ranging reforms aimed at disbanding the encomienda elite. But while Toledan reforms opposed encomiendas as archaic, feudal systems, their proposed wage system was itself based on Incan forced labor drafts (the *mit'a*) for maize production in the Cochabamba valleys. (This term *mit'a* was further retained in the twentieth-century name for women hacienda servants, *mitanis*). Spanish colonial elites and administrators studied systems of precolonial agrarian exchange, seemingly recognizing that colonial authorities would have to integrate aspects of a preexisting exchange tradition to maintain legitimacy. Resettled into *reducciónes* organized around churches and far from precolonial ritual sites like mountains, people who cultivated land or herded animals in the mountains or on distant plots would be more easily integrated into colonial life. The rural settlement shifts elicited by these reforms were dramatic. In the Valle Bajo of Cochabamba, *reducción* policy converted 130 hamlets into three villages.[9]

While nucleated towns and "Indian communities" were to replace dispersed and fragmented land-use practices (including *mitmae* settlements), other migratory cycles were partly maintained in the form of new arrangements of *mitayo* labor in the mines and encomienda labor in the valleys.[10] This policy also responded to administrators' effort to replicate an earlier subsistence equilibrium that Spaniards attributed to Inca life and sought to study through ethnography (Mumford 2008). Toledo passed regulations requiring chiefs' obligations to organize collective work parties to repair churches, build roads and bridges, and to reciprocate labor through feasting and the sharing of drink, food, and seeds with workers.[11]

Reforms in this era reshaped labor and land use into more bounded entities, in turn stigmatizing migratory laborers as shirking tribute obligations, saddling kin and neighbors with heightened labor and tax burdens. Yet efforts to secure the territorial integrity of newly resettled "Indian communities" were not always successful, especially in the outlying provinces of the Cochabamba valleys, such as Ayopaya. Census data from 1618 shows that Tapacarí ayllus in Cochabamba maintained *mitmaq* "colonists" (*colonos*) into the seventeenth century, with satellite communities located principally in the fertile river valley of Ayopaya.[12] Field hands but also herders, weavers, and domestic servants had to be secured from a pool of laborers classed as "itinerant and seasonal."

Haciendas housed many such mobile laborers, including escaped *mitayos* (bonded mine workers), *forasteros* (landless persons), *yanaconas* (indentured agricultural laborers) as well as those born out of consensual or coerced unions between Indigenous women and Spanish or Mestizo landowners and priests.[13] According to census material, in the Cochabamba valleys at this time *yanaconaje* grew, with colonial estimates of fifty thousand *yanaconas* in the Spanish colony of Peru.[14] These changes introduced new tensions in rural life. Community leaders shared reformers' anxieties about the onerous burdens that tribute evasion introduced for colonial subjects who had not managed escape to "free" territories and hacienda estates. Rising numbers of *yanaconas de servicio,* unpaid hacienda servants whose status was passed on to their children, created difficulties for tribute payments.

Recounting this early colonial history sheds light on the Cochabamba region as a place where a servile agrarian order flourished; yet it also created new ethnic alliances that linked colonists and colonized. A "regional tax rebellion" in 1730 arose when reformers sought to impose *mita* and tribute payments upon *forasteros* or landless groups. This event further secured administrators' impressions of Cochabamba as a special place, a "Mestizo province" given to dramatic forms of anticolonial violence, one whose mobile labor economies challenged tributary and census categories. Caciques deemed these subjects "proto-*hacendados*" for they had been granted village land "in return for favors or loyalty to their *patrón*."[15] This discourse stigmatized the asymmetrical exchange relations discussed earlier instead as evidence of a feudal order premised on "personal service"—that is, servitude. It also recast earlier practices, such as the expectation that rural Indians loan draft animals or perform domestic work and field labor for the cacique in exchange for land use, as instances of servitude or even "slavery."

These arrangements were especially significant in the Cochabamba region to which Ayopaya belongs, a region populated by migrating Quechua field hands and later itinerant *yanacona* laborers who, well into the colonial era, made claims to land on the premise of earlier Incan land gifts to loyal workers. Although these colonial arrangements were deeply exploitative, they also maintained and configured new opportunities for servants to build alliances, to access land, and to escape state tribute burdens for other labor ties. Seen in this longer frame, *hacendado*-worker alliances raise questions about the staying power of an older tradition of asymmetrical exchange, one that came under new fire during labor movements in the 1940s.

INSTITUTING PAID LABOR AND DISPLACING HACIENDA AUTHORITY

In the late 1930s and early 1940s, growing Indigenous and peasant unrest in Ayopaya led to labor stoppages and strikes upon haciendas and rural activist claims to land and calls for land collectivization.[16] In a 1942 petition, Hilarión Grájeda and other union leaders complained of cases of rape (*estupro* or *violación*) of "single and married women" and the whipping of *colono* workers.[17] These petitions adopted reformist language of subjective transformation externalized in labor, yet the appeals against *mitanaje* also demonstrate how, in this province, *pongueaje* and sexual services continued to be practiced despite their earlier abolition by the Ministry of Labor in 1940.

First in the 1938 Congress and then in 1941, General Peñaranda sent a memo to prefects requiring them to officially announce the prohibition of *pongueaje*. These announcements were accompanied by the circulation of printed copies of the "law" among local leaders and with the aid of urban, progressive lawyers. Rural organizing on the part of hacienda workers increased following the 1938 constitutional assembly, with its formal abolition of forced labor, and leading up to the National Indigenous Congress in 1945. Labor organizers often made use of reformist languages of land rights as a means for rural groups to reconfigure themselves as modern citizens. Wálter Guevara Arze wrote in his treatise on agrarian reform in Ayopaya that land should be distributed "so Indians can 'dress like we do,' 'improve their condition as men,' and become an 'integral part of the nation.'"[18] Despite legislators' opposition to "personal service," they upheld *pongueaje* for its civilizing possibilities, specifically as a means to facilitate contact between Indians and cities.

In Ayopaya elderly Quechua villagers with whom I spoke recalled the first wave of antihacienda organizing as beginning in the mid-1940s, spurred in part by connections to new political networks linking hacienda *colonos* to sympathetic union groups, Indigenous leaders, and *indigenista* officials, particularly in La Paz. In 1947 *waychus* (armed militias) arrived in Ayopaya from La Paz. According to Don Felix Rocha, a prominent union official in the 1950s, peasant militias chased out recalcitrant *hacendados* in the 1940s.

Encircling the property by night, militias would demand of the hacienda owners: "Masters take leave this good night or die here. Or all of you die here, because now there is the agrarian reform!"[19]

However, in many cases insurgents arrived at a vacant house, as masters had been tipped off by loyal servants and escaped to Cochabamba. And so the militias came to villagers' homes. According to Don Felix, the *waychus* "entered houses and took food, beds, and blankets. They also assaulted villagers. After this, the masters returned anew to their lands." Yet, while *waychus* nominally supported the peasant cause, Quechua villagers viewed their arrival with fear and worry. Epifania, Don Felix's wife, had been a child at the time. "They came in through open doors and found the food hidden in the back," she recalled. "They would escape with clothes and food. They came with machetes." She continued: "My grandfather escaped with my grandmother through a path in the ravine. People escaped to many places."

Other villagers recalled the "revolutionaries" who came and hid in their villages, eliciting confrontations with the armed guard who was sent from Oruro and La Paz. In one memorable case in the village of Tiquirpaya, an Indigenous leader called Sabino Wallku was being hunted down by troops. He hid himself under a woman's layered *pollera* skirt, shooting his rifle from under the bountiful layers. After shooting and killing two officials, one a police leader and another a teacher who tried to intervene, the man was shot and killed. While he was heralded as a martyr—the elementary school now bears his name—villagers' accounts suggest uncertainty about where leaders' allegiances rested. On the one hand, villagers noted that rebels were fighting "for liberation"; on the other hand, they seemed unconvinced of whether this liberation was their own. The uncertainty of these new political alliances for local villagers is clear in their accounts of rebels who subsequently "switched sides" to support masters and who, as evident in the above case, used villagers both as camouflage and fodder. Far from a consolidated block in favor of reforms or collectively supporting unions or peasant militias, then, villagers' accounts of 1947 unrest displayed great fear and ambivalence.

For hacienda owners in Ayopaya, too, February 1947 was a month of grave destruction, when an Indigenous insurgency (*Indiada*) descended upon towns and villages, haciendas and farmlands. Several masters were killed, houses destroyed, burned, and pillaged, violence often understood by surviving *hacendados* and their kin in terms of an age-old "race war" between Indigenous peasants and Mestizo or Criollo elites.[20] Ayopaya is remarkable for the magnitude of the 1947 rebellions, which drew between three thousand and ten thousand individuals and as centered on the hacienda of Yayani, located on the border with the La Paz province. For a week beginning on February 4, *colonos* attacked and pillaged haciendas including that of Yayani and eight others. In addition to killing the hacienda master of Yayani, lawyer José María Coca, and his assistant, Lt. Col. José Mercado, who had been employed to guard the hacienda in the months before, rebels also destroyed a school and threatened to hang its teacher, also employed by Coca. In addition to killing Coca and his legal adviser, insurgents visited the office of the local corregidor where they destroyed paperwork and ransacked the office. Next they visited the tax collector where they "charged [their] own tax" and recovered goods, mostly clothing, that had been confiscated in cases when *colonos* had failed to pay *muko* and *chicha* taxes (e.g., the requirement that Indigenous villagers chew a certain amount of *muko* corn paste and produce a given quantity of *chicha* beer for annual religious holidays).

Hilarión Grájeda, known to have been one of the leaders of the 1947 revolt, was a key figure in the 1945 Indigenous Congress. At the time of the 1947 revolt, he had been evicted from the hacienda of Yayani and was in hiding somewhere in Ayopaya, accused by *hacendados* of holding secret meetings with *colonos*. Grájeda was not the only local leader who had been involved in the 1945 Indigenous Congress. Angelo Choque, a prominent Quechua union leader in Sarahuayto then in his late seventies, recounted that his grandfather had been brutally punished by the Rodriguez master for attempting to participate in the first National Indigenous Congress in La Paz in 1945. As a rural Indigenous leader, the man had been expected to travel to La Paz, bringing musicians and dancers to the congress. The group was obstructed in Independencia, a town governed by wealthy masters and merchants opposed to the MNR government. Later, the hacienda masters regained their strength and the communal mayor, Angelo's grandfather, was tied to a nearby elder tree and beaten, "like a slave." To that day, Angelo noted his sense of "vengeance for the masters." This conditioned a militant stance toward the living kin of *hacendados*: "I am of this blood, so you will pay for this with me."

The MNR government was overthrown on July 21, 1946, and President Villarroel's body was hung from a lamppost in La Paz. Following Villarroel's death, a wave of repression swept the countryside. Despite military intervention, antihacienda mobilizations continued in the countryside, as peasant militias attacked haciendas and forced their owners to flee at gunpoint. Elderly villagers and townsfolk remembered this period, including involvement in peasant militias or as the wives and children of *hacendados* who fled to the city fearing for their lives. According to Angelo, after this military junta of 1946, organizers against hacienda servitude were persecuted. In one case the new renter of a hacienda in Yayani reimposed the obligations abolished earlier, noting to his *colonos*: "Your President has died....Everything has changed."[21] When a *colono* representative went to the renter Ramos bringing documents or "papers of guarantee" provided by the lawyers of the Defensa Gratuita, a free legal defense service provided by the state, the renter simply confiscated them.

Many scholars of Bolivia's revolution often emphasize shared political dissent culminating in peasant mobilizations; however, in Ayopaya many villagers characterized the early revolutionary period in terms of strangers and *revolucionarios* who appeared overnight, advising and organizing villagers. Gregorio Condorí, a former union leader whose father had been pivotal in antihacienda organizing in the 1950s recalled the year of 1950, just as he began school. "With President Villarroel, people had to work only five days, not six. Later it was further reduced to three. They punished the union leaders, who were not permitted to meet. So they met in the night, secretly, in the mountain, where no one knew. But then the very same *colonos* would tell the master that there had been a meeting." Gregorio here drew upon his father's account of agitating for hacienda abolition. His father had been a prominent union leader whose name (Condorí) appears in signed documents in the INRA archive that I consulted.

Gregorio recalled how it was that the landlord learned of secret meetings. "One *colono* would betray [the others], to be recommended for better treatment. There was spying too." This changed in 1952, when "people arrived saying 'There is no slavery anymore,' and everything flipped around. The *colonos* and *sobra runa* [overseers] were left with all of what the master had previously received. They worked the master's lands collectively. The master had to escape, for those who came were well armed." Anticipating the fleetingness of these political gains, Gregorio continued: "Afterwards, the *hacendados* made themselves union leaders, and in this way returned. Then the master's properties were sold, but he ended up with the best lands."

MNR attempts to gain power during this period were largely unsuccessful. Following the death of Villarroel and the 1947 rebellions, which for some were understood as a reprisal for his death, rural repression was extreme, particularly in Ayopaya. Along with the formation of military brigades to detect insurgents, there was the formation of civil agents, voluntary corps made up of young men who were given arms by the military and charged with finding the Indians who had killed Lt. Col. Mercado in Yayani. An attempted MNR coup in 1949 failed, as did its attempt to take office after an electoral victory in 1951, as Bolivia's communist party (El Partido Comunista de Bolivia, PCB) aligned itself with the outgoing president and convinced the military to step in and block the MNR from assuming office. It was not until April 1952, after an armed rebellion in La Paz in which miners seized arsenals and distributed weapons to civilians, and following three days of fighting, that the army surrendered and the MNR was able to take office, and Victor Paz Estenssoro became president. In March of the following year, the MNR passed a national Agrarian Reform Law that abolished forced labor and set up a program to expropriate and redistribute land from hacienda masters to rural, Indigenous farmers. Doña Maria Ayala, one former servant, recalled the relief accompanying news of hacienda abolition: "We said, 'It is good that they leave. Now we will rest.'"[22] She paused, as if savoring the memory. "Let them leave, we said. That they may suffer like we have."[23]

ABOLITIONARY INSTABILITIES: THE TRAGEDY OF THE ROTTING OCA

But this relief was short-lived. In Sarahuayto, the abolition of forced labor was complicated both by *hacendados* who aligned themselves with Indigenous peasant unionists but also by the loyalty some workers felt for prior masters and estate lands. According to Quechua villagers with whom I spoke, preceding the reform a peaceful, even "saintly" brother was left in care of the hacienda. Because of this, and since he was not "culpable for earlier suffering," *colonos* and villagers could not bring themselves to harm him, and he was warned of impending attacks. By virtue of what they characterized as his peaceful nature, the workers at the estate did not rise up again until they became aware of Estenssoro's signing of a national land reform law in August 1953. This decree formally abolished hacienda servitude, declared hacienda lands to be the formal property of hacienda laborers, and assigned peasant unions the task of overseeing the process.

Despite this decree, many Indigenous workers' retained formal support for former masters, and expressed abiding attachments to the land and crops they cultivated prior to hacienda abolition. This was especially clear in Angelo's account (recounted to me in Quechua in his home in 2011) of the labor strike carried out in Sarahuayto upon news of Estenssoro's decree. Angelo and his wife recalled the difficulty that the strike posed for the harvesting of oca (an Andean tuber). Angelo described that day: "Up there, a little up there in the mountain, there appeared a *compañero* with a *pututu* [conch shell]. After playing the *pututu*, he shouted, 'Come *compañeros*, come we will meet here.' Some went, and some were paralyzed by fear of what might happen now. They gathered like that, gathered all together. 'We were required to,' people say. There this Vitalio Condorí [Gregorio's relative] blew the *pututu*, grabbing his rifle, and said, 'On this day the work we have to do on the hacienda is over! For now and forever, there is no more hacienda. From this day onward, it is abolished.' And so the people said, 'What will happen with the oca?' A whole section of oca was ready to be harvested. 'Now who will collect it?' There the oca remained, rotting." Oca does not dry like potatoes; tubers must be laid out to drain and dry. Angelo recalled: "There was a whole section, all of it, all of it, the earth ready. The only thing left to do was to collect it. All of the ground, the oca all yellow [*ch'iqchiriq karqa*]!" Angelo's wife Laura shook her head sadly, recalling in Quechua how on that day she "felt bad for the oca, just lying there."

In Sarahuayto, villagers recalled hacienda abolition as a chaotic, violent moment in which everything flipped over and reversed. Laura Choque continued, emphasizing the discomfort of the strike for hacienda laborers: "It was the people's work to collect the oca. Why not collect it?" To leave the fruits of physical and ritual labor out to rot was unimaginable. Higher-status hacienda workers, *hilicatas* and *mayordomos*, had tried to no avail to compel the villagers to collect it. Angelo recalled: "Like this it all stayed, they say. Neither the *hilacatas*, nor the *mayordomos*, wanted to leave it there, on the ground, around the field, turning yellow. 'Come, come let's gather it!' they said capriciously. People say the *hilacatas* and *mayordomos* begged the people to harvest it. The people did not pay them any attention. Some came to collect the oca with their woven blankets to carry off what they had collected. Most said, 'It's finished,' and left the oca on the ground. Then there was no one, just the *patrón* in his house. The people returned his animals and his cows, as servitude had ended [*tukukapun servidumbre*]. They said, 'If he has sheep, he has to herd them. If he has cows, he must herd them.'" *Colonos* were caught between the expectations of their now-obsolete lords and the demands of new union leaders. Some people arrived, with their *q'ipiris* or woven blankets, to carry off the oca, while the majority refused. Then everything was still. The estate, formerly an operation with more than four hundred laborers, dissipated overnight.

This account hints at the ambivalence villagers felt: they experienced hacienda abolition simultaneously as a moment of promise and fear, relief and tragedy. On the one hand, the event culminated villagers' earlier efforts to take up arms against hacienda masters. Yet, on the other hand, jubilation was tempered by great fear of reprisal for collaborating with "strangers." People hid in their homes, hoping to escape the violence of revolutionaries or counterattacks by the ruling *hacendado* class. Such fear was warranted. Earlier work stoppages, strikes, and attempts at claiming hacienda land had resulted in lawsuits, fines, and the imprisonment of union leaders. Similarly, this lost harvest was later the catalyst for legal charges that the master pressed against union leaders, accusing them of fomenting unrest and of encouraging people to pillage hacienda property, such as the oca harvest. As punishment for his complicity in the strike, Angelo was charged with labor agitating and spent three years in prison in the 1980s.

However, workers' discomfort with letting the oca rot must also be understood in light of the ethical and religious dimensions of agrarian practice throughout the Andes. There, harvesting belongs to ongoing cycles of ritual exchange between the Pachamama or earth mother and highland communities. Ideals of reciprocity informed hacienda laborers' understanding of their work; indeed, haciendas labor was often conceived of as a gift or repayment of debts accrued through *hacendados'* favors.[24] Seen in this light, it is possible to surmise that the labor strike disavowed people's attachments to the earth and the religious and ethical significance of working the land as a relation not only to a material object or product but also as an upholding of continual, reciprocal exchange relations to earth-beings and deities associated with soil, fertility, and specific places. This made the strike gravely problematic to future agricultural yields but also to community health and well-being as contingent on attachments to place-based beings or spirits.[25] Abandoning this harvest compromised relations to masters but also offended other entities whose support materialized in abundant harvests. To this day, trees felled by the former master's family in the 1990s had been left to rot, an abiding tribute both to the severe disciplinary force that accompanied the strike and to lingering uncertainties of ownership in the aftermath of formal abolition (Figure 4).

Instilling these more secular orientations to labor in servants and workers was the duty of new agrarian advisers who were to oversee the transition to paid work. Don Adolfo Camacho, now eighty-four, came from a Quechua family in the region and had been a union representative of the local

FIGURE 4. Abandoned felled trees in Sarahuayto, Ayopaya province, 2011. Photo by author.

branch of the union during the 1953 land reform. His parents had been hacienda *colonos*. After military training, he had worked as an agrarian inspector. He described the nature of his work: "The agrarian inspector commanded the peasants, teaching them to work well, to produce." That is, he specified: "The agrarian inspector instructed the peasants so that they would work well and not do any work for free. They had to be paid." Adolfo had returned from military service in the early 1950s and the physical and political training received in the military made him, like many others in leadership positions, a desirable candidate for the local union. His parents had labored on the hacienda but with revolutionary hacienda abolition, Adolfo took on the responsibility of uprooting earlier, servant mentalities. Here young men in their early twenties were made responsible for reforming the actions of their fellow villagers, including their elderly parents. The revolutionaries, those strangers who appeared overnight and made new demands on rural peasants and former servants, were now one's children, one's brothers, and one's neighbors. The state, once embodied by the distant INRA institute in La Paz, became a proximate, even familial, presence.

While the formation of peasant unions and rural reform certainly reflected a form of grassroots organizing that was driven by local interests as well as by urban and unionist discourses, the Ayopayan case also demonstrates the multilayered and sometimes internally fraught nature of the "local" unfolding of such organizing.[26] Bolivian unions initially furthered the political goals of the earlier MNR (Movimiento Nacional Revolucionario) government, specifically its aims to convert Indigenous subjects into peasants. In many cases, however, *sindicatos* also often maintained and revived community and ayllu-based governance systems at the village level.[27] Moreover, in Ayopaya laborers had long drawn from Quechua notions of attachment to land and soil, or *jallp'a sangres* (Quechua for "the blood of the earth"), as a basis for union appeals for land rights (Ari 2014). In this regard, Andean *sindicatos* often departed notably from more secular institutions of labor organizing in other parts of the world.

In the Ayopayan region nascent peasant unions in the 1940s were headed by militant hacienda farmers, especially tenant farmers. With the 1952 revolution, however, these authorities lost power and local *hacendado* masters (and their sons) came to assume prominent roles as their leaders (Rivera Cusicanqui 1997). In fact, many Quechua villagers like Angelo privately complained that in the aftermath of abolition it was the relatives of former *hacendados* who fashioned themselves as peasants and took over key leadership roles in the nascent unions. This allowed them to shape hacienda land distribution, often to their own benefit. The peasant unions hereby assumed new importance as sites of state discipline aimed at producing new, less servile laborers. These unionists saw some laborers' sense of obligation to work for the master, or to harvest the *oca*, in the same light as their later desires to maintain ties to *hacendado* families—as grotesque remnants of premodern slavery. This view authorized more militant antihacienda unionists' violent attacks on loyal servants.

Don Humberto Huarachi, now in his nineties, had been one of the master's favored *pongo* servants. While Humberto grew up in a Quechua family, he learned Spanish at the estate, where the *hacendados* insisted servants speak Spanish. He had shouldered the domestic work of the estate and assisted the master Don Carlos Rodriguez in his day-to-day work. Humberto recalled the day of hacienda abolition: "There were lots of people gathered into a large group. They told us 'You are not to attend to this mill.' From there they went to the mine, saying, 'Get out of here!' They told us we had to go to the mine, to the mills, and then they blew on their conch horns. I came to the house. It was full of people. Then, someone announced, '*Compañeros,* this is the day *compañeros.* From tomorrow onward you will not work for the masters. You will not pay them any mind. There is no hacienda anymore. The masters have to plant their own corn. You will not work anymore.' People were chanting, 'Down, down with the hacienda.'"

Waking up the next morning, the master and Humberto planned on leaving. But that morning all the villagers of Sarahuayto were there with horses, already mounted. As Humberto recalled, they shouted: "That's it! There is no hacienda anymore. The hacienda is gone." He went on to describe how the elderly master fled for Cochabamba: because rebelling laborers had taken the master's horses and the master was too old to walk, Humberto and another *pongo* servant carried him in a chair to a nearby town some 20 kilometers away.

In Ayopaya, villagers commonly remarked that the cruel masters were killed while the peaceful or generous ones survived. Like other *hacendados*, Don Carlos had been an authoritative at times violent master to the several hundred Quechua and Aymara *colonos* who labored on his lands in exchange for meager subsistence plots, while a handful of domestic servants and *colona* tenant women provided "personal service" in the home. However, some local Quechua villagers recalled that in addition to medical care, he offered people rides in his truck, sponsored patron saint festivals, and supplied other amenities, like schooling for the sons of farm workers. He had also informally adopted several children into his household, as discussed further below. Unlike the older style of agrarian patronage of his father, Don Carlos lived in the area and managed the property himself.

Thus Carlos was a good or "all right" (*waleqlla*) master insofar as he had shared in the lives of local communities and provided the aid expected from a privileged *hacendado*. Others echoed this assessment. For instance Emiliano, a former hacienda *colono*, noted that the area of Arani originally had three landowners. "One master was cruel," he explained. "The other two were good." These accounts shared the curious description of masters as being not only cruel or "*malo*" but also good or "*bonito*." This assessment of violent authoritarians as "good masters," like the workers' sadness about the rotting oca, illuminates the challenges that faced unionist discourses that emphasized disrupting enduring ties to *hacendados* and converting servitude into paid labor. To return to the question of asymmetrical ties to masters, described in the previous chapter, these conversations point to a broader tendency for Quechua workers to personalize assessments of specific masters in light of their distinct relations to neighboring Quechua communities and workers. While nationalistic and Aymara discourses of peasant rebellion tended to ontologize Mestizo and Criollo landlords as *q'aras* (peeled, naked, unethical), former servants with whom I spoke in Sarahuayto expressed a more ambivalent set of relationships.

Villagers' memories of abolitionary violence and their discomfort with the rotting oca harvest highlight the instability of the introduction of a new language of national peasantry and its liberation through paid labor and titled land, especially in hacienda strongholds like Ayopaya.[28] In Bolivia, twentieth-century debates about citizenship and hacienda *pongueaje* popularized a new temporal frame, reordering history into a new typology opposing animal-like slavery and modern citizenship.[29] During this popularization both time and people were newly differentiated into distinct categories: people of the present, citizens, were distinguished from the walking dead, those slave-like souls still bound to the hacienda. These divisions paralleled centuries-long tensions between a more mobile hacienda labor force (*yanaconas, forasteros, mitanis,* and *pongos*) and more firmly rooted highland communities, many of whom also worked as tenant farmers on haciendas. While both nominally Indigenous (Quechua and Aymara), these two groups were rarely aligned and frequently diverged in their political loyalties. In the context of those older divisions, hacienda abolition promised freedom from an entrenched system of labor extraction and violence but also further destabilized villagers' relationships to each other and to a surrounding landscape, recoding the lived present into a past that had not yet been eradicated.

UNCERTAIN ADVANCES: "SLAVERY RETURNED FROM AFAR"

Haciendas in most of Cochabamba already showed multiple signs of decline by 1916, including masters' inability to pay mortgages, frequent leasing and rental, and estates' subdivision into medium-sized properties.[30] Nevertheless, in the most entrenched hacienda regions of Ayopaya, Tapacarí, Arque, and Mizque, *colonaje* remained a dominant labor form until at least 1953. After agrarian reform that year, *colonaje* formally gave way to sharecropping, an arrangement that shifted the burden of supplying tools and seeds away from *hacendados* and peasants without removing the personal services typical of *colonaje*. Those who did not have land worked "in company" with former masters, relying on former masters for seeds and plows in exchange for a share of the crops. Even in their absence, however, many former masters remained the legal owners of the land. Thus, the revolutionary period began with grand declarations of historic rupture and servitude's end, but by the 1980s it had withered into prolonged legal battles. It followed that, in Angelo's words, "slavery returned from afar."[31]

Thirteen years after hacienda abolition, in 1965, with land redistribution stunted by legal battles, the master and his family returned, bringing with them legal documents validating their land possessions and engineers who "took the villagers' titles and measured everything." From 1965 to 1983, Mestizo landowners continued to work in the region, relying upon the labor of local Quechua villagers. At this time the process of land division and retitling of parcels was initiated. Redistribution was complicated by the appeals of two distinct groups, not only former laborers but also returned migrants and Chaco War veterans. This created a shortage of lands to be redistributed. In addition, the land reform stipulated that if the landowners could prove "personal intervention in the work of the hacienda," the estate would be declared a "medium-size property" rather than a "latifundio."

In this manner the Sarahuayto *hacendados,* like many others in the province, maintained rights to 200 square hectares of land (of their choosing). This left only the higher, dryer, and poorer quality land to be added to a lottery for redistribution. Furthermore, if any *colonos* happened to be working lands that were of better quality, these parcels would be taken from them and added to the lottery. What followed was mass bribery of INRA technicians by union leaders and by masters, group alliances with *patrones* to secure more desirable lands, and land grabbing among villagers. In the end, Angelo explained: "People divided [*qichuy*] up each other's lands and not those of the *patrón.*"[32]

In this way, land redistribution reproduced and aggravated existing labor hierarchies originating in hacienda servitude. Those Quechua workers with ties to *hacendados,* like overseers or *melgas,* aligned themselves with the engineers and collaborated with the *patrones* to obtain the best lands. The *colonos* and *pongos,* in contrast, were left with the small parcels they had worked before the reform; if they had no land at all, they were subject to the whims of the lottery. The reform thus actively facilitated a process of land grabbing among villagers rather than simply—albeit imperfectly—dividing up the landowner's estate. As a result of these land shortages, many Indigenous villagers worked in a sharecropping arrangement with the former *hacendados* throughout the 1960s and 1970s; unpaid labor and "personal service" did not end until 1983.

With the fall of Estenssoro in 1964, and the later Military-Campesino Pact, peasants were painted as traitors of the nation, and a wave of repression spread across the countryside. Indeed, former servants recalled being beaten brutally by hacienda masters under President Barrientos (1966–69). Yet rural residents continued to mobilize for land redistribution. In July of 1983, Angelo visited Don Carlos on behalf of local villagers, chastising him for continuing to exploit local villagers. Angelo implored the master to renounce such injustice and sell the villagers his lands. When they next met, the master told the union leader that he did not want to sell the land, for "the hacienda is my pride." Angelo then made a legal and moral appeal, asking the *patrón*, "How is it that you want to continue enslaving us?" He added: "The time of slavery has long passed."[33] Invoking the 1953 agrarian reform law, he repeated once again: "That time passed long ago."[34]

With the late master refusing to leave the area and continuing practices that had been legally abolished, including free services and tenant-like farming, Angelo threatened him with legal action. He headed to La Paz the very night of the dispute, bringing a legal claim against Don Carlos. However, while he had expected the support of local villagers and former laborers, the opposite happened. Half the people "turned on us to favor" the *patrón*.[35] The traitors were a couple who live "above," a part of the village located on the opposite side of the river. These were the *yanqhas* (good-for-nothings) who supported the master.[36] Angelo continued: "All of them turned into enemies."[37] In this case, neighbors and fellow villagers suddenly turned (*kutirin*) against him, becoming (*rikhurinku*) enemies. For Angelo this shift from friend to enemy led to his being charged with attempted homicide, a charge for which he spent three years (1983–86) in prison. While he was in prison, the lands were sold to his enemies. Now, those who lived across from the river (including Oscar and his father) were cut off from Angelo and the villagers below. To this day, Angelo noted: "We are enemies" (*Enemigos kaq*). Even today, he said, "We do not give them even a thing."[38] Seen in this broader frame, contemporary disillusionment with MAS land titling (discussed in the preface and introduction) likely stemmed both from pessimism about the capacity for institutional reforms to interrupt racial hierarchies and from earlier experiences of fragmentation and betrayal among Quechua workers and villagers that followed Bolivia's mid-twentieth-century land redistribution.

Humberto Huarachi, the servant who had carried the master to safety in a chair in 1953, recalled the 1983 occupation of hacienda lands very differently. "The Sarahuayteños wanted to take the lands," Humberto noted. He had gone to Sarahuayto to buy oca seeds. As he was returning to the house of the hacienda to sleep, Don Carlos told Humberto: "'Now, secure the hacienda building with another padlock, and secure the doors. There are lots of people outside. Don't leave until the morning. Come and sleep in my room.'" Humberto continued: "We were really careful. 'No one should be let in,' the master told me. In the morning we left for the cornfield, and just then Angelo appeared, saying, 'That's it!' There was the sounding of *pututus* all around and there were a lot of people. They grabbed and hit me again and again, [yelling] 'Get out of here! Suck my dick!' This time they got us. This street is the last I remember. Afterwards I woke up all bloody. I was told I had been beat by Angelo." Here, then, antihacienda militants beat hacienda servants, confronting them on the street outside the hacienda building. The gendered quality of these worker confrontations—ones that pitted tenant masculinity against feminized domestic labor—are evident in union leader Angelo's insult to Humberto, a former hacienda *pongo* and longtime servant: "Suck my dick."

In Sarahuayto the mid-twentieth-century land struggles awakened and reentrenched enduring divisions not only between Mestizo masters and Quechua laborers but also among villagers in accord with families' prior positions as servants and laborers. This divisiveness was illuminated in particular by discussions with Angelo about the hacienda labor system. One evening I joined Angelo and his wife for dinner. As we squeezed together on a low bench in the kitchen area, Angelo outlined what he called "four classes" of labor, or *runa ruwaq,* "people that work." These labor classes were *pongos* (peons or male servants), *mitanis* (female domestic servants), *melgueros* or *melgas* (hacienda overseers), and *jatun melgas* (hacienda managers or bosses). *Jatun melgas* were akin to what were elsewhere known as hacienda *kipus,* men selected by the master to manage work over central agricultural plots and whip noncompliant workers.[39] Those who served "lived off the hacienda's scraps," yet these same laborers employed weeklong laborers who "lived off them." Thus, while the master "had" his *melguero,* this *melguero* also "had"— that is, employed or called upon the labor of—his weekly laborer (*semanero*). Because of the extensive burdens or "personal services" of hacienda tenantry, tenants often relied on *arrimantes,* landless men and women, often kin, to fulfill duties they owed to the *hacendado.*

Angelo's description raised questions about the ways that land and people came to be analytically intertwined in hacienda life. In fact, people used the same the terms for hacienda parcels and labor positions, ones that then later came to determine land distribution with the 1953 reform. As Angelo recalled: "In the agrarian reform *jatun melgas* [managers] were handed over large lands, while *sobra melgas* [submanagers, literally "left over" *melga*] were handed over only leftover lands."[40] In this formulation laborers were valued (and received land) according to their labor positions in the hacienda. The lowest rung of this labor hierarchy were *pongos*, which Angelo viewed with palpable disdain: "pig farmers and chicken farmers" who tended to animals and had no lands. He then added: "The *pongos* ate in the hacienda. Today we still scorn them. 'Your food was from the hacienda, what did you earn?' Today we still talk like this."

Don Angelo's account replicated a distinction, crucial to midcentury labor debates, between tenant farmers and hacienda servants. He considered it deeply problematic that *pongos* did not own land or animals but instead depended on hacienda masters for food and resources. This grotesque dependency was inscribed in their title, *pongo,* derived from the Quechua *punku-rina* or *punku puerta* (doorman), alluding to the person who slept by the door of the hacienda in the place of, and sometimes alongside, the dog.[41] In a cultural milieu where personhood was configured through reciprocal ties, relying on others for food, clothing, and land excluded hacienda servants not only from money or prestige but even from full personhood.[42] As Don Angelo's account reveals, in villages like these the gendered stigmas associated with servitude outlasted formal conditions of forced labor and continue to influence relations and generate bitter animosities among the families of former hacienda workers and servants.

In Ayopaya hacienda abolition created the conditions for new sorts of political claims yet also generated rifts in rural life and "scorn" for former servants who were cast as complicit with the reproduction of an unjust, feudal era. Remarkably, in contemporary villages rural subjects on opposing sides of this historical and labor divide, such as Angelo and Humberto, continued to reside in close proximity. It resulted that the problem of history's displacement (or not) haunted contemporary understandings of collectivity. Villagers were adamant that things had changed, that they were no longer unpaid servants. As the daughter of a *mitani* servant who had grown up in the hacienda household explained: "Before, all this land belonged to Don Carlos, and after the Agrarian Reform they divided it among the workers. Before, the earth was good but now it is dry and is falling. Before, we worked *qasiy* [in vain, unpaid]. Now we are paid. We are no longer like we were before."

This explanation suggests the ways that people grappled not only with political disappointments but also with the broader ethical questions of continuity and change, the before and the now. Yet the "we" forged through this divisive past was felt to be possible precisely because all traces and vestiges had not been erased; in this regard, it was a "we" that was also deeply exclusionary and that followed the well-worn tracks of older divisions between what labor organizers characterized as resistant, masculine tenant farmers and submissive, feminized hacienda servants. These distinctions continued to cast a long shadow over village land politics, often determining alliances and underlaying support for, or opposition to, regional land collectivization measures as well as new Mestizo bosses and mine owners.[43]

LAND GIFTS AND SERVANT CLAIMS

If Angelo disparaged servants for their slavish dependency on hacienda masters for food and livelihoods, Quechua villagers who had worked within haciendas narrated this history quite differently. Doña Ormega Chura, an elderly woman who worked alongside her parents as a child "serving" the master, recalled how her family moved from one hacienda to another, leaving when conditions were too extreme. Her mother had been a *michiq*, herding animals, and her father transported goods for the landowner. She herself had been a *mukoq*, chewing dried corn to produce *muqu*.[44] Other *colono* families were quite literally burdened with the task of transporting goods for *hacendados*, serving as *kachaqs* or carriers.[45] This arduous labor required them to travel dangerous roads with heavy loads strapped to their shoulders or loaded on their own mules or horses. The severity of this earlier labor had left lasting traces on their bodies, earlier subjection causing back pain, rotten teeth from *muqu* chewing, and soreness of the feet and joints, particularly in cold weather.

Given the tragic nature of these accounts, I was surprised to hear that former servants' children tended to dismiss their elders' suffering under the hacienda system. Doña Carmenia Montero was a monolingual Quechua-speaker in her late eighties, one of the last villagers who had lived under the former system of indentured labor. We spoke when I was visiting Sarahuayto for several days in 2011, staying with Don Angelo. At that time, Carmenia recounted her work as a *mitani* (unpaid domestic servant) in a nearby hacienda, from the time of her childhood until the 1953 abolition of servitude. "I tell my children about the hacienda," she lamented, "but they say: 'If the hacienda were to return, I would escape!' They ask: 'How could you have called the masters mother and father?' and tell me that to call someone mother or father, that person must have conceived me." Carmenia sighed. "I don't think today's children would *aguantar* [endure] this. I'm already old. The masters left everyone fighting." She paused and then continued: "I herded pigs and sheep. I made cheese for the *patrón* [master]. Now sorrow returns to me, confronting what was." Carmenia's account illuminates how the divisions produced by the region's history of labor bondage and reform came to refract families. The now-adult children of former servants imagined themselves as incapable of bearing the subjection their elders lived, claiming a virility and a refusal to submit to the power that cowed their ostensibly more passive, unawakened relatives.

These rifts between different classes of hacienda laborers and distributed across generations fueled objections to contemporary land titling efforts. I spoke with Doña Josephina Zarate, an elderly woman whose father had worked as a *melguero* or hacienda overseer. She was joined by her *comadre* and friend Rufina Calderon. We had been discussing the state's land regularization initiative, but when Doña Josephina was out of earshot washing their pots from lunch, Rufina hurriedly spoke to us in a hushed tone, asking me: "Why would we want her to get a title for that land?" In this case, villagers worried that by registering land with INRA, fluid land use practices associated with hacienda land gifting would be reified and formalized, thereby making permanent what many perceived to be unjust land use arrangements. These included instances where *hacendados* left higher-status hacienda laborers, particularly *melgueros* and *hilicatas*, expansive plots of fertile land that were not divided up in the 1953 reform.

These disputes indicate the conflicts generated by INRA land formalization efforts, which went against the reformist premise that land titling could resolve conflicts derived from ambiguous land ownership. By rejecting this idea that clarifying property ownership would bring justice or make land use fairer, villagers pushed back against the key logic underpinning land titling: the idea that more absolutely binding individuals to land through property regimes was a good thing. That which made titling necessary for land reform officials—the promised eradication of messy, irrational land use arrangements and the accompanying ability to bring all land into the orbit of government knowledge—was precisely the source of some rural groups' opposition to it.

Such rural reticence toward agrarian reform was likely also aggravated by the fact that initial surveying was a technique of colonial tribute collection and, as such, it was deployed to combat the patterns of labor mobility and tribute avoidance by Quechua valley populations. The first survey of Ayopaya occurred in 1550, under Pedro de la Gasca, then president of the Audiencia of Alto Perú. These surveys sought to detect people who had escaped to haciendas from state mines or from resettled, tribute-paying native communities.[46] In the 1950s, when the engineers charged with surveying former hacienda lands arrived in the countryside, their presence paralleled the earlier *visitas* of *hacendados* and their *cacique* and *mayordomo* managers.

According to peasant unionists in positions of leadership at that time, such as Don Angelo, villagers responded to these early INRA survey efforts by tearing up maps and chasing engineers from the region. In a record I accessed at the INRA archive in Cochabamba, one engineer charged with drawing up a field report complained that "conflict made topographical work impossible" in the area.[47] Given this history, it was little wonder that rural villagers were profoundly mistrustful of agrarian reformers, above all survey technicians and engineers. Not only was agrarian reform perceived as an instrument of state control, but it also threated to solidify hierarchies generated through the hacienda labor past and inscribed in landscapes through practices of informal land inheritance related to adoption.

Land use in Ayopaya remained determined in part by earlier hacienda labor hierarchies that bound ownership to fluid systems of usufruct rights obtained through hacienda labor positions, as demonstrated for instance by the land conflicts recounted by Doña Flora in the preceding chapter. The ways that practices of adoption within haciendas continued to determine contemporary land use arrangements upon former estate lands in Ayopaya was especially apparent in the cases of Federico and Franz Salas, two Afro-descendant men who were adopted by Sarahuayto's former hacienda master Don Carlos Rodriguez in the 1980s. Their mother had been a laborer on the family's coca plantation in the lowland part of La Paz.[48]

I had arranged to speak to Federico one afternoon. As we waited outside his home, a one-room adobe building with an aluminum roof located about a half mile from the former estate building, my research assistant Sylvia and I busied ourselves fending off an aggressive dog. Federico's neighbor Julio Romero, a man in his seventies, approached us and, after learning about my research, explained that had worked as a hacienda *melguero* or overseer. As Federico sauntered over, Julio turned to us and gestured toward him. "He was brought from the jungle when he was just a boy," Julio said. When Federico joined us, he recounted to us that his mother had worked for the master Don Carlos in the lowlands, where he had a second hacienda for growing coffee. "It was just us, my brother and I, those who wanted to [come]," Federico explained. In this manner they "came to live" with Don Carlos at his hacienda in Sarahuayto. Unable to provide the children with food, much less an education, their mother "gifted us" to the hacienda master, Martín's grandfather.

Federico, now in his mid-forties, was adopted in the early 1970s, after formal hacienda abolition but prior to the height of community-*hacendado* land conflict in the mid-1980s. The area retained the original hacienda building and 200 hectares (just under 500 acres) of cropland, which the master's grandson, Martín Rodriguez, had inherited when his grandfather died in 2010. Taking up the language villagers commonly used to describe informal adoptive relations, I asked Federico whether Don Carlos had "raised" him and his brother. Federico answered ambiguously. "Yes, since we were little, we raised ourselves with Don Carlos." By using the reflexive form "we raised ourselves with," Federico distanced himself from the potential intimacy associated with the term *criar*, to raise.[49] This subtle change demarcated this adoptive practice in the hacienda from other arrangements of child circulation that were decoupled from oppressive labor regimes. At the same time, by qualifying the term *criar*, Federico also dispelled suspicions that the adoptive relation had merely been one of forced labor. In fact, in its Spanish usage the substantive of this word, or *criada,* can refer either to a person raised, fostered, or adopted or to a maid or servant.[50]

Sylvia, my research assistant, knew the brothers from her work in the nearby municipal center. Before I could discourage her, she asked if they had wanted to go. Squinting up at the sun, Federico answered: "Hmm, I don't remember well. I was only five." Likely thinking of her own child, who was only a few years older at the time, she further conjectured: "But it must have been hard, no? One misses one's mother." Federico nodded. "Yes, at first. You have to accustom yourself to the people here. And being just a child, people can be abusive." He described how Don Carlos had traveled for months at a time, leaving the boys under the supervision of a senior female servant. Having heard elderly *mitani* servants describe raising orphan children in haciendas, I asked whether these women were ever "like mothers." Federico replied: "Some, yes. But they rotated and did not stay. Some were good and some were bad. Nowhere does everyone have the same character."

This occasion was a rare moment when people who had been incorporated into hacienda households recalled the move from natal home to agrarian estate. In Ayopaya, Quechua villagers and Mestizo townsfolk described this adoption of "orphans" into haciendas as common. Nonetheless, people were reticent to speak about specific cases lest they incriminate kin or, in the case of former servant families, imply a parent's victimization by earlier labor and sexual violence. Like the practices of aid that I discussed in the previous chapter, these arrangements were subject to diverging accounts. While the children of hacienda masters romantically recalled long childhood days spent playing with servants' children, others like Federico emphasized the logistical dimensions of hacienda life, with systems of rotating domestic labor. Rejecting kinship-based sentiments of care or love, Federico instead described getting himself used to (*acostumbrarse*) shifting, at times abusive, domestic arrangements. The children were integrated into the household, the master providing food and clothing but ultimately leaving the children to fend for themselves; they quickly learned to avoid especially strict overseers and *mitani* servants.

Federico's case demonstrated how aspects of an earlier land-labor nexus continued to shape the terms of rural authority and Indigenous claim-making in the present. These attempts to negotiate the obligations associated with an entrenched servile labor order were especially urgent in Sarahuayto, where servant, tenant, and master families continued to reside in close quarters and at times made claims to the same land. Like my discussion of godparenting relations in chapter 1, my argument is not that these gift relations were untouched by deeply disturbing racial hierarchies. Nonetheless, Ayopayans still drew upon elements of this asymmetric exchange tradition as the basis for relationships that could be remade in order to transform their present. The ethical and political aspects of these enduring ties were disavowed by unionists and contemporary MAS officials who saw aid alliances as hindering the realization of a more liberated form of Indigenous agency centered on paid labor and land rights.

CONCLUSION

This chapter has tracked the historical precedents of asymmetrical aid relations in Bolivia's central valleys and Eastern Cordillera from the late precolonial era on. In Ayopaya colonial value systems were shaped by regional traditions of asymmetrical exchange centered on the circulation of servants, children, gifts, and food. The longevity of these hacienda aid relations in Ayopaya complicates familiar historical genealogies of colonial labor subjection and its cultural and economic afterlives. While commonly associ-ated with a "feudal" hacienda system, in this part of the world exchanges of labor for land access can be linked back to precolonial agrarian systems that Spanish colonialists purposefully drew from and supported.[51]

Those networks became newly problematic within mid-twentieth-cen-tury labor movements and socialist agrarian reforms, with divisive conse-quences for life among villages of former servant and tenant farming fami-lies in Ayopaya. Here Quechua villagers' views of fellow neighbors as traitors retained a view of hacienda servants as ethically compromised, as treacher-ous subjects who privileged self-benefit over that of the collective.[52] Legally defined property—both as a promised overcoming of hacienda subjection and as a form of self-possessed citizenship that would displace it—required eradicating kinship-based attachments and aid relations between servants and masters. For former servants this displacement was profoundly wound-ing as it disavowed shared expectations of beneficent authority and upended networks of asymmetrical aid without installing anything satisfactory in their place. Moreover, as apparent in my conversation with Angelo, even as such networks of alliance and benefit were largely dismantled, the gendered stigmas associated with hacienda servant status remained firm.

In Bolivian national politics under President Evo Morales, the hacienda past arose as a powerful synecdoche for Indigenous subjection. Land reform was cast by Morales as an act of bringing longtime Mestizo masters to their knees. Conversely, pro-Indigenous activists and MAS supporters sought to craft militant Indigenous citizens by displacing hacienda dependencies, syn-thesized in the *colono* or forced hacienda laborer. For instance, a meme that circulated widely on Facebook by the user Ayni Digital pictures a man in traditional ritual dress. Above, to his right, it reads: "We are neither *colonos* nor human beasts," and below, to the right, "We are Bolivians, and millenar-ian children of this earth."[53] Here, *colono* status is likened to the not-quite-human, the "human beast." Like the Cochabamba activist's characterization of elderly Indigenous farmers who do not willingly speak Quechua in urban spaces as "dogs," recounted in this book's introduction, this meme cast rural subjects at odds with new forms of revitalized Indigeneity as somehow less human, even bestial. Yet, in a subtle departure from nationalist and activist tendencies to align hacienda *colonos* with sheer victimhood—often described using the language of "slavery"—former servants and hacienda adoptees in Ayopaya held much more ambivalent recollections of labor conditions pre-ceding 1953.[54]

The experiences of former servants like Humberto and Federico depart notably from widespread narratives of victimization. They instead highlight how the circulation of child and women laborers arose as partial outcomes of choice that, while constrained, also afforded new possibilities for alliance with and support from hacienda masters.[55] However counterintuitive to scholars, many servants and their kin were both technically "landless" and were at times privileged recipients of masterly aid. These cross-cutting practices of land gifting and aid between Mestizo bosses and Indigenous workers became key targets of legal refashioning in late twentieth- and early twenty-first-century Bolivia. In their place, reformers sought to install more bounded orientations to land and labor but also to racialized trajectories of belonging. As I next discuss, this occurred through a nationwide land titling initiative that promised to upend hacienda-based racial hierarchies even as it treated forced labor as a basis of legitimate ownership in the present.

PART TWO

Property

THREE

Producing Property

Ruben Arpasi and I met in his airy office on the fourth floor of the Instituto Nacional de Reforma Agrarian (INRA) headquarters in Cochabamba city.[1] A lawyer by training, Mr. Arpasi was in his thirties and had grown up in a rural Quechua agricultural community before migrating to the city for schooling. He sat on a swiveling office chair while I perched on a folding seat, my notebook and tape recorder at hand. Through the expansive windows behind him, I could see a dusty horizon of dry hills and ocher-colored adobe settlements. We were discussing INRA efforts to "regularize" (*sanear*) land by distributing new property titles to rural farmers. "Peasants," Mr. Arpasi noted, "don't use documents to account for property." This had caused "irregularities" in land use, in turn limiting the government's ability to aid farmers who suffered crop failures from frost or blight.

A blight the previous year had imbued land titling with new urgency, as the state could not subsidize losses unless land was registered. In Ayopaya more than one hundred communities were affected, and 87 percent of crops perished. In Arpasi's formulation, for the state to mitigate such risks required property formalization. Or, as Mr. Arpasi put it: "The land has to have its identification document just like people do." While ostensibly aimed at securing the well-being of Indigenous peasants, such efforts were also crucial to governmental efforts to paint itself as a legitimate seat of political authority by way of its capacity to provide basic services, and especially food, to Bolivia's needy.[2]

It was November 2011 when I first met with Mr. Arpasi, then director of the Cochabamba branch of INRA. The meeting was the culmination of a months-long process of my gaining research approval. This process was especially fraught given MAS party opposition to NGO workers as covert agents of capital expansion and accumulation from the elite North.[3] In addition, titling programs were politically delicate at that time, as they synthesized growing rifts between the MAS government and rural Indigenous and peasant constituents. Since Morales's 2005 election, peasant and Indigenous associations have demanded that the state establish new protections against land encroachment and property dispossession. These efforts have cast a harsh light on broader tensions between MAS party ideals and popular orientations to justice after hacienda servitude. INRA efforts to address the agrarian vulnerabilities of Indigenous Bolivians by titling property were related to longstanding governmental promises to remedy the injustices of the earlier hacienda system by redistributing land. In Arpasi's words: "Land regularization is important because it can resolve internal conflicts. With private property rights, you regularize [*sanear*] a parcel." Land with a valid title is considered *saneada* (literally "sanitized" or rationalized), and that land is then assumed to be free of conflict.[4] Officials thus saw titles as a way to intervene in entrenched regimes of racialized inequality that underlay early twenty-first-century hierarchies of land ownership, glossed by Arpasi as "internal conflicts."

Here and elsewhere, INRA officials used the term "conflict" as a veiled reference to untitled land use arrangements and abiding systems of Mestizo authority rooted in hacienda agriculture and reproduced under military dictatorships. As Arpasi explained: "These are conflicts that have continued for years and years and nobody resolved them. For example, in some places people still do not touch the master's lands even though he left years ago. Only after we arrive and tell them that the land is theirs now, will they use the lands. If not, they say, 'How could I? This belongs to the master [*patrón*].' They respect this." By contrast, under INRA stipulations land must have a sole owner and property boundaries must be delimited and mutually exclusive. Yet, as Arpasi noted: "You go and ask a local where his land is, and another person points to the same land. *The two are owners*. For this reason, we are regulating and perfecting. We make declarations and we resolve these problems."

As his comments demonstrate, within INRA's institutional vision, titles arose as a crucial mechanism by which to disrupt servile agrarian orders and imbue peasants with new understandings of land as alienable property. Moreover, titles supplied key opportunities for state actors, here INRA staff, to shore up discrete models of ownership premised upon an expectation that a single person would own a single parcel and that such ownership would determine the use of land over a person's lifetime. However, these efforts to smooth over conflicts by more tightly binding paper to land did not always work out as planned. Most notably, titles were meant to resolve "conflicts," but they also produced *new* conflicts. As Arpasi explained: "People say that before INRA arrived they did not have a single problem, and now they have problems. Before, they did not have property rights, they were planting on what they had inherited, and they made their own documents. With land regularization there are problems and conflicts that we have to regulate."

This chapter demonstrates how, for INRA reformers, land titles arose as crucial mechanisms for disentangling land from earlier histories of usage and abuse (including relations of asymmetrical aid, adoption, and informal land gifting discussed in the preceding two chapters). Scholars have illuminated the multiple meanings that land and territory take on in social movements, particularly in the Bolivian lowlands.[5] However, these works often leave unexamined the idea that those movements ultimately boil down to competing claims to *resources*.[6] Yet farmers inhabit Andean landscapes not only as the raw material to be cultivated or farmed but also as relatives who need to be cared for, fed, and relationally sustained in ways that blur the long-standing legal conceptions of a divide between nature and culture, kinship and capital.[7] Modifications to landscapes, and to accompanying devotional practices, have long been described by local populations as disturbing those relations.[8] In fact, while rarely included in accounts of Indigenous ontologies, practice of *wak'a* sacrifice and ritual were common upon agrarian haciendas.[9] This raises new questions about the ways that property titling initiatives interface with vernacular traditions of land and water management by which Indigenous residents have long negotiated questions of access and usufruct rights in former hacienda regions.[10]

In Bolivia, property titling arose as a mechanism by which INRA reformers sought to enclose space but also to newly delimit *time*. As Arpasi's comments made evident, within INRA programs, property titles are valuable in that they can clarify the terms of ownership, resolving uncertainties of land use and spatial boundaries. Officials like Arpasi often invoked rural conflicts to justify further interventions and, in some cases, to seize land. They were authorized to do so by Article 169 of Bolivia's 2006 Agrarian Reform Law (3545), which stipulates that land must serve a "social and economic-social function." Where it does not, that land must be redistributed or become state "fiscal property."[11] INRA officials, working with peasant union leaders, hold the power to decide on land's legitimate "function."

As Pablo Mamani Ramírez (2015) has noted, this process introduces new divisions around the kinds of people, and (Indigenous) collectivities, deserving of government aid.[12] It also more tightly defines what kinds of relations to place count as a basis for ownership. In what follows, I consider how INRA officials produced property both as an object in the world (titled land) and as a quality of agentive self-mastery or self-possession that the relatives of indentured hacienda laborers were felt to lack. Property's promise here lay in its supposed capacity to secure spatial but also temporal fixity through the bureaucratic process of title processing, revealingly termed *saneamiento de tierras* (literally: land cleansing or purification).

The analysis offered here ethnographically tracks three competing paths for the production of property in INRA's land titling program: property as *displacement*, property as *overlay*, and property as *promise*. Briefly, these paths refer to how titles simultaneously strive to uproot a bonded past (*displacement*) yet remain beholden to hacienda agricultural systems as models for legitimate ownership (*overlay*). Where alienable property was absent, this called forth new kinds of institutional intervention focused on liberating Indigenous farmers by transforming rural orientations to labor and history (*promise*). These efforts assumed special weight in former hacienda provinces like Ayopaya, which reformers had long seen as defined by peasants' anachronous ties to hacienda authority. Attending to this tripartite process of land titling reveals how property organized new kinds of spatial enclosure but also promised to rewrite the relation of past to present, bondage to liberty. Titled property afforded a mechanism for disentangling land from the arrangements of *hacendado* authority and asymmetrical aid discussed previously.

However, despite reformers' insistence on displacing earlier labor and kinship knots rooted in hacienda servitude, the technical process of "pulling" a new title relied on "superimposing" survey maps (*replanteos*) of hacienda labor in ways that revealed titled property as contingent on that labor past. While this land titling program pivoted on a logic of property as a universal form that did not rely on specific labor itineraries, the technical dimensions of "pulling" a new title showed how, less than an abstract object, property too cohered through the stitching together of bodies and landscape over time.[13] Legitimate land ownership was that which ascribed to forms of familial inheritance on the part of specific hacienda laborers. Through the GIS mapping function of overlay, the concrete dimensions of hacienda servitude continued to animate "sanitized" land maps, albeit as a trace of earlier passages and labor itineraries that were ultimately erased by the forging of a new title.

While the conditions of property's utopic production are specific to Bolivia, this case holds broader theoretical ramifications for scholarly understandings of property. It reveals how property is forged through the utopic untangling of earlier asymmetrical attachments, including the kinship-based knotting of wealth to obligation and land to history described earlier. However, it also demonstrates the threads that obstruct property's birthing as a discrete object, thereby allowing us to rethink contract's relationship to social and labor forms that precede it.

TITLING PROPERTY, DISPLACING SERVITUDE

In Bolivia, collective land rights have been a rallying cry for lowland Indigenous movements since the 1980s.[14] In 1990, Bolivians organized the First March for Territory and Dignity. The years that followed saw the development of various Indigenous rights–based movements that pushed for the land rights of "displaced" populations, including for the descendants of hacienda workers and other migrants, voluntary or forced, who came to the lowlands to work on sugarcane plantations. In 2005 activists, students, union workers, and Indigenous farmers organized Bolivia's Fifth National March for Land and Territory, which took aim at stalled agrarian reform measures and the state's failure to recognize collective Indigenous territories.[15] Marchers also opposed the state's waning support for *latifundio* land seizures since 2003. These mobilizations abetted Evo Morales's rise to the presidency and supply the political background for the MAS party's passing of a new Agrarian Reform Law in 2006.

In 2006, in a speech announcing the new agrarian reform, President Morales promised to title 20 million more hectares in the next five years and vowed to appropriate land from those who had obtained it illegally through alliances with former military leaders. When a rainstorm interrupted his speech, Morales added: "The great *patrones* of the Oriente are crying. They are hysterically crying because they know that their glory days are over.... We will seize their unproductive land and give it to poor campesinos!"[16] Nonetheless, Morales offered only limited support for the legal breakup of *latifundio* lands, a feature crucial to the earlier 1953 reform. Like INRA's 1996 law, the 2006 law promised redistribution yet often merely titled smallholder lands and existing Indigenous territories while upholding protections for large landowners.[17]

The MAS party government's property regularization program (2006–19) sought to title property in accord with land redistributed following hacienda abolition in 1953. The earlier Movimiento Nacional Revolucionario (MNR) government's agrarian reform established the institutional framework within which MAS agrarian reform initiatives unfold, including the institution charged with overseeing land titling today, INRA. The 1953 Ley Del Servicio Nacional de la Reforma Agraria abolished hacienda servitude, declaring landlords' agrarian parcels the legal property of their *colono* tenant farmers. This reform was widely popular in the countryside, especially among hacienda *colonos* (tenant farmers).[18] For Aymara and Quechua community members (*comuneros*), it offered a crucial legal vehicle for reclaiming land from hacienda masters.[19] These dual workings of agrarian reform, both as a mode of implementing statist designs of property and territory and as a channel for Indigenous claims to land and political sovereignty, continued to define rural Indigenous relations to MAS land titling during my fieldwork in Ayopaya.

Bolivia's 2006 Agrarian Reform Law drew together processes of land titling, legal aid and institutional support for collective land titling, and new legal protections for rural agricultural and domestic workers. It hinges in particular on the promises of paper titles as a means to land rights and, with them, broader kinds of posthacienda liberty (Figure 5).[20] It seeks to complete the stalled titling of agrarian lands redistributed in Bolivia's 1953 land reform, while also expanding community and Indigenous land titling.[21] In fact, the "incomplete" nature of the 1953 reform has long been a rallying cry for activists and sympathetic scholars who found earlier hopes of structural change stifled by delayed land titling, as discussed in Theodoro's case in the preface.[22]

During the time of my fieldwork (2010–12) INRA titling brigades and staff (including engineers, survey technicians, lawyers, and volunteers) were initiating visits to rural areas, surveying property and determining whether land use aligned with the redistributive land maps drawn up after hacienda abolition. In new "information campaigns," officials explained the procedure in Quechua or Aymara and encouraged women to have their names included on titles. Alongside land titling, the law emphasized the eradication of unpaid and servile labor arrangements. A 2008 amendment, a Supreme Decree called "Relations of Servitude and Verification of Their Existence," empowered land reform officials to "reverse haciendas with systems of servitude [and] to liberate captive families." It defined "servitude" (*servidumbre*) as conditions of indentured labor including any arrangement where people

FIGURE 5. A pocket-size pamphlet outlines 2010 revisions to the 1996 Land Reform Law, produced by El Instituto Nacional de Reforma Agraria (INRA). Photo by author.

work in exchange for necessities, such as food, or to repay outstanding debts. In addition, MAS passed a new child labor bill in 2013 that prohibited work for children ages five to fourteen; this was rescinded after popular outcry, including mass protests on the part of unionized child workers.

Despite their initial popularity, these land and labor reform programs subsequently faced severe criticisms by union, peasant, and Indigenous groups, who accused MAS of unduly accommodating wealthy lowland elites and their property regimes.[23] Critics argued that it made concessions to conservative groups, including term limits to Morales's presidency, new departmental autonomy measures including the right of departments to administer their own revenues, and the retraction of state support for landless movements, which had previously relied on INRA legal support to seize and title "unproductive" *latifundio* land. Instead of supporting the seizure of *latifundio* land, INRA redistributed state "fiscal lands."[24] Properties with large landholdings were grandfathered in, and the limit of 5000 hectares per property was not imposed retroactively. This served to further marginalize elderly populations and women, who did not qualify for land in early mid-twentieth-century agrarian reforms.[25] Moreover, the agrarian reform targeted "servitude" in ways that criminalized informal aid networks in which children circulate in exchange for room and board (see chapter 2). It thus required a new fixity of persons not only in space but also in accordance with more reified definitions of ethnicity and biological descent, particularly paternity along recognized heteropatriarchal familial lines.

MAS's agrarian reform, initiated in 2006, understood a greater spatial fixity of land use and territorial sovereignty as a precondition for overcoming the nation's unjust, bonded past. This required securing modes of Indigenous territorial rights in ways that were more absolute than they had been under the 1953 reform. While community lands were historically of pivotal concern for Indian and peasant movements and were hotly contested within the midcentury congressional debates preceding the 1953 reform, the midcentury reform did not actually introduce juridical mechanisms for the government recognition of collective landholding.[26] By contrast, land reform efforts under MAS included the titling of Tierras Comunitarias de Origen (Native Community Lands, TCOs), a process first initiated in 1996. This coupling of property formalization and community self-determination has created new legal channels of claim-making, including *saneamiento interna* (internal regularization), wherein union or community leaders solicit a review of land titling from INRA.[27] Despite their "self-determined" nature, these initiatives can also marginalize vulnerable community members by newly privatizing shared-use areas, like pasturelands, and by rewarding farmers and villagers with closer ties to union leaders.

As Andean historians have pointed out, the model of a spatially bounded and representative "community" was itself initially instituted by Toledo during his resettlement policy in the late sixteenth century.[28] Recalling the reconstitution of ayllus by colonial and Republican administrators, MAS agrarian reform initiatives treated community recognition as a means to modernize the countryside and encourage democratic values.[29] For example, current INRA policies combine collective land titling with an emphasis on securing land's "social and economic-social function," productive labor arising as crucial to legitimate property ownership. Under MAS tutelage, Indigenous land titling promised to remedy a bonded past, but it also offered a mechanism for increased economic and political control, much as property did for earlier modernization campaigns.[30] In this way, MAS labor laws and antiservitude campaigns replicated earlier colonial anxieties about forced labor as holdover of feudalism. While these initiatives often cast community in a romantic light, as a solution to inequality in land ownership, titling programs in the post-2006 era also reentrenched disparities related to hacienda labor hierarchies. These included solidifying racialized divisions between former master and worker groups as well as among former worker and servant families.

At the same time, to merely equate highland community with a reformist model implemented by Toledo overlooks more than five hundred years of political struggle in the Andes. As historians, anthropologists, and pro-Indigenous *Indianista* authors themselves insist, community—despite its transformation into a more bounded spatial unit under colonialism—has and remains a crucial political tool both for reclaiming Indigenous value systems and for staving off land dispossession.[31] Community, as a recognized juridical unit under Spain's dual republic system, afforded a certain degree of autonomy and independence from colonial ways. This is apparent in the Taki Onqoy ("Dancing Illness") rebellions of the eighteenth century, in which the failure of Indigenous leaders to uphold Andean qualities of proper leadership and to assume Spanish ways led to highland Indigenous uprisings against native caciques that anticipated the larger Túpaj Katarí rebellion of the 1780s, discussed in the introduction.[32] Because of the centrality of land sale in encomiendas, contesting private land through articulations of community belonging and self-rule has been an indispensable site of Indigenous resistance to colonialism, in the Andes as elsewhere.[33]

Community, however, has never been limited to a structure of collective land rights. Rather, as a range of anthropological and historical studies demonstrate, it has and also remains a relational center and structure for the elaboration of Aymara and Quechua value systems and religious practices.[34] Hence, as Esteban Ticona Alejo has argued, community cannot be reduced to a means of production model because it refers also to a broader "sociospiritual space."[35]

In the Ayopaya region specifically, community was also a key rubric through which hacienda laborers organized, making claims to land based on attachments to soil derived both from racialized status as Indians and from their labor as hacienda workers.[36] Moreover, while union structures have frequently been viewed by scholars and pro-Indigenous authors as impositions—part of the violent installing of "peasant" over "Indigenous" in the 1952 Socialist Revolution—in many parts of the Andes, above all the highland altiplano, unions took on aspects of traditional Andean organizations or, in other cases, remained less important than local ayllu and community relations.[37] In fact, for many Katarista activists and scholars, it was through this attempt to render community into a secular model of production that the Morales government revealed itself to be "neoliberal" in ways that went against earlier promises of Indigenous-led decolonization.[38]

Putting aside the question of how peasant union forms have absorbed aspects of ayllu leadership structures, both offer key mechanisms by which Indigenous people navigated, and continue to navigate, political power. Union and ayllu leaders alike are crucial figures for the navigation of relations to outsiders, including Mestizo bosses but also city lawyers, government ministries, or agrarian reform offices.[39] In fact, this remains the case as peasant union leaders were often those charged with visiting the INRA office to resolve competing land claims or to gain clarity about land collectivization processes. These relations of leadership are based on reciprocal expectations of support for an ayllu or union head and, in response, leaders' willingness to sacrifice time, money, resources, and labor on the community's behalf.[40] Some MAS critics used a similar argument as a basis to challenge Morales's leadership in the terms of community obligation to followers—in short, as a sort of extractivist or negative reciprocity model.[41]

Despite the importance of community organizations for Indigenous political negotiations with colonial and contemporary governments and governmental institutions, land titling processes also encouraged a firmer definition around community boundaries in ways that, paradoxically, used earlier hacienda labor practices as their precedents. This defining of community worked both spatially to differentiate one peasant community from another, but it also implied a division between hacienda-based and community-based landholding that did not hold for Ayopaya. In this regard, and like individual land titling, land collectivization efforts mimicked the logics of property as contingent on transforming both spatial and temporal relations in ways that risked dispossessing Indigenous villagers of land. Despite these painstaking technical mechanisms that sought to produce regularized property, this model continued to confront dramatic challenges in posthacienda regions like Ayopaya. There, Quechua unionists used land titling processes as opportunities to redefine community in ways that departed notably from familiar framings of ayllu collectivity in Katarista and Aymara-centered political discourses.

PROPERTY AS DISPLACEMENT

My conversations with officials at the central INRA office in Cochabamba provided insight into the importance of property regularization as a way to rationalize land but also to remap rural orientations to authority and history. In the second of our meetings, Ruben Arpasi outlined several challenges facing land regularization since its inception, under the parameters of Bolivia's new constitution, in 2010. At that time the MAS government had been forced to extend INRA's existing mandate for an additional three years and then, in 2013, for another four.[42]

INRA officials saw this delay as an effect of the mistrust (*desconfianza*) caused by misinformation about the regularization program. According to Arpasi, this mistrust "comes from a lack of information. Sometimes we are [in rural parts] explaining and they do not understand. It is like they are in the first grade. They don't understand. So we have to explain four times, in different ways, with examples. And afterwards, they still don't understand. It's like this. [He gestured at his blank computer monitor.] Blank. Nothing. Because of this, it is difficult. They belong to another generation. In other places [outside Ayopaya] it is not so much like this. Their children have already left to study in the city. They say, '*Papiy*, I want to [title the land]' and it's done. But in other cases, no. We have to enter, speaking Quechua, in order to explain."

In this account Arpasi dismissed rural skepticism toward land titling as a misplaced reaction spawned by slander and ignorance toward INRA. In invoking blank computer screens or uneducated children, his words eerily echoed earlier colonial visions of hacienda workers as immature, even non-human, in their inability to recognize or ameliorate their own condition. In this context Arpasi viewed land titling as a key method by which to displace anachronous affects: emotional attachments to authorities and to land at odds with an ideal of alienable property. As evident in the abandoned wood in Sarahuayto, discussed in chapter 2, these affects had dramatic material effects, above all that of peasants avoiding parcels that, for a variety of reasons, they saw as still belonging to earlier masters. Land titles promised to resolve this issue on both fronts, installing regularized land tenure arrangements and introducing a broader historical awareness of political change. With the virtues of alienability firmly planted in their minds, rural peasants would be able to dispense with anachronous affects like *hacendado* "respect" and instead adopt critical outlooks grounded by values like self-determination, economic self-sufficiency, and Indigenous autonomy from non-Indigenous elites. Where these affects persisted, officials narrated them as obstructions to the expansion of titled property.

It was not the first time I had heard MAS officials, including people from rural backgrounds like Ruben Arpasi, liken rural peasants to children. Julio Calle was in his late thirties and had held MAS government posts in multiple provinces. He was a self-proclaimed Trotskyite, and when I met him, he was employed in Ayopaya's municipal government. To Julio, Bolivia's history of military governance had ingrained peasants with an appetite for demanding resources and aid, encouraging what he called an obsession with "having" (*tener*). "They say 'I want, I want,' like a child," he told me. "This seems very spoiled, like children." In particular, Julio saw peasants in Ayopaya as constrained by a clientelist imaginary produced by their encounters with the populist Movimiento de Izquierda Revolucionaria (Revolutionary Left Movement, MIR) party, founded in the 1970s. MIR campaigns employed a transactional framework in which leaders appealed to voters with promises to provide a direct, unmediated line of dialogue with politicians and, in turn, promised heightened responsiveness to voters' demands for aid.[43] Following this mind-set, peasants frequently pestered party officials for development projects yet lacked "a vision of how [the project] would benefit them." Julio had struggled to change this outlook in his work coordinating local development projects. "It is difficult to change this mentality," he acknowledged. "Therefore, I have to plant and propose ideas [of] how they can change their form of life, of organization."

Julio, like Ruben Arpasi, was a progressive official of rural Quechua background who sought to inculcate new values of Indigenous autonomy and self-determination, which he deemed to be sorely lacking among rural farmers. Once again recalling the sentiments of eighteenth-century colonial administrators and governors, these INRA reformers understood their task as one of aiding rural Indigenous groups by incorporating those groups into more progressive configurations of labor and rights-based citizenship.[44] This effort to endow peasants with new political knowledge was ostensibly for their own good. For instance, in Julio's view this clientelist outlook made rural groups vulnerable to corruption and abuse. "You go to the masses [*bases*] and if they are not politically well-armed, the bureaucrat will distort reality," he said. "But other sectors are well-educated politically—that is, they know where they want to advance to, and so they are in opposition [to a proposal]."

To avoid manipulation by smooth-talking bureaucrats, peasants had to be "armed" politically. Development projects, rural education funding, and INRA workshops on land rights and constitutional changes were only some of the methods of *capacitación* (legal training) officials used to inculcate peasants with the political know-how to avoid manipulation. Despite these efforts, however, Julio found that peasants continued to expect state hand-outs, just as they had during the era of military rule. This confirmed the idea that grassroots political change first required external intervention on the part of trained political leaders and state officials.

Unlike Julio, however, Ruben Arpasi at the INRA office saw hacienda servitude as the root of rural dependency on political and economic elites. To him, it was "childlike" dependencies on authorities—state and nonstate—that had prevented rural groups from assuming a more agentive role in land and labor conflicts. As Arpasi put it: "It is not just that the *patrones* [hacienda masters] left. People come here and say, 'This *patrón* did this,' and we say, 'But there are no *patrones* anymore.' It's not the *patrón* but rather his son or grandson, but people [continue to] think like this." In former hacienda regions like Ayopaya, new titles supplied mechanisms for teaching people to change their modes of thought and, in doing so, to shed ingrained dependencies on agrarian masters and political elites. Only when those dependencies had been dissolved would land relations be regularized and rural peasants cleansed of a divisive past.

Knowing that I spoke Quechua, Arpasi noted, with a playful sparkle in his eyes, that the goal of land titling was to make land *chuya* (pure, crystalline, unpolluted). Using a Quechua term allowed a play on the dual meaning of *saneamiento* (regularized or, literally, "sanitized"). Like scholars supportive of land redistribution, Arpasi hereby implied that land titling could have potentially healing effects.[45] In this case, INRA officials' understandings of bureaucratic transparency drew upon and recast Quechua notions of "cleansing" as an absence of foul emotions of greed, jealousy, and resentment.

For INRA staff and MAS officials in the countryside, land regularization promised to produce titled property but also to generate new, less entrenched, orientations to land and authority. By displacing older hacienda attachments, officials hoped to allow rural groups to come into their own as awakened, liberated Indigenous subjects. These efforts resonate with what scholars have described as the reification of ethnicity within anticolonial projects of national healing in Bolivia and other Latin American nations.[46] Despite what both officials and rural populations defined as their risks, however, titling programs also carried notable ethical weight as mechanisms for state decolonization, as apparent in Arpasi's account. Supporters of this progressive project tended to view elderly peasants, including their own parents, as tragically oblivious to political change—a position that warranted intervention. By characterizing rural opposition to land titling in this way, however, officials overlooked legitimate rural objections to reform, including suspicions stemming from the fact that land that officials deemed unproductive could be seized by union officials, or even the MAS government. Arpasi invoked this productivist stance in his defense of land titling as enabling state subsidy programs and agronomical training. Quoting then President Morales, Arpasi noted: "Land is like a person, you have to feed it. If you give it better food, it works better, it produces more."

These conversations with INRA staff demonstrate how, under MAS rule, the former hacienda province of Ayopaya retained its place in the national imagination, for which it has long served as a foil to progressive ideals of rationalized land and "free" (i.e., paid) labor. By shedding this false sense of "respect" for former hacienda masters, rural farmers in places like Ayopaya would be able to assume their rightful place in the nation as more efficient, independent farmers. It might seem that this focus on productive citizenship went against a liberating gesture in which land titles promised reparation for hacienda subjection. However, in Bolivia these two impulses have never been wholly decoupled. INRA land regularization, for officials, offered a way to increase agrarian outputs but also to install a more egalitarian rural agrarian order. Titles historically arose as a way to naturally expose rural groups to the "civilizing influence of the market" and, with it, for peasants to untether themselves from abusive masters.[47] Recalling Bolivia's 1874 Law of Unchaining the Peasant Communities, INRA officials cast land titles as mechanisms for liberating peasants. This in turn raised renewed concerns, for INRA workers, with the obstructions to this process: the persistence of non-propertied orientations to land and authority. Abiding attachments to inherited patterns of land use and authority were seen to slow agrarian production, but they also limited rural groups' ability to find their footing as new, more liberated Indigenous citizens.

Officials acknowledged that adopting these new ideas of alienable property and self-determined citizenship would be jarring for many. As Arpasi explained: "I am from *el campo* [the countryside], from a region that had haciendas. We had to walk one-and-a-half hours to school each day. Today, there are better schools. Things are changing. Before, people were used to accepting [development] projects, of being told what they needed. Now, they have to decide. As the government tells them, 'I don't know what you need in your own house, that is for you to decide.' So, they have to decide if they need schools, medical posts, a new sports stadium, it is up to them. This is a momentous change, and often they object, 'But before...' However, in the end, they are pleased with it. They say, 'We didn't have this before.'"

In this account Arpasi invoked the need for autonomous decision-making on the part of rural people who must figure out "what you need in your own house." Unlike the dependencies of hacienda life, property would make rural Indigenous people owners of their own "house." Here, recalling the connotations of the English word "home," "house" evoked family but also nationalist visions of self-determined, Indigenous collectivity. In this way, to rework Lewis Henry Morgan (1868) and Gayle Rubin's (1975: 46) insistence that kinship be seen as a domain of economic production and value creation, the Indigenous "community" was to displace the hacienda household as a reserve of value, both civic and economic.

Arpasi narrated this process as a subject who had weathered this "momentous change," who had learned how "to decide." Although he was aware of the discomforts involved, he saw these interventions as necessary. Land titles promised to clear the air, displacing dreamlike spaces of historical entrenchment with the ethical and empirical transparency of law. In achieving newfound self-mastery as "well-armed," capacitated subjects, a younger generation of farmers would part ways with their grandparents (*los abuelos*), who had labored on haciendas and called the master *Taytay* (my father). Against the hierarchical intimacies and illicit genealogies of hacienda servitude, the Indigenous community as "house" was to offer a more democratic, horizontal model of belonging and political deliberation.

This deployment of property as a way to transform historical sensibilities was not new to MAS. As for late colonial agrarian reformers (see chapter 2), INRA land titling promised to reorder land relations but also to displace aid arrangements that officials aligned with an antiquated, feudal system. Moreover, much like the period of the 1950s, when the children of Quechua hacienda workers became unionists who policed the terms of rural labor, this effort at rural uplift and political awakening held generational consequences. Notably, both Ruben Arpasi and Julio Calle came from Indigenous hacienda worker families. As such, it is hard to imagine their critical evaluations of *los abuelos* (grandparents, the elderly) as not also an affront to their own relatives in the countryside.

Property was hereby conceived as a mechanism for crafting resistant, militant citizens who would work together and deliberate peacefully as members of an exemplary Indigenous community. However, officials' efforts to craft alienable property out of older labor hierarchies and kinship genealogies also hit snags, particularly in a reform climate in which legitimate land ownership paradoxically depended upon its alignment with earlier hacienda labor practices. What fell away from this official record of forced labor tenantry, however, were the arrangements of domestic servitude and land gifting relayed in previous chapters. This raised a crucial question about the interface of titled property and abiding land use practices that could not find historical affirmation in the INRA archive.

PROPERTY AS OVERLAY

INRA's regional branch office occupies all five floors of a new cement building in the bustling commercial district located south of the city center in Cochabamba. When I visited on Friday March 9, 2012, the building was packed, common in the days preceding the nearby open-air market at La Cancha. After checking in with the security officer in the entrance area and garage, I passed through a main hallway before ascending four flights of stairs to the Oficina de Saneamiento (Land Regularization Office, LRO). On the stairs I pressed past the bustle of men in slacks and pressed shirts and women in *pollera* skirts carrying toddlers in woven *aguayo* blankets. On the fifth floor, Huascar Delgado, who worked in the Property Regularization Department, waved me into the office that he shared with three other engineers. Together, the four men were responsible for conducting the "topographic review" of lands currently undergoing regularization (*saneamiento*). Huascar pulled up a seat next to his computer station, having kindly agreed to walk me through the technical process of "regularizing" a given file. As we got situated, Huascar chatted with Germaine Ruiz, an engineer who led teams of INRA workers (known as "field brigades") to conduct surveys in the countryside. There they combined photogrammetry, Geographic Information System (GIS) and digital mapping, and cadastral surveys to determine property boundaries. These technologies allowed hacienda labor histories to appear (and disappear) in the archive, whose recombined maps determined the parameters for legitimate property ownership that guided state land regularization efforts.

Ascertaining the *precise* location and boundaries of each parcel started with the collecting of "clerical information," accumulated maps and survey information since the 1950s that came to serve as a cartographic blueprint for later field visits by INRA "brigades." The technical process of "regularizing" land hinged on correctly mapping earlier hacienda and plantation labor practices. This was done by consulting land surveys conducted in the late 1940s and early 1950s (Figure 6). By processing their raster data and vector data, these maps could be assimilated into the pixilated grids that appeared on Huascar's computer. Using the overlay function of ArcGIS, these muddy, antiquated maps were enriched with satellite-derived images of the earth's surface, which corrected for the earth's curvature and also for transforming geologic features such as shifting rivers or eroded land.

It was through this process that the outlines of "regularized property" emerged. The process ended with the addition of latitudinal and longitudinal coordinates using Global Positioning System (GPS). Later, trained engineers, agronomists, lawyers, geographers, and survey technicians would conduct surveys in the countryside. A new map of the "regularized" property was shared with Indigenous political authorities (*mallkus*) and peasant union leaders. This process allowed INRA officials to gauge whether existing titles corresponded with existing geographic space and, furthermore, whether their boundaries matched those established by hacienda redistribution in 1953.

Huascar initiated the "regularization" of the file with a series of mouse clicks, which he methodically narrated for me. The first step involved dragging a digitized image of the map contained within the older agrarian file (*expediente agrario*) into the GIS program. On this occasion, Huascar was working on a file concerning the town (and former coffee plantation) of Buena Vista, located in the coca-growing Chapare province. I suspected that, given the officials' uncertainties about sharing information with me, he elected to use this file rather than one located in Ayopaya. After converting the image, Huascar spent the next half hour or so reworking these now-digitized "original agrarian files" (*expedientes agrarios*, or files drawn up by

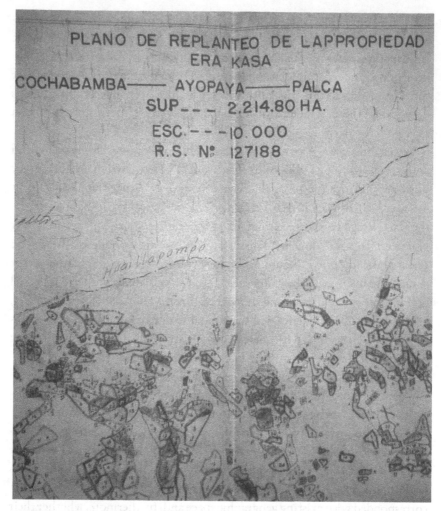

FIGURE 6. Portion of 1954 Instituto Nacional de Reforma Agraria (INRA) map of Era Kasa (Ayopaya province) showing hacienda agricultural parcels for redistribution to workers. Photo by author.

INRA survey technicians and engineers in the 1950s) into a pixelated image in which thin black lines and numbers divided parcels worked by former hacienda laborers. By using these mapping programs, he was able to convert digitized post-1953 survey maps (raster data) into GIS information (vector data), which could then provide a more accurate, "objective" representation of a given piece of land.

After converting the file map into raster data (Figure 7), the second step was to overlay this data with survey material in the form of vector data: a

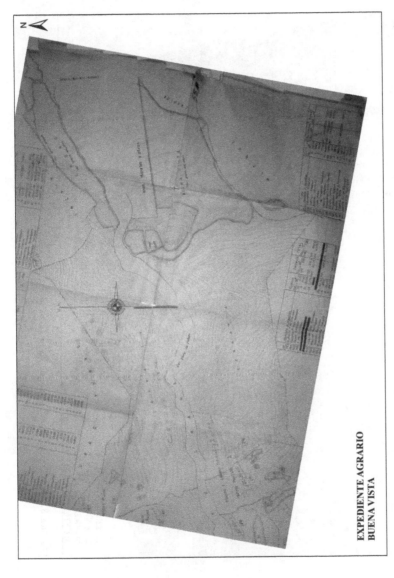

FIGURE 7. Visual depiction of the initial step of the GIS overlay process, showing 1950s province map, prepared in March 2012. Courtesy of INRA.

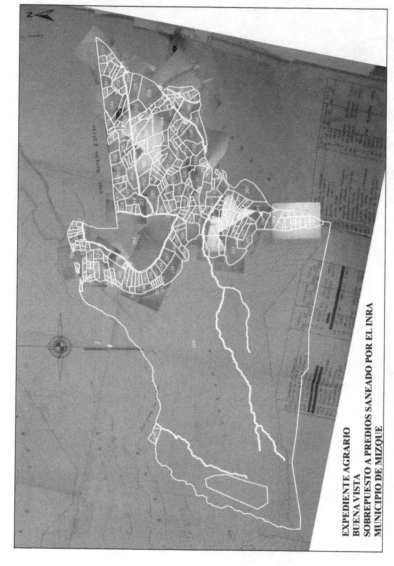

EXPEDIENTE AGRARIO
BUENA VISTA
SOBREPUESTO A PREDIOS SANEADO POR EL INRA
MUNICIPIO DE MIZQUE

FIGURE 8. Province map and compressed hacienda survey files, prepared in March 2012. Courtesy of INRA.

series of points, lines, and polygons superimposed in white atop the earlier, digitized map (Figure 8). The original agrarian file map, damaged and showing signs of wear along the creases, became the backdrop for a GIS-generated outline. Its outline, in white, marked the periphery of the former plantation property and the individual plots allotted to each worker and servant upon land redistribution in 1953. These lines were based on digitized versions of hundreds of hand-drawn survey maps that were now crammed next to one another in miniaturized form, jostling for space as their original paper expanses exceeded the allotted GIS plot lines. As an image, the antiquated map was now visually overlaid by property lines established through prior INRA surveys and indexed through miniaturized versions of individual plot maps from separate agrarian files. By virtue of this layering of survey maps and georeferenced data, the older agrarian map was made compatible with "objective" global space, a technical process of assigning coordinates. This process reconciled raster data (e.g., the scanned map) and vector data (assigned spatial coordinates) into a digitized file.

In the third step the smaller survey maps of worker plots disappeared; only the white border lines (confirmed via georeferencing) remained (Figure 9). As the compressed images disappeared, the physical maps were abandoned for the fully translated digital vector data. Engineers at INRA described this process as the "superimposition" of data that allowed for multiple, otherwise incompatible kinds of data to be held together in image form. When done correctly, this overlay of various kinds of vector and raster data promised to leave those information paths undisturbed and accessible in their original form. That is, data linked to titles and physical lands were to be preserved within the file. In this regard, the process of GIS overlay brought together multiple spatial knowledges without collapsing them—an alignment that did not require mediation by a third term. Although the earlier archival map was eventually displaced by the new, regularized property boundaries, at this stage both historical and geospatial data coexisted.

In the fourth step the represented ground of the image shifted from the antique manila color of the paper file map to a landscape of dark greens and blues afforded by satellite imagery (Figure 10). The original topographic map was replaced by an orthophotographic image obtained through GIS. Derived from an aerial photograph, an orthophotograph adjusts for topographic relief, lens distortion, and camera tilt. By way of uniform scale the photograph allows a measure of "true distance."[48] The individual plot lines and larger property boundaries remained unchanged, but viewers could

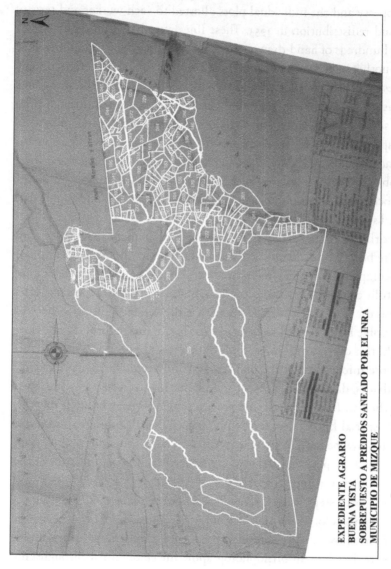

FIGURE 9. Province map and enumerated parcels, prepared in March 2012. Courtesy of INRA.

PLANO DEL POLIGONO 032 BUENAVISTA
SOBREPUESTO A LA ORTOFOTO
MUNICIPIO DE MIZQUE

FIGURE 10. GIS-enriched orthophotograph and numbered hacienda plots, prepared in March 2012. Courtesy of INRA.

now discern that the property was wedged between two rivers in the northwest and southeast, with pasturelands stretching across a mountain ridge to the west of the hacienda property. As this geospatial information was integrated, the map's point of view moved outward into a more abstract, "bird's eye view."[49] But while offering an all-inclusive picture, the new map also integrated granular detail from earlier plot maps. At this stage translation into abstract geographic space was not absolute; a roughness remained.

In the fifth and final stage (Figure 11), once again, vector data was converted into raster data. The orthophotograph had to be made compatible with points, lines, and polygons. In the process, forms of knowledge afforded by a satellite image (similar to the view on Google Earth) were translated into a more abstracted model of bounded territory in earthless space, the greens and blues erased in favor of golden tan. Blue lines denoted the southern and northern limits of the two rivers, and green lines marked the points of highest altitude in the more mountainous, westernmost expanse of town. In this last step the topographic map was delimited as a discrete representation of the property, no longer accompanied by the rest of the landscape, with its geologic features, but by longitude and latitude lines. The map was tilted so that north corresponded with the top of the image, the bottom with south, and so on.

In the process the granular details of the orthophotograph, used to align the earlier map and the recent survey data, fell away. Land was represented as uniform and coherent, colored beige, and beyond the boundaries of the town. Its periphery was undifferentiated white, except for blue rivers. As in the original maps, each plot of subdivided land was spatially divided as a numbered bundle attributed to specific original owners (i.e., hacienda tenants). Thus, while the image retained the boundaries of plots defined by the toil of *colono* bodies, its form was domesticated via its required compatibility with "objective" global, geographic space.

After this superimposition of older and new "sanitized" maps through digitized overlay, the GIS data was enriched with the use of GPS technology. This allowed reform officials to detect geologic changes since the survey was initially made in 2005. As he worked, Huascar explained that orthophotographs were often inaccurate due to the earth's curvature as well as to geologic changes in altitude. He showed me an image of a river but noted that the GIS data was now inaccurate as the river had changed course. "The river changed course and, with it, the land was reconfigured," he explained. "As a result, it is difficult to account for these [new geologic] conditions, the topog-

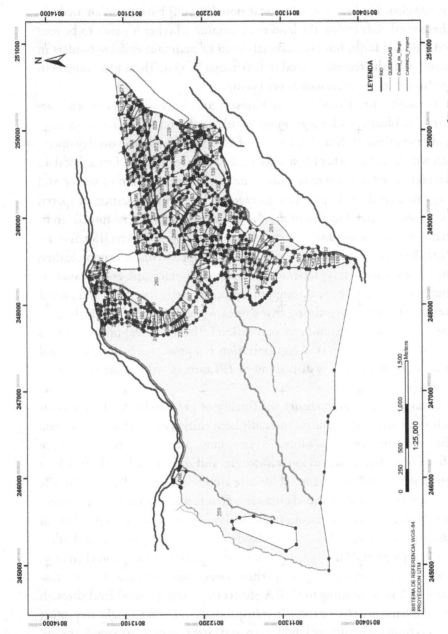

FIGURE 11. Redistribution plan and numbered properties to be titled, prepared in March 2012. Courtesy of INRA.

raphy." These changes posed challenges to 1953 property lines. For instance, shifting river courses created islets that could not be farmed and so must be left untitled. In these cases, Huascar noted, "[you] have to do an analysis, whereby officials review the land to determine whether it needs to be retitled." By and large, however, officials tried to maintain existing borders in accord with the records of land redistributed in 1953. These plots ranged in size from 7 to 25 square meters per person.

Through this clerical process Huascar and his colleagues crafted cartographic blueprints for legitimate, regularized land titles. To do so, they made use of the technical aptitudes of GIS, specifically the overlay operation which, unlike other file storage tools, produces archives formed of data overlaid or sedimented over time. Due to the organization of vector and raster data in the GIS program, storage is never only a question of spatial boundaries or files but also of *depth*. As the program's online tutorial indicates: "'within' is just another way of saying 'on top of'" (ArcGIS 2019). By using these innovative technologies, officials hoped to improve upon earlier, imprecise manual survey techniques and hand-drawn maps. For instance, as Huascar was guiding me through this process, Germaine came and peered over our shoulders, explaining that this cartographic work "makes the process more exact and eliminates corruption." This technical process of GIS overlay revealed INRA land regularization as a process of historical accrual that, in a final moment of displacement, fell away in order to produce "regularized property."

Huascar's job was to ensure the fidelity of present-day land use to this archive, ensuring that land had actually been turned over to former hacienda laborers or their children. Moreover, new, more precise calculations of space offered by global information technologies and software allowed officials to detect and stamp out corrupt or abusive land relations. It responded to the fact that in the 1950s hacienda masters often bribed engineers to misrepresent the size of their estates and individual land plots. During Bolivia's era of military rule (1964–1982), Mestizo landowners assisted government leaders in offering up rural farms where political defectors were imprisoned and tortured. As a reward, military sympathizers were often gifted land.[50] This history gave a new meaning to INRA efforts to cleanse (*sanear*) land through new mechanisms of bureaucratic transparency, ones that sought to protect farmers from manipulative landowners and bureaucrats. Cartography promised to shield land relations against corruption or abuse.

Despite the importance of the earlier agrarian file and its survey maps for regularizing property, Huascar was adamant that original and "regularized" maps were distinct: "We differentiate the two." After integrating topographical data and enriching it with aerial photographs, survey maps are "regularized" (*saneada*) and are defined as distinct from "the original." This separation occurred in the final stage of overlay, when the original map background (based on the post-1953 agrarian file) was replaced by a beige shade with black dotted coordinates for longitudinal and latitudinal axes. This "regularized map" was then distributed to residents, constituting what Huascar called an "archive."

This alignment was politically significant as it supplied the basis for settling competing land claims. After aligning the original *expediente* map and the GIS data, the next step was for Huascar to write up an *informe* (report). In this report Huascar addressed "whether the current beneficiaries coincide with the initial beneficiaries"—that is, whether contemporary land use conforms with the redistributed hacienda plots afforded by the 1953 agrarian reform. Where they did not, officials investigated the source of this variance between file and world. For this reason land regularization was a high-stakes process, forming the technical basis for determining legitimate, titled property. After this regularization earlier property titles were annulled.

The delicacy of this process for land claims made INRA officials particularly hesitant to grant me research access. In 2011, during my first meeting with INRA's president, he explained that the director had recommended denying my request for access to the archive. "There is a worry that you will take data from the archive and use it to create problems," he said. "For instance, there are some communities that were originally haciendas and were one property. The property was later divided—that is, the community divided into two or more separate villages with their own union and village authorities. Today, there are efforts to consolidate each of these separate villages into their own community, despite the fact that the archive says that the land was originally one community. People in the community today say that no, we are not one community anymore. But the data in the archive says something else."

While ostensibly detached from the hacienda and plantation past, processes of GIS regularization reveal how earlier labor patterns served as precedents for legitimate property in the present. Even as officials maintained a view of an original file and regularized land as distinct, earlier survey maps of indentured labor tenantry nonetheless continued to determine the bounds of recognizable territory and land claims. This has to do with the technical qualities of GIS, wherein data is not just stored but rather layered both as image form and as file content.[51] The insistence on aligning hacienda land use and present-day property rights remained the case even as MAS politicians emphasized land titling as a means to *displace* a bonded past.

Conversations with Huascar and his colleagues in the Land Regularization Office drew my attention to the ethical connotations that maps, and titles, assumed within a reformist climate marked by a shared sense of the tragic belatedness of hacienda property redistribution. For Huascar, GIS and GPS-based mapping techniques offered methods for correcting distortions due to corrupt politicians or inaccurate survey data. By eradicating such distortion, it would be possible to establish property as a discrete object and empirical referent. For instance, the day before, Huascar had explained that several original *expediente* maps were scaled inaccurately and would have to be redrawn. I asked him how such cartographic problems affected land retitling. He explained that if the maps do not coincide, they again do away with them and a new land survey has to be approved. "What I do is to verify, to ask 'How is this?' 'Is it true what they are telling me?' Are the superimposed graphics and orthophotos lining up? If it is not true, then I ask, 'What happened here?'" In the case of divergence, Huascar phones the union leader and asks, "Why this variation?" If the union leader agrees, the regularization process is redone, and INRA officials supply the union leader with a new survey map that reflects changes that the leader can then accept or reject.

For Bolivian interlocuters in the INRA office the importance of getting a map right had to do not only with the promise of cartographic representation as "truth," but also the fairness of land redistribution as a path to posthacienda justice.[52] Establishing regularized property was bound up with belated state promises to make former *colono* families formal "owners" of their plots, thereby realizing the promise of the earlier 1953 reform. Conversely, variations across overlaid maps and in land use practices were associated with corruption, bribery, archival tampering, or even lingering servitude—including the abiding effects of hacienda favoritism and land gifting. Yet while the promise of property regularization lay in titles' promise to secure a break from the bonded past, IRA officials' technical work of crafting, mapping, and titling property relied on those labor histories for their form and legitimacy.

For them, determining legitimate property rights hinged on investigating the relation between the former *colono* workers whose names appeared in the original agrarian file and present-day owners—presumably either kin or people who had bought the land from original title-holders—that is, hacienda tenants. Here, as in Paul Carter's (2009: 4) discussion of the precedents for coastal map-making in Central Australia, "the lines on the map, the outlines on the urban plan...contain within them a history of earlier passages." Bodies were therefore not absent—they were crucial to survey maps as cartographic determinants of legitimate property.

These mapping practices provide insight into a mode of producing property as an exemplary accrual of labor in space, echoing Lockean understandings of land improvement as a basis for possession that have circulated in this region since the colonial era (Herzog 2015). The stitching of these labor histories into landscapes through cartographic processes destabilizes the idea that maps are ubiquitous in their workings as a means to differentiate land and people, instead drawing our attention to modes of geographic representation as the threads and traces of earlier passages and labor relations, or what Tim Ingold (2000: 149) calls "landscape" as a relational product as opposed to land as an external object that stands outside of time. This raises several crucial questions: What kind of property was being produced through INRA's titling bureaucracy? More broadly, what qualities—ethical valences and future aspirations, but also ideals of labor continuity and collectivity—come to embed themselves in property as a utopic political instrument? For officials at INRA, property assumed key significance in its promise to allow rural Indigenous people to reassemble modes of collectivity that were disrupted by the colonial expansion of encomienda and then hacienda agriculture.

PROPERTY AS PROMISE

On the first floor of INRA headquarters in Cochabamba, visitors could consult an Archival Records office, which opened promptly at nine a.m. The floor also held public restrooms and a photocopier available for use with a small fee. Inside the Archival Records office, the director Carlos Delgadillo spent his days seated at a desk flanked by three younger officials who clicked away diligently at their computers. In the back of the room several rows of gray metal bookshelves were stacked high with thread-bound files organized numerically by case number (Figure 12). The sheer scale of paperwork, especially for files concerning land collectivization in Ayopaya, attests to the stakes of the archive as a space not only for research or storage but also of

FIGURE 12. Bound stacks of agrarian files, 2011. Photo by author.

active political deliberation and organized resistance. I spent the days at a desk in the back of this room, browsing the dusty files and observing interactions between visitors and staff.

One morning, an older gentleman in a white shirt and baseball cap and a younger man entered the office and approached an elevated counter where Carlos attended to them. The older man spoke Quechua, with his younger companion translating his statements into Spanish. The younger man explained that they had come to inquire about a land dispute and wished to see the corresponding file. Files referred to "original agrarian files," which included titles distributed by executive order after 1953 land redistribution, letters scripted by peasant union leaders and INRA lawyers, survey maps and topographical reports, news clippings, and—in cases of new land conflicts or collectivization proposals—related legal records for proposed or actualized ownership changes. That day, these guests also wished to submit a complaint against an INRA engineer who had unduly demanded a fee for a legal certificate. Carlos retrieved the file, and the visitors spoke in hushed tones as they reviewed its pages in search of a document that would settle a land dispute. Lingering on one page, the younger man explained: "See? That is your signature." However, the key document was missing. Turning to Carlos, the younger man pointed: "It should be here."

Carlos, trying to get a handle on the situation, asked the older man: "You're a former union leader, right?" The older man nodded yes. The younger of the two, whom I guessed was his son, relaxed a bit and smiled at Carlos, who continued to leaf through the bound file looking for the missing document. The older man then complained, to his son but at a volume loud enough for everyone in the room to hear, that "the engineer" overseeing the land survey process had recently come and billed them seventy bolivianos (about ten US dollars) for a Certificate of Validation. The younger man followed up with Carlos. "But the certificate should be free, right?" The older man additionally objected that the engineer "doesn't come to the [union] meetings at night, although he should." After some time, with Carlos patiently leafing through the file, the younger man phoned an acquaintance, to whom he spoke at booming volume: "We want to defend our government, that's why I need your help, my brother." By ringing this acquaintance, someone who was politically connected, I guessed that he had hoped to elevate his case with Carlos, thereby securing his help in contesting this property regularization outcome. Evoking his desire to "defend our government" positioned him as a MAS supporter (MASista) whom Carlos should therefore assist.

This interaction in the INRA archive illuminated the public use of earlier survey records and files as political instruments for contesting state titling outcomes. The office's open-door policy was meant to counteract past corruption, responding to MAS commitments to make administrative and bureaucratic spaces more accessible to marginalized Indigenous publics: in short, to decolonize bureaucracy from its earlier trappings in colonial and then Republican racial hierarchies.[53] As part of this broader shift, the archive was newly accessible as a site that the people could consult if they hoped to contest land reform proceedings as well as institutional abuses, such as payments for authentication certificates, or other instances of extortion, bribery, or corruption by state officials or local Mestizo elites (often the children or grandchildren of masters). During my time at INRA, I noticed that visitors brought with them copies of case documents, signed agreements, petitions, and even land titles.

This agile maneuvering in institutional spaces went against more familiar anthropological portraits of rural people as naïve and of bureaucratic spheres as facilitating the interests of elite, lettered populations. Of course, in Latin America as in other parts of the world, scholars have long noted that documents, including petitions, have been central mechanisms by which Indigenous groups challenged imperial violence and land expropriation.[54] Likewise, while land titles had long been yoked to earlier projects of modernizing state intervention, they also could be made to circulate in ways that posed challenges to top-down, legal interventions.

The route for contesting state land regularization outcomes followed the spatial layout of the INRA building. The INRA archive, conveniently located on the ground floor and with a photocopier on site where a woman could be paid twenty centavos (about three cents) per page for copies, constituted the initial landing-place for popular efforts to contest or make land claims. As the lowest rung of the building, the archive served as an institutional hinge linking members of the public to agrarian files and easing their insertion into what could be a lengthy process of legal and political posturing. The next step was a day's wait in long lines and overcrowded rooms upstairs, a process often repeated for days until the proper official was available and willing to meet. In this way the archive offered a testing ground for potential claims, a place to gauge the chances of its approval, as well as to "arm oneself" with the right papers. Land disputes began with a consultation with Carlos in the archive and later, in especially conflictive cases, might culminate with a meeting with Land Regularization Office (LRO) staff on the fourth floor. In rare cases visitors requested a meeting with INRA's director on the uppermost fifth floor. There, visitors could request a review of a given property and, in cases of corruption or distortion, the issuing of a new title.

Alongside its use as a public resource and service, the archive was also a place where Carlos—who had fashioned himself as an outward-facing representative of INRA—could educate newcomers and visitors about land regularization processes. One morning, a young man wearing a baseball cap and jeans came to the office, concerned with a land collectivization proposal that would affect his land. The man complained: "They want to be one unified community [TCO] and we don't want it.... Where are the documents? In *saneamiento* [regularization]?" Patiently and pedantically, Carlos explained how, with land titling, "you will all gather together and decide how you want it to go. If there is no existing dialogue, they will make you meet collectively. Like other divided communities, you will all meet up to see whether you would like to remain as one or become two." After all, Carlos clarified: "It is up to you how you want to be organized." When the man repeated his concern to Carlos, Carlos patiently repeated: "If you are like two communities now.... Well, it depends on you. If they are fertile lands, you will take advantage of *saneamiento* to discuss [ownership of these lands]."

This interaction signaled the importance of the archive as an informal site of legal counsel and political consultation as well as a space for educating rural people about the parameters of self-determination. With the phrases "they will make you meet collectivity" and "you will take advantage of regularization," Carlos insisted that people take up and enact a position as self-determined agents of titling, even where the parameters of that process were firmly established in INRA's 2010 Agrarian Reform Law. In his tone and language Carlos insisted that visitors take up the position as agents even as he revealed this agency to be defined and constrained by reformist designs. Land titling here arose as a collaborative exercise in self-determined Indigenous governance, an opportunity to learn how to reach a collective agreement on divisive matters like land ownership. Before new "sanitized" files could replace hand-drawn, 1953-era maps, a new map had to be "validated" or approved.

A "Land Regularization Committee" made up of five people from the community or village in question carried out this validation. Of course, reformers themselves have acknowledged that actual land practices often vary from cartographic ideals, for, as Huascar noted, "people work the land by use and custom [*por usos y costumbres*]." Drawing upon deliberative traditions, rural community members "more or less reach an internal agreement about who will work [the land]." Because of the government's commitments to self-determination, this process entailed new kinds of interplay between government agencies and engineers, Indigenous community members and union authorities. Despite his diplomatic, helpful tone, Carlos's account attested to the difficulty officials confronted in their efforts to portray regularization as something other than a top-down process.

Carlos's insistence on the need to deliberate collectively echoed Ruben Arpasi's account of how peasants must "decide for themselves" how they want to organize and what they need, even where that requirement might be experienced as unpleasant or even painful. This insistence on self-organization, however, took for granted the ease or naturalness of rural community.[55]

Assuming the organic qualities of community overlooked how rural labor and political orders had been reshaped by late twentieth- and early twenty-first-century land collectivization policies, including municipal decentralization (specifically the Law of Popular Participation, 2004) and its accompanying mechanisms for legally recognizing "autonomous" Indigenous territories (Orta 2013). Together, these processes cohered into a legal portrait of Indigenous community that could not account for the fragmentary qualities of rural life, particularly noteworthy in regions like Ayopaya where earlier labor hierarchies pitted servants and unionized laborers against one another (see chapter 2). From within the INRA archive, practices of hierarchical land gifting and aid appeared largely through their absence—that is, as suspicious misalignments between paper and practice. Yet in order to uphold community as a basis of civic virtue and Indigenous democracy, it was necessary for INRA officials to downplay land "conflicts" as exceptions to an otherwise communitarian rule or as effects of peasants' incapacity to organize or deliberate appropriately.[56]

As an institutional setting, the Archival Records Office offered a place where officials like Carlos advised rural farmers on how to proceed in initiating a land dispute. Even as land regularization was meant to empower Indigenous peasants, it ended up reinstalling hacienda systems of agrarian settlement and labor as blueprints not only for land ownership but also for property as a quality of self-mastery. Property was thus imagined as a utopic form that would break the bonds that tied former hacienda worker populations to masters' families or corrupt bureaucrats. To meet INRA criteria, peasant collectives needed to conform to the terms of hacienda resettlement or, if they could not, perform a nascent kind of unity by realigning the archive's dusty pages. That is, for rural groups to effectively mobilize these documents, they had to configure themselves into collectivities whose historical dispossession and then repossession of land the archive could prove and which could be further legitimated through formal titles.

This called forth new kinds of discipline, apparent in INRA staff's frequent insistence that rural farmers learn to deliberate as members of new, virtuous collectivities. Where maps and land use practices departed, residents might face accusations of corruption, bribery, untruth, or problematic entrenchments of hacienda subjection. Despite the specific utopic qualities that property assumed in these Bolivian agrarian reform efforts, it still operated as a mechanism for isolating not only land from networks of hacienda exchange but also, and with it, deserving from undeserving owners—where deservedness depended upon a given subject or community's continuity with earlier labor subjection under the hacienda system.

FROM OBLIGATION TO RIGHT

These concerns with titled land on the part of INRA reformers shed light on the importance of property not only in the colony but also, thereafter, in nationalist efforts to supersede and undo earlier and ongoing colonial injustices. Here land titling was not just about securing rights to resources or land; property's fixing in paper was also a crucial mechanism of developmental uplift by which to assure the displacement of backwards feudalism by modern citizenship and Indigenous inclusion. While scholars like Manuel Bastias Saavedra (2020) challenge the relevance of property—as opposed to *dominio* or possession—for early colonial navigations of ownership in the Andes, my work at the INRA office demonstrates how Lockean conceptions of agrarian improvement as modernization remain firmly entrenched through often naturalized paradigms of rural development.[57] Without private right, land could never be improved as property and a nation would never belong to the "civilized part of mankind."[58]

Yet, as these INRA land regularization efforts showed, to implement alienable property also required the disruption of abiding aid networks. While the civilizational dimensions of John Locke's optimistic enshrining of property as a basis for firmer citizen rights and protection from labor abuses has been dramatically contested, less noted are the ways modern property rights were legally elaborated against a set of less firmly defined privileges.[59] Along with converting informal exchange practices (the socially sanctioned pilfer of wood and fruit) into "theft" as a crime, Karl Marx ([1842] 1975: 235) argued that legislative shifts at his time allowed what had been a "customary right of the poor" to be newly monopolized by the rich in the form of private property.[60] In this process the law came to stand on the side of property in the abstract, and not people. By protecting property's value in the penal code, inequality was newly fixed and entrenched by law.

Understanding this legal production of property as contingent on eradicating feudal obligations helps clarify the stakes of Bolivian agrarian reforms which, in a quite different context, sought to install titled property against agrarian customs of asymmetrical aid. Such customs, as in Locke and Marx's times, were identified with the barbarous before of feudalism. Read along-

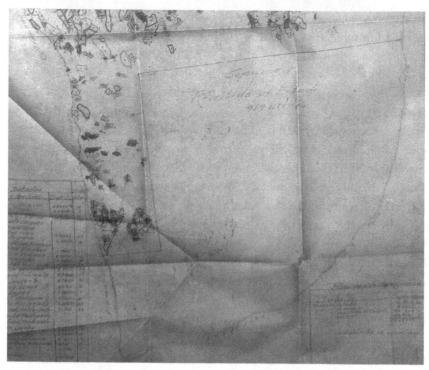

FIGURE 13. Map of collective pastureland from Era Kasa (Ayopaya province) to be "reverted to the state," 1954. Photo by author.

side my ethnographic account of Bolivian land titling, these texts encourage renewed attention not only to what property generates but also to what it displaces or disrupts: here unpropertied exchange relations against a discrete conception of an object that has one owner and can be transferred only via contract. As for Locke, for officials at Cochabamba's INRA office property promised to clarify land ownership in order to afford them both land rights and, with them, a new vision of liberty as self-possession. Moreover, where land was not improved or cultivated in accord with a developmental ethos, INRA officials were imbued with the power to have that land transferred to the state—thereby paralleling Locke's view that "waste land" should turn over to the Crown. This is apparent in an archival file map that marks an enormous tract of former hacienda land (989 square hectares, or almost 2,500 acres) as reverting, not to the peasant laborers who are listed beside the map, but to the *state* (Figure 13).

The reliance of INRA notions of deservedness upon earlier hacienda labor arrangements attests to the challenges that face the fixing of property as an ostensibly discrete, ahistorical object, even from within government corridors and reform offices. While the kind of property generated through land regularization could not fully account for the arrangements of asymmetrical aid described in chapters 1 and 2, INRA land titling nonetheless depended upon revealing land's mediation by earlier hacienda labor practices. The requirement of that labor mediation was especially problematic for the children of domestic hacienda servants, both *pongos* and *mitanis*, who had not held assigned agricultural parcels and hence whose labor could not be recorded—or redeemed—by consulting earlier INRA land surveys.

In this regard, the Bolivian case demonstrates the risks of an overly objectivist account of property. Treating property as an object (land) rather than a process overlooks the injurious qualities of property's forging not only as hinging upon labor admixture but also as eliciting a transformed orientation to hierarchy. This raises the further question, which I discuss in chapter 4, of how property, rather than only affording citizens more rights, can also reentrench inequality while criminalizing exchange relations—including among former masters and those domestic servants who could not find the grounds for land restoration in the archive—that did not take that false equality as their premise.

CONCLUSION

This chapter has traced the reformist production of property through the binding of paper titles to land through three central mechanisms: displacement, overlay, and promise. The micropractices of mapping reveal how these efforts departed from familiar fantasies of terra nullius—unpeopled space and unsettled, unproductive lands—by instead elaborating titled property through earlier practices of agrarian labor. As such, they demonstrate the work it takes to make property stick; despite that work, property has remained tenuous, at times failing to materialize. Many INRA officials framed property as an empirical object in the world that officials could regulate, title, and re/distribute, yet this objectivist orientation was belied by their quotidian office work. Property had to be continually produced as engineers, bureaucrats, survey technicians, and field brigade leaders layered survey data, consulted and reordered archives, collaborated with union leaders, and taught stubborn Indigenous farmers about the virtues of individually fixed and transferable land rights.

Against familiar understandings of property as an ahistorical object (land) that is decoupled from human histories and relations, twenty-first-century agrarian reformers crafted property as an outcome of purposeful engagements with regional labor histories. If, for these INRA reformers, titled property promised a vehicle for enacting new spatial and temporal logics of alienable ownership, it was one that was lifted from the inscriptions of hacienda sexual and labor violence on midcentury survey maps. As elsewhere, here the utopic promise of property lay in its capacity to disrupt servile agrarian orders. Both as a resource and as a quality of self-mastery, property promised to install a break in time, detaching land from people and, with them, from relations of exchange and kinship forged within haciendas.

Yet that INRA honored earlier laws that allowed master families to keep up to 200 square hectares, while *colono* laborers received a maximum of 20 square hectares each, called into question MAS party claims that property regularization would secure more equitable land access. Thus, despite MAS discourses centered on liquidating the hacienda by "regularizing" property, for INRA reformers legitimate land ownership had to be appropriately mediated by hacienda regimes. Hacienda labor practices were the basis for legitimate "property" but were ultimately disappeared from the record with the processing of new titles and maps. In this way, just like it did for Karl Marx, liberation required passing through and suffering dispossession by property.[61]

The spatial constrictions of environment, land, and resources through legal mechanisms of territorial and property enclosure are well-documented.[62] In Ayopaya, however, efforts at producing and fixing property in space and time interfaced with entrenched legacies and genealogies of labor and sexual violence. This province had long thwarted governmental efforts to disaggregate agrarian estates and thereby check the power of an influential landed Mestizo elite.[63] In this regional and historical context, property offered a crucial mechanism for recrafting an earlier custom-bound subject into a new subject of rights, here developed through a national model of Indigenous citizenship. INRA titling efforts assumed that racialized contestations of power and land could be easily resolved through formal land rights, yet in Ayopaya former master families had stayed on after hacienda abolition and other heirs returned after the 2008 global downturn. The return of Mestizo elites, coupled with the kinship-based networks, muddied the lines between Indigenous and non-Indigenous groups that guided reformers' maps. They also cast doubt over promises of Indigenous sovereignty on which land collectivization schemes were modeled.

Turning to these local engagements with INRA land titling, the next chapter shifts from my focus here on the technical aspects of land regularization (*saneamiento*) to the ways titling initiatives were taken up and renegotiated in Ayopaya. As Ayopayan farmers navigated the state's land titling program, they pushed back on land titling and its accompanying normative assumption: the argument for a natural, even absolute, securing of liberty through alienable, bounded possession.

FOUR

Grounding Indigeneity

On a humid morning in December 2011, Pavel Camacho and I accompanied his uncle on a drive to their family's land.[1] Pavel was in his early forties and came from a family of Quechua agricultural farmers. He had recently returned from Spain, where he had been working in construction to send money home to his wife, a local *chicha* brewer, and their three young daughters. After he parked the rusty jeep at the cemetery, we stepped out and stood by the roadside, surveying the sprawling agricultural valley below. The fields were green from the rainy season, which was fully under way. Pavel's uncle Ernesto pointed out various *terrenos* (land parcels) below, listing their names as well as the hacienda families associated with them.

To the north, the village of Chullpani used to be owned by Carlos Espada, a Mestizo master whose land stretched from there to the village of Pampa Redonda, barely visible from where we stood. Ernesto recalled how their family had come to own some of that land. In the late 1940s Pavel's grandparents, Pedro Soliz and Sabina Quirosa, received land in Chullpani from Espada. According to Pavel, it was an "inheritance" from the master acknowledging his grandfather's "good work" as an (unpaid) *mayordomo* or hacienda manager. Later, the land was passed on to Pavel's parents. His father, an influential unionist, had worked as an agrarian inspector under the MNR state in the 1950s, which enabled him to obtain a title for it. When Pavel's parents died, the plot of fertile land was then bequeathed to him.

Pavel had worked this plot until dwindling returns related to the global recession in 2008 drove him to leave for Spain. However, he struggled to find work in Spain and in 2011, Pavel returned home, in financial ruin. He set about preparing his land to plant *chirimoya*, a coveted tree fruit for which the region is famous, and which is celebrated in an annual fruit fair hosted

FIGURE 14. Municipal government flyer for the XIII Feria de Chirimoya, 2013. Municipio de Independencia.

by the municipal government of Independencia, the Ministry of Autonomy, and, after 2015, INRA, each May (Figure 14). For several months Pavel spent his days preparing the soil for planting, using a hatchet to remove stumps and trees as he did not own animals or a tractor. Just as he was ready to plant, and amid swirling worries about INRA land titling, the provincial union (Central Sindical Única de Trabajadores Campesinos Originarios de Ayopaya, CSUTCOA) intervened. Invoking the new 2010 law—specifically its requirement that land serve a "social and economic-social function"— another family of farmers approached Pavel and insisted that the land was theirs.[2] With the peasant union's approval, this family later seized the plots Pavel had so carefully prepared for the fruit planting.

Recalling Mr. Arpasi's language at INRA (see chapter 3), in this case land had "two [competing] owners." Pavel's grandfather had been a hacienda over-seer (*mayordomo*). In the 1940s, due to growing civil unrest and antihacienda militias in the countryside, many *hacendados* quickly sold off their land.[3] This enabled Pavel's grandfather to buy a parcel himself, becoming the "small master" (*juch'uy patrón*) of the remaining laborers. The other claimants were grandchildren of former hacienda tenant farmers (*colonos*) who had worked for Espada and, after him, Pavel's grandfather. Before he died, Pavel's grand-father left land to his godchild, the son of favored workers. This man had since died and his children migrated to Chapare to farm coca and start a gas-oline transportation business, leaving the land fallow.

Pavel, seeing this plot unused, considered it "abandoned" and available for appropriation through labor. Invoking the legal language of "function," Pavel argued that since the rightful owners had not cultivated it for twenty-six years, he had the right to farm it. This arrangement was tenable until 2011, when, encouraged by the prospect of regularizing the land through INRA's property titling program, the other (former hacienda servant) heirs returned, insisting that the land was theirs. After a drawn-out process the union deter-mined that the land belonged to the other family. In a provincial meeting, a union representative went to some lengths to explain that, counter to Pavel's argument that he had rightfully appropriated the unused land, "these lands [*terrenos*] will belong to [the former hacienda *colono* family] even if one hun-dred years pass."

Pavel experienced these land regularization efforts as affronts to what he saw as his legitimate land rights deriving from his relative's work in a nearby hacienda estate. Looking out over the green hills below, he insisted that the land had been recompense marking his grandfather's unpaid labor as a *may-ordomo*. Blinking away tears, Pavel mumbled: "What jealousy." He felt bit-ter that the new owners had waited until he finished the arduous process of removing stumps before submitting their claim. Disgruntled, he approached the union, which promised to "find a solution" together. But Pavel soon learned that the legal owners had supporters in the union. To Pavel, the peas-ant union was unevenly upholding the law, using legal stipulations about "function" as a pretense to expropriate land from people not aligned with them. Pavel noted: "The Central [union] wants to help *campesinos*. They can easily take lands. Yet, for me, they did not make justice." This, he added bitterly, is "community justice." Climbing back into his rusted jeep, Pavel reflected on the decision to head to Spain "While I was there, I thought, 'Why work in Spain, when I have land in Bolivia?" He paused. "Perhaps

I should never have left." But it was too late. His much-awaited *chirimoya* orchard was lost.

The Chullpani dispute over ownership offered insight into the kinds of land transfers encouraged by prospects of INRA property regularization, as well as the ways those titling processes subtly recalibrated popular attitudes toward regional histories of land gifting and hacienda aid. The union here creatively recast the 1996 Agrarian Law's stipulation about "function" to include the political value of redistributing land to the kin of former hacienda tenants. This required seizing land from the descendants of other labor classes, including Pavel's grandfather, a landless herder (*forastero*) who was later hired by the landlord as a *mayordomo*. In this case, his family's position as *forasteros* and then hacienda managers put Pavel at odds with unionist ideals of peasant subjectivity premised on descent from hacienda tenant farmers. Despite his Quechua dialect, his dark skin tone, his families' position as rural farmers, and his wife's renown as a favored local *chicha* brewer, the union's decision placed him outside the ambit of their benevolent assistance.

Although Pavel diverged from the type of Indigenous supplicant the union would defend, he was still vulnerable to the underlying kinds of *hacendado* racism that structured daily life in Independencia. This was apparent one evening in a local *chicharia*. Near Pavel and me, two older gentlemen— cousins and direct descendants of a notorious *hacendado* family—were playing a game of *cacho* or dice. As all the tables were full, the men invited us to join them. Over the next hour, one man chastised Pavel for not addressing him with the formal title, Señor. Later, during a game of *cacho*, the other man berated Pavel for his unfamiliarity with the rules of the game. "What did you play with when you were a child?" he asked. "Shit?" This question indicted Pavel's childhood (and his parents, Quechua farmers) for his ignorance of the ways of civilized Mestizo sociality—in this case, dice. The interaction showed how Pavel—and the relatives of other former hacienda servants, especially overseers and managers—inhabited a liminal space beyond the frames of either Mestizo belonging or Indigenous collectivity.

This chapter draws from archival and ethnographic materials to track the ways that Indigeneity as a model of aspirational belonging—as a racialized accompaniment to reified property—came to be rooted in place against governmental efforts to impose a more expansive, homogenous vision of national ethnicity.[4] In the course of his presidency, Evo Morales famously declared "todos somos indígenas" (we are all Indigenous). This declaration reveals how, as Indigeneity moved from the periphery to center stage in Bolivian political discourse, it assumed new characteristics, and exclusions.[5] As Esther Lopez Pila (2014: 431) has argued, while ostensibly expansive or mobile in its capacities to travel, a more reified formulation of Indigeneity under MAS was also beset by new divisions as Bolivians continued to invoke regional-based understandings of legitimate Indigeneity. In Ayopaya these divisions were less of a *regional* sort than they were defined by abiding distinctions stemming from varying hacienda labor tiers and related to the specific history of Quechua agrarian labor.

Pavel's case, and the disagreements about legitimate land use that underpinned it, highlights the reverberations of twentieth-century titling programs in the countryside. It demonstrates how, even where INRA's techniques for mediating land through titles and survey maps had not succeeded in establishing sole ownership, their titling agenda nonetheless subtly shifted the terms of belonging on the ground. Such an atmosphere of historical revelation had divisive consequences for rural life, not only among former masters and workers but also among Quechua agriculturalists in the province. Convulsions about legitimate land ownership hardened the lines dividing families of hacienda *colonos* (tenant farmers) from those of domestic servants, favored overseers, and managers like Pavel's grandfather.

As Pavel learned, MAS support for Indigenous land claimants meant that Lockean ideals of cultivation alone held little meaning. In this case, the vulnerabilities of Indigenous tenant farmers and indentured servants trumped the claims of higher-level hacienda workers like overseers and managers. Rather, it was the quality of that labor as earlier violence compressed in the object form (here land) that mattered. These earlier relationships of force were compressed in landscapes and contemporary land relations but risked being elided by an objectivist account of property as land—that is, as detached from earlier human labor.[6] Union leaders' insistence upon land's timeless belonging to the former *colono* family instead highlighted the rearticulation of legitimate Indigeneity as forged through spatial histories of labor subjection in hacienda estates. This reveals how land regularization efforts performed a set of temporal reinscriptions as much as spatial ones.

Building from cases like Pavel's, my discussion examines rural Ayopayan critiques of governmental formulations of abstract Indigeneity as a racialized accompaniment to recovered property. While Pavel found the union unreceptive to his land claims, Ayopayans' navigations of state land titling initiatives at other times also contravened in more homogenous elaborations of Indigenous belonging as celebrated in MAS political designs.[7] Quechua unionists contested this governmental model of reified ethnicity in part through their invoking of place-based belonging in Ayopaya. They did so by *grounding* Indigeneity to place, specifically to Ayopayan histories of labor violence and antihacienda militancy, in order to further a distinct vision of posthacienda justice while also eliciting new, sometimes painful, divisions between villagers who inhabit servitude's wake.

LAND COLLECTIVIZATION AS COLONIAL DESIGN

In May 2011, after receiving death threats from his constituents, union representative Eduardo Choque signed a document formally annulling the process of land regularization in Ayopaya.[8] In a signed statement, Choque noted that he supported recent efforts to convert the subprovince into collectively titled Native Community Lands (Tierras Comunitarias de Origen, TCO). However, following escalating rural land conflicts and growing popular opposition to the plan, he was now formally requesting its nullification. The file for the case, located in the INRA archive in Cochabamba city, bears the traces of this conflict. Its bound pages hold letters, union petitions, and legal denunciations challenging the administrative process of property titling. In the annulment letter, Choque and other union leaders criticized INRA for its collaboration with a university-supported agrarian institution, the Center for Communication and Andean Development (CENDA), noting that the Center misrepresented the process of land collectivization to garner popular support for a regional TCO. Invoking villagers' traditional rights to individual land ownership premised on "local uses and customs," leaders rejected land collectivization that they equated with "being managed like a park."

That this union representative was led to fear for his life for his earlier support of the land collectivization proposal attests to the intensity of the rural "conflicts" generated by INRA land regularization in Ayopaya. A close reading of the bureaucratic record reveals the range of fears over land dispossession, violated Indigenous sovereignty, and INRA efforts to impose a romanticized model of Indigeneity that assumed all Indigenous people would be opposed to resource extraction, economic development, and urbanization. This initiative responded to a key aim of INRA's land regularization program, the "community renewal" goal outlined in Law 1715, passed in 1996, and given heightened priority by MAS since 2006. This focus on reviving a community model underpinned new legal support for community and Indigenous land titling in Bolivia's new 2010 constitution, yet rural Indigenous unionists feared that land regularization was a cover for state efforts to reinsert themselves into matters of local government and economic life.[9] Unionists worried about the implementation of a more restrictive ideal of Indigenous community in which possibilities for future resource development, urbanization, and development opportunities would be constrained. This spatially bounded model of "community" was at odds with former fluid patterns of migrant labor and land use. Implicitly evoking earlier territorial resettlements and land dispossession campaigns carried out in the name of expanding property rights to peasants, Choque went so far as to compare the TCO proposal to a "return to colonialism."

The agrarian file for the proposed TCO in Ayopaya consisted of twenty-eight thread-bound booklets, each organized by case number (see Figure 14).[10] The claimant in each case, as listed on the title page, was CSUTCOA, and the file was marked "urgent." The second page, dated May 11, 2011, consisted of a form listing blank boxes that allowed the reviewing official to select a level of importance for the document. In this case the boxes "Regularization Unit Valley Region" and "Urgent Attention" were checked. Most of the file consisted of correspondence between the CSUTCOA peasant union and INRA, including the Land Regularization Office (LRO) and the Legal Affairs unit. The most recent document, at the time I consulted the file in late 2011, was a letter written to the General Director of Regularization, Giovana Mallea Valencia, on May 11 of that year. It was penned by Dr. Juan Manuel Zurita Portillo, INRA's General Director of Legal Affairs, and contained a threefold request: (1) for additional information concerning the TCO proposal's annulment, (2) for INRA's release of any executive files collected in preparation for their replacement by a collective title, and finally (3) for a formal statement prepared by the Legal Affairs unit addressing the current stage of land regularization in Ayopaya given "conflict in the process of titling."

The file also held an earlier letter drafted by the union of Altamachi (one of the subprovinces) noting that they had unanimously voted to cancel land regularization in their region and attaching a report on the results of the vote. The letter stated that "following the organic analysis made by all of the participants in the meeting, the social sectors that make up the regional union of Altamachi unanimously determined the [in bold] Annulling of Land Regularization of the TCO and furthermore the definitive expulsion of the SENDA [*sic*, CENDA] institute from the region." This decision was ratified by the eleven subcentral [unions], thirty-three *sindicatos* of the Altamachi region, and the municipality of Cocapata during an "ordinary congress" in the region on March 28 and 29, 2011. The letter listed the reasons for the annulment request: "With regularization as a TCO, our region would become considered and regulated as a park and in accordance with the Law 3545, article 44." It continued: "With regularization as a TCO we would be returning to the era of colonialism where residents [*compañeros*] or each affiliate of the region would no longer be owners of their lands and/or no longer have titles to their individual properties."

The letter expressed concern about the inability to "urbanize" (line 3), limits on children and grandchildren's ability to inherit land since land would be "indivisible" and the "property right of the community or region" rather than individuals (line 4), and about risks that some individuals could be expelled or stripped of land given the primacy of the "right of the collectivity" (line 5). The letter accused the NGO of "advancing a false discourse [*discurso falso*]" that promised locals could "recuperate natural resources (mineral and petroleum concessions) through regularization" by being titled as a TCO.[11] In addition, because of TCO status, people worried there would be inadequate public funds for road improvements and public administrative tasks (line 7). The letter concluded with the union seal, centered in the bottom margin, including the phrase: "Struggle for Power, Territory, and Sacred Coca" and below it "United, We Shall Overcome!"

The next page of the union letter requested the process of regularizing the region as a TCO be halted and that the newly processed titles be nullified (see chapter 3). It furthermore called for the ejection of the CENDA institute from the Ayopaya province "for having deceived people in their explanation of the entailments of a TCO." It then made a set of positive requests, including calling for the "respect for consuetudinary tradition" of each region and for the "regularization and actualization of individual titles." Next, it requested the certification of property registers in each union part of the region, as conducted by INRA. The document concluded: "Because of the above, we consider and reiterate that by unanimous decision [we] have determined the annulling of the process of regularization as a TCO [bold, all capitals, and underlined] of the executive titles collected, and if our petition is declined, we will be obliged to undertake direct action with the participation of our bases [peasant groups], against the Departmental INRA, the National INRA, and other Institutions that are participating in TCO regularization." This document was signed by the executive leader of the Altama-chi union, his signature followed by the seals and signatures of government officials, union leaders, and subcentral union leaders who supported annul-ling the INRA/CENDA land regularization initiative.

The annulment letter was accompanied by documents noting the steps already taken to reverse the retitling of the land as a collectivized TCO. A final document, a letter prepared by Choque, recounted how the proposal of a TCO came about, the challenges faced—including popular worries that "titles from fathers and grandfathers would not secure land ownership"—as well as problems with several mine owners, and the reasons why he with-drew his support for the proposal, which had subjected him and his family to threats against their life and welfare.[12] The letter signaled the deep famil-iarity of elected union leaders with legal and bureaucratic processes, evident in the invocation of legal codes and Bolivian constitutional law to challenge governmental (INRA) and nongovernmental (CENDA) claims about the benefits of collective land titling. Alongside this legal language of represen-tative democracy, the letter invoked threats of "direct action"—that is, rural mobilizations, road blockades, and the storming of buildings. Importantly, these were tactics successfully mobilized during the earlier period of antiha-cienda uprising in the 1940s and in early twenty-first-century anti-neoliber-alism protests that brought Morales to power.

In this legal correspondence, Ayopayan unionists challenged the claim that collectivization was a result of, or compatible with, Indigenous self-determination and sovereignty. Against the institutional focus on reviving Indigenous community, the union letters raised the possibility that Que-chua residents in Ayopaya, in some cases, might prefer *individual* titles and seek out developmental endeavors like urbanization and resource extraction. Given that farmers here cultivated their land by household (e.g., spouses and children) and the virtuous associations between former tenant farm-ers and the individual executive titles they won after the 1953 reform, col-lective rights at the community level were not only undesirable; they risked erasing the hard-won gains achieved through the union's history of antiha-cienda mobilization in the region. In doing so, the union highlighted INRA and CENDA's problematic assumption that Indigenous groups would natu-rally be opposed to capitalist resource development or land privatization. In Ayopaya it was not self-evident that tenacious structures of hacienda bond-age would be best remedied by reassembling highland ayllu communities. Instead, unionists turned to another nationalist figure elaborated in earlier labor struggles: the male tenant farmer as defender and protector of the Indigenous peasant cause.

While the union's language in their letters called out and ultimately rejected a romantic ideal of Indigenous collectivity as community, it nonetheless performatively invoked a different shared "we," apparent in the phrase "we would be returning to an age of colonialism" and in the seal "United, We Shall Overcome!" These Ayopayans did not view themselves as a fragmented scattering of individual servants or capitalist victims; instead, they drew upon shared histories of labor violence to articulate an alternate political collectivity in the present.[13] Moreover, the rural unrest that culminated in INRA's ejection from the region in 2011 sprung from rural worries that by collectivizing land, farmers would be denied formal property rights. This fear was justified; in the Cochabamba valleys Spanish administrators' assessments of Quechua and Aymara groups' exposure to or unfamiliarity with property was used as a basis for legally honoring or denying them usufruct land rights.[14]

The union's redeployment of legal languages complicates more deterministic, top-down theories of "the state" as an outward flow of legal ordinances and rules—via documents—from center to periphery. Instead, this correspondence brings into view new questions about the affective and ethical attachments that emerged from the failed alignments between INRA cartographic models and existing lives.[15] If Ayopaya unionists rejected the state's proposal to title their region a Tierra Comunitaria de Origen (TCO), they simultaneously elaborated an idea of regional "unity" rooted in a shared history of hacienda violence and political struggles against labor subjection as well as a sense of abiding "distance" from or marginalization from governmental zones of rights-based remediation.

FUNDING SELF-DETERMINATION FROM AFAR

Just as I was sending my proposal to conduct research to INRA headquarters in Cochabamba city, Ayopaya was gripped by a scandal involving local villagers, INRA officials, volunteers and university students at a Bolivian agrarian NGO in Cochabamba, and a Dutch humanitarian aid organization. The crisis centered on the question of funding for a land collectivization proposal. I first gained wind of the dispute when, at the union meeting I was invited to attend, a provincial union leader approached me to ask, "Who sent you?" On account of my pale skin and fleece sweatshirt, he assumed I might be a representative for the NGO involved in the land collectivization proposal. Learning I was unaffiliated, and that I had been invited as a guest by the member beside me, the union leader invited me to stay. While I was not able to gain access to the accounts of NGO officials or the Dutch government, over the course of the next year I would learn more from conversations, interviews, and by attending union meetings in Ayopaya. These encounters provided insight into the complex ways pro-Indigenous funding programs play out on the ground, with their mixed stakes for rural Quechua and Aymara farmers.

It had begun innocuously enough, with a grant from the Dutch government in 2003. The offer followed decades of international aid, configured as a Dutch bilateral development initiative.[16] Dutch funding in the early 2000s supported a range of programs related to agricultural resources, civil society, water sanitation, documentation and anticorruption, education, environmental policy, and other unspecified sectors.[17] I had the opportunity to interview someone who had been working in the Cochabamba municipal government in 2003 at that time. He noted that 8 thousand US dollars was specifically earmarked for aid in a project of instituting and titling a region of Ayopaya as a TCO. The project was proposed in the northern part of Ayopaya, the municipality of Cocapata, in a predominately wooded, semitropical region that borders the La Paz jungle, and it had a range of local sponsors and collaborators.[18]

In 2011 the Dutch funding was still on the table but had not been integrated into a viable land collectivization project. According to elected officials in Ayopaya's municipal government at that time, while the money aimed to support a TCO in northern Ayopaya, to secure the funds several individuals proposed that the TCO region could include swaths of land to the south, thereby blanketing the entire Ayopaya province. This generated difficulties, in part because Ayopaya is formed of small towns populated both by Quechua farmers and by the Mestizo kin of former *hacendados* who opposed the liquidation of private property titles. Skepticism about the proposed project was sharpened by assertions of corruption linked to earlier international development funds in the region, which critics argued were merely pocketed by union leaders and municipal officials.

When I stayed with him at his home in the village of Sarahuayto, Angelo Choque, a former union leader in Ayopaya (see chapter 2), explained that villagers had become suspicious of NGO institutions like CENDA when after grand announcements of well-funded development projects, nothing changed: nothing was done. "What happens to the money? *This* is the question," he put it glibly. Because of this, Angelo explained, there's "a lack of trust" (*confianza*) in NGOs. In addition, he himself had firsthand experience with fellow unionists forging his signature to accept a German development project from which they hoped to benefit. Likewise, the terms of the TCO project proposed in 2011 had been changed in order to secure access to the funding—8 thousand US dollars, an enormous sum in Bolivia. Learning of this funding possibility, several municipal officials and unionists expanded the initial TCO proposal to all of Ayopaya province without the union's authorization. This angered many of those involved. Former *hacendado* families and Quechua and Aymara villagers alike worried about losing land and being barred from leaving land to their children. More broadly, the proposal drew condemnation among Ayopayans who emphasized the paradoxical fact that Indigenous sovereignty seemed to rely on *foreign* funding.

But beyond this funding question, villagers and leaders also opposed the proposal for its misfit with the mosaic, interspersed patterns of land use and labor ties that continued to organize people and agriculture in the region. Next I turn to union meeting debates to elucidate the perceived problems with this reformist model of Indigenous community. In these debates unionists challenged available avenues for Indigenous recognition and collective land rights, but they also elaborated alternate understandings of Indigeneity that took the region's history of labor subjection and antihacienda struggle as formative of present-day political belonging. These debates offer insights into the ways that land regularization processes, even where contested and rejected, reshaped local discussions about the history and future of the province.

THE "PAIN" OF REFORM

About a month after I had arrived in Ayopaya, a union leader with whom I had become friendly invited me to join him at a daylong provincial union meeting. On the second Sunday of April 2011, about eighty people crowded into the union building in the municipal center of Ayopaya, the smell of corn beer (*chicha*) still thick in the air from participants' festivities the night before, for what would become a grueling eight-hour meeting. The meeting opened with a presentation by a MAS party government representative from

Cochabamba, who stood in front of the hall holding a bound file of photocopies of laws. Recently passed legislation included a new development law, measures against narcotrafficking, and a new border control policy.

In Spanish, but with a smattering of Quechua, the official noted that there had been over one hundred new laws passed since the union's last meeting, with eighty to discuss today. He remarked that the union had met only three times in 2010, and that its president had changed several times. The official implored the audience "to meet a bit more often [as] you are lacking order." Finally, he discussed several proposed development projects, including a potato commercialization project. As he passed around pamphlets summarizing new legislation, including a participatory Autonomy Law, the official returned to the topic of the potato project.[19] "You have to coordinate with the state if you want to do the project," he noted. "I'm not saying you have to accept it, but if you do, you have to coordinate with the state."

Recalling INRA officials' views of the requirement for rural groups to assess what they need and to deliberate collectively about land conflicts (see chapter 3), the government official's comments at this meeting highlighted the paradoxical place of Quechua farmers in the province, who were simultaneously being encouraged by MAS party institutions to take up a new stance as empowered Indigenous citizens yet were also dictated to on how to organize—for example, in coordination "with the state." Such projects can end up strengthening state institutions as legitimate mediators of rights and culture even where they are challenged or ultimately rejected. The government official's insistence upon "coordination" with the state followed in part from widespread MAS party government concerns that humanitarian institutions were acting as a covert means for foreign powers, especially the United States, wishing to unduly influence national politics.[20] However, the official came bearing pamphlets outlining more than one hundred new legal ordinances, thereby demonstrating the dizzying effects of bureaucratic and legal changes under MAS rule. Fully reviewing these new ordinances would be a challenge, especially as they were written in Spanish—about a quarter of rural farmers in Ayopaya are monolingual in Quechua. These prolific legal ordinances, coupled with the official's insistence on "coordination" with the state, illustrate the heavy mediation of new legal pathways to Indigenous autonomy and self-determination by government officials and bureaucratic languages.

The government official took his seat, and the head union representative rose from his chair on the stage (the union hall was also the elementary school performance auditorium), calling on the audience to discuss and evaluate "whether there are advances in the government or not." In addition, he called on audience members to consider the "spirit of the law"—that is, its broader intentions. Another representative encouraged greater patience, noting that people "want projects for the future, but they want results now." At this point a petite woman who had entered late with her baby stood up and took the floor. A provincial representative of La Confederación Nacional de Mujeres Campesinas Indígenas Originarias de Bolivia "Bartolina Sisa" (National Bartolina Sisa Campesino, Indigenous, and Native Women's Union), the women's branch of the national COB, she wore a velvet *pollera* skirt with a woolen checkered blanket over her shoulders.[21] She noted that "in order for us to advance [*avancanapaq*]," changes would have to be made to acknowledge that leaders have babies—a reference to nationwide debates over childcare and free bus passes for working mothers on union-controlled transport.

Calling on her peers to support these initiatives, she added: "We need good unity [*sumaq unidad*] as Andeans." For "just as there have been divisions in the Andean zone, so too with Ayopayans." She ended by expressing the hope that COB could provide more aid to women leaders with children. This is necessary as "in the Andean region, people don't often question or ask why [*tapuy*] things are as they are." In contrast to the earlier union representative's call for patience in light of the law's intention, the Bartolina Sisa representative challenged her peers to adopt a more critical stance. Evoking "good unity as Andeans," she encouraged them to find unity in a willingness to question the status quo. A proposal for free bus passes for union representatives had been voted down at the national level earlier that year. In a subtle challenge to the earlier speaker's call to not allow presentist critiques to get in the way of "projects for the future," she implored her peers to voice their critiques even when it required a departure from national peasant union agendas.

This question of the union's relation to central state and union institutions lay at the heart of the next topic, the Estatuto Organico de Ayopaya, recently passed national legislation outlining the avenues for legal autonomy in Ayopaya. Participants discussed the worry that the regional COB union, by way of *técnicos*, engineers, and agronomists, sought to intervene in subprovincial affairs. Autonomy at the municipal level would prevent this. A village *alcalde* (Indigenous leader) addressed this situation: "Ayopaya is a big province, and sometimes there isn't enough information about the national situation." How, participants wondered, could Ayopaya secure its representation in the national union? The regional union representative agreed: "The [COB] is forceful and can instruct the government. If we don't have a representative at the national level, we cannot call on the government or the president [Morales] to help us." What was needed was someone from Ayopaya to represent the province in the national union and to carry weight in government debates. His tone shifted and he spoke rapidly in Quechua about COB opposition to the MAS government, including proposed cuts to food and gas subsidies as well as the state's approval of a proposed highway through Indigenous territory (Territorio Indígena Parque Nacional Isiboro Sécure, or TIPNIS) in the eastern lowlands. In Quechua, he noted: "There have been problems with the [COB], problems with the marches and blockading of roads. People were directed [to participate] by the Federación [regional union]. We have to evaluate what the government is doing. We have to remember the passivist march. This work is hard; there are provincial problems."

The comments of the union leader as well as the Bartolina Sisa representative highlight the ways Ayopayans negotiated problems of local Indigenous sovereignty in terms of regional "unity." Here, unity supplied a language through which to make sense of the province's relative marginality vis-à-vis both to the national COB union and the national MAS party government. In these comments participants contemplated the problem of how to "advance," proposing "good unity" (*sumaq unidad*) as a way to secure political representation at the national level and, with it, the opportunity to pursue economic development in the region. In addition, the final speaker questioned whether autonomy of Indigenous territory was desirable given that this status had not protected TIPNIS from external federal state interventions even as it had imposed constraints on local pursuits of economic and resource development in the region.

More generally, in this conversation unionists debated how close an alliance they wanted to foster with the national-level COB. In an atmosphere of suspicion and doubt about the utility of political ties to national union and political institutions, some speakers challenged their peers to take a critical stance toward the political present. This involved critically evaluating why the government had rejected the bus pass proposal or why it was forcing a road through TIPNIS against the will of local Indigenous political leaders.

Concerns about unity as a means to secure the provincial union's power loomed large given local anxieties over the union's vulnerability to political manipulation, both by the COB and by government ministries. Encouraging his peers to evaluate the position of Ayopaya's subprovinces in relation to one another, one man noted: "Ayopaya and Cocapata are doing well, but where is Morochata? It has help from certain groups. We have to make sure to defend the land titles. There is the problem of social control as [COB] directs [us from] the department level. We and our problems are very distant as a province [from COB]." With respect to international aid for local development projects, he insisted that "we have to ask whether [these groups] respect the communities or not, for instance [one NGO] wants to start working here in February 2012 but they never informed us, they just informed the regional union [CSUTCC]." These concerns were especially crucial given recent disagreements about land titling.

Shifting to the topic of titling conflicts regarding Ayopaya's land collectivization as a Tierra Comunitaria de Origen (TCO), another speaker described "problems" concerning a doctoral student who, with help from the agrarian institute CENDA and the Bolivian University of San Simon, proposed to study collective land use in Ayopaya. The CENDA's director had received permission only from the regional, not provincial, union level. As the study began, it became clear that it was aimed at establishing a TCO. Discovering this, the regional union moved to eject CENDA and INRA from the province. One man stood up, raised his fist, and said: "We have to kick out all the people doing theses with CENDA." Another man rose, and said: "They took peoples' land titles. This has consequences. What are they going to give their children? This has caused division and discrimination." Another speaker expanded on these concerns, linking this scandal to the lack of Indigenous political autonomy. According to him, CENDA released a public *denuncio* of Cocapata regional authorities when they opposed the land retitling efforts as a TCO. This, he implied, constituted a violation of the right to autonomy. He held up a document—a copy of the recently passed *Estatuto Organico*—and noted: "This [law] says that each form of autonomy has to be within the other." That is, regional municipal autonomy must be respected and cannot be subverted by international or national institutions, including CENDA and the INRA administration. Land regularization must begin from within.

One man in tattered clothes stood up to speak in support of collective land titling. He countered the earlier speaker's critique, asking how collective titles would affect everyone. The original speaker replied: "It will affect us because we have property titles and instead, we will have just one title for the province. We know this will affect us. What sacrifice, what pain [*dolor*] will be caused by this [legislation], signed by our president? And knowing this we told people and started to question the study and project to create an autonomous Indigenous area. Our grandparents got this land as it is, individually, and that is how we want to walk forward together [*purishanchis*]." Speaking in Quechua, he invoked the past suffering of "our grandparents" as a basis to argue that institutions respect private *individual*, rather than collective, land ownership. Another unionist characterized this institutional push for collectivization as unjust: "Decisions must come from our union center. These gringos are interfering with our lands, as they have in the past."

In this discussion farmers called on their peers to recall their parents' and grandparents' suffering during the hacienda era and, later, their armed struggles against hacienda subjection and for land and rights. The province's labor history hereby was presumed to pose distinct challenges for collectivization. In an atmosphere of expected future land regularization, the region's hacienda past became key not only as a basis for elaborating a countervision of Indigenous belonging, but also in the material challenges land exchange traditions posed for MAS party autonomy law.

This was apparent in the final discussion topic that day: a border conflict between (or rather, overlapping) two subprovinces, Cocapata and Morochata. The land in question had been a hacienda, but after it changed owners, people were unclear as to where the border lay and to which subprovince it belonged. One man claimed that legally it belonged to Morochata. Another man disagreed, not with his claim but with its premise: "The problem is not one of law but one of customary use [*usos y costumbres*]." Although the land formally fell within Morochata's boundaries, farmers from Cocapata had been farming it for some time. Echoing understanding of property as dependent upon usage discussed in the preceding chapters, this speaker articulated existing *labor* rather than land titles as a precedent for legitimate ownership.[22]

This discussion encouraged participants to draw new, more absolute distinctions between customary and legal forms, with the latter taking precedent as a basis for settling land disputes. In this case, hacienda laborers were natal residents of Cocapata, yet by virtue of labor their children felt they had a claim to land in Morochata. At stake was a disagreement not only about who owned the land, but also through what process, or what institution, people should try to resolve the matter. Another man rose and, in Quechua, suggested: "You need to write up a document outlining the border and calling for repercussions if these borders are not heeded. The municipality is incompetent to solve this problem. So how else will we solve it?" Others reiterated the argument that the land belongs to Cocapata through *usos y costumbres*.

Around me, participants grew increasingly impatient. One man whispered loudly: "What they are saying amounts to a proposal that the land is theirs. This is not the appropriate place to introduce such a proposal." Depending on how the land came to be titled, members of the other subprovince would have limited claims to the land, whether as owners or to pasture animals.

The border dispute illuminates the paradoxical ways land collectivization proposals meant to strengthen Indigenous sovereignty ended up weakening the authority of union leaders and their ability to settle land conflicts. In the absence of land regularization opportunities, it is unlikely that these more amorphous, "traditional" arrangements would even rise to a level of supra-provincial legal conflicts. These overlapping, cross-cutting arrangements of land use were especially delicate matters given that, within MAS autonomy law, autonomous Indigenous regions must subscribe to existing municipal lines.[23] "Uses and customs," in this case, did not supply clear-cut answers to questions of legal ownership and therefore appeared increasingly inadequate to the problem at hand. The challenges facing a conception of Indigenous sovereignty based on discrete territory are laid bare by archival maps for the hacienda in Santa Rosa, which borders the land in question in Pavel's case. There, small segments of land were worked by *hacendado* masters and then, after land redistribution in 1953, turned over to individual workers or, more realistically, male heads-of-household.

Despite farmers' wariness and even widespread opposition to INRA land regularization, new titling processes lent urgency to the problem of determining absolute ownership, including delineating municipal lines and property boundaries. These uncertainties were answered by imbuing the MAS party state, especially INRA, with renewed authority as the legitimate arbiter among competing claims. The practical result of this process was the circumscription of the scope of legitimate union authority and, relatedly, the normalization of MAS government institutions as necessary, even inevitable judges of legitimate land use.

In these disputes, Ayopayan farmers and unionists negotiated "the law"—embodied in a bound booklet of recent legal decrees and used linguistically to connote broader formations of MAS governance and bureaucratic regimes bent on greater transparency and regulation—as double-edged. On the one hand, new legal codes could be mobilized in defense of the region's rights to autonomy and in opposition to meddling from national and international institutions. On the other hand, the processes for pursuing a degree of autonomy only reinforced the fact that Indigenous recognition was conferred by (non-Indigenous) state institutions, such as INRA and its associated bureaucratic processes. This dynamic persisted despite widespread opposition to land regularization. In this case, union participants recognized the shortcomings of institutional solutions, while at the same time perceiving those interventions as increasingly inevitable, shoring up INRA's power as a mediating body able to determine Indigenous land rights.

Recognizing waning political authority in this new reform climate, participants evoked the need for "unity" as a province (Ayopaya) and as a people (Andeans). Unity, if reached, could protect farmers from foreign development plans and corrupt authorities scheming with state agencies or NGOs. The source of such unity lay not in an externally imposed model of Indigenous territory defined by timeless, transhistorical ties to the land but rather in local languages of community and regional unity that reflected Ayopaya's distinct history of hacienda violence and militant land struggles. The region's history of subjection and bloodshed here showed all too clearly the risks of relying on outsiders for political and economic "advancement."

GROUNDING INDIGENEITY IN AYOPAYA

In Ayopaya, where rural land use departed from national ideals of ayllu-based collectivity, attempts at collectivizing land appeared to be yet another rotation in an ongoing cycle of governmental attempts to fix rural subjects in space in order to integrate them into legible systems of centralized political rule. Anthropological concepts of culture haunted these discussions about Indigeneity, demonstrating the power of Mestizo and settler legal bodies in adjudicating and mediating the terms of Indigenous sovereignty and rights. This was apparent in a racialized slur—"son of a bitch" (*hijo del patrón*)—an epithet used by unionized farmers to describe disloyal peasants, including people born from master-servant sexual relations and farmers like Pavel; by virtue of his grandfather's position as a hacienda manager, unionists saw him as an outsider to a legitimate Indigenous peasantry.[24]

Yet these union discussions also supplied occasions for advancing an alternate understanding of regional belonging as Andeans and as Ayopayans. In lieu of romantic conceptions of *lo Andino* or the Andean as an authentic reserve of Indigenous tradition and sentiment (see Starn 1991), unionists in this meeting put forth an alternate notion of Indigenous belonging as configured through long, overlaid histories of labor violence and dispossession.

These debates highlight the ways that union participants were appropriating and reconfiguring community as a basis for pursuing a form of affective belonging, even "unity," at odds with the spatially integrated model of a Tierra Comunitaria de Origen (TCO). Ayopayans mobilized unity not only to appropriate and deploy community but also to recalibrate this vision to better account for the region's history of antihacienda union militancy and overlaid spatial ties related to the specificities of hacienda farming across regions.

Such creative, critical redeployments of Indigeneity in dialogue with conceptions of Andeanness are not new. From the sixteenth century on, Spaniards assembled and applied local laws in ways that made colonialism an ethnographic project. From its inception colonial litigation was an ethnographic enterprise that worked both through Spanish efforts to determine Incan customs and through Andean articulations of their practices as continuities of the customary.[25] Litigation constituted a space where ideas alien to colonial legal thought become lodged in that tradition, particularly the notion of Inca authority as a basis for legitimate land ownership.[26] Litigants invoked the authority of Inca custom to argue that *mitimaes* held special legal status that exempted them from the need to be incorporated fully into new town settlements or to return to their communities of origin.[27]

Likewise, these border disputes and accompanying concerns with provincial unity may be understood as vernacular productions of Indigeneity in dialogue with legal institutions but with precedents in earlier Quechua valley populations' claims to land (see chapter 2). Like the *mitimae* settlements that colonial litigants in the sixteenth century confronted, in twenty-first-century Bolivia farmers evoked provincial histories of labor bondage and land struggle as the basis for land claims yet in ways that challenged reformist mappings of bounded property and Indigenous collectivity.

As scholars of agrarian reform under the MAS party government have pointed out, new autonomy measures create limits in spatially sundering Indigeneity as community and in decoupling land from subterranean resource rights.[28] Moreover, autonomy measures also infringe epistemologically in defining what can count as legitimate Indigeneity, requiring territories that wish to be autonomous to be thoroughly mediated by bureaucratic protocols.[29] Drawing from century-long ideals of community that had underpinned antihacienda organizing in the region (Ari 2014), Ayopayans evoked a more fluid understanding of regional collectivity that could accommodate both spatial mobility and a looser orientation to the COB or central peasant union, from which they felt marginalized.[30] To do so, Ayopaya unionists put forth a vision of provincial collectivity based on refashioning and redeploying elaborations of Andean difference as established by colonial systems of governance (especially tribute taxonomies).[31] They did so in ways that allowed them to unsettle and contest homogenous framings of Indigeneity guiding new land rights regimes.

Rural demands for the abolition of hacienda labor after 1938, and later demands for hacienda land distribution culminating in the 1953 agrarian reform, were driven by appeals to the state as a source of beneficent protection and aid. At the time of my fieldwork, in contrast, rural union groups and peasant associations seized upon the paper form to challenge and obstruct property regularization as collective lands. For instance, formal letters addressed to INRA officials carefully outlined the union's rejection of the TCO proposal, all the while citing the possibility for "direct action." In Ayopaya rural supplicants maneuvered existing bureaucratic processes to articulate and insist upon an exemplary regional self-determination defined by "distance" from the central union and the state.[32] In its corporeal, material dimensions, regional unity translated into political power as it allowed union members to fend off encroaching state institutions. The dynamic qualities of such legal negotiations were clear in the union meeting, where participants evoked Andeanness not as a romantic precolonial culture that survived colonial incursion but rather as a precarious living-together generated by shared bloodshed at the hands of *hacendados* and recent military governments.[33]

Farmers seized upon this history of political violence as a lesson about revolutionary state commitments and as a reason to regard the MAS state with caution. In fact, these concerns were all very proximate at that March 28, 2011, union meeting, as the national COB was gearing up for mass protests that swept Bolivia beginning April 7, 2011, and that, among other things, demanded a 15 percent wage increase for all workers. When the union participant implored his fellow farmers to "remember" the marches, he was inviting them to recall the rewards but also the risks of direct action as a diplomatic tactic. Union *denuncios* and legal briefs supplied a space of bureaucratic maneuver within and around broader national climates of political unrest and, at times, state violence. Importantly, this violence did not end when the MAS party assumed leadership in 2006. In Bolivia clashes between antigovernment and pro-government forces in Cochabamba in January 2007 left three people dead. Protesters collided with government troops again in Pando in September 2008, resulting in the death of twenty protesters. Farmers' memories and continued experiences of political violence made bureaucratic instruments particularly appealing as modes of deliberation and contestation that viewed direct action tactics as a last resort that came at a cost, including, at times, protestors' lives.

But these institutional negotiations, too, incurred their own cost. Despite local caution about alliance with federal government and labor institutions, understandings of INRA land titling as inevitable led Ayopayan unionists to normalize the MAS state's heightened mediation of rural lives, and land relations. In this case, *usos y costumbres* were newly configured as legally wanting—insufficient grounds from which to decide matters of land use and ownership. This in turn led people to press for firmer subprovincial boundaries and, in the process, to normalize INRA as a legitimate arbiter of rural land and bodies. In fact, by the conclusion of my fieldwork in Ayopaya, the province was undergoing the process of being "regularized" as a series of individual properties. However, discussions at the CSUTCOA meeting suggest that changes in provincial conceptions of custom preceded government agrarian reformers' entry into the region. This raises broader questions about the subtle ways that institutional approaches to reparative justice can recalibrate local relationships to history and to land even where they are rejected or refused.

CONCLUSION

This chapter has examined the various practices by which Ayopayan farmers have reshaped reformist projects of ownership both over land as property and over people as Indigenous citizens. In peasant unionist debates, participants articulated a vision of Quechua Indigeneity as premised on people's rootedness in place through shared histories of labor servitude and antihacienda militancy. Drawing upon earlier nationalist discourses of hacienda tenants as virtuous laborers and exemplary proto-citizens, CSUTCOA unionists argued that theirs constituted a distinct mode of Indigenous belonging forged through a divisive history of dispossession and armed political struggle. In this way they reworked a history of dispossession into a narrative of overlapping, dynamic spatial attachments and labor practices. I call this process one of *grounding Indigeneity*: a practice of binding Indigeneity to history and place by way of its articulation through fluid, cross-cutting spatial ties and overlaid histories of labor violence.[34] Against INRA land titling initiatives as projects of installing Indigeneity as racialized property and spatial enclosure, Ayopayans put forth a vision of Indigeneity as contingent upon and reshaped by bloody struggles against hacienda labor subjection in the region. In doing so, they defined a mode of regional belonging at odds with the romantic ideals of ayllu community that center Aymara revivalism and which they encountered in land collectivization schemes.[35]

Ayopayan land conflicts reveal the cunning ways that governmental rights-based efforts subtly reshaped local understandings of legitimate ownership and history but also how farmers creatively reworked this politicized past to articulate a vision of belonging that contested those interventions. CSUTCOA unionists evoked an older twentieth-century ideal of the peasant supplicant: an ideal of virtuous agricultural labor set against unvirtuous kinds of work as hacienda servants, mistresses, managers, kin, and adoptees. The securing of a legitimate form of Ayopayan belonging required distinguishing exemplary peasants from those characterized as having betrayed the Indigenous-peasant cause. Subjects who had not been able to sustain a more masculinist ideal of the militant peasant unionist were characterized variously as defectors of pro-Indigenous socialism, as "sons of bitches" (*hijos del patrón*), and as colluding with hacienda elites for their own self-interest. Even as Ayopayans pushed back on models of Indigeneity undergirding land collectivization, then, their negotiations with MAS institutions in this reform climate normalized increasing governmental influence over rural life. This was especially evident in Pavel's case, whom unionists saw as unfitting given nascent elaborations of posthacienda Indigeneity and Ayopayan "unity." Here, a given subject's deservedness of Indigenous status was interrupted both by his or her family's sexual histories, including children produced from *mitani* rape, and by forms of friendship and aid (including land gifting) between Indigenous workers and Mestizo bosses.

In the course of land collectivization efforts, the reifications of Indigeneity as community and of ownership as titled land intersect.[36] This is not unprecedented; as Brenna Bhandar (2018: 150) and Cheryl Harris (1993) have shown, historically the reification of property has been accompanied by the shoring up of discrete conceptions of race. The Ayopayan case advances our understanding of the dual reifications of property and race in regards to Indigeneity in particular. Restorative approaches to land redistribution in Bolivia were mediated by a homogenous, unified vision of Indigenous collectivity premised on kinship-based ayllu community. In this case, an essentialized idea of Indigeneity as culture destabilized local Quechua and Aymara control over land adjudication disputes, challenging rural leaders' sense of authority over the terms of legitimate property rights.[37]

However, farmers contested these more reified models of property—both as titled land and as a homogenous Indigenous territory. In the context of a rapid slippage toward heightened governmental adjudication of land and people, unionists reworked twentieth-century visions of peasant militancy as the ground of countermemory projects that rearticulated Indigeneity through the region's hacienda past in ways that refused its abstraction in land collectivization efforts. In Ayopaya this remaking of history allowed farmers to push back against top-down reform agendas, but it also created new distinctions in rural life, ones that cast some Quechua farmers and workers aside. In this context older networks of asymmetrical aid retained their appeal, for some villagers, as ways to demand Mestizo accountability not only for earlier labor violence but also for the risks of an extractivist present.

PART THREE

Exchange

FIVE

Demanding Return

To the grating rhythm of an air compressor outside the gold processing plant, René Cruz recounted how he came to purchase the gold mine in Sarahuayto back in 2002.[1] René initially learned about the mine from Fabio Rodriguez, Martín's uncle and the earlier hacienda master's nephew whom I introduced in chapter 1. The friendship between René's father and Fabio went back many years, as the two had been schoolmates in Cochabamba city. So, when René was in the market for a mine, he reached out to his old friend for guidance. Not long after sending off a chunk of stone for a mineral analysis, René and his two male cousins bought the mine. Fabio advised them and collaborated as a local business partner but also sought to retain his authority over the mine. To this end, he reminded the mining novices how important their relationship to him was as a basis for their work and safety in the region. According to René, Fabio told them: "It would be impossible for you to work here without me. I was a master. They've known me all of my life. They would throw you out." René continued: "Fabio inculcated us with this [fear]. We were afraid."

In this case, mining endeavors in Ayopaya relied on earlier social and economic ties related to hacienda servitude. Ties to former masters allowed prospective business owners to learn about and then purchase the mine, and it was through upholding such attachments that the newcomers could feel safe working and living in this rural, Indigenous-majority province. Yet the nature of these ties binding new mining economies to the earlier hacienda system were also sources of local contention and disagreement.

René and his cousins had only worked the mine for several months when a dispute arose between two villages that border the mine, located on former hacienda estate land now owned by Martín. One village had historically maintained amicable ties to the Rodriguez masters and was peopled these days by the families of former servants whose homes and fields bordered the original estate. The other village was situated on a drier, more distant mountain slope above the estate, on land that former tenant farmers and their children had inherited. Tenant farmers in the upper village had been involved in legal and armed disputes with the hacienda masters since the 1940s (see chapter 2). Divisions among peasant families rooted in earlier hacienda labor hierarchies and inegalitarian land inheritance patterns remained consequential to the two villages' divergent orientations to the new mine owners. When the lower village negotiated with René to have him install a water turbine to be used to gain electricity, the upper village objected. Since the water flowed through their land, they noted that they too should gain access to electricity.

In the spring of 2003 the turbine issue erupted into a regional conflict that eventually halted René's mining operation. Frustrated that they had been excluded from new, if not unprecedented, aid relations between the lower village and the new mine owners, people from the upper village took about blocking off the road linking the mine to the nearby town of Independencia. Using boulders, sticks, and their own bodies, they effectively closed off access to the mine, making the road impassable even for the mine owners, maids, and miners. Union-affiliated villagers worked in shifts patrolling the roadway, searching passing vehicles to ensure that no one from either village was hidden inside. In this way the mine lost its best workers, miners who had worked since the hacienda era and had valuable knowledge of the inner "veins" of the mine. René and his cousins felt this loss profoundly given that they had no prior experience in gold mining, much less at that mine. Dependent as they were on the older miners and their technical knowledge, the novice owners worried that their loss might devastate the mine's output. Eventually René agreed to pay the higher village 4,000 bolivianos for a second turbine, and corresponding water plant, to be constructed in the lands above. Only by accommodating villagers' demands in this way did René ensure that he, his workers, supplies, and *el mineral* (gold, antimony, lead, and other metals) would be able to enter and leave the mine. However, the senior miners never returned.

That former hacienda elites like Fabio Rodriguez continued to live in Ayopaya, a province where enduring tensions concerning earlier hacienda labor abuses met new questions about Indigenous resource rights, was itself remarkable. It pointed to the Rodriguez families' relatively amicable relationship with local farmers. For, as Angelo (a Quechua former militia leader) pointedly explained, after the 1952 Socialist Revolution only land-owning families who fostered amicable relations with rural villagers were allowed to remain in the countryside: the rest "would have been killed."[2] René's mine raised questions about the constitutive role of Ayopaya's earlier hacienda system in shaping and enabling contemporary extractive relations. Hacienda infrastructures laid the groundwork for new mining pursuits, supplying roads, mining caverns, buildings, and cheap labor. Likewise, René's access to dirt roads and water channels needed for gold processing was contingent upon his ability to stay in villagers' good favor by upholding aid relations that preceded him. This involved supplying money, meals, and rides as well as aiding villagers in gaining access to electricity and water. Here, the hacienda's afterlife was double-edged. It supplied owners with resources, roads, and labor while also enabling miners' demands that owners provide aid and assistance to Quechua villagers to whom they would otherwise feel little obligation.

Expectations that Mestizo elites supply aid to Indigenous residents have precedents in a set of exchange relationships elaborated in Bolivia's early colonial period, and reconfigured since (see chapter 2).[3] Quechua and Aymara workers on the province's haciendas, recalling earlier Incan systems of political rule, have long insisted upon "verticality" as a practice that binds political and religious authority to acts of material redistribution.[4] Likely drawing from institutions of authority on agrarian estates owned by encomenderos, Indigenous miners too stipulated that rural bosses provide them with corn beer and coca, wool, and cloth.[5] Likewise, in colonial-era Bolivia, miners were traditionally allowed to collect leftover stones and ore and of hacienda workers to glean the harvest. Well into the twentieth century, related frameworks of redistributive authority guided Quechua workers' relations to Mestizo bosses and to their own labor.[6] Such arrangements of symmetrical aid and kinship ties, where spurned by hacienda masters, lent further support for militant labor movements in which hacienda workers laid claims to hacienda estates by appealing to their unique attachments to land as forged by agricultural labor.[7]

In various ways contemporary workers in Ayopayan gold mines creatively recast aid relations that had linked masters and servants during the hacienda era, reworking aid relations and labor-based alliances to demand historical redress and accountability for present-day racial hierarchies.[8] If within haciendas labor was often cast in terms of workers' divine gifts to *hacendados* as living embodiments of Catholic beneficence, in the wake of hacienda abolition those debts were reversed, imbuing wealth with new, deeply vexed connotations as an artifact of earlier racial violence.[9] Drawing from earlier forms of labor resistance in haciendas, miners and servants made use of labor mobility to express preferences for certain bosses. In subsequent months, growing consensus about René's shirking of aid obligations led miners and mine servants to flee the mine and call for his removal from the region. Workers' demands for aid from René raise questions about the critical refashioning of earlier practices of agrarian labor resistance in which people voted with their feet, electing to take up work elsewhere if conditions were too severe.[10] In a region with abiding labor shortages, such acts of labor retraction could have dire consequences for the success of rural mines.

Attention to these disputes about the relational qualities of wealth reveal quotidian practices that accompany paid work—including gendered forms of affective labor and informal demands for money and rides—as crucial both to capital's production, and, in cases of labor strikes and road blockades, its interruption and refusal. These disagreements about mining bosses' proper ways of embodying economic authority reveal power as contingent upon relations that would seem to fall outside it, in this case, dispositions toward neighboring villagers and workers.[11] Given continued state violence against peasant labor unions under MAS, workers' relations with mine owners remained crucial to their abilities to renegotiate the terms of local extractivism. It supplied an alternate frame of political critique that was calibrated to the government's efforts to brutally quash union activism in the region. In the disputes about racialized wealth that I describe, Ayopayans took as an open question, rather than a given, the volitional and temporal qualities of contract through and as property.

The centrality of earlier exchange ties to contemporary mining economies problematizes a familiar narrative of capitalist progress as built upon the inevitable dissolving of earlier labor ties.[12] Instead, they highlight what Marcel Mauss ([1925] 2016: 58) called an "enduring form of contractual ethics" that blurs what are otherwise taken as the appositional domains of volition and duty, constraint and interest.[13] Yet, while Mauss theorized the passive enduring of noncapitalist exchange regimes, in Ayopaya contemporary workers critically reformulated and extended older agrarian ideals. Rather than take alienability as a primary route of historical redress, residents emphasized the violence of "free" labor in its legitimizing of bosses' shirking of an abiding ethos of Mestizo repayment for earlier hacienda sexual and labor violence.[14] Against presumptions of the discrete nature of profit that accompany a paradigm of modern property, many of the Ayopayans working in provincial gold mines insisted that Mestizo bosses share *returns* from profits built upon the relational and infrastructural tracks of preceding Indigenous labor subjection. In doing so, they put forth a distinct vision of Indigenous redress premised on the tethering of wealth to history where property required their disentwinement.[15]

"THE BLOOD OF THE EARTH": LABOR MILITANCY AND CLAIMS TO PLACE IN AYOPAYA

Farmers in Ayopaya have long organized against land dispossession by reframing their labor-based proximity to soil and earth as the basis for regional belonging, one that warranted special land rights (see chapter 4).[16] In the 1930s, Quechua laborers in this province organized in part by drawing from a conception of hacienda laborers as *jallp'a sangres* ("the blood of the earth"), members of an Indigenous collectivity bound to the landscape through agricultural labor rather than timeless residence. A similar language of blood-based reckoning underlay former Indigenous labor militants' deep-seated anger about the tenacity of hacienda domination (see chapter 2). Angelo Choque insisted, for instance, that as his grandmother was tied to a nearby tree and whipped by the hacienda master, he would continue to seek vengeance for this bonded past from contemporary hacendado heirs, for "I am of this blood."

Laborers' attachments to land here operated as more than a strategic fashioning of collectivity garnered toward legal recognition; insistence on villagers' rootedness in place and to earlier hacienda economies also operated as a basis for making demands on new Mestizo elites. In the case of Martín's mine, for instance, workers extended a logic of agrarian obligation to his new business, implying that he must uphold lines of aid and accountability to villagers that had defined his grandfather's earlier position in the countryside. This formation was also recast and extended to make new mining bosses, like René Cruz, beholden to workers in ways that he saw as undesirable and deeply problematic. To understand the bases for such claims, it is necessary to examine how Ayopaya's agrarian estates gave way to distinct contemporary mining businesses. These businesses held vastly distinct relations to Quechua workers and villagers, ones conditioned by alliances and antipathies toward earlier masters.

The village of Sarahuayto was until the late 1950s the home of an agricultural hacienda upon which some sixty-seven tenant farmers labored for

FIGURE 15. Entrance to the chapel yard in Sanipaya (Ayopaya province), 2011. Photo by author.

the Mestizo master. To this day, a small chapel that was built on the hacienda for Catholic services that workers were required to attend stands atop a hill in the center of the village, with a new entrance that was recently built to enclose the patio for religious festivities (Figure 15). In 1961 the estate was divided and its land distributed among sixty-nine peasants (male heads of household and widows) and six Mestizo co-owners, the latter consisting of the children and descendants of former *hacendados* (see chapter 2).[17] Even at that time, there were dramatic disparities in land redistributed to former tenant farmers and land maintained by the kin of Mestizo *hacendados*.[18] This has driven villagers' and unionists' protracted legal battle to reclaim title to land left to hacienda heirs.

At the time of research, those efforts had proven largely futile. The master's grandson Martín retained fertile land in the region but also two mines, one of which was sold to urban mining entrepreneurs, namely René and his cousins, in 2002. He continued to live in a building surrounded by villages that had taken up arms against his grandfather. This fact put pressure on him to attend to the demands of neighboring villagers, many of whom worked in his mine.

Alongside Martín's familial ties to the region's agrarian past, relations among Quechua workers and Mestizo bosses bore the markings of the province's specific history of asymmetrical aid from the Inca period on.[19] The Incas worked mines in the Ayopaya river valleys. Subsequently, following Spanish imperial incursions, these mines came to be owned and used by Jesuit missionaries even before the territorial boundaries between Portuguese and Spanish colonies were established.[20] In both periods lords and encomienda masters were expected to distribute precious stone, food, and brewed corn beer to worker-subjects. During the colonial period, *minga* workers or *kajchas* (silver thieves) continued to lay claim to abandoned or extra chunks of ore (*la corpa*) to augment their salaries.[21]

Hence, while elsewhere mining and agriculture were parallel endeavors, in Ayopaya they have been (and remain) structurally linked. Mines like Martín's are situated on former *hacendado* lands and operated by *hacendado* heirs. Moreover, miners were often the children of earlier hacienda tenant farmers and servants. In these cases in particular, bosses' use of mines and their access to proficient workers depended on their upholding of older aid relations with villagers.

Ties between Mestizo bosses and Indigenous workers have also been impacted by the state's brutal suppression of mining unionism in the late twentieth century. Mining occupations and strikes in 1918, 1923, and 1942 culminated in massacres against labor activists and organizers. Agrarian unions were popularized throughout this region in the 1930s, and in 1947 a rebellion of forty thousand hacienda laborers, union activists, and Aymara and Quechua farmers led to the deaths of two hacienda masters and the sacking and burning of countless haciendas. Following hacienda abolition in 1953, many former hacienda masters became unionists, and military governments supported the interests of Mestizo leaders who required peasants' submission in their role as unionists, godparents, and former masters.[22] With the coup of General René Barrientos in 1964, Bolivia underwent a turn to military rule and the violent suppression of unions. Later, the state's brutal repression of mining union movements, including military-union confrontations at the Catavi and Siglo XX mines in Cochabamba in 1967, culminated in Colonel Hugo Banzer's 1971 coup. Banzer's government repressed peasant and union movements, leading to the death of more than one hundred peasants as well as an unknown number of miners in Cochabamba.[23]

During a three-day coup in 1971, hundreds of people were murdered, universities closed, and students, workers, labor leaders, and political activists were imprisoned and tortured. Under Banzer the National Workers Union (COB) was subsequently declared illegal in 1974, and in its place state-sanctioned *coordinadores laborales* were set up. Banzer's government framed this program as an attack on Communism, one for which it received substantial financial assistance from the US government.[24] Peasants unwilling to join these official trade unions were arrested and, at times, tortured. In fact, Quechua villagers recounted that allies of military leaders had received large swaths of land in the region and that peasants had been tortured in their homes.

In Ayopaya, Banzer's dictatorship consolidated former *hacendados'* land claims, encouraging migration from city to country on the part of new agrarian and mining elites. This appeared, to many Quechua farmers, as a perilous reversal of the revolutionary gains made by earlier antihacienda mobilizing. Relatedly, this situation of political uncertainty and repression caused by Banzer's military government imbued existing ties to former *hacendado* families with new importance, as Mestizo elites could act as powerful allies and even protectors against the abuses of military rule. Although Banzer's dictatorship ended in 1978, with General Padilla gaining power, this earlier period of military dictatorship and its accompanying forms of union repression and Criollo agrarian settlement had lasting effects in Ayopaya. Twentieth-century political repression and state violence against peasant unions often made villagers hesitant to use institutional channels, including national unions, as political tools against agrarian elites who in some places like the Amazonian lowlands have remained at their helm.[25] This was even more so given that Evo Morales, in his second term in office, held an increasingly combative orientation to Bolivia's national union association, evident in police repression of mass mobilizations against the TIPNIS highway in 2011. In April 2014, after my fieldwork had ended, police clashed with miners who were blockading a road outside of the mining town of Kami in Ayopaya, leaving two miners dead and forty injured.[26]

Like the earlier period of mid-twentieth-century revolutionary upheaval in the early 1950s and the later political repression of labor movements in the 1970s, Morales's rule at this time was experienced by many peasants as an uncertain gamble. In fact, rural Quechua villagers expressed concern on various occasions that Morales's government might crumble and that they would be left, as they had before, abandoned in the face of severe political violence and a conservative backlash or retribution for their earlier support for the MAS party. These risks meant, quite simply, that ties to Mestizo and Quechua elites could not be summarily abandoned. Nonetheless, these alliances with elites were not without their own forms of critical pushback and opposition. As laborers organized against René's mine (but not Martín's mine), they adopted earlier techniques of antihacienda militancy like strikes, blockades, and workers' movement from one site of employment to another to contest abuse. These practices can be understood as militant engagements with economic inequality, ones that took the form of quotidian demands based on understandings of places as conditioning unwilled obligations to others, and to history. In their insistence on historicizing capital, workers pushed back on ideals of alienable ownership that treat value as separate from place and history.

OF FAILED PARTAKING: PROXIMITY, AID, AND THE DEMAND FOR RETURN

René was in his late thirties and had grown up in the city of Cochabamba. He was from a wealthy Mestizo family, his grandparents having been owners of hacienda estates in the eastern part of the city and shareholders in one of the city's largest newspapers, *Los Tiempos*. In 2002 René and his two cousins bought a gold mine in Arapampa (Ayopaya), on estate land originally owned by Martín's grandfather. The village, like most, had earlier housed hacienda servants and farmers and, before that, had been the site of a Jesuit mission whose church still stood. During my fieldwork René employed about thirty workers and seven domestic maids, members of local Quechua families as well as migrant laborers from Oruro and La Paz. Workers slept in shared rooms in housing quarters bordering the processing plant, beside a private apartment where the owners stayed during their rotating shifts overseeing the mine. Martín, the master's grandson, also owned a mine, though of smaller "artisanal" style (e.g., using a nonmechanized water panning system) and employing about fifteen workers and two maids. The two mines differed both in the quantity of workers and in technology—Martín's mine contained dilapidated sheets of tin roofing, while René's boasted a new processing plant and a mechanized panning system.

Given the region's history of militant antihacienda organizing against the Rodriguez masters, I was surprised to learn that Indigenous peasant unionists sought to unseat René, and not Martín, from his mine. To this day, Martín (like his earlier *hacendado* grandfather) was a favored godparent and reg-

FIGURE 16. René's gold processing plant, K'uti (Ayopaya province), 2011. Photo by author.

ularly doled out money for beer during regional fiestas and patron saint's day events. René, by contrast, did not come from a family of Ayopayan *hacendados*, although his wealthy Mestizo family had owned several estates closer to the central Cochabamba valley. The cause for his targeting might be understood as an outcome of sheer monetary worth—for example, his mine with its modern technology was worth much more than Martín's (Figure 16). Yet my conversations with maids and miners from both mine centers suggest that it had to do also with his broader affective disposition toward local villagers. René and his cousins had provided miners with watches, food, mining uniforms, helmets, and flashlights as well as aid in obtaining water and electricity, even hiring a van to transport miners to and from the mine. However, they never socialized with villagers like many other Mestizo elites did, and René in particular was known to speak in highly derogatory terms about Indigenous workers at his mine.

When René and his cousins first began working the mine, they followed advice they received from Fabio, the former owner. Fabio was Martín's uncle and belonged to a *hacendado* family. As Fabio was childhood friends with René's uncle, he advised the fledgling owners to generously provide aid to miners and villagers lest they oppose his ownership of the mine. The men complied. "We helped [the workers]," René said. "The first thing everyone asked for were watches. We bought watches as a gift...then boots, helmets, and overalls. They were very happy." They also brought electricity to the mine, extending the powerlines outward to two neighboring villages. These aid relations drew in explicit ways from earlier hacienda exchange practices between masters and servants, evident in Fabio's insistence that workers uniquely respected him since he had been a master. Many miners came from local Quechua villages of earlier hacienda laborers; others had worked in this mine since before unpaid labor ended in 1986. This blurring of the lines between hacienda and mining economies complicated new bosses' arguments that a property sale obviated their need to uphold existing structures of obligation and assistance to Indigenous workers and villagers.

After the turbine conflict was resolved, the gold extraction at René's mine came along smoothly until the final months of 2011, when René and his cousins confronted opposition from workers and neighboring villagers. A road blockade followed from a growing consensus that despite the aforementioned efforts, René had rescinded on promised aid projects of electricity and potable water. I learned more about villagers' opposition to René's mine when I joined several of his employees and friends outside a dry goods store in Independencia one Sunday morning. Severino Colca, who spoke Spanish and Quechua and lived in town with his wife, had been hired by René to transport dry goods to René's mine. He had previously worked in the mine as a child, and his father, Ramón, continued to live in Sarahuayto, supplying Severino and his wife with insight into villagers' feelings about René (see chapter 2).

Outside Severino and his wife's dry goods store, Severino was hurriedly preparing a delivery of dry goods for René. After securing a tarp over the goods, Severino collected a large manila envelope holding legal documents from René's lawyer. René planned to circulate these documents, which proved his legal ownership of the mine, to union leaders, villagers, and municipal officials in order to quell further opposition. Upon seeing the envelope, Severino's wife, Magda, commented sharply: "René had better consult well with his lawyer." Martín's godson Edgar, a heavy-set man in his early forties who owned a bee aviary in town and from whom I had initially learned about Martín's agrarian estate (chapter 1), chimed in: "Yes, but if all his legal business is in order, there should be no problem." Martín, who had been supervising his workers as they loaded goods into his truck, interrupted: "His legal matters are in order. But this has to do with more than law: If the campesinos are frustrated with him, they will not let him work. They could take over his equipment or attack the mine. He has the law on his side but that doesn't mean anything." His godson nodded: "The people probably heard exactly what René says about them, all his talk of Indios." Martín countered that René had promised villagers "a thousand *huevadas* [a lot of nonsense]" but delivered nothing.

According to Magda, Edgar, and Martín, workers' opposition to René's mine was not principally rooted in popular assessments about formal property rights. He had the property deed and could show evidence of the sale. Rather, villagers seemed to challenge to the presumption that this formal legal status could settle matters. In particular, they took issue with René's position that because of his documented ownership rights, he could dispense with his earlier promises to supply aid and infrastructural support to Quechua villages neighboring the mine. This revealed how his own ownership was at once more socially embedded, and precarious, than legal property regimes could admit.

Over the following weeks, the union ratcheted up its opposition to the mine, unsatisfied by René's legal documentation. Local residents circulated a public denunciation calling for his expulsion from the region. In a letter to the municipal government penned by the provincial union, unionists complained that René's mine—owned as it was by three relatives who had only recently bought it from Fabio—violated new legal restrictions on family-owned mining. A formal document was posted publicly, with a copy also delivered to René, that described him as persona non grata and called for his immediate departure from Ayopaya. Faced with mounting opposition and worried for his life, René left for Cochabamba and hired a lawyer. As the dispute escalated, legal maneuvering was coupled with displays of force. Drawing from earlier tactics used in the 2003 turbine conflict, unionists used tree trunks and boulders to block off the road to René's mine. Receiving the letter and learning about the road blockades, René had fled the village at nightfall, driving the long way through Morochata to avoid the town of Independencia, where the union had organized protests. Unluckily for him, he had an accident on that drive, totaling his vehicle and scarring his face.

Despite these threats to René's life and business, Quechua villagers remained supportive of Martín's mining business. In fact, rather than breaking off ties to the family, they began lobbying Fabio Rodriguez, the former master's nephew, to reclaim his position as the legitimate mine owner and to form a new mining collective with them. By founding such a collective, villagers hoped, they would be able to regain control of the mine and, at the same time, ensure René's prompt departure. The proposal became irrelevant after René enlisted the help of a lawyer friend in Cochabamba to legally consolidate his mine as a nominal "collective." Nonetheless, it was revealing of how Ayopayan workers were creatively recrafting older ties to *hacendados* in order to dispute new and, to many villagers' minds, more pernicious arcs of extractivism in the region.

This proposal to form a collective with Fabio drew from the new mining law that put limits on the inheritance of mines within families and encouraged their collectivization by workers. A MAS government decree (Decreto Supremo No. 1308) sought to "nationalize" Bolivian mines and support mining collectives, subsequently implemented in August 2012. This decree was followed by a mining law (Ley 535 de Minería y Metalurgia), passed in 2014, which limited foreign ownership of mines. These new reforms—first as decree and then as law—introduced limits to the purchase, sale, and private ownership transfers of mines, instead encouraging miners to establish "collectives" (corporate or cooperative entities).[27] However, as the effort to forge a collective with Fabio demonstrates, in an atmosphere of entrenched racial hierarchies and uncertainties of legal ownership, Quechua workers' appropriation of mines from Mestizo bosses was deemed unlikely without leaning upon alliances with former master families. This casts also in a new light the land disputes described in chapter 1, in which the *hacendado*'s daughter Flora retained significance for Indigenous villagers navigating new land claims including on the part of the relatives of children born out of wedlock in provincial haciendas.

Given my own position as a White foreigner, villagers were not especially keen to discuss René's case with me. Instead, they offered up more general statements about greedy elites that, I believe, acted as coded critiques of René. As we stood in his front yard about a kilometer from the mine, I asked Severina Calderon, a Quechua farmer who lived only steps from Martín's estate, about recent "mining conflicts" in the area. Without going into details, she said there had been some "problems" at the mine. When I asked what they concerned, she replied pithily: "It's that the rich get richer, and the poor stay poor." In other conversations villagers evoked the fact that René spoke no Quechua—a staple marker of *q'ara* (White exploitative) subjectivity. Beyond his linguistic and physical difference as a well-to-do Mestizo urbanite, locals found his guarded nature off-putting. When I stayed with Quechua acquaintances in the nearby village, one man noted that René did not "*compartir*" (partake, share) with them.

In Ayopaya this term *compartir* was commonly used to describe occasions when people who occupy differential positions in racialized hierarchies nonetheless came together in close quarters to drink *chicha* (corn beer), to eat steaming plates of food prepared in large cauldrons for the feasts that accompany religious fiestas, or to dance and play guitar and *charango* music together.[28] As made apparent in Flora's relations to former servant villages (see chapter 1), occasions of shared sociality like these folded within them redistributive aid relations, including distributions of *chicha*, heaping plates of food, but also money, dry goods, medicine, and patronal support (Ramírez 2002). In Ayopaya such practices were aligned with a position as a good boss or leader. For instance, a construction manager in Ayopaya explained that monthly *cha'llas* in which bosses purchased dinner and drinks for workers were necessary to ensure workers' continued motivation and willingness to work. Given these widespread practices of shared sociality and redistributive aid, René's more isolated demeanor struck many workers as unusual and deeply offensive.

Villagers' perception of René's frugality were aggravated by the fact that his mine was located on former hacienda land whose former master and his kin (Fabio and Martín) remained deeply involved in village affairs. Martín's grandfather had been celebrated by many villagers as a "good [*sumaq*] master" who commonly invited workers for meals and drink during holidays, such as Christmas, and also acted as a godparent and source of medical care (he had medical training), and laid roads throughout the region. Compared to him, René's failure to greet workers, much less act as religious sponsor or godparent, appeared deeply transgressive of local aid customs. Taken in this broader context, villagers' complaints of René's unwillingness to *compartir* also expressed an ethical evaluation of his greedy character, one interpreted through the figure of earlier Mestizo overlords who for centuries prospered from the unpaid labor of undernourished workers. René's tactlessness and guarded demeanor positioned him as a negligent, greedy *q'ara*—a White person who profits by exploiting Indigenous people.[29]

During fieldwork at René's mine I gained some insight into his treatment of workers. René commonly invited friends and acquaintances to his living quarters on the mine for weekend barbeques, but workers were not welcome. On one such occasion, not only did he not extend an invitation to the miners, who were just getting off of work and whose kitchen he had his maid use to prepare the food, but he also displayed a near-paranoia about the workers' theft of food. After we ate, René instructed a maid to quickly store the leftovers lest workers steal away with a plate. By contrast, *hacendado* kin like Flora or Martín commonly invited Quechua villagers to *ch'allas* and, in Flora's case, offered poor farmers a free meal. René's frugality during this event was especially striking given that his workers were already complaining—to Severino, Magda, and anyone else who would listen—that their daily work meals lacked meat.

This withholding of sustenance to workers contrasted sharply with René's proclivity for overconsumption, especially of drink. By 5:00 p.m., when miners got off of work and retreated to the worker quarters, René would be slurring his speech, stumbling, and cursing loudly. René also spent weeks in the city—a common feature of the cruelest hacienda masters who left it to their overseers to discipline laborers—arriving at the mine late at night at an unsafe speed, often inebriated. When René passed by people, villagers complained, he never offered so much as a hello or a wave. These qualities only increased existing frustration about René's empty promises to complete a bridge across the Sacambaya River and to expand electricity to several villages.

My conversations with René suggested that his treatment of workers was not a matter of ignorance so much as a principled stance deriving from his progressive emphasis on citizenship rights as welcome displacements of earlier hacienda hierarchies. As René sipped whiskey in the living room of his housing quarters at the mine, my tape recorder perched on the coffee table in front of him, he discussed "problems" plaguing the mine. Mixing Spanish and English (he had gone to school at Cochabamba's American International School), René described his outrage about workers' expectations that he offer up his truck-bed to give workers a lift from town to the mine. Leaning forward, his hands clasped, René explained: "Look—the times change, and I'm all for them changing, but I am not okay with people walking all over you and violating your rights. Because I did not do anything to them. I did not enslave them. I pay taxes. I am legally established. It is ridiculous that because I work in this region they think they have a right to climb up and travel in my truck. After all, *I'm* the one who pays *them*. Yet I'm supposed to be at *their* service."

Here, René cast aid relations between bosses and workers as a "violation of rights" that went too far in reversing the terms of earlier servitude, a position that recalls conservative White supremacist critiques of US affirmative action policies as overcorrections for slavery.[30] Like liberal arguments for colorblindness, equality here offered a shield against taking seriously demands for historical accounting for racial oppression.[31] René's account included several references to the hacienda system, including allusions to "the times changing," "enslaving people," and to the problematic reversal of labor "service" in the posthacienda era. Lamenting that he was now to be "at [workers'] service," he implied that earlier Mestizo hacienda masters had become servants and the servants masters. In the posthacienda period, René hinted, bosses like him had become newly, and grotesquely, subject to their workers' whims and demands.

In this conversation René contested but also revealed the reparative connotations of aid relations like offering rides or supplying meat to workers. While his orientation to authority departed starkly from those guiding the actions of former *hacendado* family members like Flora or Martín, René's narrative recognized that aid was not just about material resources; it served as an acknowledgment, for Mestizos, of the historical debts they bore as continued beneficiaries of earlier hacienda servitude. In this way his narrative confirmed what I had heard from relatives of hacienda masters and servants: asymmetrical aid relations among Mestizo elites and Indigenous workers could be interpreted as key sites of vernacular historical redress and even reparation.

René summoned a narrative of equal citizen rights to his defense against such historical acknowledgment. Invoking his unmitigated rights as a citizen ("I pay taxes") and, in turn, to secure ownership ("I am legally established"), he rejected the tacit premise that Mestizos like him should heed aid commitments related to Mestizos' benefit from forced Indigenous labor in the hacienda era. Hence René was not innocent of the ethical valences of aid so much as dismissive of their applicability *to him*. As an urban elite who, he insisted, had not personally enslaved anyone, workers' demands for rides, meat, beer, or shared sociability appeared anachronistic and even unjust. And although he was willing to take part in standard arrangements of managerial aid, distributing uniforms, helmets, flashlights, and watches, workers' expectations of ride-sharing and shared feasting crossed a line.

To workers and villagers, René's unwillingness to *compartir* attested to his depraved, greedy character and his flagrant violation of provincial aid customs, qualities that together canceled out claims to legitimate ownership conferred through his earlier alliance with *hacendado* relatives like Fabio. In the climate of national mobilizing against private mine ownership and for

Indigenous resource rights, these ethical failings assumed heightened political dimensions. This made René's mine the object of increased union scrutiny and ultimately dramatic worker opposition and resistance. René's ejection from the countryside despite his firm ownership of the mine demonstrates how Mestizo authority in Ayopaya remained contingent upon relations to Indigenous workers and, with them, to the region's brutal labor past, a contingency that frameworks of naturalized property deny.

THE LAST MASTER: AID AS AN ETHICS OF WEALTH

Quechua villagers' steadfast support for Martín came as a surprise to me given his direct ties to earlier Mestizo hacienda masters. He came from a solidly middle-class Mestizo family who had initially received land in Ayopaya through Jesuit land grants in the late eighteenth century. As the hacienda master's grandson, Martín had spent summers visiting the estate since he was a child and knew long-term workers and fieldhands by name. In fact, Martín had been involved in the suppression of earlier land conflicts at his grandfather's estate. In 1984, when he was just twelve, Martín had accompanied his grandfather and military police when they approached Angelo Choque's home, arresting Angelo for threatening Martín's grandfather the late master, for organizing strikes, and for pillaging estate produce. In keeping with his grandfather's ways, Martín continued to offer rides to miners and villagers, including his employee and Severino's elderly father, Mario, in his rusty truck-bed. Alongside cultivating agricultural produce that he sold at regional markets, Martín employed people to work several "artisanal" (low-technology) mines. The gold and other valuable metals like antimony were processed at a mineral processing plant made up several shack-like buildings (Figure 17). There, Martín presented to me the shiny, gray substance that they process (Figure 18).

Perhaps related to the time he had spent at the estate as a child, Martín prided himself in reproducing *hacendado* ways as a mixture of generosity and force that, as with his grandfather, was befitting of a "good master" (*waleq patrón*). In fact, Martín boasted that he was "the last *patrón*." And he fit the part, carrying a rifle in his truck at all times and routinely making a show of conducting target practice on the outskirts of the former estate, in earshot of neighboring villagers and agricultural workers. Yet despite this palpable sense of racialized superiority, Martín was sought after by villagers as a god-

FIGURE 17. Martín's gold processing plant, K'uti (Ayopaya province), 2011. Photo by author.

parent and religious sponsor. On Sundays, he could be found in his usual drinking place, the curb of a humble store in Independencia. On the cement stoop outside the store, beer in hand, Martín caught up with his uncle and godchildren. One day, he was seated on the curb when Mela, a shy schoolgirl of thirteen, approached and greeted him. Her hair was separated into two neat braids, and she wore a dark maroon *pollera* skirt, an embroidered white shirt, and black shoes. Martín introduced her to me as his goddaughter, explaining that he pays for her room and board as well as schooling costs. He dug into his pocket for a crumpled twenty boliviano bill (worth about three US dollars), which he gave to Mela, instructing her to buy coloring pencils and a new notebook for school.

After she left, Martín explained that Mela was the eldest of seven children, from an extremely poor family. Her father was one of the best workers in Martín's gold mine; he had previously worked for Martín's grandfather and so had a detailed knowledge of the internal channels or "veins" of the mineshaft. When Mela turned thirteen, her mother came with her and asked if Martín would be the *padrino* (godfather) of Mela's education. Martín spoke fondly of Mela, noting that she was hardworking and sharp. He added that

FIGURE 18. Antimony mined at René's mine in K'uti (Ayopaya province), 2011. Photo by author.

he came to town and visited her school every week, chatting with her professors to hear how she is doing and to make sure she is behaving herself. "She has to study and go to school, that's all," Martín noted. "That's what I am paying for." On other occasions, I joined Martín, his partner, and Mela for lunch. Over lunch he explained that he saw Mela as an investment. By helping her, he would provide her siblings with a positive model of upward mobility and education, thus also "transforming their lives." In fact, Mela was about to graduate from middle school and would attend high school in Cochabamba. There, she planned to live with Martín's parents while she continued with her education, a pattern familiar in the region.[32]

Like Flora's adoption of her half-siblings (see chapter 1), Martín's position as a godparent to Mela attests to the unsteady ways that aid relations followed the grooves of earlier agrarian hierarchies. But seeing their bond as a case of sheer historical continuity is misleading, for neither Martín nor Mela had lived during the period of forced labor. And despite parallel kinds of asymmetrical aid relations across the hacienda era and the present, for villagers it was crucial that labor conditions had changed. Indeed, while to me Martín's continued presence in the countryside seemed uncanny, even traumatic, this was not the case for his Quechua neighbors. I asked Doña Severina Moya, who lived near the former estate, whether it had been strange to see someone return to the hacienda building in 2002. She answered in an unconcerned way: "Don Martín is good. When Don Carlos died, he [Martín] returned. But only to mine. He plants potatoes to eat is all. He doesn't make anything [from farming]." In addition, villagers described appreciating his frequent offer of rides, always at issue as the municipal center is some 15 kilometers away and there is no public transport. As Doña Juana Soruco, an elderly woman who had worked as a domestic servant for Carlos Rodriguez, explained: "Don Martín is good; he is not bad. He carries us in his vehicle. He pays us and helps us. He is good." These commentaries suggest that it was by virtue of, rather than despite, his upholding of some *hacendado* ways—aid relations, but not labor arrangements—that many tolerated his presence in the countryside.

Martín's relations with neighboring villagers recall Andean notions of authority that liken *hacendados* with positions of saintlike beneficence while, conversely, equating mineral wealth with greed, avarice, and alliance with the devil.[33] If having spent the summers in Ayopaya with his grandfather as a child had made Martín's skilled at negotiating this relational milieu, René, by contrast, disdained but also underestimated this milieu. To better understand this stance, I consider how this older authority paradigm departed from views of proper, unmarked authority on the part of progressive, educated Ayopayan elites. This raises new questions about the friction between liberal conceptions of undifferentiated citizenship and aid-based paradigms of redress across racialized hierarchies.

DISPLACING MASTERY: EQUALITY AS DISAVOWAL

These older hierarchies and asymmetrical aid relations elicited discomfort for the descendants of hacienda masters who imagined themselves, and the political present, to have overcome the trappings of hacienda servitude. One afternoon Alejo Ramirez, the director of a Catholic school for Indigenous girls, and I sat together on a park bench in Independencia's central plaza. He explained that while his parents had been hacienda masters, he belonged to "another time." "I don't discriminate," Don Alejo said, defensively. "I belong to another epoch. I recall my father's character, for instance, as quite different from my own because he lived another time." He added: "Furthermore, it's my position based on what I've seen and heard that the systems they [*hacendados*] maintained were unjust."

Despite this, however, rural Quechua villagers continued to treat Don Alejo differently on accord of his perceived lineage as a member of a powerful *hacendado* family. He explained: "For example, there are still several elderly villagers who call me *niñoy* ["my child," -*y* being the Quechua first-person possessive suffix], and they greet all the masters' children with this title." Other times, he noted, they simply call him *patrón* (master). Such customs elicited surprise and consternation from German philanthropists with whom Don Alejo worked at the girls' school. "When I'm working next to Europeans people call me *niñoy* and the Germans are surprised," he recounted, "but this is something that has stayed with them [villagers] and although you tell them 'Don't say it, I am not your child nor your master,' you can't erase it."

For progressive Mestizos, being associated with this older paradigm of mastery could be profoundly disturbing. As for INRA reformers and municipal staff who blamed the formerly enslaved for upholding anachronous orientations to authority, here educated Mestizos like Alejo blamed Indigenous peasants for maintaining racialized inequalities by way of their stubborn dependencies on Mestizo elites (see chapter 3). This was apparent in Alejo's account of an interaction he had with a Quechua farmer. Enrique Torrez, a man who worked with Alejo at the Christian girls school he had founded, and Alejo were working in a rural village where they stayed with an acquaintance, an elderly Quechua villager. In the course of their stay, this villager called Alejo "my child" (*niñoy*). Enrique asked the man why he called Alejo "my child" and not him. The man turned to Enrique and said: 'You are an Indio just like me. He [pointing at Alejo] is a son of masters.'"

Don Alejo turned to me pointedly. "This stays with them. And you can't take it away." He continued: "Look, the [agrarian] reform happened some fifty or so odd years ago, but it [hacienda authority] remains, at least for some, for the people who served the master. I haven't had tensions with people here, neither with the elderly nor the young." But he had encountered requests for aid. "In many cases," Alejo explained, "people see the child or descendent of the master as a person who would make a good godparent of their child, who could help [them] in baptism or to build a house. This, too, continues to be the case."

My conversation with Alejo helped me to understand hacienda-based traditions of authority as a frame within which Martín could pursue and, in part, achieve authority in the eyes of local villagers and workers. This was a frame in which hierarchy was presumed as a starting part for social relations that could not be erased or elided despite some elite Mestizos' discomforts with them. Similarly, and like his grandfather, Martín was a godfather to local villagers' children and had aided villagers in establishing electricity and water in the villages bordering the mine. This aid was combined with an aggressive, even violent demeanor toward these very same subjects, particularly to his own agrarian workers. For instance, on one occasion, neighboring villagers had let their donkey out to graze, and it had eaten some of the vegetables in Martín's garden. In response, he shot the animal and drove through the village with its body tied to his truck. The latter incident resulted in a formal complaint, in which the municipal government charged him a fine and required him to pay the villagers a sum reflecting the worth of the dead donkey.

Newer mining elites like René and his cousins were both unsettled by, but also fetishized, this form of authority configured by the duality of force and generosity. One day I sat with René Cruz and his cousins Roberto and Enrique in the living room of the mine's housing quarters as they discussed Martín. Roberto recalled that they been out drinking one day when Martín asked him what sort of a gun he carried. Roberto had shown him his gun, and Martín had laughed, taking the gun and firing it into the air. He raised his own gun and fired, the echo of the shot contrasting sharply with the hollow *put, put* sound of Roberto's more modest weapon. Martín warned Roberto: "Your gun won't do anything to these Indios." Martín had mimed the act of brushing dirt off one's chest, explaining, "They have skin as thick as animals." This had so disturbed Roberto that he was left speechless. Martín, noticing villagers at an adjacent table staring at them, turned around and asked, "What are you looking at?" One man had responded deferentially, "Nothing, Don Martín."

Roberto expressed his shock to me about this incident, which he saw as evidence of Ayopaya's backwardness. "When I first arrived here," he recounted, "I realized that there was something I didn't understand, something of *el campo*, the countryside, which is more akin to what relations to *hacendados* were like in Cochabamba fifty or more years ago. It's a different world." Roberto's brother Enrique added, thoughtfully: "What is so sick is that even as we know that Don Martín is the worst, we also want to be like him." Roberto objected, loudly interrupting: "No!" His brother cut him off. "Well," Enrique continued, "it's Don Martín they respect. They say, 'Oh yes,

Don Martín, of course, Don Martín.' And to us? They show up late to work and take two-hour lunch breaks. There is something that has stayed with Martín, something of the haciendas, that we don't have." Enrique continued: "And while Don Martín's name is always uttered with deference and respect, if we try to give us orders, they just laugh at us."

As this disagreement lays bare, for more progressive urban Mestizos like Enrique or Roberto, Martín embodied a form of masculinity and authority that they themselves neither could achieve nor could ethically accept. Despite this, that mode of authority retained appeal to them. Like Alejo, Enrique too described hacienda authority as a sentiment that had "stayed with" people even after the formal abolition of hacienda servitude. Mestizo townsfolk and bosses like them saw hacienda mastery as an institution that had problematically outlived institutional efforts at its displacement by a more horizontal model of equal citizenship. However, for some this displacement was profoundly ambivalent. For Enrique, Martín embodied the limits to his own authority, modeled as it was on urban progressive ideals of managerial authority and an accompanying focus on fostering a friendly work atmosphere.[34]

In fact, Roberto and his brother went to great lengths to be likeable, sharing rides as well as *pikchando* (coca-chewing breaks) with workers. If Martín's relation was marked by an exemplary division and hierarchy between Mestizos and Indigenous workers, these young mine owners instead tried to collapse or implode such division. To their consternation, however, friendly interactions in the workplace did not confer respect compared to Martín's gun-wielding ways. Neither did this lenient managerial style cancel out workers' demands for aid and resources. This background clarifies René's complaint about aid obligations. Treating workers as equals here involved a purposeful disregard for the hacienda past—one that the young mine owners expected would lead Quechua workers to do the same.

For progressive Mestizos like these, this wedding of wealth and aid, care and violence, belonged to an earlier time of injustice that should have been supplanted by a more liberal order of natural rights as citizens and humans—what Alejo revealingly referred to as an "equality of blood." However, Martín's case made clear that these patterns of masterly aid and violence not only "stayed with" former servant groups but also with masters' kin. Conversely, the duties that followed from earlier hacienda violence could not be evaded by recourse to a language of unmarked citizenship. Despite René's attempts to dissipate expectations for aid or to do only the necessary to placate miners, for workers and villagers the mine's location on former hacienda lands introduced obligations, binding place and aid in ways that went against a naturalized ethos of alienable property. That René and his cousins bought the mine, transferring title and ownership from the earlier hacienda masters, did not neutralize their position as Mestizo bosses, a position understood to carry responsibilities of supplying aid and help to neighboring villagers. The toppling of René's mine after his failure to uphold these expectations of asymmetrical exchange as historical return highlights the precarity of Mestizo authority in the countryside. Likewise, it destabilizes more formalistic definitions of property as an orientation of expected benefit whose possession could be assured simply by firmer ownership rights.[35]

That unionists in Ayopaya came to organize against René's mine, and not Martín's, suggests that what was at stake was not resource rights or capitalism in the abstract but rather a particular texture of provincial relations through which authority was crafted and its legitimacy conferred. Martín, with his authoritative if generous demeanor, was intelligible to workers given enduring paradigms of economic and racialized mastery molded on hacienda owners. René and his cousins, in contrast, tried to be sympathetic and to craft more horizontal ties to workers. Nonetheless, their practical disregard for existing traditions of asymmetrical aid smacked of disavowal—however liberal or progressive—of the reparative dimensions of hierarchical aid relations in the present. Here, abstract ideals of rights and citizenship were invoked in ways that denied existing asymmetries between bosses and workers, Mestizo elites and Indigenous villagers. By denying that inequality, René and his cousins also sought to reject villagers' insistence upon their abiding responsibility to the region's past.

While deeply problematic in their reinscription of racial hierarchies, in Ayopaya relations of asymmetrical aid also offered pathways for workers and villagers to demand elites' accountability to a violent past, one that was not possible from within a new, more horizontal rights-based framework of unmarked citizenship and progressive management styles. These inherited frameworks of wealth held the power both to confer authority and to undo it, to make masters and unmake them. Here, Quechua farmers and mine workers used traditions of aid and labor circulation as leverage to negotiate and renegotiate the terms of extractivism. Against alienation, these workers and miners demanded return as a willingness to *compartir*, to share resources and sociality with Quechua neighbors and workers. Rather than being inherited wholesale or reproduced as an intact cultural system, return was an outcome of the ways contemporary workers creatively refashioned older patterns of labor mobility. Wielding, withholding, and transferring their own labor from one mine to another allowed workers to challenge owners who did not heed workers' demands for aid as forms of repayment for abiding hacienda debts. Workers hereby activated mobility not only to refute territorial containment and homogenous Indigeneity (see chapter 4) but also as a technique for contesting capital as an abandonment of place-based obligations.

LABOR MOBILITY AND THE DISRUPTION OF CAPITAL

Formal union challenges to René's mine were accompanied by the flight of local miners and domestic servants from the mine. One morning my research assistant and I squeezed into René's truck to accompany him and one of his miners (a new worker hired to drive the tractor) to the village of Sarahuayto, where I planned to spend several days doing research. Along the way René slowed as we met another vehicle going the opposite direction. The vehicle belonged to one of the managers at Martín's mine. The drivers lowered their windows, and the driver of the other vehicle turned to René and said: "We are carrying off all your maids. They are not going to work for you anymore."

At first, I imagined the exchange to belong to the kinds of playful banter with which people, especially Mestizo men, often negotiated tense racialized dynamics in the region. However, subsequent conversations with local women employed to cook and clean René's mine confirmed the information imparted in this earlier encounter: laborers were leaving René's mine to instead undertake work in Martín's home and mine. These practices raised questions about labor mobility—a variation on a labor strike—as a technique by which local Quechua residents sought to destabilize production at this mine. Such practices of labor retraction might be seen as a mode through which workers enacted their support for Martín over René and, with him, their insistence that for new bosses to operate in the region, they must embody authority in a way that heeded to the lessons of the region's turbulent history of antihacienda mobilization and violence. Recall, here, Angelo's insistence that in the 1940s as newly formed peasant labor militias swept across this landscape, it was only the "good" [*waleq*] masters who had been allowed to stay on.

The union's drafting of a letter declaring René a persona non grata had been accompanied by a peasant union vote in which Quechua and Aymara villagers agreed to stop working at René's mine. One Quechua mine worker explained to me that the laborers preferred Martín, the former master's grandson, whose truck was always full of villagers and whose workers' midday meals always included meat. Likewise, one Quechua maid whom I spoke with noted in exasperation of René's mine: "We don't want to cook for the miners anymore. We've had enough."

René's primary maid, Rosalin Roque, had recently left his mine, choosing to work for Martín instead. When I spoke to her at her new place of employment at Martín's estate, Rosalin explained that the idea of leaving her post at René's mine first arose after several occasions when René had tried to enter her room at night, presumably for sex. She shared a room with an older female cook, a woman *de pollera* (of the traditional multilayered skirt), who had been notably shocked to find her boss, René, standing there, half-naked and drunk in the doorway to her sleeping quarters. Rosalin had told him no, but he had been relentless, inviting her to share a drink with him in his bedroom. Rosalin had always declined. As a small act of revenge, Rosalin informed René's then-girlfriend that her boyfriend was bringing other women to the mine when she was not there. To drive home this point, Rosalin purposefully did not clean up a used condom from René's visit to the mine with another woman. When René confronted Rosalin, accusing her of lying to his girlfriend, Rosalin retorted: "Then why do you always bother me in your underwear?" Here the form of agency that Rosalin enacted, like the retraction of labor on the part of the mine workers, relied on inaction: namely, the refusal to clean up the condom.

When we spoke, Rosalin bemoaned the fact that René assumed that his Mestizo status would result in unlimited sexual privileges. She likened René's behavior to that of the earlier hacienda masters. Of earlier *hacendados* and their sons, Rosalin noted: "They think it's like that, that they can just have sex with whomever [they want]." This expectation of sexual access seemed to spring from the earlier commodification of domestic laborers [*mitanis*] in haciendas (see chapter 1). Into the present, domestic laborers, particularly women, continued to be treated by employers as extensions of hacienda or mine property. When Rosalin up and left her place of employment at René's mine, it elicited a lot of gossip. She had been, as Severino and his wife at the dry goods store in Independencia put it, "de René"—that is, of René.

I had encountered this language earlier at a birthday party when Severino's elderly mother described herself to Martín as "de Carlos"—that is, implicitly belonging to the hacienda master, Martín's grandfather. This use of the possessive preposition *de* reveals a specific attribute of sexualized ownership (with implications of concubinage at times) that extended over hacienda workers and that, Rosalin's experience showed, persisted under new conditions of mineral extractivism. To be "of René" here connoted the fact that, as his principal female maid, Rosalin was to ensure his comfort and fulfill his domestic (and, to his eyes, sexual) needs. This dynamic had not ended even after she gave up the job. During a visit to drink with Martín, René had tried to "get her back" again. Hiding in her room with the light off, Rosalin had heard him shout repeatedly that he was going to "bring her to the mine below," angrily insisting that she come "work" for him again.

The question of the sexual violence perpetrated by Mestizo bosses and workers was a topic of great concern in the countryside at that time. In fact, accusations of rape were crucial in the peasant union's decision to organize a strike against René's mining business. Reportedly, a hired tractor driver from Cochabamba city had raped several elderly Quechua women, including the mother of a well-known and well-liked rural schoolteacher. (In fact, the man who joined us in René's truck that morning had been brought on to replace this previous tractor driver, who was gravely injured when a group of villagers—led by the rape victim's son—confronted him. He later died of his injuries after fleeing from the hospital in Cochabamba to avoid being charged.)

Similarly, unionists had worried that Martín's godparenting relation with Mela, discussed earlier, was sexually exploitative. Later that month, just as miners began blockading the road to René's mine with rocks and boulders, Mela returned home. Her father, hearing rumors of sexual impropriety at Martín's house in Cochabamba, went to fetch her. However beneficial this higher education might be to her, for her father it was not felt to outweigh the risks of sexual predation that young Indigenous women frequently faced in urban Mestizo households. These various cases—of Rosalin, of the accusations of rape leveled against the tractor driver, and of Mela—shared a concern with sexual violence as the most egregious of a broader set of labor continuities spanning earlier hacienda agriculture and new mining economies. The shoring up of property through Mestizo possession here operated through bosses' ownership of land but also, and with it, hierarchical control over people and laborers, especially as sexual access to women.

Villagers' understandable outrage about these labor abuses honed in on René, who despite his status as a stranger in the province nonetheless embodied what villagers saw as the most repulsive qualities of older *hacen-*

dado patrones: material greed and a lust for local women. In an atmosphere of growing anger, women's domestic labor (whether paid, in Rosalin's case, or folded into informal sponsorship arrangements, such as with Mela) and the movement of miners' bodies arose as critical sites of intervention and power. By leaving one mine or one mining encampment, as Rosalin did, she was able to actualize her preference for employment under Martín over Rene and, at the same time, weaken or render precarious his presumptions of bodily access and control. In the aftermath of state violence and union repression, these microlevel, intimate zones of claim-making appealed to miners as a way to reshape extractive economies absent the power to fully displace enduring, racialized inequalities. By withdrawing labor and blocking the mine, villagers reminded René of the contingency of wealth not only on the qualities of the world—the percentage of gold or antimony in the ore—but also the labor that allowed that ore to be removed, processed, transported, and sold for profit.

Labor here arose as a tool of political maneuver, a form through which to expose the historical and relational underpinnings of wealth: what Marx ([1867] 1972: 320, 323) described as the "secret" of social character of labor hidden within the commodity. Where those demands went unheeded, workers sought to reclaim control over the terms of their own labor, drawing from hacienda-based patterns of peasant mobility to disrupt flows of bodies, *minerals*, and affects on which profit depends—in short, to reveal temporal and spatial slippages against the material boundedness and ahistoricity of capital. To use Nancy Munn's ([1986] 1992) language, in these cases an informal set of exchange relationships (of meat, patronal support, and rides) emerged as modalities of "positive value creation" that articulated a mode of subjectivity defined by extension—here of material obligations—over time and space. Like Ramón Colque's insistence that the relatives of earlier masters for whom he worked continue to "give" to him in more capacious ways than that of a daily wage, René's employees here seemed to insist upon the insufficiency of formal labor contracts or ownership documents in establishing legitimate authority.

Of course, an alternative way to understand this conflict might be as evidence that nascent discourses of Indigenous land and resource reclamation had rendered fragile, even foreclosed, Mestizo mining. Yet that miners and domestic workers selectively opposed René, and not Martín, casts doubt over an interpretation of this dispute as a culmination of Indigenous opposition to resource extractivism as such. Rather than taking issue with mining at large, workers opposed the expansion of a new, more progressive orientation to profit that saw wealth as necessarily disentangled from older patterns of redistributive aid and sociality. Instead, and drawing from the broader range of kinship and exchange relations described in earlier chapters, it seemed that workers imbued asymmetrical aid as a way to honor obligations to wealth derived from place. Cast in this broader light, the demands for assistance that René casually dismissed constituted, for workers, an insistence that former hacienda lands carry with them enduring obligations to local Indigenous people and to the region's brutal labor past. Aid here assumed important connotations as a reparative device premised upon Mestizos' expected redistribution of wealth to Quechua villages residing adjacent to the mine.

Redistributive aid relations hereby acted as a countergift or a repayment of debts accrued through Mestizo elites' earlier benefit from forced Indigenous labor and sexual violence. To evoke the language of knotting laid out in the introduction, this case demonstrates how rural villagers and workers mobilized exchange as a way to navigate the relational terms of provincial gold mining by insisting that economy retain the trappings of an earlier paradigm of kinship-based alliance and aid rather than the discrete orientations to money and wages captured in a modern ethos of property.[36] Claims made through these practices of labor mobility and aid relations were especially important for people who, related to legacies of labor mobility and hacienda servitude in the region (see chapter 4), did not find opportunities for access to redistributed land or Indigenous recognition through MAS agrarian reform programs.

Against ahistorical ideals of disembedded capital, apparent in René's appeal to his unequivocal rights to profit and labor, villagers' actions revealed his authority and business as contingent on arrangements of aid and domestic labor that are commonly excluded from the category of commodities as such. In doing so, they exposed how Mestizo masculinity in and as property derived as much from *expectations* of benefit (e.g., sexual access) as it did from material control over resources and land.[37] A crucial if undervalued dimension of these rural mining camps was domestic labor: women maids cooked for miners and bosses, cleaned bosses' living quarters, and provided emotional support, companionship, and, at times, sexual favors. Theirs was the labor that lubricated rural mining regimes, allowing the motors of extractivism to whir uninterrupted and without snags. When Rosalin left, she turned René's attraction and affect against him, exposing his reliance on forms of attachment that, in his formal approach to workers, he had consistently eschewed.[38] This in turn unraveled René's more myopic vision of profit as a form of value produced through what Nancy Munn ([1986] 1992: 13) has termed the "'contraction' of spacetime"—one echoed in René's insistence that he "did not enslave them" and thus needn't uphold aid relations as devices of historical repair.

CONCLUSION

Despite the legal abolition of hacienda servitude in 1953 and the subsequent shift from "unfree" to "free" (wage-based) labor, extractive relations in Ayopaya did not undergo an absolute break from "vertical" relations to a more atomized individualism. The Ayopayan miners and servants with whom I spoke drew from their experiences of this continuity to reject the naturalness of property as a model of ahistorical wealth and profit generated by the internal makeup of resources rather than qualities of labor or infrastructure. Given the infrastructural and labor continuities linking hacienda economies to mineral extraction, mine owners' visions of wealth as a private matter rang hollow to neighboring villagers. Drawing from older paradigms of wealth that articulated both authority and aid (see chapter 1), villagers instead insisted on places (and mines) as bound to hacienda-era debts in ways that interrupted the smooth extraction of profit.[39] The hacienda system's linking of authority and redistribution here operated as a lively ruin—an accumulated set of redistributive social ties—that could be seized upon to unseat new Mestizo bosses' notions of individual gain absent a broader accountability to Quechua workers.

Workers' and villagers' demand that elites uphold inherited duties stood in tension with reformist efforts to solidify new kinds of rural political consciousness and Indigenous agency through the displacement of earlier hacienda labor and social ties via land titling and through reclaiming ownership over mines. As in other postplantation regions of the Americas, in Ayopaya Quechua villagers experienced the shift from older regimes of agrarian aid to new arrangements of labor contract and rights as profoundly wounding.[40] Liberal labor contracts introduced new possibilities of rights but also naturalized Mestizo bosses' disavowals of earlier obligations to workers and neighboring villages. Exchange provided a creative mechanism by which workers sought to uphold a specific texture of historical continuity, insisting that new mining economies maintain a broader, relational orientation to wealth. Such disagreements over the ethical entailments of wealth in Ayopaya thereby demonstrate how relations of economic abandonment and social undoing that often appear natural to scholars are not experienced as such everywhere.

This mode of mining activism forces a rethinking of political agency in its relation to colonial history, highlighting a practice of Indigenous critique centered on the creative reactivation of an inherited exchange paradigm. In this case, political action did not require a historical break from what preceded it but rather emerged from the reworking of hierarchical forms people were trying to contest.[41] These practices reveal how exchange operates as a mediatory form by which Quechua Ayopayans navigated the ethical possibilities of property and kinship as contrasting models of historical redress. Finding property-based reparation efforts sorely inadequate, Indigenous workers sought to extend arrangements of aid to new mining elites, thereby binding wealth to rural histories of labor violence and Indigenous dispossession that could not be dislodged or overcome through time's passing or a property sale.

Ayopayan gold miners' ejection of René for failing to uphold this paradigm problematize a familiar historical telos wherein contract overtakes other relations of exchange such as gifting or religious sponsorship. Thus for Marx ([1867] 1972: 433) it was the dissolution of feudal ties that cut loose the fetters on exploitation, thereby sending a "free and 'unattached' proletarian' onto the labour-market."[42] Miners and maids challenged the very premises of "free" labor—both as wage work and as bosses' disattachment from the plight of workers and neighboring villagers. They did so by putting forth an understanding of economic contract—namely, paid mining and domestic labor—as bound up in and thereby accountable to racialized labor orders, including those grounded by predatory Mestizo masculinity. Even if new mining bosses were not personally implicated in hacienda subjection, their mines rely on roads built by indentured laborers at the behest of hacienda masters, and villages of earlier hacienda worker encampments continue to supply the labor power for the mines; mining economies, however "free," are not disjoined from ongoing histories of Mestizo settlement, labor exploitation, and Indigenous land dispossession. By insisting that new bosses heed the duties established by hacienda subjection, Ayopayan workers revealed the embeddedness of capital in forms of history and sociality that proponents of unmitigated rights to profit, such as René, denied.[43]

These mining conflicts hold broader significance for rethinking the politics of capital in late liberalism. If the fantasy of capital in neo/classical accounts rests on the refusal of temporality—the idea that profit is something generated from the quality of the commodity itself as a matter of exchange value, not compressed labor over time—workers' demands for aid instead drew upon the region's labor history to contest a dehistoricized orientation to money as individual profit. Echoing Karl Marx's ([1867] 1972) challenges, in *Capital*, to liberal political economy for veiling the force needed for capitalism to gain hegemony in history, workers and villagers rejected the idea of money as an autonomous substance organized around its fundamental alienability from histories of labor and residence. As a form of strike calibrated to the region's history of labor shortages and mobility, Indigenous workers' withdrawing of (gendered) labor allowed them to hold bosses to account for their insertion into racialized structures of hacienda labor and Indigenous dispossession. In cases where villagers found mine owners unwilling to embody such answerability to the past, workers retracted their labor, thereby revealing the centrality not only of domestic labor but also of kinship-based claims and alliances, for the making and unmaking of racialized property.

Despite his efforts to distinguish himself from backward bosses, René's work and person here remained weighed down (even haunted) by the figure of the earlier hacienda master: Mestizo men who "enslaved" Indigenous villagers and raped Indigenous women. René seized upon languages of discrete capital and unmarked citizenship in his attempt to avoid that apparition. Yet he could not escape what many villagers saw as the unavoidable social costs of mining: a short life and a lonely death. When we met at a sports bar in Cochabamba's elite El Prado neighborhood in 2015, he was despondent. Sipping whiskey, his face illuminated by intermittent flashes of light from a TV broadcast of a boxing match, René lamented: "My children don't even like me." He wished he had not spent their childhood at the mine or allowed his focus on his company to compromise his marriage. In this regard, René himself acknowledged that he embodied the risks of an unsavory mining life—wealth without history, property without relation. These uncertainties about the historical trappings of authority assumed new shape in rural debates about MAS governance, as embodied by then President Evo Morales.

SIX

Reviving Exchange

In early February of 2012, members of the municipal government in Independencia invited me to a *ch'alla*, a drink-based offering used to consecrate buildings, crops, mines, vehicles, and homes. The *ch'alla* that day was hosted by the municipal government office, and guests included leaders of the Central Sindical Única de Trabajadores Campesinos Originarios de Ayopaya (Central Union of Campesino Workers of Ayopaya, CSUTCOA), rural government staff employed in the Independencia mayoral office, and friends and family of both these groups. We met in a government parking lot that was empty except for three tractors recently acquired through Bolivia's new 2010 Agrarian Reform Law.[1] There I joined several young men in slacks and cotton coats, accompanied by two women, one in jeans, another in a pollera skirt with a woven shawl pulled tightly across her shoulders. This group included Oscar Torrico, whom I introduced in chapter 2, who led the municipal government's Projects Division. We stood around, smoking cigarettes to ward off the cold, and chatting in hushed voices about then President Evo Morales's visit to the neighboring village of Cavari earlier that day. He had arrived late and departed early, skipping a carefully prepared feast. This disappointed his hosts, including the municipal workers who later gathered for the *ch'alla*; some were long-term MAS supporters who knew "Evo" from tending their coca fields in lowland Chapare, other municipal officials felt more ambivalent about MAS party orders and governance projects.

Our discussion ended abruptly when Julio, a municipal worker in his late twenties, approached the lot guiding a white llama. Wordlessly, people gathered as Julio Calizaya knelt beside the llama and, after a brief pause, gently lowered it to the ground. Lifting a knife, he began slitting the llama's neck, working with another man who nimbly collected its blood in one bowl then another. The overflow formed dark rivulets that streamed toward the road, attracting two stray dogs. After the bowls were filled, Julio handed one to the mayor and another to the president of CSUTCOA. In turn, they cast the blood in the direction of the three tractors and a white four-wheel-drive Toyota truck, also a municipal vehicle. Once the bowls were empty, the process was repeated, the blood leaving marbled blotches on vehicles. With each casting, the officials shouted: "Jallalla! Jallalla!" (which is used like the Spanish "viva" or "long live").[2] The guests repeated this phrase with varied referents: "Jallalla Bolivia! Jallalla MAS! Jallalla Evo!"

Sunshine parted the clouds just as the two men began skinning the animal. They cut carefully so that the fur was removed intact, while others went about removing the heart, which must still be palpitating when placed in the sacred *q'oa* bundle. The ritual ended with the burning of the *q'oa*, a folded paper packet holding the heart and hoofs of the llama as well as coca leaves, incense, confetti, anise candy, and other offerings, recalling *q'oas* I had attended on the part of pro-Indigenous activist organizations in Cochabamba (Figure 19). Guests made gifts of *trago* (alcohol) and *chicha* (brewed corn beer) to the Pachamama, dripping liquid on four points around the bundle before polishing off the rest.

Then the mayor, a Quechua man in his forties who had grown up in a nearby village, addressed the group: "Good, well today our president Evo came to Catavi. We offer you this *q'oa* so that these projects yield success, and so that there will be more projects in the future." Silvio Campos, a weathered man in a camel-colored *sombrero*, continued: "This *q'oa* is for the Pachamama, asking for help in our municipality and with the Process of Change."[3] More coca was distributed. Alluding to the ongoing risks posed to workers from perilous road-building efforts in the region, the mayor dripped *chicha* on the bundle. Approaching the *misa* (ritual table), he said: "To the projects in Catavi, may they go well." The men lifted the wet bundle into the embers, the color of its ash taken as an omen for the year ahead.

This municipal *ch'alla* belonged to a broader set of phenomena wherein Bolivian state agencies and bureaucratic institutions under Evo Morales's Movimiento al Socialismo (MAS) party government (2006–19) sought to incorporate and "revive" hitherto marginalized, disparaged Indigenous traditions.[4] The event centered on making a sacrificial offering of the llama's blood and heart to the Pachamama, part of ongoing, reciprocal cycles of ritualized gift-giving in exchange for abundant harvests as well as human and animal health. Seeking extra protection for municipal vehicles and their drivers and passengers was especially urgent in this mountainous province, where

FIGURE 19. *Q'oa* offering during Indigenous Rights March in Quillacollo, a suburb of Cochabamba city, 2012. Photo by author.

unpaved roads descend steeply into deep ravines and river valleys, causing frequent accidents with multiple casualties.

In this bid for protection through rural traditions of *ch'alla* offering, these municipal leaders yoked revived rites to new developmental agendas, requesting the Pachamama's "help" in securing future development funds and rural aid projects. In Ayopaya these revivalist efforts were complicated by the religious connotations of exchange—both among humans and with more-than-humans—as upheld and refashioned under conditions of bonded servitude on agrarian haciendas.[5] Usually *ch'allas* were performed by local villagers and townsfolk, including the families of former hacienda masters (see chapter 2), rather than by municipal officials. This municipal *ch'alla* was in fact only the second event of its kind.

The municipal *ch'alla* and similar political events in Ayopaya offer insight into the ways that residents remade kinship-based paradigms of asymmetrical aid as the basis for new demands and contestations centered on seeking accountability from state political authorities. As historians and anthropologists note, *ch'allas* have been commonly performed in the Andes since the colonial era, leading some scholars to speculate that they constitute a sort of Andeanist refashioning of baptismal rites.[6] Into the twentieth century such *ch'allas* are often performed as supplications to El Tio, a figure often associated with the Devil, said to preside over mines.[7] While initially reserved for agrarian and mining settings, from the 1980s on such practices are also common in urban settings—for instance, to bless a new business or home.[8] But the performance of this rite in Ayopaya was related to the renewed centrality of sacrificial offerings like these in Indigenous revivalist contexts.[9]

Reception of this revivalist agenda was especially vexed in the province of Ayopaya, where the divisive effects of earlier hacienda bondage had complicated traditional structures of highland community, foreclosing easy claims to Indigeneity as collective being "in-ayllu."[10] In a province where hacienda labor systems continued to palpably shape landscapes, labor relations, and attitudes to earthly and more-than-human authority, Indigenous traditions could not be clearly cut off from the non-Indigenous without rearranging the material texture or shape of a given life-world. This inadequacy of revivalist approaches lent urgency to other efforts to negotiate and bear colonial history and, in turn, to reelaborate Indigeneity in a place and among subjects who continue to navigate the multivalent entrenchments of a recent hacienda past.

This chapter considers the ways that Ayopayans took up and repurposed aspects of the asymmetrical exchange tradition discussed in preceding chapters in order to critically assess and contest MAS political authority.[11] I argue that institutions of exchange like patronage aid, godparenting, and distributions of money and resources by authorities retained a privileged place in rural Indigenous assessments of legitimate political and economic power in the province. In the course of rural visits from government officials, including the president, Ayopayans implicitly drew from broader practices of food sharing and godparentage to evaluate such officials premised on their as capacities and willingness to redistribute aid across hierarchy.[12] Exchange emerged not as a cultural relic but rather as a purposeful binding of political authority to earlier structures of patronage and their distinct grammars of accountability to the lives of largely impoverished Quechua villagers. Looking at how this exchange configuration shaped rural engagements with MAS party officials reframes Indigenous revivalism not only as the imposition of identarian meanings atop existing lifeways but also as Quechua residents' efforts to critically refashion historical institutions of authority in order to define and challenge the terms of revolutionary governance in Bolivia's present.

That morning, President Evo Morales's rural hosts had been alarmed when he cut short his visit to Catavi, a neighboring village, leaving cauldrons of steaming soup, rice, and meat untouched. I had caught a ride to the village, about forty-five minutes' drive from Ayopaya, with several acquaintances, squeezed between a young man who worked in Independencia's Public Records office and an older woman *de pollera* in her sixties who had been hired to cater the event. As we drove, I noticed that my leg was burning against a large tin pot near my legs. As I stuffed my scarf beside my leg to protect myself from the hot metal, the woman beside me explained: "It's food, for the president!" With this, her face brightened, and she smiled. For the next few minutes we joked about the luck of traveling with "Evo's meal," leg burns included.

In Catavi village officials and school staff bustled around hurriedly, adorning a table with white balloons and preparing wreaths of flowers to place around the president's neck to welcome him. The event would occur at the village school and union building, both located on a high mountain peak with a striking view of the river valley below. Villagers and their schoolchildren waited uncertainly for an hour, until someone called out "helicopter!" Expectant faces turned toward the northeast cordillera. The helicopter drew near, its rhythmic whirring audible, before turning and landing in a field below. Not long after, a group of three white SUVs (telltale indicators that Morales was near) approached the school, their progress slow due to the dramatic altitude climb. Morales made a brief speech from the head of a table adorned with loaves of *T'antawawas* ("bread babies") brought by the schoolchildren, which are often modeled after important Indigenous political leaders and martyrs like Túpaj Katari (Figure 20).

When Patricia Diaz, a Mestiza municipal employee from Independencia, approached the table carrying drinks, she was briskly shooed away. Tito Arancibia, a friend from Independencia, leaned over to explain that this was "because of the photos," which were to show Evo with rural union leaders and schoolchildren, not blonde-haired women in windbreakers. On earlier visits he had also been welcomed by a group of young women known as *cholitas*, a racialized term used to describe unmarried Indigenous women, but rumor got around that he pursued them and then left. They had gotten sick of that arrangement, so this time there were no *cholitas*.[13]

After the photos, Evo was whisked away in one of the white SUVs, leav-

FIGURE 20. "Bread babies" (*T'antawawas*) on display in Sacaba, Bolivia, including one depicting Indigenous Aymara leader Túpac Katari, 2012. Photo by author

ing dust and palpable disappointment behind. Although staff from Independencia's municipal government did not explicitly address this issue, Morales's swift departure may have been a reaction to the relatively small crowd of supporters at the event that day. Like the unwillingness of young women to welcome Morales and make themselves available to him sexually—a practice that followed from patterns of sexual benefit commonly enjoyed by hacienda masters only decades earlier—the sparse crowds in Catavi pointed to proliferating disenchantment with Morales in Ayopaya at that time.[14] Organizers' unwillingness to provide the president with *cholitas* also occurred in the context of recent scandal in which Independencia's mayor was accused of having sex with underage girls at a hotel in a neighboring mining town. Rumor had it that the girls had been manipulated to accept the arrangement by an older woman whom the mayor paid.

These contemporary rumors about the mayor's sexually predatory behavior and Tito's explanation for why there was no *cholita* welcome committee cast in a new light Morales's abrupt departure. While this fleeting appearance likely reacted to the sparse attendance at the event, itself a response to the rumors of sexual impropriety outlined above, Morales's hasty departure and growing evasiveness among rural supporters further indicted him. Above all, from the perspective of rural attendees, it recalled the elusive character of the most violent landlords and the aloofness of new Mestizo bosses (see chapter 5).[15]

Municipal staff likewise critiqued Morales's hasty departure, not least for its reproduction of gendered labor dynamics among government workers. Elvira Tapia—a Quechua woman in her thirties who worked in Independencia's municipal Records Office and would later attend the *ch'alla*—and two women coworkers were left to clean up a large hall where a banquet for thirty guests had been prepared. With Morales's early departure, tables, chairs, plates, napkins, and streamers had to be unceremoniously cleaned up. Elvira and her coworkers spoke in hushed tones, discussing their frustration that Evo had left without eating and that they had been left with the thankless task of breaking down tables and chairs and discarding steamers and balloons so that the hall would be in order for the next school day. The men, in contrast, had cracked into a case of beer intended to be shared with Morales and his staff during the day's festivities.

Morales's visit to Catavi belonged to broader patterns whereby the MAS party engaged rural supporters in events that reproduced familiar traditions of reciprocal, hierarchical authority (especially a form of immediately remunerated labor, or *mink'a*) including the hosting of meals and collective feasting. In Aymara and Quechua communities across the Andean region, acts of providing and sharing food have historically been key to establishing legitimate authority, placing a person in an asymmetrical relation to his or her subjects or workers.[16] When Morales left early and without eating, he reneged on the duties elaborated within that authority frame. However, this did not prevent Ayopayans from bringing expectations of asymmetrical return to bear on their understandings of MAS political events. More broadly, events like these and participants' evaluations of them raise questions about how agrarian traditions of authority were reclaimed and reworked as evaluative frames for judging MAS political leaders in the present.

Elvira's annoyance seemed to have stayed with her later that day, when staff gathered for what was supposed to be a celebratory *ch'alla* to mark the president's visit. After the llama sacrifice and the burning of the *q'oa* bundle, people broke into smaller groups to smoke hand-rolled cigarettes, chew coca leaves, and drink *chicha* and beer. As we stood around, Elvira asked (in Spanish): "Why do we say 'jallalla, jallalla'?" An older Quechua and Spanish-speaking unionist looked at her quizzically: "I don't believe that you don't know." Elvira sipped her beer defiantly and said: "I don't ask questions for which I know the answer." The question struck me as a remarkably strong expression of doubt about the meaning and fittingness of elements included in the event. While participants often took time after a *ch'alla* to discuss its relative strengths or a healer's individual style or materials, asking a question like this while still in a formal ritual context was unusual.[17]

Dressed in jeans and a leather coat rather than a *pollera* skirt, Elvira might be taken to have been expressing urban disdain toward Indigenous customs like sacrifices. She was college-educated and originally hailed from Oruro, but she came from a rural village and spoke Quechua fluently—key factors in popular evaluations of Indigeneity in Ayopaya. Unlike many of her municipal peers for whom this government post followed earlier work in their natal region, Elvira had lived in Independencia for fifteen years and her grandparents were from the area. Moreover, she was well versed in and sympathetic to *ch'alla* rites; we had attended several together earlier that spring. As a Quechua woman who was deeply familiar with such rites, publicly asking a clarifying question like this signaled a strident challenge to its organizers. It drew attention to a misfit between the variant of Indigeneity organizers had summoned and those sacrificial practices with which local guests were more familiar.

Elvira was not alone in her skepticism toward the event. A few minutes later, Julio came around distributing anise candy to guests. Still holding the anise in his cupped hands, Enrique Roca, a Quechua union leader in his forties, eyed his doubtfully. "Why do we eat these when we *ch'allar*? Is it because it is for sale, or what?" Echoing Elvira's skepticism about officials' use of the Aymara term *jallalla*, Enrique challenged the use of anise candy in the rite. His suggestion that the candy was used "because it is for sale" implied that its presence was a matter of convenience rather than a necessary or traditional aspect of the rite. That he added "or what" afterward, however, implied that such a reason was problematic and insufficient. This in turn surprised me given that ritual accoutrements like llama fetuses and coca have long been sold in regional markets, traveling on merchants' backs long distances from the high Andean mountain plateau (*puna*) as far as the subtropical low-lands (*yungas*). This question, like Elvira's, pointed to the broader concerns about origins fueled by MAS revivalist efforts, but it also illuminated a critical practice of public questioning. Neither Enrique nor Elvira were *ch'alla* novices; both were surely familiar with the use of nonlocal materials that in many circumstances underpin the potency of ritual forms.[18] As such, these two questions, asked in brazen earshot of other guests and the mayor, acted as dramatic public expressions of displeasure and skepticism toward the event and its government hosts.

This municipal event, and the questions that ailed it, occurred during a national moment of ever more explicit dissatisfaction with MAS party policies and leadership. Earlier that fall, Bolivia was gripped by nationwide protests opposing first the construction of the Villa Tunari–San Ignacio de Moxos Highway through the Isiboro Sécure National Park and Indigenous Territory and later the MAS party government's violent repression of protests opposing the road. A march of Indigenous associations and union groups reached the Presidential Palace in La Paz in October 2011, and protests continued through April 2012, a month after the *ch'alla*. In this atmosphere of heightened opposition toward MAS, particularly state development projects centered on road building, the mayor's appeal to the Pachamama to help secure road construction was risky. This event elicited doubt and worry about the variant of Indigeneity underlying MAS party policy designs, whether that vision of Indigeneity and its accompanying agendas aligned with local Ayopayan understandings of what it meant to be Indigenous and how that form of Indigeneity should shape the province's future.

Positioned in this broader context, Elvira's question about the term *jallalla* took as its jumping-off point the fact that this term is rarely used in rural locations and does not actually exist in Quechua, the first language of most municipal officials and the majority language in Ayopaya province.[19] *Jallalla*, generally used in an analogous way to English- or Spanish-language expressions like "long live" or "viva," was common at political rallies but not rural *ch'allas*. For instance, pro-Indigenous activists I knew in Cochabamba often used the phrase "Jallalla Bolivia, Jallalla MAS" as they dripped beer, alcohol, or *chicha* as an offering to the Pachamama during Friday evening *q'oa* events that drew together activists, volunteers, tourists, and interested cityfolk, and which were advertised in posters hung in the central plaza and shared zealously on the group's Facebook page. But Ayopaya was not the city, and the municipal parking lot was not a pro-Indigenous activist setting.

It was this slippage between rural and urban, governmental and nongovernment spaces that seemed to be at issue in Elvira and Enrique's questions. With its rash proclamations of life, this phrase lacked the humility usually modulating such rites—ones that treated life cycles as precarious and therefore incapable of being secured beforehand, either by sacrificial offerings or devotional languages. Likewise, participants' questions at the *ch'alla* hinted at the public discomforts MAS efforts to marry revivalist and extractivist ventures elicited. While everyone present was at least nominally a supporter of the MAS party (an unspoken condition of work in the municipal government at that time), participants' comments suggested palpable feelings of doubt and suspicion toward MAS revivalist agendas.

Against MAS party claims to be reviving Indigenous traditions, participants in this event seemed worried that living traditions were being ossified in problematic ways. Revivalist agendas that rural people were encountering made it newly necessary to draw firmer divisions among existing practices (usually cast in the legal language of "uses and customs") either as precolonial institutions worthy of protection or as colonial derivatives requiring displacement. As apparent in the union debates about municipal lines and valid land use configurations described in chapter 4, this split confronted limits in Ayopaya, a place where villagers frequently identified as Indigenous, Quechua, and/or Aymara, but also retained deep attachments to forms of authority, land tenure, and peasant collectivity crafted by earlier hacienda servitude and antihacienda militancy. It was not simply that such ossifications of tradition were wrong or overly simplistic, but that they were also being applied in ways that took political control away from Indigenous groups whose forms of political and social order did not ascribe to those models enshrined in various MAS government policies, including land collectivization, the integration of agrarian rituals in political events, and Indigenous language revitalization. My conversations with a municipal official and friend, Oscar, further clarified doubts about revivalist rituals—namely, about the conjoined risks of essentialism and division.

EXTRACTING THE HEART, RUPTURING A WORLD

Later that month, I joined Oscar Torrico (a member of Ayopaya's municipal staff) to discuss government revivalism projects, like the *ch'alla*. As we gripped hot mugs of *mate de coca* and sat around our friend's kitchen table,

Oscar described the difficulties facing institutional projects of Indigenous revivalism. When I asked him about his position on MAS efforts to revitalize or dig up (*rescatar*) marginalized Indigenous traditions, Oscar paused. "Look, it is difficult to recuperate something that is already lost," he said. "Only the activities that remain will be cordoned off, and thereby somewhat 'recuperated.' Because really you don't have anything you can recover." Despite his pessimism, Oscar took considerable pride in his rural upbringing, even recounting how he had donned a traditional Quechua poncho and sandals during his final oral exam for his master's degree in sociology.

Two weeks earlier, we had visited Sarahuayto together when I accompanied Oscar, who had returned for the Virgen de Candelaria saint's day celebration, playing the pan flute with his father. Despite originating in earlier hacienda servitude, villagers still honored the saint during two nights of raucous merrymaking centered on copious drink, flute-playing, a chapel service, and an animal sacrifice. Oscar did not, however, see those practices as confirmation of a governmental model of Indigeneity. He explained: "The whole record is lost and that's it; the only things that remain are attitudes, fiestas, for better or for worse. Perhaps before it was different. We do not know. The *q'oa* [a sacrificial offering] was more spiritual and was a calling to the Pachamama for equilibrium so that she gives you results. It was sacred, and the fiesta was only a complement. Now, people trade the *moseñada* and *tarqueda* [highland dances] for flags and brass bands. This is how you mix in other things while always preserving your form, the rhythm, its qualities."

Oscar's account raised doubts about MAS claims to recuperate an ostensibly "pure" Indigeneity, a pillar of MAS governance since 2006 and also a key aspect of late twentieth-century missionary activity in the region.[20] Such projects sought to counteract the losses and transformations wrought by Spanish colonialism, with its violent extirpation of non-Christian "idols" and associated superstitions, including animal sacrifice.[21] Elsewhere, in Cochabamba city, I had spoken with pro-Indigenous activists who saw patron saints, particularly the Virgen del Carmen who was housed in the church in Quillacollo, as unwelcome Spanish incursions that should be displaced and Indigenous people encouraged to pay their respects to precolonial deities, like the Pachamama, instead. By contrast, Oscar emphasized enduring attachments to forms of devotional practice that he had grown up with in the village of Sarahuayto (see chapter 2). These included annual festivities for the Virgen de la Candelaria, a saint said to have been introduced or "carried" from the La Paz lowlands (*yungas*) to the village by the hacienda masters. As elsewhere, in

Sarahuayto the hacienda masters had required workers and servants to attend fiestas to pay their respects to the Catholic saints and church.[22] Despite her local origins in the hacienda system, Quechua villagers in Sarahuayto (and elsewhere) retained strong attachments to this saint, casting doubt over governmental efforts to bifurcate present-day life into two categories: "purer" Indigenous traditions and imposed colonial institutions.

In our conversation Oscar made explicit his discomfort with state-led Indigenous revivalism, a discomfort shared by other government staff attending the municipal *ch'alla*. While hybridity is a hallmark of Latin American *mestizaje* (racial admixture as cultural assimilation), Oscar's vision did not imply a smooth unification of colonial and native pasts.[23] He instead emphasized the difficulties of translating (or assimilating) Quechua and Aymara ritual practices into non-Indigenous frameworks of thought, including the general concept of Indigeneity. To Oscar, Indigeneity as an abstract category was an outcome of officials (and anthropologists) "cordoning off" exemplary institutions from broader domains of cultural overlay and historical amalgamation.[24] For this reason he challenged the Bolivian state's co-optation of Indigeneity as a means to constrain and domesticate Indigenous difference. His account resonated with long-standing scholarly critiques of Andean revivalism as the spatial imposition of a romanticized, bounded model of Indigeneity. For instance, Thomas Abercrombie (1998: 22) warned, there is a danger that scholars write "a cultural-resistance success story solely by privileging terms that carry 'indigenous' inflections: ayllu rather than *cantón*, *jiliqata* instead of *cacique*, rituals directed towards mountains rather than towards saints." While these critiques were initially expressed several decades ago, Oscar's critique demonstrates that they remain pertinent given the centrality of these more bounded ideas of culture in guiding MAS revivalist policies.

Whereas many of the scholars, including anthropologists, employed in the MAS party government during Morales's presidency tended to foreground continuities in rural highland practices and social institutions from the precolonial era to the present, Oscar instead emphasized the difficulty of establishing any kind of certainty about traditions that were substantially transformed more than five centuries earlier.[25] Addressing the violent processes of transformation and loss elicited by the region's colonial and more recent hacienda past did not, for Oscar, require disavowing the continued significance of certain Indigenous traditions for rural life in the present. As he explained, Quechua and Aymara forms like *ayni* (reciprocity), *mink'a* (labor exchange), or *mit'a* (rotating labor) "are very ample [*complejo*]. Until now I do not have a concrete definition of what these words are.... They can be very large or very small. They exist within an attitude."

Oscar's background as a monolingual Quechua-speaker here made him skeptical about the revivalist assumption that vast, overarching Quechua concepts could be smoothly translated into Spanish, and into Spanish-language ideas of labor and exchange institutions. (Oscar learned Spanish relatively late in life, in middle school, where classmates bullied him for his Quechua accent.) In light of this background, Oscar saw Quechua forms such as *ayni* not as circumscribed cultural institutions but as *sensibilities* to be cultivated at the level of bodily attunement and sensing (*palpar*). For this reason, he had argued, their conversion into reified institutions required them to be artificially "cordoned off" from other practices to be protected.

Alongside this critical stance toward MAS revivalism, however, Oscar elaborated a deeply felt form of Indigeneity that persisted and was open to reelaboration through bodily practices, including fiestas. Oscar had been among the tireless dancers—what participants called *chiriguanos*—whose melodic flute play persisted into the early dawn hours.[26] When we spoke, Oscar explained the reasoning behind the flute-play. "You begin to blow [on the flute] so that the winds calm themselves," he said. "This is the idea. This is why we blow, we blow. It begins to rain in the first weeks of December and so we begin to blow and to help, we climb until Piña Laguna [Angry Lake] and play *pinquillo* [a six-hole flute]." While the festivals of the dry season, including the Fiesta de la Virgen de Guadalupe, seek equilibrium, in Candelaria "you're looking for conflict." Oscar continued: "If there is a good fight it is a fertile year, [the harvest] will be good."[27] Despite his concerns about romanticized governmental treatments of Indigeneity and the changes that revivalist projects could elicit for given practices, Oscar emphasized the existence of rural Quechua and Aymara collectivities forged through tragic histories of colonial loss and recombination. This perception explicitly drew from his background in Sarahuayto, which had been among the largest of the hacienda estates in direct proximity to the municipal center of Independencia and where his own grandparents had labored (see chapter 2).

In this account Oscar held up aspects of the Virgen de la Candelaria festival, including devotional flute-play and dance, as exemplars of the possibility of fostering Quechua and Aymara forms of collectivity—marked in his evocation of "we"—in company with figures and entities introduced by Spanish colonialism, in this case Catholic saints. This festivity for the saint Candelaria, he explained, has "existed and is a cultural expression, obviously of an existing culture transplanted here or brought from another place. But as far as I have been able to tell... There are clues, you can intuit, feel [*palpar*], see." Here, the pause in his speech can be perceived as an effort to place into language a fraught sense of attachment to Candelaria despite the fact that she belongs to a broader set of impositions that occurred through the extremely oppressive hacienda system. That religious figures like her were initially bound up in forced servitude, including of Oscar's grandparents, did not foreclose lingering attachments to them as key sites for cultivating a regionally grounded sense of Indigenous belonging. Rather than seeking to erase practices introduced by the expansion of Mestizo landholding and forced labor, including saints and labor gifts deriving from hacienda patronage, Oscar outlined a form of rural belonging defined by double-edged attachments to these impure pasts.

My conversations with Oscar and the skepticism expressed at the municipal *ch'alla* showed how government-sponsored rituals supplied occasions for new revelations about the disjuncture between revivalist approaches to Indigeneity and on-the-ground attachments to history and Quechua belonging. Recalling Elvira's question about *jallalla* and Enrique's doubts about the anise candy, Oscar critiqued MAS's revivalist agenda for constraining, rather than merely recuperating, existing Indigenous practices of feasting, sponsorship, and ritual as they were converted into more reified, bounded objects that could be celebrated and circulated in media coverage of rural MAS events (such as in photos of Morales with the *T'antawawas* or "bread babies" in Catavi, described in the opening to this chapter). Combined with widespread outcry about recent INRA land collectivization schemes (chapter 4), many participants at these events were deeply skeptical about the government's proclaimed defense of Indigeneity, and of the consequences of its revitalization for local control over the terms of land use and belonging in the countryside.

In these governmental attempts to draw new dividing lines between a hybridized present and a purer past, MAS policies produced a form of Indigeneity that was difficult, if not impossible, for contemporary people to uphold. In part attesting to this difficulty, Oscar narrated the Sarahuayto festivities we had recently participated in as somehow anachronistic, characteristics of a lost "before." The Candelaria celebrations had not included flags or brass bands but rather pan flutes. However, Oscar's emphasis on devotional activities focused on saints also showed the obverse to be true. In the face

INDIO HERMANO, TU NOS HAS ENSEÑADO
A RESISTIR CON DIGNIDAD . . .
POR NUESTRAS VENAS CORRE
SANGRE DE LIBERACION . NUESTROS
ANCESTROS NOS PROTEGIERON Y
GUIARAN A LA RESISTENCIA CONTRA
LOS GOLPES Y PALOS DEL FASCISTA
QUE NO PODRAN CALLAR NUESTROS GRITOS
DE REBELDIA, IGUALDAD Y LIBERTAD
¡JALLALLA PACHAMAMA!

FIGURE 21. Graffiti pictures ancestral Indigenous struggle against Criollo and Mestizo violence, Cochabamba city, 2010. Photo by author.

of well-publicized efforts to portray Evo's support for Indigenous revitalization, Ayopayans like Oscar nonetheless expressed deep attachments to religious figures that overspilled the trappings of this revivalist frame of national Indigeneity, one that pitted Indigenous ancestors against Mestizo fascists. Oscar summoned an ethical debt to saints, and not only Quechua ancestors and kin (Figure 21).

The divisive impacts of the MAS government's increasing influence over ways of defining and reviving Indigeneity worried people at the Institúto Nacional de Reforma Agrarian (INRA), too. When I was conducting fieldwork at their headquarters in Cochabamba, I met Ricardo Quispe, a bilingual Quechua official and Spanish-speaking INRA official in his late sixties. At that time, he led rural "field brigades" to places slated to be titled in the state's land regularization program. As we waited for lunch one day, Ricardo shared his thoughts about the government's new bilingual education program. I learned that Ricardo was particularly alarmed by the government's new requirement that written Quechua adopt a standardized alphabet based on a three-vowel orthography established in Peru in 1985, a process Ricardo equated with the violent splitting of an existing body or life.[28] Repurposing the sacrificial logics that guide *ch'allas*, he noted: "This is like extracting a heart and putting it in another body. This *crime* is being committed against us." The program sought to standardize Quechua, but it also imbued state and international authorities and rights-based commissions with the power to oversee and adjudicate proper usage and orthography. Ricardo perceived this move as criminal, revivalism acting as a perversion of sacrifice.[29] If, in *ch'allas*, animals are slaughtered and their hearts offered to deities, this policy instead guts living languages in favor of a new hybrid that strives to pass as a recuperated Indigeneity.

For both Oscar and Ricardo, state Indigenous revitalization programs risked producing a new kind of Indigeneity that was uncanny, organized around an artificial purity that made it unfamiliar to its ostensible bearers. Oscar shared these concerns, but he also offered a more hopeful alternative to Ricardo's vision of Indigenous revitalization as violent dissection. This alternate centered on what he called the "form" of devotional practices, a term that drew together villagers' deep affective ties to a set of ambivalent colonial inheritances including Catholic saints, Indigenous highland traditions of flute-play, and asymmetrical exchange traditions. Against urban accounts of Ayopayans as pathologically "determined by [their] hacienda past," Oscar reclaimed these felt attachments to places and histories as a basis for Quechua belonging in the present. His account helped me to understand how the doubts expressed by participants did not foreclose deeply held attachments to the practices in question.

This was particularly true of *ch'allas*, which, like Candelaria and other devotional festivities, were widely popular and highly valued in Ayopaya. Agrarian rituals offered venues for contending with environmental and social risks, including those produced by the mercury runoff from neighboring mines, but they were also sites of revelation about the transformative impacts of MAS revivalism.[30] Against MAS efforts to cleave the revolutionary present from a recent hacienda past—an effort apparent in the use of property regularization to alienate land from hacienda labor economies—Ayopayans like Oscar reframed Indigeneity in light of Quechua villagers' attunements to their abiding attachments to religious figures and exchange practices that had been introduced in the course of the province's unsettling labor past. This suggests how new relations, and new relations to tradition, came into being not only through revivalist state programs but also through the critiques and historical revelations they elicit.

This municipal *ch'alla* and the debates that accompanied it reflected a novel political moment centered on governmental efforts to rewrite the boundaries between Indigenous traditions and the Bolivian state.[31] Key to this project was Bolivia's 2009 Constitution, with its inclusion of Quechua and Aymara concepts, as well as the Law of the Rights of Mother Nature (Ley 71 de Derechos de la Madre Tierra), passed in December 2010. Cast in a broader historical frame, the municipality's hosting of the *ch'alla* was unprecedented, given earlier colonial extirpation of non-Catholic religiosities and colonial approaches to Indigenous sacrifice in particular.

However, while these ritual forms were being drawn into state spheres in more explicit ways under Morales, their inclusion in institutional politics was not new. Agrarian rituals have long been crucial to Andean people's engagements with productive landscapes, materializing relationships between authority, exchange, and sacrifice (see chapter 2). Such rituals assumed new importance in twenty-first-century projects of Indigenous revivalism and Indigenous rights-based development.[32] To acknowledge the crafting and recrafting of Indigeneity through legal systems is not to deny the existence of alternate value systems or ontologies, but it does force a rethinking of the romantic account of Indigeneity as a subterranean force that has waited, intact, outside of state forms and only now erupts onto the scene of legal and political history.

Events like the municipal *ch'alla* and Ayopayans' reworking of existing models of magnanimous authority complicate an understanding of emergence as a reconnection with Indigenous roots elicited by ethnic revivalist movements.[33] In these cases it arose also as a mode of political intervention with which to demand structural transformations and to challenge Indigenous peoples' erasure from institutional centers of political deliberation within an earlier liberal-democratic order as well as in more recent identity-based reform projects in Bolivia. Attention to the critical workings of ritual offers a crucial guard against the tendency, apparent in many works of the new "ontological turn," to romanticize Indigenous being and attachments to other-than-humans as a salve for the disorders of a late liberal, capitalist present.[34]

By casting Indigeneity as largely external to modernity, such arguments risk perniciously constraining what can count as legitimate Indigenous political engagements only to those that uphold an impossible standard of purity from colonial history.[35] These debates hold special significance in the Andes, where religious practices and meanings have long been used to challenge the expansion of Spanish colonial power through capitalist systems of property but where early Spanish administrators also explicitly incorporated and repurposed precolonial and Incaic religious traditions, as I discussed in the introduction.[36] As such, characterizing such *ch'alla* rituals like these as moments of insurgent Indigeneity (an appearance of a concealed but intact Indigenous ontology) are deeply unsatisfactory.[37]

In the municipal *ch'alla*, villagers and government workers used the occasion to engage critically with the inconsistences of MAS's political project. This included posing questions about the proper performance of the rite but also, in other occasions, questioning the paradoxes of MAS's revivalism. Governmental support for Indigenous land collectivization here went hand-in-hand with the violent repression of Indigenous protesters opposed to the TIPNIS highway. For critics of MAS in Ayopaya these recent events complicated a revivalist narrative of Indigenous culture as something "outside" of the state that the state now was going to integrate or revive. These risks have been especially palpable in Ayopaya, where Quechua villagers have long been characterized by progressive reformers as problematically entrenched in Mestizo institutions, and where the immersion of Indigenous communities and Mestizo landholders foreclosed the ability to gain recognition as an Indigenous territory. Essentialist ideals of Indigenous alterity mobilized within MAS revivalism, like romantic academic models of Indigenous culture, can here end up producing "new regimes of inequality or hyper-marginality of supposedly insufficient or 'decultured' Indigenous populations."[38] Remaining vigilant about this romantic separation of state and Indigeneity was, for people like Oscar, especially urgent given how such romances had legitimated MAS policy interventions while masking the government's brutal repression of Indigenous movements at odds with its policy designs.

Put simply, rural Ayopayans took issue with the ways that, within MAS revivalism, Indigeneity itself came to be hardened or reified in ways that approximated the fixing of property. While that reification did not fully succeed—apparent in the sharp critiques made by participants in the municipal *ch'alla* and at INRA like Enrique, Elvira and Ricardo, MAS revitalization efforts still did politicize older practices and subject them to new structures of evaluation based on the criteria of authenticity linked to an aspirational continuity from the precolonial era. The anise candy, devotional languages

(Jallalla), musical instruments, dances, and even saints here arose as "quasi-objects" (Latour 1993: 137) that circulated in MAS-led Indigenous revivalism but also operated as sites for contesting and recasting the meanings underlaying that project. In the municipal *ch'alla*, as in Oscar's account of Candelaria, such practices served as tangible sites for destabilizing the value systems introduced through MAS revivalist projects. Enduring attachments to forms of practice derived from a history established through the uneven conjuncture of colonial and precolonial practices could not be accounted for by the presumptions of purity that implicitly underlay MAS's pro-Indigenous stance. That stance denied forms of belonging rooted in villagers' deeply felt attachments to institutions that escaped classification either in Bolivia's colonial or precolonial pasts.

In this regard, the *ch'alla* ritual can be interpreted as an occasion for metacommentary on the place of tradition in MAS political designs, and, for Ayopayans in particular, on the revivalist erasure of regional expressions of posthacienda Indigeneity. While Ayopayans at this *ch'alla* used the occasion to point out the MAS government's imperfect ascription to revivalist ideals, at other political events they also drew from regionally elaborated exchange traditions as evaluative paradigms by which to judge and destabilize the legitimacy of MAS party leadership.

EVO AS GODFATHER, OR NATIONALISM
AS FAMILY ROMANCE

Every year before Christmas, rural villages and towns prepare for one of the most important school events of the year, the *fiestas de promoción* or graduation ceremonies in which school-age children are celebrated for their educational progress. As celebrations for first generation graduates, these occasions supply important opportunities for families to—literally—shower schoolchildren in money, confetti, and affection (Figure 22). A push for rural, Indigenous education was a staple of MAS policy, and state development initiatives around rural schooling supplied robust educational possibilities for many Ayopayans.

In December 2011, I traveled from Independencia to Rami, a small village and former hacienda a half-hour trip away, with Pavel Camacho and his wife, famed *chicha* brewers. (Pavel was the gentleman who lost access to the land he hoped to convert into a chirimoya orchard, as I discussed in chapter 4.) They

FIGURE 22. The *madrina* of the fiesta makes her way to a graduate's home, Santa Rosa (Ayopaya province) 2011. Photo by author.

came with a truck-bed filled with gas cylinders of home-brewed corn beer to sell. Sandra Hinojosa, a Quechua businesswoman and business student in Cochabamba, approached the truck to buy a pitcher of *chicha*. We began chatting, and I learned that she came from a family of hacienda masters in the area, who, like Pavel's family, had started out as Quechua *forasteros* who gradually were able to buy their way out of servitude. Sandra held a vital role in the festivities, where she had agreed to the "cargo" of serving as the *madrina* (godmother) for the event. Later that day, more than two hundred guests gathered at the school soccer stadium for a graduation ceremony in which education officials delivered speeches and handed out degree certificates. Afterward, families hosted guests for meals and drink; guests in turn gave the graduates money gifts to be used for continued schooling or to aid with the transition to a permanent job.

Celebrations at the village level are typically sponsored by a former alumnus, a wealthy resident or relative, or even a state official. The *promociones* in

FIGURE 23. A sign marks funding through the Bolivia Cambia. Evo
Cumple program, Independencia, 2011. Photo by author.

2011 were sponsored by two people: Sandra and President Morales. To fulfill
her duties for this role, Sandra had paid village administrators two hundred
dollars, a sizable chunk of money in these rural parts. The *padrino* (godfather) of the *promociones*, as the school's principal announced loudly through
crackling speakers from the roof of the school beside the stadium, was "President Evo Morales Ayma." Although Morales was personally absent from
the event, his administration had supplied funds to the school, aiding in
the construction of a new soccer stadium earlier that year. The stadium, like
Independencia's new stadium and a regional hospital, was funded through
a new rural development program supported by the Morales government
(Figure 23).

These infrastructural initiatives belonged to a policy "Bolivia Cambia.

Evo Cumple" (Bolivia Changes. Evo Complies), active in the countryside from 2007 to 2018.[39] While government funding for such rural development initiatives was unsurprising, I was struck by the announcement of Morales as the *padrino*. This was a position typically reserved for the wealthy kin of former *hacendados*, like Sandra, or well-off newcomers, such as myself (I had been asked, on another occasion, to serve as the *madrina* of music for the saint's day celebrations in the neighboring village of Machaca). In this event old *hacendado* families and new political leaders inhabited parallel positions of leadership. As formal cosponsors, moreover, they partook of similar paradigms of authority—deploying the idiom of parental beneficence afforded by the language of godparenting.

This event, with its facile likening of President Morales to the usual wealthy rural sponsors, highlighted how populist leaders sought legitimacy in part by embodying older figurations of *hacendado* generosity. While Morales was not present, casting him as a godparent made institutional distributions of rural development monies legible within existing idioms of rural sponsorship rooted in kinship imaginaries. Even though he was physically absent, this recourse to a familiar, kinship-based language of vertical aid personified rural development programs. Elsewhere, I had heard his supporters explicitly compare Morales to a struggling "father," challenging critics for placing undue burdens on him with requests for additional subsidies and government support.

While part of Morales's appeal in the countryside has always been rooted in a sort of populist discourse characterizing him as a people's leader, however, I was surprised to find state programs of Indigenous aid formulated through this vertical kinship language of godparentage—especially in view of the objections to clientelism voiced by office workers at INRA (see chapter 3). Sponsorship practices are common throughout Latin America, but in Ayopaya these relations were colored by earlier arrangements of *hacendado* sponsorship in *ch'allas* and religious holidays. For instance, political leaders and union officials are celebrated in much the same way as late *hacendado* sponsors and *patrones*: publicly adorned with wreaths of flowers, confetti, and usually but not always, an appreciable degree of drunkenness. This is also how Morales was received upon earlier visits to Independencia as well as in Catavi, described earlier, as was Sandra, the *madrina* of the festivities that day.

This idiom of redistributive aid based on sponsorship shaped the official events that day, but it also provided a framework of sociality within which other guests, including me, engaged with graduates. That afternoon, people made house visits to relatives and acquaintances. Both in houses and in the village public market—converted into a dance floor—local adults, guests, and government officials showed their support for schoolchildren. They stood in a reception line waiting to shake hands with the graduates, receiving a flower necklace and a handful of confetti on their head, while bills of five, ten, or twenty bolivianos were pinned to the graduates' shirts. In the *promociones*, monetary distribution was given individuated form in the bodily proximity of host and guest/sponsor. Bills accumulated, flapping in the wind on graduate's shirts and dresses, as if illustrating the ability for bodies to be transformed by money. Here, as Jonathan Parry (1989: 65) pointed out, money in the shape of banknotes were not just accompaniments but themselves agents: by way of this practice, not just the students but the money was being "baptized"—a process that then allowed for future offspring to breed and grow.

As a guest, I too was summoned to this role, carefully pinning a twenty boliviano bill to one graduate's shirt as he sprinkled confetti on my head as a gesture of thanks. In Bolivia, like elsewhere in Latin America, money and representations of money—especially paper money or cash—is key to devotional offerings made to the Saints as located in *imágenes* (figurines) (Figure 24). Devotees leave them bills or miniature versions of the objects they hope to obtain.[40] The graduates' bodies, recalling devotional figurines like the Virgen de Carmen, hereby carried money but also the potential for future, accumulative wealth.

On the one hand, this event can be understood as evidence of the MAS party government's effort to instrumentalize rural kinship regimes to gain rural support and to remind villagers of Morales's importance as a political leader sympathetic to their plight. However, on the other hand, the *promociones* also allowed Quechua villagers and their children to make claims upon well-off Mestizos and national political leaders. For rural Quechua schoolchildren these bills can assure a smooth transition to urban centers for further education or permanent work. On both fronts—as a structure of rural political legitimacy and of sociality among unequal parties in the countryside—these sponsorship practices highlight aid relations in Ayopaya that shared with hacienda customs an arc of asymmetrical aid across entrenched hierarchies (made most explicit by Flora Soliz in chapter 1).

Most notably, through this process political leaders in the MAS party, including Morales, came to occupy structurally similar positions to former

FIGURE 24. Imitation US bills offered at a shrine for the Virgin de Urkupiña in Quillacollo, 2011. Photo by author.

hacendados and their living kin. Despite centuries-long agrarian reforms oriented toward dismantling hacienda mastery, both the kin of earlier *hacendados*, like Sandra and government officials, drew from and recast earlier paradigms of asymmetrical aid. This in turn illuminates the incomplete displacement of asymmetrical exchange relations by liberal, rights-based reform projects from the early twentieth century onward.

Disagreements about how people in positions of authority should embody their power and what duties, if any, this might entail to those in subordinate positions, were at the heart of a conversation I had with Ayopayan interlocutors about the nation's famous tin baron, Simón Iturri Patiño, born near there. We had gathered to carry on merrymaking after the town's Carnival celebration in February 2011. As the night drew on, a heated debate arose concerning Patiño—known as the Andean Rockefeller. Patiño was born in Santiváñez, in the high mountains of the southern Cochabamba region, and several of his tin mines are located in Ayopaya. These mines have been riddled with political conflicts since the 1940s. In 1941 a Patiño-era mine was the site of violent labor suppression during the "Catavi massacre." Most recently, in 2014, clashes between unionized miners and military police left forties miners injured and two dead. Likewise, the Kami mine in Ayopaya, which was still used to mine tungsten and tin at the time of my fieldwork, was blockaded by unionists who were violently dispersed by armed military and police in 2011.[41]

Likely elicited by recent tumult at his namesake mine, the conversation that evening hinged on how to position Patiño in the nation's past. After a game of cards among eight of us, two men in their late thirties—Doña Flora's son Paco Soliz and Tito Chambi, the grandson of hacienda workers who was designing Independencia's new MAS-funded hospital—debated Patiño's place in Bolivian history. Both, educated men who had been raised speaking Quechua in Independencia but now resided in Cochabamba and Oruro respectively, agreed that Patiño had been a grand figure. Tito, however, noted that Patiño had been a wonderful nationalist who supported the growth of Bolivia's economy and the arts, while Paco recalled that Patiño had sent all his riches to Spain: he was hence a "Criollo type." Disagreeing sharply, Tito replied, allowing his fist to fall heavily on the table to punctuate the italicized word: "No, he was an *Indio,* an *Indio* like you and me."

Like historians of Patiño, Tito and Paco could not agree on how his biography should be told—namely, it was unclear whether they should remember Patiño as a Cholo, an illegitimate child of mixed Quechua and Spanish heritage who grew up working in his mother's store in Oruro, or rather as a Mestizo, a person of Spanish descent, who attended private schools and went on to become, during World War II, one of the wealthiest five men in the world. As this case lays bare, here local assessments of authority also set the terms of self-identification: an "us" built on shared commitments to a model of generous leadership.

In this discussion Tito appealed to asymmetrical aid as a distinctly Indigenous system of leadership, and in turn the basis of true Bolivianness. To be a true Bolivian, a nationalist, was to keep and invest one's wealth in the motherland, to support the arts and economic growth: in short, to make wealth the basis for a patronal position, as Rockefeller had in the United States. Both men were at that time supporters of Evo Morales and on other occasions had expressed to me their "pride" (*orgullo*) for their Quechua Indigenous heritage. However, in this conversation Paco challenged a national historiography to reframe Patiño as an extractivist colonizer who made money off the labor of underpaid Indigenous Bolivians. Tito, by contrast, reclaimed asymmetrical aid as an Indigenous sensibility and the basis for judging a subject's ethical character. More than a colonial holdover that "stays with" peasants for better or for worse (see chapters 3 and 5), Tito instead saw a willingness to embody wealth with generosity as the basis for a sensibility that he cast as properly "Indian." Tito implied that, if a leader retained felt attachment to rural Bolivians and their plight, that sentiment would stand in the way of his support for the neocolonial extraction of minerals—in the case of Patiño, imperialist lines of flight that transported tin from Bolivia to Germany, England, and France.

Alongside recent labor-based conflicts at Patiño's former mines, this disagreement occurred at a time of growing nationwide dissatisfaction with the Morales regime, which, many felt, had reneged on earlier promises of rural aid. That same month of February 2011, widespread protests by union groups, students, and middle-class Bolivians challenged state cuts in national subsidies to sugar, grain, and other food staples.[42] These protests recalled earlier conflicts over the "nationalization" of natural resources at stake in Bolivia's water and gas wars, in 2000 and 2003, respectively. Tito had taken part in the 2000 uprisings against the privatization of the city's municipal water supply company, avidly recalling his escape behind the hospital in Cochabamba to avoid the tear gas and enclosing police barricade.

While neither Tito nor Paco mentioned Morales by name, their argument touched on delicate questions of redistribution and return that were crucial to broader debates about MAS leadership at that time. Cuts to food subsidies elicited strong feelings of betrayal for rural constituents; they took the cuts as evidence of MAS's growing indifference toward Morales's so-called Indigenous or peasant base, including people who knew him from his childhood as a llama herder and, after that, his time spent as a coca-grower in the Chapare lowlands. This sentiment was stated most strongly in publicized comments by Guaraní political leader Celso Padilla, who in 2010 charged Morales for "thinking himself a king, and new master of indigenous peoples."[43] Morales, he concluded, therefore "needs to be decolonized."

In their argument that night, Tito and Paco offered a way to make sense of Morales's position in the Ayopayan countryside in light of earlier, if conjoined, histories of colonial mastery and Andean redistribution. During his visits to the province in 2011, President Evo Morales fashioned himself as a benevolent leader in ways that recalled earlier, "good" hacienda masters:

municipal officials formally declared him godfather of education in Rami, he hosted a feast in Catavi, and he was a sponsor of a range of infrastructural projects ranging from the new schools celebrated in the graduation *promociones* to a new hospital and new soccer stadium in Independencia. Rather than liken these practices to clientelist political manipulation, Tito instead reclaimed asymmetrical aid as part of a distinctly Indigenous sensibility and orientation to wealth at odds with colonial frugality and greed. Partaking in this exchange tradition, to his mind, was what made certain authorities *Indian* and not problematic "Criollo types." Tito's effort to bind generosity to true Bolivian *Indio*-ness, combined with critiques of Evo for his shirking of feasting duties and his self-fashioning as a greedy master, highlight the ways that people drew from older figurations of *hacendado* mastery in their judgments of MAS governance and of President Morales himself.

In these narrations Ayopayans expressed felt attachments to forms of history at odds with a more hegemonic nationalist archive of precolonial institutions that MAS party programs aimed to revive. Notably, this paradigm's efficacy as an evaluative frame did not rely on origins. No one claimed that this aid tradition had roots exclusively in the precolonial Andes or in colonial subjection. In this regard, Tito's elevating of aid to an evaluative frame points to the dynamic ways that people reclaimed seemingly impure histories of hacienda authority, like Oscar's earlier evocation of his felt devotion for the saint Candelaria, as rightfully Indigenous. These critical appropriations highlight the continued importance of rural attachments to paradigms of authority and ethical behavior at odds with modernizing ideas of horizontal citizenship and equal rights. These sensibilities toward power and wealth continued not only to organize people, money, and labor but also shaped rural Ayopayans' critical evaluations of the failures and abandonments of contemporary economic elites and political leaders in the province.

While labor organizing from the 1940s to more recent, post-2006 antiservitude land titling sought to dismantle hierarchy as oppression, some Ayopayans instead wielded ideals of asymmetrical aid as a basis on which to judge MAS party leaders. Earlier and ongoing forms of racialized dispossession would not be resolved by property alone, either as land rights or assurances of individual profit. Rather, for many interlocutors in Ayopaya, legitimate Indigenous political leadership hinged on return: the flow of money, resources, and developmental aid back to impoverished Bolivians. To my surprise, these ideals of return revived an older figure of the fatherlike *patrón* or master, the godparent that had long been central to rural Indigenous families' ability to secure their children's education. Here, the knotting of exchange—the binding of authority to redistribution, of present to past—operated through a critical and expansive refashioning of earlier idioms of kinship-based aid in the countryside.

INDIGENIZING BUREAUCRACY: FROM OPPOSITION TO CO-ELABORATION

Following Evo Morales's election to the presidency in 2005, MAS political legitimacy was bound tightly to the common argument that Morales not only represented Bolivia's Indigenous poor majority but *was* himself part of this population. By way of his personal biography, the argument went, he embodied the average impoverished, Indigenous Bolivian.[44] In Ayopaya too, villagers claimed "Evo" as their own. In Bolivia, as in other earlier cases, like Eva Perón in Argentina, this relation implied a presumption of unmediated access to leaders.[45] This was achieved in part through a series of local media productions on the part of regional supporters of MAS.

A historical reenactment coproduced by Independencia's municipal government and a local filmmaker titled *Q'arwa Awatiris* (2008), Aymara for "llama herders," combines photographs, video interviews with villagers, and historical reenactment to trace Evo Morales's early life shepherding llamas in the region (Figure 25).[46] The cover for the DVD portrays Morales as a rural Indigenous farmer familiar with the challenges of llama-herding and as someone integrated into provincial customs of sponsorship and aid—the photograph shows Morales dancing, adorned with a wreath of flowers. This image implicitly links into highland understandings of herding as a metaphor for leadership.[47] The municipal government's production of this film suggests how, in Ayopaya, there was significant interest in Morales, not only as a sympathetic political leader but as one of their own—as someone who superseded the constraints of Bolivian racial and class hierarchies to become *their* Indigenous president.[48] The film, importantly, also served as a venue to speak directly to the president. As an interviewee notes in the film 7:35-minute mark: "I would like for him to visit us, to remember the places where he walked, and perhaps to help us in some way."

At the time of my fieldwork, Ayopayan villagers and townsfolk in Independencia often expressed deep ambivalence toward Morales, whom they both celebrated as their own but whose growing distance and seeming aban-

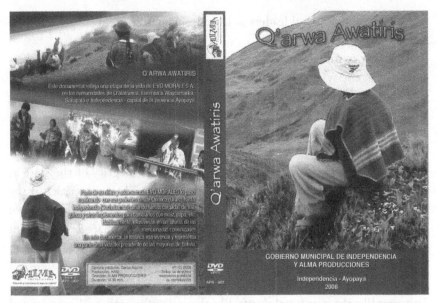

FIGURE 25. Cover jacket design for the 2008 film *Q'arwa Awatiris,* filmed and produced in Independencia, 2012. Photo by author.

donment of connections to his childhood home struck them as deeply problematic. In Ayopaya the state's appeal to constituents through idioms of elite sponsorship also carried with it possibilities for evaluating the president and what appeared to many as his rebuff of a more exemplary embodiment of leadership premised on direct answerability and remembered obligations to place.[49] These models of magnanimous authority were frequently applied both to earlier hacienda masters and populist political leaders.

According to elderly people who worked in agrarian estates, masters invited servants for Christmas and patron saint's day holidays, where they shared food and drink. Later, in the 1950s, political leaders also feasted with rural families. Among others, revolutionary president Victor Paz Estenssoro and earlier president Gualberto Villarroel (1943–46) both acted as godparents and ritual sponsors for rural union leaders and peasants. In addition, at that time INRA engineers were welcomed with feasts of chicken. Regional elites like Doña Flora or the mine owner Martín kept up these traditions, butchering animals and hosting villagers both to honor the Pachamama and to mark their relations as *waleq patrones*—generous, responsive masters. In this broader historical context the municipal *ch'alla*, Candelaria festivities, and practices of ritual feasting worked to position MAS municipal and federal political leaders as beneficent masters who supported their subject-citizens.

One way to understand these practices is to accept a discourse of assimilative Indigeneity as put forth by MAS's project of revivalist governance: the argument that Indigenous forms of knowledge and tradition too long excluded were now, under President Morales, finally gaining recognition, dignity, and inclusion.[50] According to such an argument, what was at stake in the municipal *ch'alla* or in Morales's posing with rural Indigenous supporters was a purposeful effort to destabilize the integrity of the state as outside, above, or merely standing for "the people." Instead, critics of the *ch'alla*, like Oscar, invite us not to lose sight of how long-run histories of colonial legal and missionary intervention shaped and reshaped the terms of Indigeneity not simply as a matter of recognition (e.g., of a tribute category) but in terms of the responsibilities that accompany specific paradigms of authority, as given expression in devotional practices and political events.[51] In events like the municipal *ch'alla*, like the earlier feasts that villagers hosted for INRA officials, participants asked questions that blurred binary oppositions between modern governance and an external Indigeneity, as well as between hacienda impositions and practices rooted in an ostensibly more pure precolonial past.[52]

That such critiques emanated from government spaces, such as the municipal *ch'alla*, raises questions about the slippages between state and nonstate places. It illuminates the MAS party's claims to sovereignty as partial, contingent on forms of reception that are outside or seemingly beyond it.[53] At the same time, an account of the increasing institutionalization of exchange would not be complete without returning to Oscar's point about the entailments of revivalist inclusion. In contrast to villagers' militant demands for aid and accountability from *hacendado* kin, demands for aid from mining bosses and political leaders required institutional affiliations and were more heavily mediated by federal and municipal governments, INRA, and the nationwide COB workers' union. In particular, government funding for schools, soccer stadiums, and a limited number of hospitals came through MAS party's ambitious rural development initiative Bolivia Cambia. Evo Cumple.

Programs like these reflected new forms of rural-government alliance, driven in turn by earlier MAS promises of accountability to vulnerable Indigenous constituents. Unlike ideals of cross-generational debt for violence and of *hacendado* accountability to people living on former hacienda lands, this more general paradigm of authority was premised on a redistributive duty to provide aid to rural constituents. Moreover, as its slogan suggests, this program reflected an interactional paradigm based on an idea that, by distributing promised money or aid, MAS officials would secure rural support for their government. With that compliance, however, they would also be absolved of future responsibilities. In fact, after nearly nine thousand mega-projects were complete, and about half of them education-related, the program ceased.

Institutionalizing these claims elided their historical precedents and instead shored up more totalizing categories of class and political party allegiance. As exchange shifted away from obligations to place to a more general structure of wealth-based duty, the claims of more liminal subjects—the children of raped servants or the relatives of earlier *hacendado* managers like Pavel Camacho—were increasingly cast aside. In contrast to the framework of governmental compliance described earlier, practices of aid between the living relatives of *hacendados* and Indigenous servant families operated not as onetime acts of compliance but rather as ongoing relations of obligation based on a capacity to be affected by history. Moreover, the arrangements of support in which Evo could be a godfather, host a feast, or promise to support his people were oddly centered on his physical absence.

In the context of institutional deliberations over aid and resource rights through this conscribed model of authority, many Ayopayans continued to summon a more diffuse notion of obligation to history, one that unsettled Morales's claims to virtuous leadership. This was especially evident in the debate about Patiño, who seemed to stand in as a synecdoche for Morales. Should Patiño, an illegitimate child of a Quechua mother, be reclaimed as a generous Indigenous leader or, conversely, should he be cast off as yet another Mestizo master? Likewise, was Morales still "their" president or, in his absent and increasingly ravenous ways, had he gradually come to resemble a greedy *patrón*?

These grounded debates among Ayopayan interlocuters corresponded to broader national conversations about what critics saw as Morales's unethical abandonment of a more militant Indigenous cause. This sentiment is apparent in graffiti I photographed in 2013 that challenged the benefits of formal "liberation" achieved by Bolivian Independence in 1825 (Figure 26). The graffiti reads: "200 years of liberation, for whom?" Beside it, to the right, is printed "10," likely referring to the years that had passed since Bolivia's "Black October," the popular uprising that was violently repressed by then president Gonzalo Sánchez de Lozada, killing more than seventy-one people

FIGURE 26. Graffiti depicting an overburdened Indigenous man: "200 years of liberty, for whom?," Cochabamba city, 2010. Photo by author.

and wounding another four hundred, and eventually leading to the rise of Morales to the presidency. Morales subsequently proclaimed October 17, the day of Lozada's resignation, a "Day of National Dignity" marking the end of Bolivia's neoliberal era and the start of a new revolutionary cycle.

Like other politicians who promised to bring justice to Bolivia's Indigenous peasantry, however, Ayopayans and many Bolivians saw Morales as corrupted by power, leaning on essentialist portraits of Indigeneity as a means of self-aggrandizement. In doing so, they charged, he had shifted the political project toward a problem of ethnic identity rather than structural transformation. This critique is apparent not only in Oscar's account, discussed earlier, but also in Katarista critiques of Morales for his reproduction of elite power relations hidden behind the veneer of leftism and Indigenous revolution.[54] As Portugal Mollinedo and Macasuya Cruz (2016: 22) wrote: "[MAS's] principle historical component was unending series of ritual acts and ceremonies directed at tourists, as if this were what the Indigenous had been fighting for, as if this were the content of their struggle."

The notion that Indigeneity was something pure, that persisted outside the state and that would only now be ceremonially integrated by MAS, disavowed the violent interventions carried out by earlier states in the name of civilizational uplift and social betterment, as Oscar eloquently reminded me. This interplay between MAS governance projects and on-the-ground engagements with those projects suggests the need to rethink monolithic ideas of governance based on a constitutive split between "the state" and "the people."[55] On-the-ground challenges to MAS narratives of Indigenous revivalism in Ayopaya show how ostensibly traditional practices were reworked into sites of critical engagement with state agents and leaders. Thus, while revivalist events like these belonged to a specific institutional effort on the part of MAS, critics too were creatively mobilizing, even *reviving*, an older exchange paradigm to judge state authorities and MAS political leaders as public servants and bosses. These mediations were effects not only of top-down governance but also of bottom-up reception, critique, doubt, and disenchantment. This suggests that while revivalist efforts to shore up Indigeneity and displace coloniality were not entirely successful, their failures were not experienced as dead ends; rather, they opened up alternate ways to bear colonial history and negotiate loss.

CONCLUSION

In multiple ways Ayopayans extended ideals of exchange-based return to national political figures and business leaders. The planned feast Morales was expected to share with rural constituents, the municipal efforts to host an animal sacrifice, and officials' recasting of Morales as godfather during rural graduation events illustrate the dynamic interplay of political authority with supposedly precolonial exchange traditions. However, aspects of those traditions had been locally elaborated through systems of hacienda servitude. This meant that elements of vertical authority that MAS officials elsewhere condemned also operated, at least for some, as exemplary models of Indigenous leadership. So, while people at INRA and in Ayopaya's municipal government bemoaned the staying power of rural regimes of authority based in earlier agrarian servitude, aspects of that order were inadvertently "revived" in MAS attempts to recuperate Indigenous exchange traditions.

This dynamic interplay of top-down revivalism and bottom-up engagements with it challenges the idea that exchange is principally recursive—that is, a symptom of earlier colonial cultures of servitude or of a twentieth-century military-peasant alliance. Instead, asymmetrical exchange emerged as a lively ruin that Ayopayans creatively seized upon to insist that elites not renege on the duties associated with power. By mobilizing an ethical frame of political judgment premised upon expectations of asymmetrical aid and consubstantiation, Ayopayan residents pushed back against more constrained narratives of Indigenous collectivity that guided MAS government agendas concerning land, language, and mediatized portrayals of Morales' presence in the Indigenous countryside.

In the context of tepid local orientations to the MAS party state, this binding of authority to return was also a challenge to logics of timeless Indigeneity afforded by tethering contemporary value systems to an oppressive political and labor past. This was clear in Oscar's insistence that Indigenous rituals' logics and practices—be they sacrificial offerings or Indigenous ayllus—could not be recuperated without appreciating the losses incurred through the nation's colonial and more recent hacienda past. In a political atmosphere defined by new efforts to shore up land rights and to free the servile, the state's instituting of property and bounded Indigenous territory ended up being remarkably similar. Both required that mobile enactments of Indigeneity be replaced by peasants' fixing to property or, in collective land titling, contained within a bounded community model contingent on giving up resource rights. These property-based models reified Indigenous life as the fragile object of preservation, an object needing protection from external predation or contamination. They also drew more absolute lines in space; they asked farmers to engage with their lands not as places of past subjection or violence but as resources to be farmed and as the raw material for crafting a liberatory form of Indigeneity that could supplant and overcome the colonial and hacienda past.

Property here organized both the fixing of objects into more constrained arrangements of ownership but also the reification of people into more delimited understandings of racial identity and privilege—what Brenna Bhandar (2018: 150) has called the "identity-property nexus."[56] In Bolivia this nexus was apparent in the ways that reformist notions of deservedness relied upon a logic of status—namely of Indigenous ayllu or territorial membership, developed through the nation's legal history of assimilative *mestizaje* and bearing the distinctive traces of Katarista struggles for community. Land inheritances stemming from sexual violence upon haciendas were not legible from within INRA archival logics of overlay (see chapters 1 and 3), suggesting how such status shapes governmental and unionist efforts to redistribute land in accordance with perceptions of warranted and wanton sexual practices on the part of Indigenous women, specifically hacienda *mitanis*.[57]

Here the paradigm of identity as property, with its accompanying racial and gendered ideals of self-possessive subjectivity, supplied a new horizon for local understandings of land justice and history, but was also critically refused by some Ayopayans whose families' labor itineraries exceeded territorial enclosures modeled on the notion of community (see chapter 4).[58] By reframing MAS revivalism as part of a longer legal genealogy of constricting Indigeneity to a spatially bounded model of difference, Ayopayans like Oscar contested romantic ideals of purified Indigeneity but also, and with them, the MAS government's efforts to cast itself as innocent of similar interventions under the banner of cultural revivalism.[59] Contesting a telos of epochal displacement that grounded MAS revivalism, Oscar instead recalled how longue durée histories of state intervention had delimited the scope of legitimate Indigeneity and erased the validity of forms of Quechua belonging forged through deeply felt attachments to imposed institutions. By recentering constraint and the residual, he highlighted the injuries of redemptive property not only through land rights but also as a vehicle of identity recovery.[60]

Yet instead of living history's weight only as a burden, the Ayopayans whom I came to know engaged the past both as a reminder to be vigilant against the historical erasures folded into revivalist agendas *and* as a site of revelation about alternate possibilities for shared life and Indigenous futurity. In this regard, Ayopayans' insistence on the binding of economy to history and wealth to obligation challenged the normative or liberatory connotations of property that animated reform efforts. In their elaborations of transracial solidarity premised on Ayopaya's labor past, unionized farmers proposed existing alternatives to the reification of Indigenous status within INRA collective titling programs. This alternative emerged out of purposeful efforts to cultivate alliances that had grown out of the region's centrality to Indigenous and Mestizo efforts to resist land resettlement and labor oppression, apparent in the municipal center's name Independencia, which stemmed from the town's primacy in national independence battles in the late eighteenth and early nineteenth centuries.[61]

Like the eucalyptus stalks sprouting in the crumbling foundations of late hacienda estates, their practices remind us how new things emerge out of inherited institutions, and even entrenched forms are creatively repurposed and refashioned. This repurposing of inherited and emergent forms—what Fred Moten has called "the critical remixing of nonconvergent tracks"— offers a powerful rejoinder to romantic accounts that yoke Indigenous vitality to cultural resilience.[62] This narrative more tightly conscribes what can count as legitimate political activity or felt collectivity while also making that delimited sphere unreachable for the majority of people who inhabit colonialism's wake. What took shape in Ayopayans' reflections upon life in the aftermath of servitude instead was an unruly elaboration of Indigeneity based on ongoing experiences of labor mobility, land use fluidity, and ambivalence toward the central government. Such belonging was forged through the creative and ongoing work of recombinant history, one that overspilled property both as a recognized mode of Indigenous identity and as a final institutional redress or closure for an injurious past.

Conclusion

PROPERTY'S AFTERLIVES

"Evo Morales wasn't *all* bad, you know," Sandra explained. This phrase, uttered with reports of violent attacks on Morales supporters and staff still fresh, offered a thinly veiled defense of the recently ousted president at a time when displaying outward support for him could have endangered us both. It was January 2020, only months after Morales's conflictive departure from the presidency, when I visited the Bolivian city of Santa Cruz de la Sierra. I joined Sandra and her sister, two women in their mid-thirties whom I knew from earlier fieldwork in Ayopaya, for fermented corn beer and a lively game of dice in their parents' restaurant. As I made my way back to my apartment through the dusty southernmost outskirts of the city that evening, I spotted nearly new billboards advertising Morales's hydrocarbon investment plan, reminders of his unfinished agenda against what observers, critical and sympathetic, had just recently narrated as a politics of forever.

The raw aftermath of Morales's ousting illuminated the fragility of the relationships that had struck me as tireless and resilient during my fieldwork. As violent clashes subsumed urban centers in October 2019, friends who used to play *charangos* together during Carnival instead mocked one another on Facebook. One man condemned his erstwhile friend for being a fascist MASista, while she appealed to him to not forget *la gente humilde*, rural Indigenous people who had benefited considerably from Morales's development rural initiative. Morales's violent and dramatic downfall shattered the fragile cohabitations that I experienced, from 2010 to 2012, as routine. They also cast in an even more sinister light the ways that histories of racial violence could be denied through myopic appeals to democracy, and how quickly proclamations of homogenous citizenship gave way to subterranean discourses of White superiority and reason and Indigenous inferiority and irrationality.[1]

Morales renounced the presidency in November 2019, after trade unions, the police, and the military suggested he resign.[2] The regime that followed was led by interim president Jeanine Añez and backed by a conservative, anti-Indigenous faction. It fed on the legal and political uncertainty of the post-electoral moment, including twenty-one days of national strike during which pro- and anti-MAS supporters and police clashed and armed motorcades pursued pro-MAS protesters, killing at least thirty-four people.[3] In WhatsApp messages I received in October and November, friends and acquaintances employed under MAS and living in Sacaba (Chapare) described being holed up in apartments, hearing military helicopters and gunfire in the streets, and receiving death threats. Morales's ousting was accompanied by racist attacks on Indigenous women in the street, media accounts portraying pro-Indigenous activists and protesters as "terrorists" and "rapists," and the public burning of icons of Indigenous power and heritage, like the *wiphala* flag.[4] This atmosphere of widespread violence makes Sandra's tepid defense of Morales understandable, especially as she and her partner had been MAS employees.

With the rapid hardening of pro- and anti-Indigenous divisions since Morales's ousting in 2019, many of the scenes of alliance and aid I have narrated in this book have become nearly unfathomable. Exchange has slipped into deadlock. Additionally, this period betrays the return of narratives that render unthinkable the ability for rural Indigenous people to support a revolutionary program of political transformation without manipulation or deception. For instance, the conservative attack on Morales was rooted in accusations of foreign interference, subsequently debunked, on the part of the Organization of Associated States (OAS), which prematurely declared that there had been vote tampering.[5] Unfortunately, however, arguments that Morales's ousting was only an outcome of a foreign-led "coup" also risk eliding Indigenous forms of agency.[6] In the initial moment after Morales's ousting, the foreign media tended to paint former MAS supporters as childlike or politically naïve, lamenting the fact that Morales's earlier extension of term limits had not resulted in a popular abandoning of support for the MAS party. Imagine their surprise when, in 2020, Bolivians elected another MAS party representative, Luis Arce, as Morales's successor.

President Luis Arce's election in 2020 confirms the enduring vibrancy of Bolivian Indigenous movements across changing regimes of state governance. Against the assuredness of foreign observers and national critics, Leftist MAS candidate Arce received an impressive 55 percent of the national vote. Following his election, he promised to "rebuild" Bolivia after a year of violent backlash against Indigenous MAS supporters, including bloody confrontations on the street between Morales supporters and armed, largely Mestizo opposition forces. Arce has pledged to work toward healing the wounds caused by the eruption of sentiments—above all conservative Mestizos's resentment about Morales's long reign and the affronts to Mestizo supremacy that his presidency brought about. For MAS supporters who grew increasingly disenchanted with Morales's abandonment of a program of revolutionary structural change, Arce presented another opportunity to realize the transformations that Morales had promised.

Given the arc of the ethnographic material presented in this book, Arce's election should not come as a surprise. As I have sought to demonstrate in the preceding chapters, in rural provinces like Ayopaya, firm political support for Morales was coupled with highly critical assessments of the shortcomings of his political agenda. Quechua interlocutors in Ayopaya with whom I spoke simultaneously harbored deep attachments to Evo as their president and were deeply critical of what appeared as another set of belated, perhaps even elusive, revolutionary promises to deliver true political and economic change to the countryside.[7] There, popular memories of having "served" the master and of the abrupt slippage from revolutionary governance to Mestizo dictatorship to Indigenous political persecution had prepared them for the rapid crumbling of revolutionary state promises and dreams of historical supplanting.

Yet neither had state political persecution been limited to the nation's past, or even to the period preceding Morales's rise to the presidency. In 2008 antigovernment crowds captured dozens of rural MAS supporters in Sucre, forcing them to strip to their waists and chant anti-Indigenous slogans, and in 2011, MAS police suppressed a pro-Indigenous opposition march against the TIPNIS highway, killing an infant and wounding thirty-seven people. As apparent in the union discussions (see chapter 4), Ayopayan farmers and villagers kept memories of racial subjection and recent political persecution close: they thereby sought to prevent becoming caught in the crosshairs of urban political violence such as that which erupted into the streets in November 2019. Even in MAS strongholds like Ayopaya, then, rural Indigenous support for Morales was never absolute or unthinking but rather calibrated to earlier abandonments and to the tragedies of overturned political orders.[8]

More broadly, this book has asked what Ayopayans' engagements with an oppressive past and an inegalitarian present can tell us about the nature of authority in practice. I have sought to unsettle the idea that power is ever entirely secure, asking instead how configurations of authority depend upon mutual dependencies and vulnerabilities that paradoxically also open them up to disruption and critique. Viewing authority as attached to place and to history in this way contravenes in a naturalized paradigm of power—such as in structural analyses of property or land inequality—in which structure is assumed to hold outside of, or above, the practices by which it is inhabited, reproduced, or potentially undone.[9] Against an increasingly technocratic state that yoked Indigenous justice to bureaucratic norms of compliance and transparency, the Ayopayans whom I spoke to insisted on political and economic elites' continued answerability to earlier—and ongoing—experiences of Indigenous dispossession and political marginalization. The tools Ayopayans mobilized for that struggle exceeded property as a civilizing mechanism of Indigenous uplift that, in late twentieth- and early twenty-first-century Bolivia, was recast by governments, peasant unionists, and many social movement leaders as a liberating project.

KNOTTING PAST AND PRESENT: KINSHIP, PROPERTY, AND EXCHANGE

The analysis put forth in preceding chapters has attended to servitude's afterness as itself something requiring explanation. That is, rather than presume structural continuity, I have looked at the mechanisms by which attachments over time and space are built and the ethical and political projects attached to those mechanisms. In particular, I have considered the interplay among three modalities of attaching past and present, what I have elaborated as processes of "knotting" that also organize engagements with Bolivia's violent hacienda past—kinship, property, and exchange. Against teleological arguments that kinship attachments wane in the face of increasingly alienated capital, I have sought to show how Quechua and Mestizo Ayopayans repurposed idioms of kinship-based support both to address a divisive labor past and to insist that recent arrivals in the countryside heed by the constraints imposed by this framework of authority. Less than an absolute shift from earlier "feudal" economies premised upon sexual and affective entanglements to regularized patterns of titled land and paid labor, the Ayopayan case illuminates both the elusiveness and the fragility of contract-based formations in determining matters of land use, kinship, and resource extractivism.

The grip of what I have termed exchange—a distinct authority complex forged by Ayopayans' purposeful extension of kinship languages to new political and economic formations—problematizes the telos of capital as the movement toward alienated ownership and disembedded economy.[10] The present was lived not as an absolute departure from the past but rather as an ongoing struggle for answerability to a violent past and its reproduction in mining infrastructures and domestic labor and resource economies. In their efforts to seek redress for an ongoing history of racial violence, Ayopayans drew upon frameworks of authority that were also entangled with earlier servitude: the generous mother or *mamitay* who bore the affective and material debts of the bonded past; the rapacious, profiteering *patrón* who at times was refashioned as the modern boss; and the sympathetic, pro-Indigenous politician who promised revolution but also sought support and pleasure through familiar *hacendado* ways. The duration of these figurations of power was double-edged. It reproduced racialized hierarchies but also obstructed property as a bounded orientation to power, requiring that authority remain tied to history and that obligations to place guard against the neutralizing of wealth as unmarked capital.

Alienated property, both as titled ownership over land and as a paragon of self-possessed personhood, has historically operated as a crucial yardstick for judging, assigning, or withholding people a place in civilized modernity. Denaturalizing this ethos of alienability, Ayopayans instead recast property as an unrealistic fantasy premised on the callous disavowal of racialized histories of violence. At the same time, their efforts to repurpose and extend kinship paradigms to urban Mestizo bosses and even President Morales challenge familiar understandings of economy (and capital) as ahistorical and abstract, and kinship as genealogical and inherently embedded in society. Detachment and embeddedness instead exist along a continuum of what are understood as desirable qualities of subjective engagement with others in a place defined by competing Mestizo and Indigenous claims to land and to history.

At the same time, INRA officials showed me the mediations that must fall away in order for property, both as titled land and self-possessed citizenship, to appear natural as a discrete entity or bundle of rights. Against tendencies to distinguish kinship as durative from property as enclosure, they taught me that property, no less than the kinship claims Ayopayans were making, was also an outcome of a purposeful accrual of labor, as stitched to the landscape through their ArcGIS mapping technologies. This insight intervenes in the assumption that property, but not kinship, allows for an atomistic expression of sovereign action or land ownership detached from an oppressive labor past. My analysis offers "exchange" as a concept that names this space of ethical and political disagreement about kinship and property, embeddedness and abstraction in time and space, as affording contrasting models of action and personhood in a deeply inegalitarian present.

In tracing nascent demands for exchange-based return on the part of rural Indigenous Bolivians, I have sought to show how kinship obligations were mobilized in order destabilize, but also to critically *reinvent*, property. This opens up a more complicated view of "the economy" as vulnerable to transformation by other orientations to wealth and history. In regard to mining conflicts in Ayopaya, demands for exchange synthesized Quechua workers' insistence that Mestizo bosses acknowledge how labor (and profits) depend upon attachments to others and the circulation of substances, objects, emotions, and power.[11] By recounting these grounded disagreements about earlier servitude in Bolivia, I have sought to illuminate how, despite its ostensible hegemony, property—as racialized ownership, as titled land, and as a route toward reparation through self-possession and identity recovery—remained precarious and subject to critique. The challenges it faced stem from more than the inherent difficulties of translating a legal or technocratic model into material reality. Rather, they speak to broader ethical uncertainties about whether, and for whom, a more constricted model of property (and of identity as a kind of discrete property) constitutes an apotheosis of the just life.

GENDER, INJURY, AND UNMARKED CITIZENSHIP

In addition to revealing property's fractures both as a historical telos and a normative ethos of wealth, my account has considered the gendered consequences of shifts in the arc of claim-making from more fluid arrangements of land gifting and Mestizo patronage to structures of institutional alliance and developmental aid. This transformation involved an increased reliance upon mediated channels of developmental aid through union organizing, INRA land claims, and MAS political alliances. As a way to contend with earlier labor violence and abiding racial inequalities, these institutional pathways depended upon more reified classifications of history and hardened ethnic lines (Mestizo, Indigenous, migrant, Quechua, landowning, servant). These new divisions had difficultly accommodating people, such as the living kin of domestic servants or landless Quechua *forasteros* turned *hacendados*, who inherited land and relational attachments from both bonded labor hierarchies and Indigenous communities. Institutional programs of aid through the MAS party development schemes opened up crucial new opportunities for rural people, but they also subtly recalibrated shared orientations to history and Indigenous collectivity in the present.

This shift toward institutional channels of claim-making had notable gendered consequences.[12] Practices of cross-familial aid that rested on kinship figures like the mother (as *patrona, madrina,* or *mamitay*) grappled centrally with the key question of who should bear the burden for the region's violent labor past. They did so in a way that accounted for the specific histories of sexual violence upon haciendas, including masters' fathering of children with Indigenous servants. As demands for aid and assistance shifted to unions and political parties and away from *hacendado* and servant families, both benefactors and the beneficiaries were increasingly male.[13] The people central to such negotiations were not the long-suffering mother, Flora, or feminized aging laborers, like Ramón (see chapter 1) or Carmenia (see chapter 2) but rather virile young men like Martín, René, or Evo Morales. Elected union leaders and municipal officials aligned with federal institutions like INRA and the national peasant union were reluctant to speak about, much less address, Indigenous women's forced (sexual) labor in haciendas, and its entailments for processes of land redistribution in the present.[14]

If the informal practices of historical obligation through kinship languages had accommodated persons and histories that blurred a reified nationalist binary of Mestizo masters and Indigenous peasants, new institutionalized channels tended to formalize that split. Instead of operating as a shared object of care and vigilance, the region's bonded past increasingly served as a stain on a more militant, purified ideal of Indigenous sovereign actors as embodied in resistant peasant-farmers. Justice, now writ large, would lie in empowering Indigenous campesinos by providing access to land, development monies, education, and health care. These initiatives were frequently cast by reformers in the language of self-determined citizenship, of learning (as Ruben Arpasi put it), what one needs in one's own "house." Mestizo elites and MAS party officials both critiqued rural "handouts" as relics of earlier military and hacienda patronage. Where they encountered poverty or dependency, government officials and rural unionists narrated it as the fault of Indigenous peasants themselves, elderly women and aging former servants who had failed to elevate themselves into new citizen-owners with the capacities to define and defend their land, bodies, and the terms of their own history.

Here it is revealing that INRA employees, Indigenous rights activists, and foreign humanitarian workers center their rural interventions around workshops focused on *capacitating* rural people through exposure to rights-based logics and legal processes. For people involved in these efforts, justice required that Indigenous groups find their own footing as awakened agents of history and possessors of property. Government officials and activists could not do this *for* them, but they could help birth a new order by encouraging their detachment from earlier aid arrangements, whether through state institutions or Mestizo elites. Hence, inequality changed from being a matter of everyday practice to that of absent state agencies funneling money into poverty relief, education, and village infrastructure. In these subtle ways Bolivia's nationalist project of Indigenous justice through property encouraged a semantic shift—from immersion in an imperfect present to a shared longing for an imminent, if elusive, future.

REFUSING PROPERTY AS HISTORICAL CLOSURE

Against this more hegemonic, teleological narrative of markets, states, and subject-citizens as traveling along toward ever-greater social and economic alienability, Ayopayans continued to demand a more entangled orientation to authority from *hacendado* relatives and mine owners as well as MAS political leaders.[15] For even as MAS leaders reasserted the telos of alienability in their arguments that, by gaining property titles and development monies, Indigenous farmers would be transformed into self-commanding, responsible citizens, people in Ayopaya found themselves in many of the same binds that they had been before Morales took power. After all, what good were property titles when the land they secured was dry, barren, and too small to feed families much less to sell for profit, or when indignant Mestizo elites could pick up a rifle and assert their own boundary lines? What use were medical centers if they were locked and unattended? What benefit were laws nationalizing gold mines if Mestizo owners merely turned to lawyer friends to capitalize on legal loopholes?

These constraints highlight how, despite idealistic assertions to the contrary, property's efficacy in the world depended also upon its instantiation through a set of relational entanglements—not only the overlay of labor at INRA discussed above, but also family connections such as between Fabio and René, and institutional alliances such as between the provincial and national peasant union. This also meant that, in the absence or given the instabilities of such attachments, property as a form of ownership and racialized benefit could also be contested and potentially undone. That Ayopayans understood this well was apparent in their insistence in the insufficiency of contractual forms in affording legitimacy to a given way of organizing land, labor, or resources. A land title, a labor contract, or (René's) documentation of a formal mine sale fell short absent their binding to materialities through continued forms of action and remaking. This also proved the case with mine owners like René, who erroneously assumed that their authority—and their right to access women and benefit from resource mining—could be detached first from rural Quechua workers and second from the obligations imposed by the mine's situation on former hacienda land.

It is ultimately within this broader conjuncture of forces that Ayopayans' waning support for Morales might be understood. Morales's departure was eased by long-run patterns of "pro-democracy" military aid and logistical support that abetted the so-called civic movement (led by Luis Fernando Camacho and Marco Pumari). Yet in Ayopaya growing disillusionment with Morales preceded these events by nearly a decade. In his skipping out on public appearances and his declining availability for unmediated dialogue, not to mention rumors of his sexual exploits and complaints of abandoned "megaprojects," it increasingly seemed that Morales had come to take his rural Indigenous supporters for granted. As I have discussed, this dissatisfaction was evident in 2011, when Indigenous rights supporters, peasant unionists, and members of the middle classes opposed the MAS party's earlier rescinding of promises of Indigenous sovereignty in its handling of the TIPNIS conflict.[16] Alongside the TIPNIS dispute, Morales's party was pushing for road expansion in Ayopaya while at the same time disavowing rural Indigenous people sovereignty over resources and land. Hence, despite Morales's nominal commitments to support greater Indigenous sovereignty, MAS legislation shored up federal control over natural resources—defined as "national property"—and introduced severe restrictions on recognizable configurations of Indigenous territory.[17]

Many commentators on Morales's ousting explained Bolivia's coup as a reaction to the threat MAS's leftist, anti-imperialist agenda posed to an international extractivist order. Yet my conversations with Quechua farmers, unionists, municipal officials, and other formal MAS supporters in Ayopaya suggested rather that Morales's reform program did not go far enough, trafficking in now familiar portraits of Indigenous ecosubjects and newfound protections for the Pachamama, while at the same time pushing forward hydrocarbon and gas extraction against the wishes of Indigenous people living on those territories.[18] The MAS government hereby promised a kind of liberty to be achieved by way of passage through and the superseding of property, but it propped up systems of dispossession and political marginalization on the part of subjects cast as imperfectly embodying a nationalist ideal of Indigenous citizenship.[19] This confirms how, as Yarimar Bonilla (2017) has argued, hegemonic projects of decolonial sovereignty are modeled upon settler/colonial ideas of agency.[20] In Bolivia in particular, rights-based models of Indigenous sovereignty have often served to marginalize and cast as listless and undeserving people who, for a range of different reasons related to labor practices and histories of movement and migration, do not fit within more purist models of Indigeneity.[21]

Like recognition-based models of colonial reparation, Bolivia's property-based project of hacienda repair sought to achieve justice, but as elsewhere it did so in the colonizer's terms.[22] Rather than being constrained to the period immediately following the abolition of slavery or forced labor, I have sought to show how property as a political formation haunts contemporary state programs geared toward securing Indigenous land rights and identity recovery. Mine is not an argument against land reparation as a worthy pursuit, either for disenfranchised groups to seek racial justice or in governmental efforts to take account of colonial legacies of violence and dispossession. To the contrary, money and land-based reparations are crucial in Indigenous and Black struggles for settler states to acknowledge colonial histories and their continued shaping of the distributions of labor, law, value, and profit in late liberalism.[23] Moreover, as I write this conclusion questions of reparation for slavery loom large in the United States—in Asheville, North Carolina, and Evanston, Illinois, and elsewhere.[24] Reparation constitutes a key first step in coming to grips with present-day hierarchies of wealth and pleasure as built upon histories of slavery and indentured servitude.

But such acknowledgment alone does not dispense with an unjust past, and reparation measures often replicate features of liberal projects of assimilative citizenship and imperial models of civilizing intervention. Property as a reparative model grows out of, and remains beholden to, these anterior political formations. In Asheville this is apparent in the fact that reparations will not consist of direct cash payments but rather of "investments" in areas where Black people live. Like insurance, *investment* implies future returns, money put down with expectations of eventual reward or profit, a connotation related to the history of property insurance on transatlantic slave ships.[25] Despite their promise, then, property-based reparations do not offer a final resolution nor inoculate the present of lingering colonial debts. In this context academics, activists, social movement leaders, and others can learn something from Ayopayans' disaffections with land titling and identity revitalization as routes of historical redress which ended up imposing impossible expectations of spatial autonomy and temporal detachment. In this regard, Morales's pursuit of property-based aid did not depart enough from familiar trajectories of political and economic liberalism. It followed that Morales, in Celso Padilla's cutting words, "need[ed] to be decolonized."[26] Reparation, including through promises of formal land redistribution, must be treated as the beginning of a longer process of addressing historical injustice, not its end.

Ayopayans' engagements with revolutionary land titling and their insistence on power as a relation of unwilled mutuality provide insights into the limits but also the creative recasting of property in light of alternate relational orientations to history and violence. These engagements point to a set of generative slippages that exceed property both as titled ownership and as discrete self-possession.[27] Enclosure here both drew firmer lines in place but also sought to newly delimit time, promising reparative closure of open colonial wounds. Recognizing the insufficiency of reparation through formal land rights, Ayopayans also insisted upon keeping open continued lines of dialogue about oppressive pasts and the obligations those pasts generate in the present. Those projects drew into their orbit neighbors and kin but also enemies and uncomfortable allies, patron saints introduced by hacienda masters and earth beings, like the Pachamama, who had been slighted by years of forbidden sacrifice. These are slower projects of repair and rebuilding that do not rely absolutely on governmental processes for their energies. In Ayopaya, addressing a violent labor past entailed walking forward together [*purishanchis*] despite fits and starts, sweat and tears, and undertaking small acts like planting a peach tree and awaiting its fruit.

ACKNOWLEDGMENTS

In the years of research and writing that have cohered into this book, I have amassed enormous debts. In Cochabamba, Luis Morato-Peña first set the tone in his garden, where we patiently endured hours-long intensive Quechua lessons, enlivened by the cackle of his parrots. In that same city, Ramiro Saravia took me in from the start, instructing me on the kinesthetic politics of drinking *api* at the 25 de Mayo market on frigid winter mornings. He also dragged me along to art openings, plaza debates, music performances, and monthly *q'oas*, where he introduced me to artists, performers, activists, travelers, *chicha* brewers, radio DJs, sociologists: the wide consortium of Cochabambinos (and foreigners) who shared deep commitments to making the Bolivia they envisioned. Ramiro weathered lively debates with me about national politics, Christianity, humanitarianism, and urgent if often-elusive projects of decolonial political change. It was through Ramiro that I had the pleasure to get to know Elias Ramirez Zoribia, Intiyawar, and Edwin Torrez Huanca, who expanded my knowledge of Bolivian history from the ground up and always supplied new reading suggestions.

Many people in Cochabamba made the city feel like home. Cynthia and Cesar Zentano Villarroel and their daughter, Shirley, and Marwin and Maria Isabel Vega S. invited me to Sunday *parilladas* to stave off my homesickness. Marisol "de la plaza" and Maria Luisa provided companionship over coffee and gossip. Florencio Condori Chavéz imparted upon me his love of Tapacarí and its pan flute traditions and, along with Sandra Carmen, helped me to expand my knowledge of how agriculture and Indigenous justice intersect. Raúl Galarza took an interest in my research and guided me through the intricacies of mapping technologies to bring clarity to issues that I would not have otherwise understood. Raúl López Soria gifted me a book of his poetry and shared with me, over coffee, his thoughts about an embattled Bolivia and its possible futures. Jesusa Delgado and Beatriz Guzman showered me with humor, friendship, and camaraderie. Walter Gonzales Valdivia provided ample *chicha* and fantastic live music at his *chicharia* Chernobyl, where I learned to dance *la cueca*. Others facilitated the institutional side of my research. Javier C. Sanjinés kindly sponsored my research at a time when research visas were nearly impossible to come by. Pablo Regalsky supplied mentorship and advice about the course of the research early on. Edmundo Arze, Mariela Arze, Marcelo Guzman, Jhonny Lazo C., and Freddy Delgado greatly abetted my thinking through their sociological takes on Bolivian politics. Antonio Camacho provided indispensable help navigating the lay of the land in the INRA archive.

Fellow social scientists and Andeanist scholars in Cochabamba helped my research questions to ripen in crucial ways, showing me a special kind of mentorship among peers: Sarah Hines, Carmen Soliz, Carwil Bjork-James, Rosalin Flores, Gustavo Adolfo Vargas Montero, Sayda Cotrina Reyes, and Jason Tockman—your keen questions are sprinkled throughout these pages. In June 2011, at the Congreso de la Asociación de Estudios Bolivianos in Sucre, I first crossed paths with fellow Bolivianists with whom I had the privilege of reflecting upon Bolivia's revolutionary present and past: Hanne Cottyn, Alessandra Pellegrini, Pablo Quisbert Condorí, Hernán Pruden, Sinclair Thomson, Tristan Platt, and Matt Gildner. In Peru, Jean-Jacques DeCoster and Bruce Mannheim provided an institutional home and allowed me to pursue Quechua study and also supplied contacts and clarity about the project early on.

My largest debts are to fieldwork interlocuters in Ayopaya, who made this research both possible and enjoyable. Zaida Elena Crespo Mendizabel, Huascar Rolando Mendizabel Chavez, Cristina Rojas, Raquel Montan Rojas, Wilder Inocente, Jose Antonio Caero Montecinos, Edgar Apata Ramirez, Rosa Montan Escobar, Carlos Suárez Montan, and Tito Lisberger Tames welcomed me in Independencia and insisted I inquire further into the region's labor history during the initial, crucial days and weeks. Jorge Aquino and Eloy Vargas provided institutional support and housing. In Ayopaya I had the luck to meet Duizan Sandra Silva Soria, Sonia Vallejos, and Patricia Janco Vera, whose friendships (and card games) I greatly miss. The majority of Ayopayan interlocuters of this project must remain nameless as labor genealogies travel to shape and potentially compromise ongoing land claims. While I must withhold names, words cannot do justice to my gratitude to union leaders at the Central Sindical Única de Trabajadores Campesinos Originarios de Ayopaya (CSUTCOA) for supporting this research and to Quechua interlocuters in Sanipaya, Tiquirpaya/Rodeo, Sailapata, Cutipampa, K'uti/Ch'allani, K'ullupaya, Charahuayto, Huancarani, and Pucara for entrusting me with their narratives and historical accounts.

At the University California–Berkeley, I encountered an intellectual atmosphere defined by equal parts philosophical curiosity and political commitment, one that allowed my initial, reaching questions to cohere into the doctoral research project that forms the basis for this book. Saba Mahmood did not live to see this research take book form, but I would like to think that this text carries the traces of her tireless inquisitiveness, her humor, and her insistence on continually subjecting one's ideas to revision and critique. Charles Hirschkind has been an indefatigable supporter and superb mentor, providing detailed comments and questions on early reaching drafts and encouraging me when writing felt insurmountable. Judith Butler, Sinclair Thomson, and Charles Briggs joined this project early on and have remained crucial interlocutors and mentors. Stefania Pandolfo, Lawrence Cohen, Marianne Ferme, Cori Hayden, William Hanks, José Rabasa, and Guillermo Delgado provided crucial insights at crucial moments.

At UC–Berkeley, I had the great fortune to share delectable meals, sundrenched hikes, intense coffee, and lively discussions with fellow graduate students, co-conspirators, and friends Bharat Venkat, Janelle Lamoreaux, Ruth Goldstein, Alissa Bernstein, Laurence Tessier, Patricia Kubala, K-Sue Park, Lyle Fearnley, Emily Chua, Bruno Reinhardt, Alisa Sanchez, Krystal Strong, Alex Dubilet, Jerry Zee, Leticia Cesarino, Milad Odabaei, Damon Young, Michael D'Arcy, Jean-Michel Landry, and Jeremy Soh. Bharat, Janelle, and Ruth waded through various drafts of this work and helped me navigate book publishing. They, along with Amy Krauss, have also been there for big questions of life and work that unfold alongside our writerly selves.

At the University of Chicago, I have been blessed with immensely supportive colleagues. Julie Chu, Stephan Palmie, Hussein Ali Agrama, Joseph Masco, William Mazzarella, Brodwyn Fischer, Judith Farquhar, Nancy Munn, and Emilio Kourí have all contributed to this manuscript in one form or another. A faculty writing group with Angie Heo, Darryl Li, Adia Benton, Alireza Mohammadi Doostdar, Sarah Fredericks, Ghenwa Hayek, Emrah Yildiz, and Elham Mireshghi has been life and work transforming, providing a space of play, complaint, creativity, and experimentation that I have found deeply nourishing. During weekly meetings as a faculty fellow at the Franke

Institute for the Humanities (2019–20), I had the opportunity to learn from a number of brilliant colleagues, whose curiosity and keen insights on the introduction made this book immensely better: Emily Austin, Jessica Baker, Larissa Brewer-García, John Muse, Anna Christine Schultz, James Wilson, Daniel Carranza, Sam Lasman, Brandon Truett, Michael K. Bourdaughs, and Richard Theodore Neer.

My development of this book's central themes was also pushed forward by the insights of several fantastic graduate students, including Emma Gilheany, Sandy Hunter, Lorna Hadlock, Inés Escobar González, Paloma Cobo-Diáz, and Sarah Shaer. Finally, I had the opportunity to build out ideas for this work through a Faculty Book workshop sponsored by the Center for International Social Science Research (CISSR) at Chicago, where it benefited from careful readings and thoughtful suggestions from Lucinda Ramberg, Bruce Mannheim, Andrew Matthews, Mark Goodale, Brooke Larson, and Joe Masco. I owe Lucinda a huge debt for her insistence that I think more closely about property in relation to kinship.

This work has also grown in conversation with colleagues at Wellesley College, the University of Illinois–Urbana-Champaign, University of California–Santa Cruz, and Johns Hopkins University, where I presented earlier versions of the research. My thinking about materiality and extraction was enlivened by participation in an Equivocal Anthropocenes workshop in Santiago in November 2018, including the careful readings and comments from Manuel Tironi, Marcelo González Gálvez, Timothy Neale, Emma Cardwell, Florencia Carmen Tola, Andrew Pereira, Ingmar Lippert, Sarah Kelly, and Pablo Howard Seward Delaporte. More recently, new collaborations have put me in dialogue with Cymene Howe, Lesley Green, Ana Mariella Bacigalupo, Daniel Fischer, and Macarena Gómez-Barris, allowing for older ideas to ferment and yield new insights about this material. In Bloomington, Indiana, new friendships with Olga Rodríguez Ulloa, Shane Greene, Olimpia E. Rosenthal, Judy Rodriguez, and Meredith Lee helped me survive the final writing push, offering sustenance through laughter and companionship in dystopic times.

The research for this book was supported by a Wenner Gren Dissertation Fieldwork Grant, a Josephine de Karman Dissertation Fellowship, and a Dissertation Fellowship from the Townsend Center for the Humanities. Writing was supported by a generous Faculty Fellowship at the University of Chicago's Franke Institute for the Humanities (2019–20). At Amherst College, I happened to take Deborah Gewertz's Contemporary Anthropology class in the spring of 2003. This class, and Deborah's superb teaching, initiated me in the alchemy of anthropological thought; without it, this book would not exist.

Kate Marshall at the University of California Press has been immensely generous with her time and insights; her firm support for this work early on, coupled with her careful guidance on writing and style, have been indispensable to this book's materialization. Detailed commentary and superb suggestions from two anonymous reviewers (who later revealed themselves to be Justin Richland and Andrew Orta) were crucial to helping the book's analytic framing cohere. Wendy Piquemal copyedited the initial manuscript but also helped me to clarify key aspects of the argument. At UC Press, Cindy Fulton and Enrique Ochoa-Kaup helped shepherd the book along and were responsive and prompt in helping me to navigate an unfamiliar process. Amy Smith Bell combed through the manuscript with remarkable attention to detail.

My parents, Bob Winchell and Leonore Hildebrandt, expertly dwell in a world made both of ideas and matter. Their painting, poetry writing, gardening, music-making, and bread-baking imbued me with an early, and abiding, appreciation for the tactile magic of world-making. They, along with my sisters Nicole, Shaina, and Emily, and made kin Mary and Robert, gave their support by humoring my undisciplined thinking and utopic impulses from an early age.

Finally, the deepest thank you to Michael, and our Henry and Arlo, who have weathered—with me—the ups and downs of writing, who have accompanied me to Bolivia and back, and who have graciously shared their lives, and me, with the phantom of this book for so long. Your love has nourished this project.

NOTES

PREFACE

1. Throughout the Andes, language is often used as principal marker of Indigenous identity (Canessa 2012; García 2005; Mannheim 1991). Gregorio Condorí, like the majority of indigenous farmers in Ayopaya, speaks Quechua as his mother tongue, and has also learned Spanish through state primary schooling, required national military service, and as a requirement to communicate with non-Indigenous people both in Ayopaya and elsewhere. In this book I identify people who speak Quechua as their primary language as Indigenous Quechua. Doing so retains the key connotations of linguistic practices for localized elaborations of ethnic and racial belonging, in this way contesting dominant nationalist narratives of *mestizaje* that have associated exposure to Spanish language and culture with a loss of authentic Indigeneity (Rivera Cusicanqui 2014).

2. In a place where racial identity is conferred as much by dress and dialect as it is by skin pigment or origin, this dialect conferred Indigenous social status upon him (Canessa 2012). For a critical genealogy of Spanish racial logics from the late medieval period on, particularly its early connotations of Christian virtue, religious orthodoxy, and unsullied bloodlines, see Martínez (2008: 80, 111, 202).

3. For an introduction to this system of bonded agrarian labor or *pongueaje*, and peasant struggles for its abolition, see Chipana Ramos (2018).

4. The most recent Bolivian census occurred in 2012. These statistics about the province of Ayopaya are taken from the 2012 census, reprinted in "Cochabamba: Principales Características de la Vivienda, Según Provincia y Municipio, Censo 2012," www.ine.gob.bo/index.php/estadisticas-sociales/vivienda-y-servicios-basicos/censos-vivienda/ (accessed January 19, 2022).

5. Encomiendas were land grants that included "native communities and their inhabitants," who were required to pay tribute to encomienda grantees (Larson 1998: 33–34).

6. For several key studies of hacienda labor violence and political repression in the Andes see De la Cadena (2014), Lyons (2006), and Mayer (2009).

7. My attention to history as materialized harks back to Walter Benjamin's focus on traces. In the essay "Theses on the Philosophy of History" (in *Illuminations: Essays and Reflections*), Benjamin warned about the risks of secular or "homogenous empty time," wherein ritual calendars and earlier textured distinctions between different moments were displaced by the qualitative nondifferentiation, or abstract, experience of time. I owe Stefania Pandolfo a huge debt for encouraging me to think further about the ethics of historical reckoning in the present. On the material afterlives of history, see Stoler (2008) and Gordillo (2014). Other anthropological works on time that have shaped my thinking are Bear (2016), Chakrabarty (1997), Chu (2014), Dawdy (2016), Fabian ([1983] 2014), Hirschkind (2016), Palmié and Stewart (2016), Scott (2013), Stewart (2016), and Trouillot ([1992] 2015).

8. My elaboration of the conditional draws from Povinelli (2016: 191).

9. On Bolivian land titling since 2006, see Anthias (2018) and Fabricant (2012). For a detailed discussion of property regularization in relation to colonial resettlement projects, see Winchell (2018).

10. On the *derecho de la pernada* (right of the first night), wherein workers' brides spent the first night of their marriage with the priest or master, see Reinaga ([1970] 2007). See also Canessa (2012: 17, 255).

11. For the challenges facing land titling as an equalizing project, see Farthing and Kohl (2012).

12. I use the term *Mestizo* while recognizing its inadequacy. The term *Mestizo* (used to denote a person of "mixed" Spanish and indigenous descent) spans colonial tribute legislation, racialized discourses of marriage and miscegenation, assimilative discourses of modern nationalism, and aesthetic movements in literature, art, and photography. See De la Cadena (2000) and Weismantel (2001).

13. Following De la Cadena (2014), I use the term "earth-being" to emphasize the inadequacy of smoothly translating persons like the Pachamama into rubrics either of natural religion or of land-based, material ontologies (see also Mannheim 2019).

INTRODUCTION

1. For antihacienda militancy in Ayopaya, see Dandler and Torrico (1987). For highland Aymara memories of hacienda violence, see Canessa (2012: 63–118).

2. Titling assumed new significance with Bolivia's 1996 Reform Law, and then with MAS government revisions to that law in 2010.

3. Leading up to Morales's election in 2005, Bolivian peasant unions, Indigenous organizations, students, and middle-class Bolivians organized into a mass political movement that contested both foreign multinational control over nat-

ural resources and government austerity programs as violations of Indigenous sovereignty (Bebbington 2007 and Perrault 2012). On twentieth-century mobilizations against neoliberal austerity that built upon anticolonial Indigenous militancy, see Thomson (2002). For the history of Indigenous rebellion from the eighteenth century on, see the edited volume by Stern (1987). For the early period of Incan-Spanish warfare and the implementation of the encomienda system, see Stern (1982).

4. On land titling as a mechanism for adjudicating multiple land claims, see Fabricant and Gustafson (2013); for the history of overlapping land claims in the Andes, see Herzog (2015).

5. These examples illuminate what Saidiya Hartman (1997: 4) identifies as the "violence perpetrated under the rubric of pleasure, paternalism, and property."

6. This insistence on reparation through action recalls Verene A. Shepherd's (2018: 41) argument that "reparation is a right to redress and repair, not an act of begging. Perhaps José Martí sums it up best: 'Rights are to be taken, not requested; seized, not begged for.'"

7. American Heritage 2019, s.v. "after," www.ahdictionary.com/word/search .html?q=after (accessed November 2019).

8. I therefore focus principally on showing how history was navigated in the present. My approach is informed by Michael Lambek's (2002) notion of "bearing" history both as burden and promise. See also Das (2006), Sharpe (2016), Thomas (2019), Nelson (2009, 2015), and Venkat (2021).

9. For laborers' accounts of hacienda servitude in Ecuador, see Lyons (2006). For Peru, see Mayer (2007).

10. While "knot" is not a term that Ayopayan interlocuters used, it does usefully draw together sentiments of historical repurposing that I encountered, including notions of being "affected," "transforming" and "improving upon" the past through present-day dispositions and actions toward those in positions of vulnerability. This usage responds to my understanding of anthropology as a necessarily collaborative exercise, in which theoretical terms and analytics—here that of knotting—emerge from dialogue and fieldwork as mutually transformative processes. This interpretation of ethnography parts ways with illusions of the researcher's transparent authority on the one hand and fantasies of racialized and gendered access on the other. See Simpson (2016: 328), Strathern ([1988] 2004), De la Cadena (2015), and Haraway (1988).

11. Unlike the imagery of assemblages (Deleuze and Guattari 1987) or friction (Tsing 2005), knots emphasize connections as partial outcomes of ongoing efforts to maintain attachments to place and to history. This approach departs from studies that emphasize the haunting afterlives of hacienda systems and architectures (Lyons 2006 and Weaver 2020). Rifkin (2017: x) describes "temporal knottings" as "connections across time and with nonhuman entities" that are a "means of envisioning futurity" for Indigenous peoples. See also Pandolfo (2018) on knotted forms of subjectivity borne of injury and violence.

12. Michel de Certeau ([1980] 2011: xv) focuses, likewise, on "the intricate

forms of...the recomposition of a space by familial practices...and the tactics of the art of cooking, which simultaneously organizes a network of relations, poetic ways of 'making do' (bricolage), and a re-use of marketing structures." In my analysis, as for de Certeau, bricolage is a "making do" that necessarily contends with existing structures of authority and hierarchy. On historical ruination, see Stoler (2008). On the emergent dimensions of ruins, see Stewart (2007), Berlant (2008), and Carter (2009).

13. There are Andean precedents for this analytic of knotting as a kind of purposeful integration over time and of matter: the *khipus* with which Quechua Peruvians tell time and keep accounts (Salomon 2004); Aymara women's weavings in which aesthetic designs denote relations to kin, ancestors, and landscapes (Arnold 1993); and *thaki* memory paths through landscapes in which piles of sticks and rocks inscribe historical events and mark ongoing attachments to place (Abercrombie 1998).

14. This accords with Deborah Thomas's (2019: 220) call to critically reassess the political disavowals enacted in the name of aspirational, rights-based justice—what she calls a paradigm of *expectancy*. Such a project was anticipated by Franz Fanon (1952: 114) when he wrote: "The dialectic that introduces necessity as a support for my freedom expels me from myself. It shatters my impulsive position. Still regarding consciousness, black consciousness is immanent in itself. I am not a potentiality of something; I am fully what I am."

15. Although these policy documents used the term "slavery" metaphorically as a provocation to emphasize the continuities of colonial labor systems among Indigenous populations in present-day Bolivia, we should not lose sight of the fact that in the colonial viceroyalty of Peru, enslaved Africans arrived alongside Spanish conquistadores. African-descendent peoples were crucial to the building of early Spanish empire in the region. Moreover, following Garba and Sorentino (2020), "slavery" always operates as a metaphor insofar that it normatively judges a given condition of subjection through reference to a figure (the slave) that should not be mistaken for an ontological condition (e.g., a mode of being). On African slave regimes in colonial Peru, see Aguirre (2005), Bowser (1974), Flores Galindo (1984), and Lockhart (1968). For an account of contemporary Afro-Bolivian racial politics and identitarian mobilizing, see Zambrana (2014), Heck (2020), and Sturtevant (2017).

16. On the characterization of hacienda servants as "slaves," see Gotkowitz (2007: 192). See my detailed discussion of this reform program in Winchell (2016). For rural Indigenous Ayopayans' opposition to imposed temporalities of progress, see Winchell (2020).

17. See Pictou (2020: 372) and Povinelli (2016). Such disciplinary projects of modern citizenship are ongoing. In 2017, for instance, sixty Indigenous women in Saskatchewan sued the Canadian government for forcing them to accept sterilization before seeing newborn babies. For a review of forced sterilization in Canada, see the 2021 Senate report, discussed in *Global News* reportage, Fakiha Baig, "Indigenous Women Still Forced, Coerced into Sterilization: Senate report,"

Global News, June 3, 2021, https://globalnews.ca/news/7920118/Indigenous-women-sterilization-senate-report//.

18. Readers might want to know whether these initiatives to have been halted following Morales's 2019 resignation. During a January 2020 visit, government staff assured me that titling initiatives were ongoing.

19. For the continuities that link colonial, Republican and liberal paradigms of Indigenous uplift and liberty, see Larson (2004), Gotkowitz (2007), and Postero (2017).

20. In this regard, such programs of uplift are to a large degree "already embedded in the structure they would escape" (Moten 2007: 2; Butler [1997] 2021). For Puerto Rico, see Bonilla (2017: 331); for Australia, see Moreton-Robinson (2015).

21. See Bhandar (2018) and Thomas (2019). For a classic approach to this problem, see Hartman (1992).

22. On Bolivian land titling and Indigenous autonomy measures, see Anthias (2018), Anthias and Radcliffe (2013), Orta (2013).

23. For the entanglements that comprise what attempts to pass as autonomous sovereignty, see Cattelino (2015: 248) and Dennison (2017). On the limits to settler-colonial regimes of recognition and reparation and the reclaiming of relation as a site of historical redress, see Rifkin (2017); Simpson (2014); Arvin, Tuck, and Morrill (2013); Todd (2018); and Thomas (2019).

24. Kinship is often imagined in Western social theory as emblematic of "primitive" life before modern—i.e., alienated—exchange relations. In the premodern era, so the story goes, the world was defined not by contractual exchange among self-interested individuals but by the bonds, at times magnanimous but mostly despotic, of kinship and family. Drawing upon Aristotle, scholars like Hannah Arendt famously argue that prior to the fifteenth century, there was no firm distinction between the domain of the household (a common spatial retainer of kinship or family relations) and economy (Leshem 2014: 128). *Oikos*, or household, here constituted a site of crucial economic activity and rationality. In fact, the modern English word "economy" comes from the Greek *oikonomia*, the management (*nemein*) of the *oikos*. Instead of separating the domestic or "private" space from that of the economy, for Aristotle the family was a key sphere for "managing the necessities of life" and in this way sustaining the *polis* or political community. Modern sociality, for Arendt, developed by leaving behind this despotic realm, wherein ordinary life was defined by biological needs, and replacing it by establishing contractual relations among citizens—horizontal members of the polis (Leshem 2014: 123). Despite its earlier despotic expressions, Arendt aligned the ordinary or the mundane (including household practices that recall *oikos*) with ethical potentiality in its contrast with the polis, a domain defined by the masculinist search for individual glory. Elizabeth Povinelli (2006, 2011) has described this configuration as a liberal imaginary of "genealogical society" in which "the prior" is yoked to kinship-based attachments and bonds, and is opposed to individual liberty by way of the self-fulfillment of the

"autological subject." See also Mahmood (2004), Strathern (2005), Mody (2019), Berlant (1998), and Scott ([1988] 2018).

25. See Povinelli (2006: 14) and her discussion of the "genealogical subject." See Gow (1991) for a study of how Peruvian (economic) history is managed from within kinship structures rather than displacing them through ethnic acculturation.

26. See Edelman (2018) for an excellent discussion of how classic studies of hacienda and plantation economies commonly treated labor relations as occurring outside of racialized structures of coloniality in ways that presumed continuity without sufficiently asking what relations of power enabled the reproduction of labor structures. The analysis offered here pushes this critique one step further to show how the centering of (male/masculinized) labor in (Marxist) peasant studies has tended to overlook the interlocking nature of economy and kinship, racialized labor oppression and sexual violence.

27. Fred Moten (2003: 18) points to the importance of such a centering of reproduction for rethinking production as capital in the following terms: "This interest is, in turn, not in the interest of a nostalgic and impossible suturing of wounded kinship but is rather directed toward what this irrepressibly inscriptive, reproductive, and material objecthood does for and might still do to the exclusionary brotherhoods of criticism and black radicalism." My approach aims to take this project one step further to decouple questions of kinship from those of (biological) reproduction.

28. This definition of the good departed from that offered by Catholic theology (Smith [1776] 1977: 13).

29. I refer here to Smith ([1776] 1977), and after him, David Ricardo and Thomas Robert Malthus.

30. Readers might object that Smith himself formally opposed slavery on economic grounds, finding it economically constraining as it limited a person's capacity to change trades as much as he wishes. However, his work belongs to a natural rights tradition that saw liberty as intrinsic to but also severable from the person (Tuck 1979: 49). Moreover, as Pagden (1995) and Harris (2016) show, Smith's ideas were used to defend slavery long after a rationale of colonial Christianization lost favor.

31. Moreover, as Bhandar (2018: 30) has argued, this subject is also thoroughly gendered. See also Iman Jackson (2020: 4, 29, 159–60) and Stoler (2002).

32. As Bhandar (2018: 8) has argued, forms of market abstraction and racial subjectivity were produced through one another in the colonial context.

33. See Pagden (1995) for a discussion of the First and Second Colonialism and the shift away from religious to commercial ideologies. Pagden (1995: 9) also discusses Smith's elaboration of a model of political rule as a departure from feudalism, seen as a Roman inheritance. On "feudalism" as a modern invention, and the normative work it does, see Davis (2017).

34. See Stephenson (1999).

35. See Stoler (2002). For a comparative account of domestic labor and colonial racial regimes, see Ray and Qayum (2009).

36. On *limpieza de sangre* and nascent property regimes in the Spanish Americas, see Martínez (2008).

37. On the interface between Andean kinship practices and rights-based legal systems of nuclear family, see Leinaweaver (2008), Abercrombie (1998), and Babb (2018). For twentieth-century women's rights organizing in Bolivia, see Gotkowitz (2007).

38. During sixteenth-century colonial rule in Peru (Burns 1999), Indigenous women were subject to patriarchal discipline related to the disruptions that daughters of Inca nobility could pose to a nascent colonial property regime. After national independence and the formal end of colonial rule in 1825, these sexual and labor relations arose as especially uncomfortable reminders of the unfreedoms that accompanied earlier colonial projects of ostensible liberation, whether from pagan idolatry or, later, from feudal hierarchy. This highlights the fact that a gendered nature/culture binary (i.e., Smith's model of the unmarked but White male exchange partner as singularly human, and others as animal, irrational, or savage) was not a universal structure or semiotic framework but rather a *colonial artifact*. For a discussion of White male humanity and the racialized, gendered figure of the nonhuman, see Jackson (2020) and Wynter (2003).

39. For colonial Peru, see Burns (1999); for modern Peru, see Leinaweaver (2008). For the United States, see Pictou (2020) and Piatote (2013); for the Americas, see Dawson (2012). For a comparative discussion of Maori Indigeneity, see Tuhiwai Smith ([1999] 2012).

40. These children, often called *criadas*, were variously incorporated into homes but also treated as servants (Burns 1999: 16).

41. See Twinam (1999), and Weismantel and Wilhoit (2019).

42. According to *mestizaje*, money Whitens and de-Indigenizes; it also genders its carrier as more masculine. See Alonso (2004), Soruco Solguren (2011), and Wade (2005); on resistance to *mestizaje*, see Safa (2005).

43. See Safa (2005) and Soruco Solguren (2011).

44. As in colonial-era Indonesia and India (Ray and Qayum 2009; Stoler 2002), in Bolivia the development of a more spatially constricted model of kinship premised on the nuclear family was a central mechanism for solidifying, and defending, colonial hierarchies built upon Mestizo superiority. In this way, nonconjugal sexual practices and related arrangements of domestic labor, adoption, or godparenting assumed notable weight in the context of historical efforts to assimilate and eradicate Indigenous people. See Simpson (2016); on Indigenous kinship in relation to legal recognition policies; also see Strathern (2005) and Povinelli (2006).

45. See Stephenson (1999) and Pacheco (2017).

46. See Gotkowitz (2007).

47. These interventions rely upon classical views of economy that position the

nuclear household as a center of property transfer, but not paid labor. See Blofield (2009); see Ray and Qayum (2009) for a review of this scholarship.

48. On the anxieties about preserving kinship as a domain of racialized enclosure in conditions of neo/colonial rule and racialized labor hierarchies, see Stoler (2002), Mody (2008), Povinelli (2006), Martínez (2008), and Boddy (2011). Contemporary citizenship-making projects in Bolivia both blur and attempt to reinscribe this boundary between private and public, making each subject also a "sexual citizen" whose forms of intimate life amplify and undo broader configurations of national fraternity and kinship. This is evident in efforts to incorporate Indigenous value systems like Sumak Kawsay into Ecuadorian state governance, which have upheld the criminalization of violence against women while at the same time reinscribing family norms and state penal structures that limit women's access to justice (Tapia 2016). See also Weeks (1998), Puar (2007), Ginsburg and Rapp (1995), and Hunt (1992). For Bolivia, see Ellison's (2018: 23) discussion of alternate dispute resolution in Bolivia, in which she describes NGO officials' insistence that inequality be resolved in the private realm among spouses. See also Canessa's (2012: 278) discussion of how former President Morales's unmarried status was felt to impact his capacity to govern.

49. Historians like Brooke Larson (1998) and Susan Ramírez (2005) showed how Spanish colonialists partly integrated and honored Incaic exchange and how recently colonized groups made use of Incaic exchange practices as a basis for demanding colonial land rights. Later works describe how, into the late twentieth-century, Incaic and precolonial exchange and kinship traditions—and not just universal configurations of feudalism and peasantry—continue to shape labor systems and Indigenous political struggles in the region. See Harris (1995), Klein (1993), Larson (1998), Rivera Cusicanqui (1987), Ari (2014), De la Cadena (2014), and Soliz (2021). Anthropologists like John Murra (1968), Jonathan Parry (1989), and Olivia Harris (1989) have argued that the region is exemplary of the embedded qualities of economy, here defined by the distinct qualities of Andean kinship, reciprocity, and ritual exchange. Michael Taussig (1991: 287, 333) took this argument to its extreme to famously contrast the demonic qualities of capital with the ethical substance of Andean landscapes and kinship relations. This work recast Andean traditions of kinship-based collectivity as reserves of ethicality and healing against the torturous abstractions of colonial capital. See also Weismantel (1995), Bolton and Mayer (1977), Isbell (1978), Van Vleet (2008), Leinaweaver (2008), Arnold (2009), Canessa (2012), and Salas-Carreño (2016).

50. See Salomon (1986: 137).

51. See de Betanzos (1551 [1996]: 102–103), as cited by Leinaweaver (2008: 5).

52. See also Urton (1991), Wachtel (1977), and Abercrombie (1998). For an archaeological study of reciprocal offering, see Lau (2019).

53. See Leinaweaver (2008) for a review of this scholarship. See also Isbell (1978), Ossio (1984), and Van Vleet (2008).

54. See, in particular, Canessa (2014), De la Cadena (2014), Ellison (2018),

Leinaweaver (2008), Spedding (1998), and Van Vleet (2008). For a review of this scholarship, see Weismantel and Wilhoit (2019).

55. See also Hurtado (1986), Weismantel (1995), Swanson (2007: 715), and Harris (2008).

56. Arvin, Tuck, and Morrill (2013); for Bolivia, see Rivera Cusicanqui (2012); for a review of women's movements in Latin America, see Fernández Anderson (2020) and Safa (1990). For Bolivian scholarly analysis of *Indianismo*, see also Apaza Calle (2011); Ávila Rojas (2017); and Pacheco (1992). For a comparison with negritude, see Oliva Oliva (2010). For the exclusion of Kataristas from MAS governance, see Calle (2011) and Goodale (2019). For English-language engagements and reviews of Katarista thought, see Stephenson (2002) and Hylton, Thomson, and Gilly (2007).

57. Schavelzon (2016). For Peru, see Valdivia (2020). For accounts centered in North America, see also Pictou (2020), Rifkin (2017), Simpson (2014), TallBear (2018, 2019), and Todd (2018).

58. For kinship in regard to Indigenous decolonial projects, see Daigle (2018), Haraway (2016), Pictou (2020), Povinelli (2006), Rifkin (2017), Simpson (2014), Stevenson (2014), TallBear (2016, 2018, 2019), TallBear and Wiley (2019: 5), and Todd (2018). In addition, scholars have pointed out kinship's centrality to reckoning with histories of Black enslavement. See Hartman (1997, 2006), Hunter (2017), Miles (2015), and Sharpe (2016).

59. While acknowledging the brutality and violence of colonial pursuits of land, labor, and minerals, critics warn that this tendency to cast colonialism as sheer displacement overstates the efficacy of modern capitalism in its capacity to supplant other exchange traditions. See Weiner (1992), Parry (1986), Graeber (2011). On Andean systems of exchange and their displacement by colonial property, see Mayer (2007), Murra (1980), and Ramírez (1996, 2016); for a critique of this presumption of the colonial displacement of kinship-based land use, see Bastias Saavedra (2020: 223). For a theoretical discussion of alienability as crucial to colonial missionization projects, see Keane (2007). De la Cadena (2014) offers a crucial discussion of Quechua Peruvian orientations to land in terms of human and more-than-human relationalities that exceed property.

60. For Quechua perceptions of "places as kin" in Peru, see Salas-Carreño (2016). The last decade has witnessed burgeoning legal claims to the "environmental personhood" of ecological entities including trees, lakes, rivers, forests (*Te Urewera* in New Zealand), nonhuman animals (in India) and, in Ecuador, the Pachamama (see Khandelwal 2020 for a review).

61. Scholars from Karl Marx on have critiqued the civilizational connotations of this telos from kinship to capital, from gift to commodity relations, pointing out that contractual exchange elicited new forms of unfreedom and suffering. Rather than oppose kinship and economy, Marx ([1867] 1972: 393) argued that the division of labor in the household constituted the original class distinction that later reappeared in the manufacturer's workshop. Later, anthropologist Lewis Henry Morgan ([1868] 1997)—and then Claude Levi-Strauss (1969)—showed

how kinship structures and imaginaries of genealogical consanguinity were crucial to exchange relations, particularly land inheritance (see also Rubin 1975, whom I discuss below). Drawing from Marx's notes on Morgan, Friedrich Engels ([1884] 2010) argued that the rise of alienable property disempowered women, eliciting a shift from an original, matrilineal-based communism to patrilineality with the introduction of farming and pastoralism. Influenced by Marx, Bronislaw Malinowski (1922) and Marcel Mauss ([1925] 2016) focused on practices of "kula exchange" in the Trobriand Islands, which they argued constituted a tradition of gift exchange that blurred the lines between individual self-interest and altruism, chiefly power, and community well-being. Others, like sociologist Karl Polanyi ([1944] 2001), drew upon this work to contest a formalist approach and argue that all economies are *embedded* in social relations. Later, Marshall Sahlins (1972a) extended these insights to differentiate exchange into three modes of reciprocity: generalized, balanced, and negative. He argued that these different forms depended on the intensity and duration of ties between the people exchanging goods. Instead of treating private and public as empirical referents, Nancy Munn ([1986] 1992) and Marilyn Strathern ([1988] 2004) have shown how descriptors of "kinship" and "economy," gift and commodity, contain normative ideals that can be mobilized to challenge the ethicality of a given practice in light of more discrete or more expansive conceptions of personhood.

62. As Andrew Orta (2013: 130) has shown, the MAS party's designs imposed dramatic limits on Indigenous autonomy, *límites* operating simultaneously as a "territorial boundary, a threshold of acceptability, [and] an act of regulatory containment." I discuss these legal constraints and Ayopayan unionists' opposition to collective land titling in Winchell (2020). See also Anthias (2018).

63. For a discussion of the private/public divide as an ideology, see Gal (2002).

64. On ideas of the genealogical subject—the subject bound to tradition and to the family—as one that is tethered to legitimate Indigeneity within settler recognition paradigms, see Povinelli (2006), Simpson (2014), and Strathern ([1988] 2004); for Bolivia, see Canessa (2012). Within Bolivian governmental and Katarista projects, ayllu-based kinship is frequently evoked as an alternative to capital and a retainer of a distinctly Andean ethos of reciprocity. See Taussig (1991) and García Linera (2009). For a critique, see Rivera Cusicanqui (2012: 105). For the legal history of reforming ayllu-based household arrangements, see Larson (1998), Gotkowitz (2007), Platt (1982), and Stephenson (1999). On the interface of hacienda and ayllu forms, see Grieshaber (1979, 1980) and Klein (1993). For the promise of modern property as a means to disrupt Church and encomienda monopolies, see Langer and Jackson (1997).

65. See, for instance, Taussig (1980: 10, 70) and Nash (1993).

66. See also Weiss (2018: 141) and Dua (2019).

67. Bhandar (2018: 17) also makes this point.

68. This key point is treated in greater depth by Brown (2008) and Mahmood (2015).

69. See Skinner (1998: 40–41).

70. See Bhandar (2018: 19).

71. In the Andes such debates are apparent in Spanish legal distinctions between *dominio útil*, which was a form of nontransferable or inheritable ownership reserved for children and immature political subjects, including Indians, and *dominio directo*, which was a more complete model of ownership or possession that was legally available only to Mestizo and Spanish subjects. See Pagden (1995) and Ramírez (2016: 46–47).

72. As Asad (2003: 130, citing Tuck [1979: 49]) notes, it was only when medieval approaches to property rights as *claims* gave way to the late Middle Ages view of property rights as freely transferred that liberty was first seen as something alienable. In this way "a theory of rights sanctioned practices—such as slavery—that an antisubjectivist theory disallowed."

73. Throughout Latin America the fiction of consent facilitated the "lawful theft of [. . .] land" (Simpson 2016: 330) through the Spanish imperial tradition of *requierimiento*, the reading of a 1513 document in Spanish to Indigenous inhabitants. See Salomon and Urioste (1991). Jurisdiction here took root also through efforts to account for its absence, and legal claims to possession appear closer to magical conjuring than to science. For magic as a microcosm of society, see Jones (2017). On the cosmological and religious dimensions of possession as *dominio* in the Andes, see Abercrombie (1998) and Bastias Saavedra (2020).

74. Goldstein (2018) and Harris (1993).

75. Harris (1993: 1716).

76. See Humphrey and Verdery (2004: 9) and Bhandar (2018).

77. Scholars like Joseph W. Singer (2000) have critiqued the dominance of this ownership model for smoothing over the ways property is based on desire and on a set of (racialized and gendered) expectations of benefit. See the edited volume by Humphrey and Verdery (2004). Property holds various, at times antithetical, connotations: as abundance, as propriety, as an analytical concept, a political category, as a folk category or cultural ideal, and as intangible heritage, image, or software (Maurer 2004: 307). See also Bhandar (2018: 19), Goldstein (2018, citing Bentham 1843), Pottage (2004), Strathern (1988), and Grey (1980: 73–74).

78. See Locke ([1689] 2001), Hartman (1997), and Hunter (2017).

79. Hartman (1997), Dru Stanley (1998), and Hunter (2017) trace the centrality of contract—including as marriage, as paid labor, and as land ownership—to postbellum conceptions of anticolonial justice. In the French Caribbean, labor contracts and property ownership arose as indispensable tools for dismantling slavery (Scott 2013). As Bonilla (2015: 13) discusses, this occurred both through "the deployment of legal constraints (vagrancy statutes, black codes, contract systems, apprenticeship systems, and anti-enticement laws) and moral compulsions to enter the wage system—the latter operating through the promotion of ideas of responsibility, self-reliance, and industriousness."

80. As Hartman (1997) has compellingly shown, in the postbellum United States this process created blame-worthy subjects, reentrenching colonial paternalism and violence. It also shored up gendered models of postemancipation sub-

jectivity that upheld earlier connotations aligning Black women's bodies with property par excellence, as lucrative reserves of reproductive labor and repositories of the natural. See Hunter (2017), Iman Jackson (2020), and Wynter (2003). For Peru, see García (2005). For Bolivia, see Stern (1987) and Medeiros (2005). For Ecuador, see Lyons (2006).

81. For how contractual ideas of possessive individuality make some injuries visible and others unthinkable, see Strathern (2005) and Weiss (2018).

82. For accounts of the erasures of rights-based conceptions of proprietorial subjectivity as liberty in two very different contexts, see Scott (2004) and Asad (2003: 24). For a powerful discussion of how human rights frameworks delimit viable from unviable injuries and constrain ethical engagements with such injury, see Clarke (2009).

83. For this problem in the French Caribbean, see Bonilla (2015: 11–12).

84. This argument was made by Mintz (1974). See also Bonilla (2015) for a discussion of the forms of sociality that were stamped out by a new model of sovereignty as self-possession.

85. For this reason scholars like Verene Shepherd (2018) have powerfully argued that property-based reparations are indispensable as routes of historical redress. See also Jordon, Mount, and Parker (2018) and McKeown (2021).

86. See Graeber (2011).

87. Larson (2014); for North America, see Greer (2012).

88. For a discussion of the German and French approaches to property, see Humphrey and Verdery (2004).

89. As Bastias Saavedra (2020: 223) has noted, narrating Indigenous communal landholding as displaced by Western frameworks of private property or Christian possession risks leaving intact Spanish systems of possession or money as consolidated outside history. For conjunctural approaches complicating historical frameworks of peasant "resistance" to colonial money systems, see Larson, Harris, and Tandeter (1995). See also Pagden (1995), Klein and Vinson (2007), Mayer (2007), Murra (1980), and Ramírez (1996, 2016).

90. As Herzog (2015) points out, at issue is not only the matter of colonial origins (e.g., Britain or Spain) but rather the need to develop a more conjunctural approach to property's trappings as historically elaborated through conquest. Acts of surveying and legal regimes of ownership belonged to this story, but so did colonial agents' legal and armed conflicts with Indigenous populations over definitions of rightful possession and its inscription in space. This complicates the tendency, apparent in the work of Marxist critics of colonial exploitation like Eduardo Galeano (1971), to view colonial ownership as universal, unaffected by the traditions of land use, exchange, and authority with which colonial authorities, missionaries, and representatives of the crown necessarily had to contend. On the intersection of precolonial and colonial exchange traditions in the Andes, see Kosiba and Hunter (2017), Mayer (2002), Murra (1980), and Ramírez (1996, 2016).

91. See Strathern ([1988] 2004: 147).

92. On the division of land through the *repartimiento* system, including its reliance on jurisdiction based on ethnography that changed local perceptions of history and time, see Mumford (2008), Stern (1982), Vanvalkenburg (2017), and Wernke (2013).

93. Ramírez (2005).

94. See Larson (1998, 2004), MacCormack (2007), and Herzog (2015).

95. These arrangements included practices of gifting and aid, including grain provisions in times of famine or drought. These relations and communal land control came under attack in the 1780s with liberal concerns about assimilating Indigenous people and the accompanying imposition of a more constricted model of native "communities" (Larson 1998 and Thurner 1993).

96. Of course, critics of Western modernity like Marx and Proudhon had long argued that property constituted a sort of despotic domination and ethical failing, a theft. See Marx ([1842] 1975: 235). On modern sovereignty as the fixing of jurisdiction over people and space, see Bonilla (2015), Ford (2010), Kahn (2018: 8, 207), and Dua (2019). On property as a solution to hacienda injustice, see Anthias (2018), Larson (1998), and Gotkowitz (2007).

97. See Thomson (2002: 11); for Haiti, see Scott (2004).

98. See Stern (1982), Vanvalkenburg (2017), and Wernke (2013).

99. This process was contested through litigation and popular Indigenous unrest (Platt 1987 and Grieshaber 1980), leading to government concessions.

100. Larson (2004: 204–15).

101. See Larson (2004: 226–27).

102. See Klein (1993: 21). On competing ownership regimes in colonial Peru's dual republic system, see Thurner (1997).

103. For the central role that Indigenous (Quechua and Aymara) peasant unions played in their shaping the terms of mid-twentieth-century agrarian reform in the Cochabamba region of Bolivia, see Hines (2022) and Soliz (2021).

104. Soliz (2021: 10) offers a careful study of this bottom-up process.

105. See Choque Canqui (1986); Saavedra (2014: 81); Pati Paco, Mamani Ramirez, and Quise Chipana (2009: 20). For an English-language history of Katarismo, see Stephenson (2002).

106. Tockman, Cameron, and Plata (2015: 40, 52); see also Orta (2013: 130). As I discuss in chapter 3, Bolivia's 2009 constitution and a 2010 Framework Law of Autonomies and Decentralization established three avenues for attaining Indigenous autonomy: municipal conversion, autonomous territory, and autonomous regions or joint municipalities.

107. Anthias (2019) has shown how lowland groups have used Indigenous autonomy programs to negotiate private mining contracts with multinational corporations. In this regard, legalistic approaches to indigenous territory in Bolivia often do not vary as substantially from private property regimes as might be expected.

108. See Lopez Pila (2014), Postero (2017), and Canessa (2012).

109. For a parallel argument about the production of Indigenous citizenship

through language revitalization efforts in Peru, see García (2005). For racial commodification as an accompaniment to reified property, see Harris (1993), Bhandar (2018), Greene (2009), and Fanon (1963).

110. Ford (2010).

111. These processes worked through jurisdiction and its absence, interdiction, as a claim about the exceptional or external status of an event, location, or case. See Kahn (2018: 8, 207).

112. For instance, Graeber (2011) discusses how contemporary mortgage-lending practices unravel ideas that modern property arrangements and leases are fully distinct from earlier institutions of tenant leasing or tithe farming. Moreover, Ferraro (2004: 83) has demonstrated how, in the Ecuadorian Andes, debt operates not only as economic dependency but also as a domain of moral or spiritual potency: for instance, it may be a condition for the land's future fertility. See also Chu (2014). On the obduracy of assumptions of property's telos, see Carter (2008: 16).

113. I discuss this fantasy of historical detachment at greater length in chapter 3. For a related critique of map-making in Australia, see Carter (2008).

114. This insight builds upon scholarship tracking practices of survey, cartography, mapping, and transnational management and interdiction as crucial mechanisms for bureaucrats, managers, environmental experts, and lawyers to produce "nature" (including oil, water, wind, and forests) as a collection of commodities and resources to be managed. See Appel (2020), Appel, Mason and Watts (2015), Mathews (2011), Ballastero (2019), Raffles (2002), Tsing (2012); for Bolivia, see Anthias (2018), Anthias and Radcliffe (2013); and Fabricant and Gustafson (2011).

115. Writing about the Indian Act in Canada, Bhandar (2018: 14, 30) aptly identifies this as the "identity-property" nexus of Indian status. For Peru, see García (2005).

116. See Jackson (1994: 182).

117. On popular disenchantment with MAS decolonization projects, see Dunkerley (2007: 148), Hylton et al. (2003), Swinehart (2019), and Winchell (2020).

118. More precisely, Marx ([1844] 1978: 73) accuses the discipline of Political Economy (and Adam Smith) of ventriloquizing the desires of capitalism and concealing those within its theoretical terms, specifically that of private property. Moten takes up this commodity speech in regard to the shriek and song of enslaved Africans who spoke, and not just as a ventriloquizing of the theorist or capital. While Moten (2003: 11) argues that their speech and sound refused or staged an "objection to exchange," my analysis draws from historical and anthropological studies of Andean kinship and exchange systems to challenge the presumption that capital's entification is the only exchange form within which enslaved and indentured peoples, and their descendants, operate.

119. As Rubin (1975: 46) reminds us, what is exchanged in kinship is not just women: "They exchange sexual access, genealogical statuses, lineage names and ancestors, rights, and *people*—men, women, and children—in concrete systems

of social relationships." Moreover, as I discussed earlier, for Smith this included a passage through slavery as a stage of racialized commodification.

120. Smith ([1776] 1977) put forth two theories of value, one for "primitive" people and another for "civilized" society. In the former, value depended on the amount of labor used to produce a given thing while in the latter, it resulted from exchange. In dialogue with Smith, Marx ([1842] 1975: 229) argued that rather than being a natural proclivity, exchange was a historical and societal construct. In fact, while critics of classical distinctions have challenged the normative connotations of modern exchange, they have left intact its telos. For instance, Karl Polanyi ([1944] 2001: 44) divided societies into three different models of integrated economy: reciprocity, redistribution, and exchange, wherein exchange displaced the former two. Polanyi saw this transformation of *sentiment* as inexorable. As he wrote, "obviously, the dislocation caused by such devices must disjoint man's relationships and threaten his natural habitat with annihilation" (Polanyi [1944] 2001: 44). Mauss ([1925] 2016: 58) emphasized the survivals of earlier exchange traditions in modern gift relations, yet he too characterized the gift as an "enduring form of contractual ethics." "Enduring" signals what was, for him, the gift's anachronous character. Marshall Sahlins (1972a: 140) similarly distinguished "primitive exchange" as community building and redistributive ethics from production-based transactions in "modern exchange." In primitive exchange, much more than modern society, the *materiality* of the forms exchanged is crucial to the social relations they produce.

121. In fact, a defining feature of a gift as opposed to a commodity is *time* (Mauss [1925] 2016). It is the delay in reciprocation that produces the gift's value in and as sociality. See also Munn ([1986] 1992), Strathern ([1988] 2004), and Guyer (2016).

122. On the temporality of injury, see Butler (1997), Comay (2008), Das (2007), and Pandolfo (2018).

123. See, for instance, Keane (2007) and Lambek (1993).

124. See De la Cadena (2014).

125. As I discuss in chapter 4, the province's history of Indigenous labor mobility, overlapping systems of land use across municipal boundaries and with multiple owners, and asymmetrical aid relations with Mestizo elites overflowed the kinds of spatial and ethnic enclosure implied by governmental programs of installing individual property and Indigenous territory. This complicates the evolutionist typology outlined above, in which modern exchange displaces redistribution and reciprocity as emblems of primitive exchange. On conjunctural approaches to exchange in the Andes, see also Larson (2004: 211), Parry and Bloch (1989), and Platt (1982). On the ethical dimensions of revived Indigenous shamanic traditions as forms of historical reckoning in Latin America, see Bacigalupo (2016), Langdon (2016), and Taussig (1991).

126. Strathern (2005: 24).

127. See Costa (2018) for how Amazonian Kanamari people refuse kinship ties to White outsiders.

128. My own approach is closest to that of Seligmann (1993), who viewed exchange as a practice by which Quechua women navigated disparate value systems related to rural Indigeneity and Mestizo markets.

129. Such a tethering of relations to place and history recalls Veena Das's (2006: 71) discussion of the case of Asha, who views her relationships through a "temporal depth" that makes her hesitant to sever ties even as she acknowledges the fragility and pain of attachment. Here, I also take inspiration from Lieba Faier's (2009: 14) study of Filipina migrant laborers in Japan, in which she attends to intimacy as a set of "social and spatial proximities" that both reproduce and at times surprisingly transform "mutual, unequal dependencies." See also Ray and Qayum (2009), Guyer (1993), Wilson (2004), Faier (2009), and Yanagisako (2002).

130. Suspending the premise of property as a normalized division or "cutting" (Strathern 2005: 24) between here and there, then and now, workers demanded a durative orientation to wealth as an outcome of racial violence in haciendas and mines.

131. See Appel (2020: 244).

132. See also Dua (2019), Graeber (2001: xii), Kahn (2018), and Appel (2019).

133. I am drawing from Hartman (1992: 3), Simpson (2016: 328), Sharpe (2016:113–19), and Moten (2003). For an argument that emphasizes Indigenous *endurance* (rather than an apolitical or passive continuity), see Kauanui (2016).

134. For this reason the authors call for renewed attention to responsibility as "grounded in actual practices and place-based relationships." Recent debates in critical Indigenous studies call for attention to relationality both as a basis for Indigenous solidarity and resurgence and as a condition of transformative Indigenous-settler dynamics (Daigle 2018, Pictou 2020, Rifkin 2017, TallBear and Wiley 2019: 5, and Todd 2018). Regarding the generative dimensions of the entanglement of Western legal systems of property and Indigenous relationalities, see Cattelino (2008), Simpson (2014), and Dennison (2017).

135. Recalling discourses of the sovereign and custom-bound subject, here kinship is "not a thing but a moving target" (Povinelli 2006: 14).

136. According to Bolivia's most recent census (INE 2012), the population of the municipality of Independencia in the province of Ayopaya is 23,658 people, 17,918 of whom listed Quechua as their primary language. The population of the municipal center in 2012 was 4,938 people (see INE 2012, http://censosbolivia.ine.gob.bo/censofichacomunidad/c_listadof/listar_comunidades).

137. I completed 120 open-ended Quechua and Spanish interviews with members of former *hacendado* and servant families, farmers, shop owners, municipal officials, domestic workers, mine owners, and miners.

138. While existing studies focus on more masculine domains of tenant farming and peasant unionism in the Andes, former hacienda servants with whom I spoke described agricultural production as sustained by unpaid domestic labor. For two important exceptions, see Gordillo (2000) and Lyons (2006).

139. By the time I wrapped up by doctoral research in 2012, however, my con-

versations with close friends and activists seemed to have subtly changed this narrative. In one weekly "popular history lesson" that I attended, the speaker spoke at length about Cochabamba's "distinct" labor history and the challenges it had raised for projects of Indigenous land recuperation.

140. The Central Union of Campesino Workers of Ayopaya, in Spanish, is the Central Sindical Única de Trabajadores Campesinos Originarios de Ayopaya. In Bolivia, unions or *sindicatos* tend to be associated with the political goals of the earlier MNR (Movimiento Nacional Revolucionario) government. However, at a village level, in Ayopaya and elsewhere *sindicatos* also uphold elements of community and ayllu-based governance systems, and in other cases have reintroduced them. See Orta (2013: 118).

141. This became clear to me during an early oral history interview with Doña Carmenia Montero, an elderly shepherdess in Sanipaya and a former hacienda servant. When I asked what the *hacendados* were like, she answered: "More or less like you...light skin, brown hair."

142. See Haraway (1988).

CHAPTER 1. CLAIMING KINSHIP

1. On twentieth-century labor discourses of hacienda servitude as "slavery," see Keith (1977). For a historical comparison of hacienda and plantation labor, see Klein and Vinson (2007) and Wolf and Mintz (1957).

2. On how sentiments shape conditions of bonded labor and domestic service, see Ray and Qayum (2009) and Yanagisako (2002). For Bolivia, see Lyons (2006) and Gill (1994).

3. On moral imaginaries of labor debt in the Andes, see Mintz and Wolf (1950: 361–64).

4. On domestic labor as a problematic feudal residue or colonial inheritance, see Ray and Qayum (2009). For Bolivia, see Gotkowitz (2007).

5. Fabio was mostly in Cochabamba those final months, accompanying his ailing wife, so I was not able to speak with him directly about this matter.

6. On how intimate relationships elicit dramatic anxieties for the rights-based project of installing political and economic liberty, see Mahmood (2015) and Mody (2019).

7. Here, as for Mariner (2019: 31), kinship involves "intimate speculation." In the context I describe, such anticipatory forms operate in an atmosphere of modernizing reform that casts speculation as irrational and immature (for India, see Ramberg 2014), and therefore confirming the blame-worthy status of its participants.

8. This extends a classic theme in economic anthropology since at least Munn ([1986] 1992: 13): the mobilization of descriptive categories (such as of kinship or capital, gift or commodity, reciprocity and hierarchy) as a basis of normative cri-

tique, not only by scholars but also by ethnographic interlocuters. For kinship-based racial justice in postslavery and settler-colonial societies, see Carby (2019), Hartman (2008, 2020), and Miles (2015). For kinship as an ethical form for nego-tiating historical violence, see Butler (2000), Das (2006), Mueggler (2001), Sharpe (2016), and Lambek (2002).

9. See Thurner (1993: 35) and Lyons (2006: 182, 185).

10. Brian Massumi (2002: 39) calls this the "felt reality of relation." Or, to use Danilyn Rutherford's (2016: 286) language, these are the "forces that move peo-ple" and lead to feelings of compelled action.

11. See Tomic et al. (2006). For Latin America, see Rubbo and Taussig (1983).

12. See Stoler (2002: 11) and Taussig (1986: 58).

13. On the modern invention of a "feudal" past, see Davis (2017).

14. In this regard, looking at how intimate ties shaped domestic labor rela-tions in Bolivia and elsewhere complicates the tendency for scholars to align the problem of affective labor with neoliberal care industries or to "postindustrial labor" in call centers, tech firms, banks, and other service industries (see Hardt 1999: 95; Lazzarato 2012).

15. See Faier (2009) and Buch (2013).

16. As Marx wrote in *Capital* (as cited in Ray and Qayum 2009: 1): "Types of work that are consumed as services and not in products separable from the worker, and not capable of existing as commodities independently of him...are of microscopic importance when compared with the mass of capitalist produc-tion. They may be entirely neglected, therefore."

17. See also my discussion of Rubin (1975) in the introduction.

18. See also Proudhon (1840 [1994]).

19. As discussed in chapter 2, in the precolonial Andes systems of vertical control were premised on notions of reciprocity organized across dispersed settle-ments (Murra 1968, 2017). Unlike nucleated settlements, such patterns were pre-mised on nested groups including ayllus, lineages, community, tribe, and ethnic lordship themselves linked by a shared ancestor-god and divided into dual moi-eties and satellite mitimae settlements (Larson 1998: 22).

20. See Lyons (2006).

21. See Tylor (1861: 250–51) and Mintz and Wolf (1950: 362).

22. See also Bolton and Mayer (1977) and Arnold (1998).

23. See also Albro (2000) and Postero (2007).

24. See Scott (1985: 162, 194–95).

25. For a detailed discussion of this "authority complex," its historical under-pinnings in Incan political systems, and its Spanish appropriations, intention and accidental, see Sallnow (1989).

26. See Allen (1982) and Canessa (2012).

27. See Gill (2004) and Canessa (2012). On twentieth-century reformist views of hacienda labor as a violation of a national ideals of the Mestizo nuclear fam-ily, see Stephenson (1999).

28. On Ayopaya's history of agrarian servitude and antihacienda organizing in

the Chayanta Rebellion of 1947, see Jackson (1994), Dandler and Torrico (1987), and Gotkowitz (2007).

29. On the expulsion of Jesuits from the region in 1767, see Larson (1998: 225).

30. Quechua servants and tenant farmers took advantage of a crumbling landholding class in the 1870s to purchase land (Jackson 1994: 86, 151–53).

31. On Andean oral and folkloric traditions concerning White or Criollo greed, see Weismantel (2001), Nash ([1980] 1993), and Taussig (1986).

32. See Sallnow (1989: 209).

33. In the Andes, *ch'allas* began as ritualized displays of tributary payment to *hacendados*, a practice wherein various villages of tenant farmers competed over who could deliver more bounty to the town home of the *patrón*. See Thurner (1993: 70).

34. On gifts, including gifts of labor, to hacienda landlords, see Harris (1989) and Thurner (1993).

35. See my discussion of Agrarian Reform Law 3545 in chapter 3.

36. On "natural children," see Harvey (1998).

37. On hacienda patronage see Mintz and Wolf (1950), Ossio (1984), Spalding (1970), Wade (2009), and Lyons (2006: 12).

38. During fieldwork between 2011 and 2012, I expressed interest in interviewing Hasintu Soliz directly, but from his unreceptivity to my interview invitations I gathered he was not keen to speak to me. As such, my account of this case draws unduly from the narratives of Flora and her son Raul.

39. On the antebellum context in the United States, see Hartman (1997: 79–114).

40. In a 1942 petition Grájeda and other union leaders complained of cases of rape (*estupro* or *violacíon*) of "single and married women" and the whipping of *colono* workers (Gotkowitz 2007: 147).

41. See Lyons (2006: 169–70) on accepting responsibility for hacienda violence.

42. Here, as for other ethnographic interlocutors, Raul used *errores* to denote sexual impropriety.

43. As I discuss in chapter 2, *forastero* was a fiscal category used to denote mobile laborers who lacked land (Larson 1998: 112) or "Indians without an ayllu" (Jackson and Maddox 1993).

44. See Thomas (2019: 212) and Nelson (2015) on the limits to reparation-based accounting.

45. See Thurner's (1993: 45) critique of the language of hacienda laborers as pre-political subjects.

46. On lowland land titling and autonomy movements, see Anthias (2018), Fabricant (2012: 158–82), and Postero (2007).

47. Echoing divine authority in the colonial past, haciendas bound wealth to redistributive practices that, conversely, aligned tribute payments with peasant land claims (Harris 1989: 241).

48. On masters' involvement in ritual practices as key to popular assessments of legitimate authority, see Harris (1989: 246).

49. See Bolivia's Childhood and Adolescence Code (2014) and Family and Relatives Procedure Code (2014).

50. On claims to dependency, see Strathern ([1988] 2004), Ferguson (2013), and Piliavsky (2020). For the Andes, see Parry and Bloch (1989).

51. While in many cases earlier servitude experiences remain opaque in the present (Lyons 2006; for a US comparison, see Sharpe 2016 and Hartman 1997), this partial unavailability of the past in the present does not mean scholars should discount people's own accounts of earlier events in which they participated, here how they narrate hierarchical aid relations and their lapses and transgressions.

52. For verticality as a structure of exchange and ethos see Larson (1998: 20), Harris (1989), Murra (1968), and Wachtel (1977: 83).

53. See Guyer (2016) for Mauss's notion of *rendre* or return.

CHAPTER 2. GIFTING LAND

1. In the early 1950s the area housed more than four hundred workers. INRA Archive, CBA.03.00010.01 Sanipaya, consulted by the author in November 2011.

2. See Orta (2013); for Ecuador, see Colloredo-Mansfield (2009).

3. Carter (2008: 83).

4. See Rivera Cusicanqui (2014: 99).

5. My discussion here draws heavily upon Larson (1998: 17–68).

6. See Lyons (2006: 36); Salomon and Urioste (1991).

7. Urton and Chu (2018).

8. Mumford (1998: 68).

9. Jackson (1994: 25).

10. Larson (1998: 68).

11. See Larson (1998: 71).

12. Larson (1998: 79).

13. Wolf and Mintz (1957) and Lyons (2006: 48) discuss forced labor and sexual ties between forced laborers and Spanish encomienda lords.

14. See Larson (1998: 83, citing Barnadas).

15. Larson (1998: 156).

16. Following the 1938 constitutional convention, *colonos* from various provinces in Cochabamba filed petitions against continued servitude, contesting the landlords' arbitrary change to usufruct plots as well as evictions, plot substitution, and continued *mitanaje*.

17. Gotkowitz (2007: 147).

18. Gotkowitz (2007: 122–24).

19. Expressed in Quechua: "Propietarios kunan ch'isi lloqsipuichis de buenas

o wañunkichi kaypi. O wañusunchis kaypi enteritunchis, porque tiyan reforma agraria kunanqa!"

20. My discussion builds heavily from Gotkowitz (2007: 237–63).

21. Gotkowitz (2007: 239).

22. This was expressed to me in Quechua as: "Allin ripunku ah, kunanqa samarisunchik ninku."

23. This was expressed to me in Quechua as: "Allin ripun niyku. Paykuna sufrichun kikin."

24. See Langer (1985, 1989), Larson (1998), Lyons (2006: 17, 19, 43), Oberem (1981), and Orlove (1974).

25. For Andean agrarian ritual practices, see Abercrombie (1998), Allen (1982), Canessa (2012), De la Cadena (2015), Earls (1969), Gose (1994), and Isbell (1978).

26. See Jackson (1994: 202) for this argument.

27. As Orta (2013: 118) has argued, despite these continuities with the past, peasant unions in the twenty-first century underwent a sort of "second reduction" related to political decentralization into rural municipalities, dividing larger villages into two parts, or cabildos, and imposing new forms of legibility on ayllus at the national level. See also Hines (2021) and Soliz (2021).

28. See Stern (1987) and Thurner (1993).

29. For a discussion of servitude as a key site of peasant and Indigenous activism leading up to and around the time of the 1952 Socialist Revolution, see Chipana Ramos (2018). For a comparison with antiservitude politics in Columbia, see Rubbo and Taussig (1983).

30. Gotkowitz (2007: 140–41) and Jackson (1994: 164).

31. On the popularization of a stigmatized idea of slavery on haciendas, see Thurner (1993: 73).

32. Expressed in Quechua as: "Kay runamanllataq jallp'asta qichunku mana patrónpata qichunkuchu."

33. Expressed in Quechua as: "Esclavitud tiempo pasakapunña."

34. Expressed in Quechua as: "Chay tiempoqa pasakapunña unay."

35. Expressed in Quechua as: "Chanta khuska runa kutirin a favor."

36. Expressed in Quechua as: "Chaykuna a favor del patrón correayqachriq kanku."

37. Expressed in Quechua as: "Chaykuna enemigosnin rikhurinku."

38. Expressed in Quechua as: "Kunawan mana quykuchu ni imata."

39. Thurner (1993: 53).

40. The term *melga* derives from a Spanish administrative system in which it denoted a single parcel of land.

41. Gotkowitz (2007: 137).

42. Lyons (2006:123) and Isbell (1978).

43. Regional land collectivization debates are addressed in detail in chapter 4, while new gold-mining economies are the focus of chapter 5.

44. Gotkowitz (2007: 138).

45. Taussig (1987: 287).

46. Larson (1998: 73). See also Wolf and Mintz (1957); for Ecuador, see Lyons (2006: 44).

47. INRA CBA.03.00010.01 Sanipaya.

48. On African slave regimes in colonial Peru, see Aguirre (2005), Bowser (1974), Flores Galindo (1984), and Lockhart (1968). For a comparison of Indigenous hacienda labor and African plantation labor, see Klein and Vinson (2007) and Wolf and Mintz (1957). In contrast to tendencies to compare haciendas and plantations, Federico and Franz's biographical itineraries highlight their mutuality as oppressive labor regimes in which laborers moved from one to another and in which Mestizo families were masters upon both.

49. See Leinaweaver (2008) and Arnold (1998).

50. Leinaweaver (2008: 164).

51. These earlier anxieties with modernizing the countryside haunted Bolivia's Socialist agrarian reform of 1953. Reformers and progressive unionists perceived hacienda servants, but much more rarely former hacienda masters, as living embodiments of the obstructions to modernity, here associated with the spread of a more disentwined, abstract orientation to money and land. See Wolf and Mintz (1957) and Lyons (2006: 73).

52. Similarly, in Chile a Mapuche man who collaborated with consultants concerning the building of a hydropower dam in Mapuche-Willliche Territory was chastised by leaders for being a "yanacona" (Sarah Kelly, personal communication with the author, 2018).

53. In Spanish: "No somos colonos ni bestias humanas" and "Somos Bolivianos, hijos milenarios de esta tierra."

54. See Fabricant (2012: 21, 122). For a critique, see Soliz (2017: 262).

55. Here, it is revealing that the colonial use of *yanacona* (indentured servant on agrarian estate) hinged on proximate residence, naming Indians who lived "near or for a Spaniard" (Larson 1998: 82, citing Murra 1968: 225–42) rather than ossified labor status.

CHAPTER 3. PRODUCING PROPERTY

1. An earlier version of this chapter appeared as Mareike Winchell, "After Servitude: Bonded Histories and the Encumbrances of Exchange in Indigenizing Bolivia," *Journal of Peasant Studies* 45, no. 2 (2018): 453–73. DOI: 10.1080/03066150.2016.1229309. I thank the journal for their permission to reprint the article in this chapter form.

2. On subsidy programs aimed at providing Bolivians' "basic needs," see Ballard and Banks (2003: 299) and Albro (2005: 442). On food-sharing as crucial to legitimate authority, see Ramírez (2005), Harris (1986, 1989), Murra (2017), and Tassi (2010).

3. MAS accused US NGOs of violating the nation's sovereignty in their efforts to affect national politics (Achtenburg 2015).

4. The term *saneamiento* is used throughout Latin America to denote the regularization of social services, including public health institutions.

5. See Wolford (2010) and Li (2014). For Bolivia, see Anthias (2018) and Fabricant (2012).

6. By contrast, classic anthropological studies of Andean and Amazonian land relations have long cast doubt over the idea that land is reducible to its productive dimensions (Abercrombie 1998, Allen 2002, Gose 1994, Isbell 1978, and Raffles 2002).

7. De la Cadena (2015) and Salas-Carreño (2016).

8. MacCormick (1998: 337).

9. Lyons (2006: 102) and De la Cadena (2015: 106).

10. See Bacigalupo (2016), De la Cadena (2015), Di Giminiani (2018), and Orta (2013). For historical accounts of twentieth-century Bolivia, see Hines (2021) and Soliz (2021).

11. See Chumacero (2011) and Lastarria-Cornhiel (2007).

12. See also Lopez Pila (2014: 431) and Patzi (2004). For Ecuador, see Colloredo-Mansfield (1998).

13. Paul Carter (2008) describes this as the "stitching" of people to landscape, one that retains its mark in cartographic maps.

14. On eighteenth-century pan-Indigenous mobilizations for collective land, see Thomson (2002). For twentieth-century Quechua and Aymara organizing for the return of land expropriated by hacienda expansion, see Soliz (2017).

15. In the lowlands protests arose in 2000 and 2005 over the fact that only 15 million of roughly 107 million hectares of land had been "regularized" since 1996 (Fabricant 2012: 138; Assies 2006; and Urioste 2007).

16. As cited in Fabricant (2012: 140).

17. This absence of legal backing for *latifundio* redistribution was a central point of contention in post-2006 reform efforts. See Zimmerer (2014: 5).

18. Soliz (2017: 66).

19. See Ari (2014) and Rivera Cusicanqui (1987).

20. This reform is regulated by a 2006 law, specifically the Ley de Servicio Nacional de Reforma Agraria and the Ley No. 3545 de Reconducción Comunitaria de la Reforma Agraria.

21. Fabricant (2012: 138).

22. See also Malloy (1970) and Chumacero (2012).

23. Fabricant (2012: 172). See also Gustafson (2010), Soruco Sologuren (2011), and Postero (2017) on constitutional land rights in Bolivia.

24. Fabricant (2012: 173); Tockman, Cameron, and Plata (2015); and Urioste (2011).

25. Lastarria-Cornhiel (2007: 9); Farthing and Kohl (2012); and González Nuñez (2014).

26. Dandler and Torrico (1986).

27. Zimmerer (2014: 5).

28. See my discussion in chapter 2 of how early colonial reforms reorganized native groups and *mitmaq* collectivities into geographically bounded territories termed "Indian communities."

29. For instance, Ouweneel (2005: 92) writes, the ayllu was "established as part of a lordship... [but then] became more egalitarian during the Spanish period because of Spanish pressure to rotate its principal office and to secure it within fixed boundaries."

30. Andolina, Laurie, and Radcliffe (2009); and Farthing (2009).

31. Hurtado (1986: 221).

32. Millones (2007).

33. Thomson (2002) and Larson (2004).

34. Mamani Ramírez (2015: 40).

35. Ticona Alejo (2010: 50). For English-language accounts of ayllu-based ethical systems premised upon asymmetrical exchange, see Abercrombie (1998), Allen (2002), Arnold (1998), Gose (1994), Harris (1978, 1980, 1986), Mayer (1974, 2007), and Orta (2004).

36. Ari (2014).

37. Salazar de la Torre, Rodríguez Franco, and Sulcata Guzmán (2012: 12); and Orta (2013: 100).

38. Calle (2010); see also Postero (2017: 14); Fabricant and Gustafson (2014: 5).

39. Carter and Mamani (1978) and Buechler (1969).

40. Yampara (2011) and Coila (2020: 45).

41. Portugal Mollinedo (2020).

42. In 2013 the newspaper *Los Tiempos* (June 30, 2013) reported that merely 30 percent of the country's land had been successfully regularized.

43. Like Juan Perón in Argentina, the MIR is known for having personal ties to citizens and, conversely, for emphasizing leaders' redistributive obligations to citizens. See Lazar (2008: 105).

44. See Canessa (2012: 214); for Peru, see García (2005).

45. See Valdivia (2010) and Rivera Cusicanqui (1987).

46. For Bolivia, see Canessa (2012: 184–215); for Guatemala, see Nelson (1999: 12); and for Peru, see García (2005).

47. Harris (1989: 239); Parry and Bloch (1989).

48. The term "orthophotograph," coined in the 1950s, refers to an image produced optically or electronically from aerial photographs that eliminates distortions related to the earth's curvature.

49. See Michel de Certeau ([1980] 2011).

50. See Fabricant (2012), Urioste (2001, 2005, 2007), Urioste et al. 2007, Soruco Sologuren, Plata, and Medeiros (2007), and Soruco Sologuren (2011).

51. For an overview of Overlay toolset, see http://pro.arcgis.com/en/pro-app /tool-reference/analysis/an-overview-of-the-overlay-toolset.htm (accessed February 1, 2019).

52. See Riles (2006) for the ethical weight of transparency-based reforms under neoliberalism.

53. See Johnson (2010).

54. Gotkowitz (2007); for Peru, see De la Cadena (2015).

55. The notion of "Indian community" was itself formalized in Toledan land resettlement policy (1569–81) and later revived by midcentury land activists and agrarian reformers throughout the Andean region (Mallon 1993 and Colloredo-Mansfield 1998).

56. See Orta (2013: 110) and Postero (2007).

57. To make sense of the civilizational connotations of property, one need only look at Locke's early 1690 work, *Two Treatises of Government*. In that work Locke ([1690] 1980: 6, 12) characterized life in the precolonial Americas and outside institutions of liberal contract "noxious," requiring eradication through the implementation of property as "private right." As the secretary to the Council of Trade and Plantations (1673–74) and member of the Board of Trade (1696–1700) responsible for the American colonies as well as a major investor in the English slave trade through the Royal African Company and the Bahama Adventurers company (Quiggin 2015), Locke surely held a personal stake in the colonial project of capital.

58. See Locke ([1690] 1980: 8, 12). In addition, Locke ([1690] 1980: 12) put forth a notion of "waste land" that could be legitimately possessed in order to maximize its potential productivity; conversely, the failure to "improve" such land meant it could be rightfully appropriated. But rather than seeing land as a latent source of property, he argued that for this conversion to occur land had to be infused or "mixed" with labor. Absent such mixture, Locke ([1690] 1980: 11) warned, "all the world would be America"—in short, it would be premised on a "state of nature" rooted in barter and trade yet without property.

59. It was this displacement of unpropertied aid relations that Marx took as his focus in the newspaper article, "Law on the Theft of Wood" ([1842]1975). This work tracks new legal understandings of property and their entailments for older customs, including in which peasants would collect fallen wood and fruit from agrarian estates. The article compares the criminalization of such practices as theft to earlier sixteenth-century supreme penal code that sanctioned the gathering both of fallen fruit and wood as needed for subsistence (Marx [1842] 1975: 225–26).

60. These reforms felt "justified in abolishing the obligations of this indeterminate property toward the class of the very poor" as an extension of the abolition of state property (Marx [1842] 1975: 230, 233).

61. Marx ([1842] 1975: 413–14).

62. For Bolivia, see Anthias (2019); Fabricant and Gustafson (2011); for comparative cases, see Appel (2019) and Mathews (2011).

63. Elsewhere in Bolivia, agricultural lands organized as haciendas underwent a dramatic process of fragmentation and decline between the early nineteenth and early twentieth centuries, but this was not the case in Ayopaya. While survey-

ors recorded 70 haciendas in Ayopaya province in 1839, by 1912 the number was 676 (Gotkowitz 2007). The increase likely stems from the division of larger properties for inheritance or sale and the creation of new properties along an expanding agricultural frontier (Jackson 1994: 182).

CHAPTER 4. GROUNDING INDIGENEITY

1. Portions of this chapter were published previously as Mareike Winchell, "Liberty Time in Question: Historical Duration and Indigenous Refusal in Post-Revolutionary Bolivia," *Comparative Studies in Society and History* 62, no. 3 (2020): 551–87. DOI:10.1017/S0010417520000171. I thank the journal for their permission to reprint it here.

2. See Urioste (2007).

3. See Jackson (1994) for the twentieth-century history of land sales in Ayopaya.

4. That my fieldwork in Ayopaya in 2011 began only days after the conflictive ousting of an NGO (spearheaded by a foreign graduate student) in Ayopaya imposed limitations on my research, eliciting questions about my presence in the countryside and my complicitly in similar development initiatives. My Whiteness and foreignness, coupled with my gender (these are largely male-dominated institutional spaces), here allowed me only a partial view of these rural orientations to INRA programs. On the reification of race that accompanied nascent modern property regimes, see Bhandar (2018: 8, 13).

5. On the hardening of Indigeneity within MAS nationalistic political discourses, see Canessa (2016) and Rivera Cusicanqui (2012).

6. Marx ([1867] 1972: 320, 323) described this as the "secret" of the "social character of private labour" hidden within the commodity.

7. My argument for the "grounding" of Indigencity parallels Greene's (2009: 17) discussion of how post-Amazonian political organizers in Peru "customized" Indigeneity as "specific acts and to a structural process of constrained creativity." In some ways my approach suggests Quechua Ayopayans' efforts to rein in and concretize Indigeneity from its capacity to travel through ethnic rights organizing, which Greene's account describes.

8. See INRA *Expediente* 58170-45974-49394 CBBA, in particular TCO03030001 I-800.

9. On community in Bolivia's new constitution of 2009, see Zimmerer (2014: 5); Urioste (2011). For the colonial history of land grants (*mercedes*), see Keith (1977: 76–79).

10. The proposed TCO would apply to the rural cantons of Cocapata, Icari, and Choquecamata. See *Expediente* 58170-45974-49394 CBBA, in particular TCO03030001 I-800.

11. The letter noted that NGO workers claimed residents "would be own-

ers of both, which is false given that these resources are administered directly by the central government following article 3, number III, of the Law 3545, and the community does not participate." See Tockman, Cameron, and Plata (2015: 52).

12. See "Ref.: Retiro de Rúbrica de la Demanda TCO Ayopaya," INRA Archive, Cochabamba.

13. See Mayer (2009); cf. Li (2014).

14. Larson (1998: 41).

15. To recall Nadia Abu El-Haj's (2002: 197) terminology, this "making of space" through cartographic technologies of property-based territory not only reproduces historical patterns of division and exclusion but also "generate[s] political possibilities."

16. According to a Ministry of Foreign Affairs report in 1996, the Netherlands provided 840 million guilders (431 million US dollars) to Bolivia between 1969 and 1996. This aid continued into the early 2000s, with Bolivia remaining the second largest (12 percent) recipient of all reported international aid in 2003. See *Bolivia: Evaluation of the Netherlands Development Programme with Bolivia* (ENDP), published in 1996 by the Policy and Operations Evaluation Department of the Ministry of Foreign Affairs, www.oecd.org/countries/bolivia/35164822.pdf.

17. According to the Dutch Foreign Ministry, the money was made available both through the bilateral program as well as being cofinanced through the Netherlands Development Organization (SNV) and multilateral organizations in Bolivia (ENDP 1996: viii). See "Aid Activities in Latin America and the Caribbean, 2001-2002." OECD 2003.

18. These included two Bolivian NGOs, one in the city of Cochabamba and the second a regional NGO in Ayopaya, leaders of the Central Union of Campesino Workers of Ayopaya (CSUTCOA), members of the municipal government in Ayopaya, and the National Institute for Agrarian Reform (INRA).

19. Decreto Supremo No. 802, passed on February 23, 2011, revised an existing Autonomy Law titled Ley Marco de Autonomías y Descentralización "Andrés Ibáñez," passed on July 9, 2010.

20. Cordoba and Jansen (2016).

21. In Spanish, Confederación Nacional de Mujeres Campesinas Indígenas Originarias de Bolivia "Bartolina Sisa" (CNMCIOB), or the Bartolina Sisas.

22. See chapter 3. For the historical precedents for this form of possession in the Andes, see Herzog (2015: 42).

23. Tockman, Cameron, and Plata (2014); cf. Orta (2013).

24. For segmentary appeals to community, see Thomson (2002: 24).

25. As Mumford (2008: 8) has shown, Inca authority was evoked by both Indigenous and Spanish litigants in the colonial era as the basis for the legal legitimacy of their position in a range of disputes.

26. Mumford (2008: 36).

27. See also Amith's (2005) account of migrant legal claims in colonial Mexico.

28. Tockman, Cameron, and Plata (2014).

29. Orta (2013) and Anthias (2018).

30. For a discussion of how such fluidity collides with governmental Indigenous autonomy measures, see Rivera Cusicanqui (2012: 98–99).

31. See Thurner (1997).

32. Unionized farmers and hacienda workers in Ayopaya have used petitions to rally for government aid and representation from at least 1938 on (Gotkowitz 2007 and Ari 2014).

33. Bolivia's episodic history of twentieth-century political violence includes the MNR party state's violent suppression of worker movements that were at times characterized as "communist organizing" from the late 1940s well into the 1980s. These include protestors' fatal clashes with state police and military in 1949, 1960, 1964, and 1967, 1970, 1978—with the 1979 military coup led by Colonel Alberto Natusch Busch resulting in some three hundred deaths. In Ayopaya many unionists had themselves participated in national strikes and direct action against President Hugo Banzer in April 2000, which left eight people dead.

34. The scholarship on the production of Indigeneity is vast. For Latin America at large, see Wynter (2003); on the Andes, see Taussig (1986), García (2005), and Thurner (1997).

35. See Choque Canqui (1986). I discuss Aymara revivalism centered upon ayllu political structures in the introduction.

36. In their analyses of ethnic movements and Indigenous reparations processes in Latin America, Ramos (1998) and Nelson (1999; 2009) demonstrated the ways such appeals reify identity and belonging with divisive consequences. In Bolivia this reification of ethnicity was premised on an Indianista vision of highland ayllu communities as the basis for legitimate national Indigeneity (Rivera Cusicanqui 2013; Canessa 2012).

37. While Povinelli (2002: 23, 42) does not couch her analysis in the language of property per se, her analysis of the cunning of recognition similarly sheds light on the ways that Indigeneity is fixed through legal recognition processes that promise new mechanisms for Indigenous people to access customary land rights.

CHAPTER 5. DEMANDING RETURN

1. An earlier version of this chapter appeared as Mareike Winchell, "Economies of Obligation: Patronage As Relational Wealth in Bolivian Gold Mining," *HAU: Journal of Ethnographic Theory* 7, no. 3 (2017): 159–83. DOI: http://dx.doi.org/10.14318/hau7.3.011. I thank the journal for their permission to reprint the article in this chapter form.

2. For Angelo's story of mid-twentieth-century labor militancy, see chapter 2.

3. Ayopaya's haciendas absorbed redistributive practices that had been elaborated through the conjuncture of Incan and Spanish religious and political orders. See Allen (1982), Bastien (1978), and Isbell (1978).

4. Parry and Bloch (1989), Lyons (2006), and Alberti and Mayer (1974). For a comparative discussion of Mexico, see Wolf (1999: 275).

5. See chapter 2. See also Larson (1998), Nash (1993 [1980]), and Taussig (1980).

6. Into the 1930s and 1940s, Ayopayan hacienda workers demanded in petitions good treatment from hacienda masters and decried labor abuses, including rape (see chapter 2).

7. See Ari (2014).

8. See Striffler (2001: 197).

9. See Langer (1985, 1989) and Orlove (1974).

10. For a comparative case in South Africa, see Donham (2011).

11. These practices of gifting, countergifting, and debt illuminate the centrality of exchange for hierarchical configurations of authority (Leinaweaver 2008; Strathern [1988] 2004: 147, 151). For a related argument concerning gold mining in Mexico and demands for entanglement, see Ferry (2019). For emic redistributive logics in regard to mining at large, see Kirsch (2006). For miners' contestations of alienability premised on alternate religious and value systems, see Coyle Rosen (2020).

12. Marx ([1867] 1972: 433) and Harvey (1989: 147).

13. Guyer (2012: 491). See also Graeber (2001: 221) and Povinelli (2011: 142).

14. For substantivist debates that argue for the embedded qualities of society and economy, see Polanyi ([1944] 2001) and Yanagisako (2013).

15. Put differently, demands for return (*rendre*) as a sort of countergift or repayment highlight a space of exchange that is temporally persistent and "laterally adjacent" to ostensibly disembedded, contractual capital (Maurer 2016: xiii).

16. Ari (2014: 4).

17. INRA Archive, File CBA.03.00018.01.

18. According to INRA archival file (CBA.03.00018.01), in 1961 a total of 200 square hectares (133 hectares of cultivated land and 67 hectares of mountain land) was titled to the co-owners and 209 square hectares to 69 peasants (former hacienda tenant farmers). In the end, peasants each received an average of 7.4 square hectares of cropland (including individual and shared plots) while the children of hacienda masters received an average of 33.3 square hectares each.

19. I discuss this enduring "authority complex" in greater detail in chapter 2. See Sallnow (1989).

20. Herzog (2015).

21. Larson (1998: 59, 121).

22. Rivera Cusicanqui (1987).

23. Nash ([1980] 1993: xi).

24. It received economic aid and loans from the US government in the amount of an initial $10.6 million and then another $4.5 million for special programs, including market reforms (Nash [1980] 1993: xii–xiii).

25. On the continuities between hacienda hierarchies and posthacienda unionism, see Rivera Cusicanqui (1987).

26. ACLO Fundación (2014).

27. In particular, Article 151 of this Law (535) prohibited association between cooperative and private companies.

28. Feasting is a common part of municipal politics in Bolivia, crucial as a device for forging notions of legitimate authority and regional belonging (Albro 2010: 58).

29. In the Andes greed is often mediated through a racialized figure of the q'ara, a Quechua term for "peeled" or "raw," used to denote a (White) person's externality from community practices of sponsorship, reciprocity, and mutual aid (Van Vleet 2008: 51; Isbell 1978; and Nash [1980] 1993).

30. West (1998: 611).

31. Jackson (2009: 171).

32. See Leinaweaver's (2008) detailed discussion of the "circulation of children" as a means of upward mobility for poor Quechua families in Peru.

33. Lyons (2006); for Ayopaya, see Aquino and Galarza (1987).

34. See Shever (2012) for a discussion of shifting labor arrangements from traditions of patronage to modern administration and bureaucracy in Argentinian mining.

35. I outline competing definitions of property in the introduction. See Goldstein (2018) and Bentham (1843).

36. These demands for material assistance premised upon the ideal that bosses *compartir* with workers recall scholarly accounts of demands for the "socially-thick" (Ferguson 2013: 203) or "embedded" qualities of capital (Polanyi [1944] 2001).

37. See Goldstein (2018) for a discussion of property as expectation of benefit.

38. On subversive demands for patronage aid, see Guerrero (1991), Spalding (1970), and Wade (2009).

39. For the "embedded" nature of economy, see Polanyi ([1944] 2001) and Mitchell (2002). For challenges the telos of alienated capital, see Wood ([2002] 2017) and Sahlins (1972b).

40. See Sigaud (2006: 17), Wolf (1955), and Scott (2004).

41. See Englund (2011) for a comparative discussion centered in Malawi.

42. For a more contemporary iteration of this argument, see Harvey (1989: 147).

43. See also Ferguson (2013: 230, 232).

CHAPTER 6. REVIVING EXCHANGE

1. See chapter 3.

2. This term is said to be mean "life" or "hope" in Aymara, although I could not find it in dictionaries.

3. "Process of Change" (El Proceso de Cambio, or "El Cambio" for short) was the official slogan and name of Morales's MAS party reform program (2006–19).

4. Postero (2007: 25) and Gustafson (2011: 121).

5. See Lyons (2006) for a detailed history of both Mestizo Catholicism and Runa religious traditions as they conjoined to define the trappings of authority, virtue, and violence upon Ecuadorian haciendas.

6. MacCormack (1991: 181). For a comprehensive account of colonial fears of sacrificial traditions and the veneration of sacred places, see Mannheim and Salas Carreño (2015).

7. Nash ([1980] 1993) and Taussig (1989).

8. Lazar (2008: 86). See also Abercrombie (1998: 350).

9. See De la Cadena (2014) and Burman (2016).

10. De la Cadena (2015).

11. Throughout the Cochabamba region, exchange has historically offered a privileged analytic for Indigenous efforts to navigate labor and sexual violence, including land appropriation, an intensifying mining economy, and the harsh refraction of highland systems of political leadership since the colonial era. See the introduction and chapter 1.

12. Ramírez (2005), Albro (2000), and Paulson (2006).

13. See De la Cadena (2000).

14. See the discussion of sexual benefit and racialized *hacendado* privilege in chapter 5.

15. Similar accusations of sexual impropriety haunted Morales after his ousting. See Robinson (2020).

16. See Gose (1994: 8–10) and Ramírez (2005). In Ayopaya these feasting practices were derived from older regimes of agrarian authority elaborated in the hacienda system but with precedents in precolonial and early colonial structures of agrarian lordship that were widespread throughout today's central Bolivia. See chapter 1.

17. On doubt in urban *ch'allas* in La Paz, see Lazar (2008: 147).

18. On the colonial trade in ritual objects (incense, dried llama fetuses, confetti, and wool), see Larson (1998); see also Orta (2004: 106).

19. According to Bolivia's most recent census for which language data available, 90 percent of Ayopaya's 26,825 residents speak Quechua, and more than 92 percent identify as Indigenous Quechua. This makes Ayopaya one of Bolivia's most Quechua-dominant provinces. See INE (2001).

20. For Vatican III's theology of inculturation, see Orta (2004).

21. See De Arriaga ([1621] 2015).

22. See Aquino and Galarza (1987); Lyons (2006).

23. On *mestizaje*, see Hale (1996), Weismantel (2001), and De la Cadena (2000).

24. Rivera Cusicanqui (2012: 98).

25. *Forma Valor y Forma Comunidad* (2009) by former Bolivian vice president Álvaro García Linera offers a snapshot of this analytic tendency to foreground and celebrate continuity of community institutions.

26. The term *chiriguano* refers to an Indigenous Guaraní group who live in the

lowlands of eastern Bolivia and other parts of South America. In the usage here the term marks a dance said to have been transported there from the lowlands.

27. On the colonial history of *malos aires*, literally "bad air," see Allen (1982) and Abercrombie (1998).

28. See Choque Canqui and Sinani (1992).

29. See Nelson (1999: 26).

30. I discuss these environmental concerns at greater length elsewhere (Winchell 2020).

31. See Sarmiento and Hitchner (2017).

32. Marisol De la Cadena (2010) has emphasized how ritual practices and ontologies (modes of being) reshape national political realities and calibrate political orientations at odds with a horizontal, contract-based model. In this context agrarian rites including *pagos*, *despachos*, and *misas* in Peru point not simply to a new way of being Indigenous but rather to the "insurgence of indigenous forces and practices with the capacity to significantly disrupt prevalent political formations, and reshuffle hegemonic antagonisms" (De la Cadena 2010: 336). See also Salas-Carreño (2016: 826).

33. On the emergence of Indigeneity as revelatory response to Indigenous rights organizing for ethnic revivalism, see Clifford (2013).

34. See Latour (1993: 34), Blaser (2016), cf. Bessire and Bond (2014), and Todd (2019).

35. Povinelli (2011), Simpson (2014), and see also Coronil (1997: 74).

36. Against characterizations of a modern divide of Nature and Culture in which religious practices by Indigenous groups were understood to belong to the former, in the Andes the religious was never cut off entirely from the political. Spanish expansion was from the start conditioned by the Christian telos of manifest destiny and by cosmological ideas of divine possession. Moreover, early Spanish administrators' understandings of Incan religiosity informed early colonial governance, taxation, and authority. They violently condemned animal sacrifices as idolatrous but also regenerated aspects of this authority complex within administrative spaces, affording land gifts to the kin of early Incan field hands in the Cochabamba valleys and requiring that encomienda owners distribute coca, wool, cloth, and grain to subject-workers. See Padron (2004) and Bastias Saavedra (2020: 223).

37. See Niezen (2009) and Clifford (2013).

38. See Bessire and Bond (2014: 445) and River Cusicanqui (2012).

39. Over this period the Bolivian government spent 2.3 million US dollars (15.6 million bolivianos) for 8,797 "mega-projects," 4,300 of which were related to education and the majority being soccer stadiums (*canchas*) (Vargas 2019).

40. See Tassi (2010) on Indigenous Aymara displays of abundance in Bolivia.

41. See CEDIB's (2013) report.

42. For an English-language account of Evo Morales's response to the protests against subsidy hikes, see BBC (2011).

43. Equipo Nizkor (2010).

44. Postero (2007).

45. Auyero (2011).

46. The film *Q'arwa Awatiris* (2008) is available at www.youtube.com/watch?v=rxyOtOsEkUc (accessed September 9, 2021).

47. See Orta (2013).

48. Goodale (2019: 21).

49. As I discussed in chapter 2, in Ayopaya agrarian rituals and broader arrangements of asymmetrical exchange have long constituted a dynamic site of interplay for national leaders' appeals to villagers and, in turn, for villagers' assessments of popular kinds of alliance and allegiance to state leaders.

50. On revivalism principally as a matter of scale—the scaling up of Indigenous traditions to institutional spheres, see Fabricant (2012: 8–9).

51. Salomon and Urioste (1991).

52. These slippages were in part targeted outcomes of 1990s efforts to decentralize governance—for instance, through Bolivia's Popular Participation Law, passed in 1994 (Orta 2013), which had encouraged municipalities to assume qualities of Indigenous community historically associated with ayllus and peasant unions.

53. Dennison (2017) and Todd (2018).

54. Calle (2010) and Winchell (2020). See also Mamani Ramírez (2020: 132) and Portugal Mollinedo (2010: 97). (I thank Jordan Cooper for introducing me to these works.)

55. See Rappaport and Cummins (2011).

56. As Bhandar (2019: 178) has noted of the Canadian Indian Act: "Indian status remains a relic of a nineteenth-century property logic, which still determines access to band membership and reserve lands." See also Barker (2011), Moreton-Robinson (2015), Harris (1993), and for Bolivia, see Van Cott (2000) and Canessa (2012).

57. For this reason, as Arvin, Tuck, and Morrill (2013: 24) have insisted, an Indigenous feminist stance insists on viewing questions of Indigenous sovereignty and gender violence together, a perspective that varies dramatically from the focus on securing subjective autonomy that has, by and large, organized White feminism.

58. On the juridical production of Indigenous identity as property through Indian Law in Canada, see Bhandar (2018: 152). For abolition as the shoring up of racialized property, see Hartman (1997) and Moten (2003).

59. My discussion of essentialism is deeply indebted to Said's (1979) pathbreaking work.

60. See Bessire and Bond (2014: 448) and Williams (1977).

61. Moten (2003: 11). I discuss colonial administrators; conceptions of Ayopaya province (and the Cochabamba region at large) as a "Mestizo province" defined by the evasion of colonial tribute categories and labor reforms in chapter 2. Like the American maroon communities described by Cedric J. Robinson, these forms of solidarity are decidedly transracial. As Robinson wrote (cited by Bhandar 2018:

196): "American marronage was not just a Black phenomenon. Indeed, American maroon communities frequently acquired the multicultural and multiracial character that liberal historians of the early twentieth century had expected of the whole nation."

62. Hence, in Ayopaya as elsewhere, attending to the longue durée emerges as a powerful method for interrogating history as teleology (Braudel 2012: 252).

CONCLUSION

1. Kurmanaev (2019).

2. See Soliz (2019), Fabricant (2019), Hetland (2019), and Zibechi (2019).

3. For a detailed account of this violence, see IHRC (2020).

4. See scholarly and media coverage of these events in Collyns (2019) and Kovarik (2019).

5. On false accusations of vote tampering pertaining to the Bolivian election, see Higgins (2020).

6. As a heuristic of political upheaval, *coup* assigns agency, once again, to the most obvious incarnations of unmitigated power: foreign governments like the United States, international military cadres, or the groups of mostly male MAS politicians who supposedly orchestrated mass protests in support of the party when the ballot results initially came under fire late on election day. See Rivera Cusicanqui (2019).

7. See my discussion of union repression in chapter 5. See also Achtenberg (2011).

8. For followers' views of Morales as a "father," see Kurmaneav (2019). As I discuss in chapter 6, the use of kinship-based models of authority is common in the Bolivian countryside, yet assertions of fatherhood or godfatherhood can be mobilized as a basis for critique, not simply adoration or unthinking respect.

9. Edelman (2018) makes a similar argument about structural studies of haciendas and plantations. The presumption of structure here can dehistoricize and weaken attention to the social and relational forms that allow structures to seemingly reproduce themselves.

10. See Williams (1977).

11. See Strathern's ([1988] 2004) elaboration of a relational notion of the self; for Peru see Leinaweaver (2008).

12. For a comparative discussion in Canada, see Arvin, Tuck, and Morrill (2013).

13. For the ways that rights-based developmental initiatives for Indigenous people frequently impose and reinforce gender hierarchies, see Pictou (2020: 373).

14. This was apparent in Carmenia's lament that her grown children chastised her for calling the master and his wife by kinship names and insisted: "If the hacienda were to return, I would escape!" See chapter 2.

15. See Parry and Bloch (1989: 5).

16. Higgins (2020).

17. See Tockman and Cameron (2014).

18. See Goodale (2019) and Rivera Cusicanqui (2012).

19. Goldstein (2018), Bhandar (2018), and Harris (1993).

20. This model frequently works to affirm the agency of those imbued with sovereign will, while casting as helpless, naïve, and innocent subjects who do not ascribe to such a model (Ticktin 2017).

21. Silvia Rivera Cusicanqui (2012). See also Sexton (2014) and Rifkin (2017).

22. Thomas (2019) and Hartman (1997).

23. For practices of human/nonhuman mutuality as they interrupt modern legal categories of nature and capital, see Daigle (2018), Haraway (2016), Pictou (2020), Rifkin (2017), Simpson (2014), TallBear (2016), TallBear and Wiley (2019: 5), and Todd (2018).

24. The city of Asheville, North Carolina, for instance, approved reparations for slavery in a unanimous council vote in July 2020. See BBC (2020).

25. Sharpe (2016).

26. See my discussion of Padilla's critique in chapter 6.

27. Daigle (2018), Pictou (2020), and Todd (2018).

BIBLIOGRAPHY

Abercrombie, Thomas. 1998. *Pathways of Memory and Power: Ethnography and History among an Andean People.* Madison: University of Wisconsin Press.

Achtenberg, Emily. 2015. "What's Behind the Bolivian Government's Attack on NGOs?" September 3. NACLA Report on the Americas. https://nacla.org/blog/2015/09/03/what%27s-behind-bolivian-government%27s-attack-ngos.

ACLO Fundación. 2014. "Conflicto por ley minera deja al menos un muerto y más de 40 heridos." April 1. http://aclo.org.bo/bolivia/index.php/noticias-nacionales-einternacionales/14-nacionales/638-conflicto-por-ley-minera-deja-al-menos-un-muerto-y-mas-de-40-heridos.html.

Aguirre, Carlos. 2005. "Silencios y ecos. La historia y el legado de la abolición de la esclavitud en Haití y Perú." *A Contracorriente* 3 (1): 1–37.

Alberti, Giorgio, and Enrique Mayer, eds. 1974. *Reciprocidad e intercambio en los Andes peruanos.* Lima: Instituto de Estudios Peruanos.al

Albro, Robert. 2000. "The Populist Chola: Cultural Mediation and the Political Imagination in Quillacollo, Bolivia." *Journal of Latin American Anthropology* 5 (2): 30–88.

—. 2005. "The Indigenous in the Plural In Bolivian Oppositional Politics." *Bulletin of Latin American Research* 24 (4): 433–53.

—. 2010. *Roosters at Midnight: Indigenous Signs and Stigma in Local Bolivian Politics.* Santa Fe, NM: School for Advanced Research Press.

Allen, Catherine J. (1982) 2002. *The Hold Life Has: Coca and Cultural Identity in an Andean Community.* Washington, DC: Smithsonian Books.

Alonso, Ana María. 2004. "Conforming Disconformity: 'Mestizaje,' Hybridity, and the Aesthetics of Mexican Nationalism." *Cultural Anthropology* 19 (4): 459–90.

Amith, Jonathan D. 2005. *The Möbius Strip: A Spatial History of Colonial Society in Guerrero, Mexico.* Stanford, CA: Stanford University Press.

Andolina, Robert, Nina Laurie, and Sarah A. Radcliffe. 2009. *Indigenous Development in the Andes: Culture, Power, and Transnationalism.* Durham, NC: Duke University Press.

Anthias, Penelope. 2018. *Limits to Decolonization: Indigeneity, Territory, and Hydrocarbon Politics in the Bolivian Chaco*. Ithaca, NY: Cornell University Press.

Anthias, Penelope, and Sarah A. Radcliffe. 2013. "The Ethno-environmental Fix and Its Limits: Indigenous Land Titling and the Production of Not-Quite-Neoliberal Natures in Bolivia." *Geoforum* 64: 257–269.

Apaza Calle, Iván. 2011. *Colonialismo y contribución en el indianismo*. Bolivia: Ediciones Pachakuti.

Appel, Hannah. 2020. *The Licit Life of Capitalism: US Oil in Equatorial Guinea*. Durham, NC: Duke University Press.

Appel, Hannah, Arthur Mason, and Michael Watts, eds. 2015. *Subterranean Estates: Live Worlds of Oil and Gas*. Ithaca, NY: Cornell University Press.

Aquino A., Jorge, and J. Galarza. 1987. "Trabajos y Materiales. No. 4. Entrevista Realizada en La Localidad de Machaca. Independencia, 15 July 1987." Independencia, Bolivia, personal archive.

Ari, Waskar. 2014. *Earth Politics: Religion, Decolonization, And Bolivia's Indigenous Intellectuals*. Durham, NC: Duke University Press.

Arnold, Denise Y. 1993. "Adam and Eve and the Red-Trousered Ant: History in the Southern Andes." *Travesia* 2 (1): 49–83.

———. 1998. *Gente de carne y hueso: Las traumas de parentesco en los Andes*. La Paz: ILCA and CIASE.

———. 2009. "Cartografías de la memoria: Hacia un paradigma más dinámico y viviente del espacio." *Cuadernos* 36: 203–44.

Arvin, M., E. Tuck, and A. Morrill. 2013. "Decolonizing Feminism: Challenging Connections between Settler Colonialism and Heteropatriarchy." *Feminist Formations* 25 (1): 8–34.

Asad, Talal. 2003. *Formations of the Secular: Christianity, Islam, Modernity*. Stanford, CA: Stanford University Press.

Assies, W. 2006. "Land Tenure Legislation in a Pluri-Cultural and Multi-Ethnic Society: The Case of Bolivia." *Journal of Peasant Studies* 33 (4): 569–611.

Auyero, Javier. 2001. *Poor People's Politics: Peronist Survival Networks and the Legacy of Evita*. Durham, NC: Duke University Press.

Ávila Rojas, Ódin. 2017. "La vigencia del debate sobre el sujeto politico indio: La crítica desde el indianismo de Fausto Reinaga al vivir bien en Bolivia." Doctoral dissertation, Social Sciences, Universidad Autónoma Metropolitana Unidad Xochimilco. Mexico City, Mexico.

Babb, Florence E. 2018. *Women's Place in the Andes: Engaging Decolonial Feminist Anthropology*. Berkeley: University of California Press.

Bacigalupo, Ana Mariella. 2016. *Thunder Shaman: Making History with Mapuche Spirits in Chile and Patagonia*. Austin: University of Texas Press.

Ballard, Chris, and Glenn Banks. 2003. "Resource Wars: The Anthropology of Mining." *Annual Review of Anthropology* 32: 287–313.

Ballastero, Andrea. 2019. *A Future History of Water*. Durham, NC: Duke University Press.

Barker, Joanne. 2011. *Native Acts: Law, Recognition, and Cultural Authenticity.* Durham, NC: Duke University Press.

Bastias Saavedra, Manuel. 2020. "The Normativity of Possession: Rethinking Land Relations in Early-Modern Spanish America, ca. 1500–1800." *Colonial Latin American Review* 29 (2): 223–38

Bastien, Joseph W. 1978. *Mountain of the Condor: Metaphor and Ritual in an Andean Ayllu.* Saint Paul, MN: West Publishing Company.

BBC. 2011. "Bolivian President Evo Morales Flees Food Price Protest." February 11. www.bbc.com/news/world-latin-america-12427057.

———. 2020. "North Carolina's Asheville Unanimously Approves Reparations for Slavery." July 16. www.bbc.com/news/world-us-canada-53435311.

Bear, Laura. 2016. "Time as Technique." *Annual Review of Anthropology* 45: 487–502.

Bebbington, Anthony. 2007. "Social Movements and the Politicization of Chronic Poverty." *Development and Change* 38 (5): 793–818.

Benjamin, Walter. 1969. *Illuminations: Essays and Reflections.* Edited by Hannah Arendt. Translated by Harry Zohn. New York: Schocken Books.

Bentham, Jeremy. 1843. "Chapter 7. Principles of the Civil Code." In *The Works of Jeremy Bentham, Vol. 1.* Liberty Fund Network. https://oll.libertyfund.org//title/bentham-works-of-jeremy-bentham-11-vols.

Berlant, Lauren. 1998. "Intimacy: A Special Issue." *Critical Inquiry* 24 (2): 281–88.

———. 2008. *The Female Complaint: The Unfinished Business of Sentimentality in American Culture.* Durham, NC: Duke University Press.

———. 2011. *Cruel Optimism.* Durham, NC: Duke University Press.

Bessire, Lucas, and David Bond. 2014. "Ontological Anthropology and the Deferral of Critique." *American Ethnologist* 41 (3): 440–56.

Bhandar, Brenna. 2018. *Colonial Lives of Property: Law, Land, and Racial Regimes of Ownership.* Durham, NC: Duke University Press.

Blaser, Mario. 2016. "Is Another Cosmopolitics Possible?" *Cultural Anthropology* 31 (4): 545–70.

Blofield, Merike. 2009. "Feudal Enclaves and Political Reforms: Domestic Workers in Latin America." *Latin American Research Review* 44 (1): 158–90.

Boddy, Janice. 2011. "Bodies under Colonialism." In *A Companion to the Anthropology of the Body and Embodiment.* Edited by Francis E. Mascia-Lees, 119–36. London: Blackwell.

Bolton, Ralph, and Enrique Mayer, eds. 1977. *Andean Kinship and Marriage.* Special Publication Number 7. Washington, DC: American Anthropological Association.

Bonilla, Yarimar. 2015. *Non-Sovereign Futures: French Caribbean Politics in the Wake of Disenchantment.* Chicago: University of Chicago Press.

———. 2017. "Unsettling Sovereignty." *Cultural Anthropology* 32 (3): 330–39.

Bowser, Frederick P. 1974. *The African Slave in Colonial Peru, 1524–1650.* Stanford, CA: Stanford University Press.

Braudel, Fernand. 2012. *The Longue Durée and World Systems Analysis*. Edited by Richard E. Less. Albany, NY: State University of New York Press.

Buch, Elana D. 2013. "Senses of Care: Embodying Inequality and Sustaining Personhood in the Home Care of Older Adults in Chicago." *American Ethnologist* 40 (4): 637–50.

Buechler, Hans. 1969. *Huaylas: An Andean District in Search of Progress*. Ithaca, NY: Cornell University Press.

Burman, Anders. 2016. *Indigeneity and Decolonization in the Bolivian Andes: Ritual Practice and Activism*. Lanham, MD: Rowman and Littlefield.

Burns, Kathryn. 1999. *Colonial Habits: Convents and the Spiritual Economy of Cuzco, Peru*. Durham, NC: Duke University Press.

Butler, Judith. 1997. *Excitable Speech: A Politics of the Performative*. London: Routledge.

———. 2000. *Antigone's Claim: Kinship between Life and Death*. New York: Columbia University Press.Canessa, Andrew. 2012. *Intimate Indigeneities: Race, Sex, and History in the Small Spaces of Andean Life*. Durham, NC: Duke University Press.

———. 2016. "Paradoxes of Multiculturalism in Bolivia." In *The Crisis of Multiculturalism in Latin America*, 75–100. New York: Palgrave Macmillan.

Carby, Hazel. 2019. *Imperial Intimacies: A Tale of Two Islands*. New York: Verso.

Carroll, Clint. 2014. "Native Enclosures: Tribal National Parks and the Progressive Politics of Environmental Stewardship in Indian Country." *Geoforum* 53: 31–40.

———. 2015. *Roots of Our Renewal: Ethnobotany and Cherokee Environmental Governance*. Minneapolis: University of Minnesota Press.

Carter, William E. 1964. *Aymara Communities and the Bolivian Agrarian Reform*. Gainesville: University of Florida Press.

Carter, Paul. 2008. *Dark Writing: Geography, Performance, Design*. Honolulu: University of Hawaii Press.

Carter, William E., and Mauricio Mamani P. 1978. "Patrones del uso de la coca en Bolivia." In *Ensayos Científicos Sobre la Coca*. Edited by William E. Carter, 177–209. La Paz, Bolivia: Libreria Editorial Juventud.

Cattelino, Jessica. 2008. *High Stakes: Florida Seminole Gaming and Sovereignty*. Durham, NC: Duke University Press.

———. 2015. "The Cultural Politics of Water in the Everglades and Beyond." *HAU: Journal of Ethnographic Theory* 5 (3): 235–50.

CEDIB. 2013. "Crónica de conflictos mineros en Bolivia (Enero—Mayo 2012)." PetroPress, pp. 41–43. www.cedib.org/wp-content/uploads/2013/09/conflictos-mineros-8.13.pdf.

Chakrabarty, Dipesh. 1997. "The Time of History and the Time of the Gods." In *The Politics of Culture, in the Shadow of Capital*. Edited by Lisa Lowe and David Lloyd, 35–60. Durham, NC: Duke University Press.

Chipana Ramos, Francisco. 2018. "The Death of Servitude." In *The Bolivia Reader: History, Culture, Politics*. Edited by Sinclair Thomson, Rossana Barragán, Xavier Albó, Seemin Qayum, and Mark Goodale, 365–70. Durham, NC: Duke University Press.

Choque Canqui, Roberto. 1986. "De la defensa del ayllu a la creación de la República del Qullasuyu: Historia del movimiento indígena en Bolivia (1912–1955)." In *Historia y evolución del movimiento popular*. Edited by Encuentro de Estudios Bolivianos, 465–504. Cochabamba: CERES.

Choque Canqui, Roberto, and Tomasa Sinani. 1992. *Educación indígena: ¿Ciudadanía o colonización?* La Paz: Aruwiyiri.

Chu, Julie. 2014. "When Infrastructures Attack: The Workings of Disrepair in China." *American Ethnologist* 41 (2): 351–67.

Chumacero, J. P. 2011. *Informe 2010. Territorios Indígena Originario Campesinos en Bolivia. Entre la Loma Santa y la Pachamama*. La Paz: Fundación TIERRA.

———. 2012. *Una Mirada a La Estructura De Tenencia De Tierras En Bolivia En Los Últimos 60 Años*. La Paz: Fundación TIERRA.

Clifford, James. 2013. *Returns: Becoming Indigenous in the Twenty-First Century*. Cambridge: Harvard University Press.

Coila, Elizabeth Huanca. 2020. "La plurinacionalidad desde abajo: Autogobierno indígena en Bolivia y Ecuador." *Estado & Communes: Revista de políticas y problemas públicos* 2 (11): 203–205.

Collins, Patricia Hill. 1998. "It's All in the Family: Intersections of Gender, Race, and Nation." *Hypatia* 13 (3): 62–82.

Colloredo-Mansfield, Rudi. 1998. "Dirty Indians, Radical Indígenas, and the Political Economy of Social Difference in Modern Ecuador." *Bulletin of Latin American Research* 17 (2):185–206.

———. 2009. *Fighting Like a Community: Andean Civil Society in an Era of Indian Uprisings*. Chicago: University of Chicago Press.

Collyns, Dan. 2019. "Bolivia President's Initial Indigenous-Free Cabinet Heightens Polarization." *La Paz*, November 14. www.theguardian.com/world/2019/nov/14/bolivia-president-jeanine-anez-cabinet-indigenous.

Comay, Rebecca. 2008. "Missed Revolutions: Transmission, Translation, Trauma." *Idealistic Studies* 38 (1–2): 23–40.

Cordoba, Diana, and K. Jansen. 2016. "Realigning the Political and the Technical: NGOs and the Politicization of Agrarian Development in Bolivia." *European Journal of Development Research* 28 (3): 1–18.

Coronil, Fernando. 1997. *The Magical State: Nature, Money, and Modernity in Venezuela*. Chicago: University of Chicago Press.

Costa, Luis. 2018. *The Owners of Kinship: Asymmetrical Relations in Indigenous Amazonia*. Chicago: HAU Books.

Coyle Rosen, Lauren. 2020. *Fires of Gold: Law, Spirit, and Sacrificial Labor in Ghana*. Oakland: University of California Press.

Daigle, Michelle. 2018. "Resurging through Kishiichiwan: The Spatial Politics of Indigenous Water Relations." *Decolonization: Indigeneity, Education & Society* 7 (1): 159–72. Dandler, Jorge, and A. Juan Torrico. 1986. "From the National Indigenous Congress to the Ayopaya Rebellion: Bolivia, 1945–1947." In *Resis-*

tance, Rebellion, and Consciousness in the Andean Peasant World, 18th to 20th Centuries. Edited by Steve J. Stern, 334–78. Madison: University of Wisconsin Press.

Das, Veena. 2006. *Life and Words: Violence and the Descent into the Ordinary.* Oakland: University of California Press.

Davis, Kathleen. 2017. *Periodization and Sovereignty: How Ideas of Feudalism and Secularization Govern the Politics of Time.* Philadelphia: University of Pennsylvania Press.

Dawdy, Shannon Lee. 2016. *Patina: A Profane Archaeology.* Chicago: University of Chicago Press.

Dawson, Alexander S. 2012. "Histories and Memories of the Indian Boarding Schools in Mexico, Canada, and the United States." *Latin American Perspectives* 39 (5): 80–99.

De Arriaga, Pablo Joseph. (1621) 2015. *The Extirpation of Idolatry in Peru.* Louisville: University Press of Kentucky.

de Betanzos, Juan. (1551) 1996. *Narrative of the Incas.* Edited by Dana Buchanan. Translated by Roland Hamilton. Austin: University of Texas Press.

de Certeau, Michel. (1980) 2011. *The Practice of Everyday Life.* Third edition. Oakland: University of California Press.

De la Cadena, Marisol. 2000. *Indigenous Mestizos: The Politics of Race and Culture in Cuzco, Peru, 1919–1991.* Durham, NC: Duke University Press.

———. 2010. "Indigenous Cosmopolitics in the Andes: Conceptual Reflections beyond 'Politics.'" *Cultural Anthropology* 25 (2): 334–70.

———. 2014. "Runa: Human but *Not Only.*" *HAU: Journal of Ethnographic Theory.*

———. 2015. *Earth Beings: Ecologies of Practice across Andean Worlds.* Durham, NC: Duke University Press.

Deleuze, Gilles, and Felix Guattari. 1987. *A Thousand Plateaus: Capitalism and Schizophrenia.* Minneapolis: University of Minnesota Press.

Dennison, Jean. 2017. "Entangled Sovereignties: The Osage Nation's Interconnections with Governmental and Corporate Authorities." *American Ethnologist* 4 (4): 684–96.

Di Giminiani, Peirgiorgio. 2018. *Sentient Lands: Indigeneity, Property, and Political Imagination in Neoliberal Chile.* Tucson: University of Arizona Press.

Donham, Donald L. 2011. *Violence in a Time of Liberation: Murder and Ethnicity at a South American Gold Mine, 1994.* Durham, NC: Duke University Press.

Dru Stanley, Amy. 1998. *From Bondage to Contract: Wage Labor, Marriage, and the Market in the Age of Slave Emancipation.* Cambridge, UK: Cambridge University Press.

Dua, Jatin. 2019. *Captured at Sea: Piracy and Protection in the Indian Ocean.* Oakland: University of California Press.

Dunkerley, James. 2007. "Evo Morales, the 'Two Bolivias,' and the Third Bolivian Revolution." *Journal of Latin American Studies* 39 (1): 133–66.

Earls, John. 1969. "The Organization of Power in Quechua Mythology." *Journal of the Steward Anthropological Society* 1: 63–82.

Edelman, Marc. 2018. "'Haciendas and Plantations': History and Limitations of a 60-Year-Old Taxonomy." *Critique of Anthropology* 38 (4): 387–406.

El-Haj, Nadia. 2002. *Facts on the Ground: Archaeological Practice and Territorial Re-Fashioning in Israeli Society.* Chicago: University of Chicago Press.

Ellison, Susan. 2018. *Domesticating Democracy: The Politics of Conflict Resolution in Bolivia.* Durham, NC: Duke University Press.

ENDP. 1996. "Bolivia: Evaluation of the Netherlands Development Programme with Bolivia." Policy and Operations Evaluation Department, Ministry of Foreign Affairs. Edited by N. Forest-Flier and A. F. Brown. Translated by A. Torres. Ridderprint BV: Ridderkerk, Netherlands. www.oecd.org/countries /bolivia/35164822.pdf.

Engels, Friedrich. (1884) 2010. *The Origin of the Family, Private Property and the State.* Vol. 3 of *Marx/Engels Selected Works.* Hottingen-Zurich. www.marxists .org/archive/marx/works/download/pdf/origin_family.pdf.

Englund, Harri. 2011. *Human Rights and African Airwaves: Mediating Equality on the Chichewa Radio.* Bloomington: Indiana University Press.

Equipo Nizkor. 2010. "APG: 'Evo se cree un rey, es el Nuevo patrón de indígenas; hay que descolonizarlo.'" *Derechos.* February 2. www.derechos.org/nizkor /bolivia/doc/apg8.html.

Fabian, Johannes. (1983) 2014. *Time and the Other: How Anthropology Makes Its Object.* New York: Columbia University Press.

Fabricant, Nicole. 2012. *Mobilizing Bolivia's Displaced: Indigenous Politics and the Struggle over Land.* Chapel Hill,: University of North Carolina Press.

———. 2019. "The Roots of the Right-Wing Coup in Bolivia." *Dissent,* December 23. www.dissentmagazine.org/online_articles/roots-coup-bolivia-morales -anezcamacho.

Fabricant, Nicole, and Bret Gustafson. 2014. "Moving Beyond the Extractivism Debate, Imagining New Social Economies." *NACLA Report on the Americas* 47 (3): 40–45.

Faier, Lieba. 2009. *Intimate Encounters: Filipina Women and the Remaking of Japan.* Oakland: University of California Press.

Fanon, Franz. 1963. *Black Skin/White Masks.* Translated by Richard Philcox. New York: Grove Press.

Farthing, Linda. 2009. "Bolivia's Dilemma: Development Confronts the Legacy of Extraction." *NACLA Reporting on the Americas.* https://nacla.org/node/6096.

Farthing, Linda, and Benjamin Kohl. 2012. "Material Constraints to Popular Imaginaries: The 'Extractive Economy' and Resource Nationalism in Bolivia." *Political Geography* 31: 225–35.

Ferguson, James. 2006. *Global Shadows: Africa in the Neoliberal World Order.* Durham, NC: Duke University Press.

———. 2013. "Declarations of Dependence: Labour, Personhood, and Welfare in Southern Africa." *Journal of the Royal Anthropological Institute* 19 (2): 223–42.

Fernández Anderson, Cora. 2020. *Fighting for Abortion Rights in Latin America: Social Movements, State Allies and Institutions.* New York: Routledge Press.

Ferraro, Emilia. 2004. "Owing and Being in Debt: A Contribution from the Northern Andes of Ecuador." In *Social Anthropology* 12 (1):77–94.

Ferry, Elizabeth. 2019. "Royal Roads and Entangled Webs: Mining Metals and Making Value in El Cubo, Guanajuato, Mexico." *Journal of Anthropological Research* 75 (1): 6–20.

Flores Galindo, Alberto. 1984. *In Search of an Inca: Identity and Utopia in the Andes.* Introduction by Carlos Aguierre and Charles F. Walker. Cambridge: Cambridge University Press.

Ford, Lisa. 2011. *Settler Sovereignty: Jurisdiction and Indigenous People in America and Australia, 1788–1836.* Boston: Harvard University Press.

Forero, Juan. 2005. "Coca Advocate Wins Election for President in Bolivia." *New York Times.* December 19.

Foucault, Michel. (1978) 2004. *Security, Territory, Population.* London: Picador.

Gal, Susan. 2002. "A Semiotics of the Public/Private Distinction." *Differences: A Journal of Feminist Cultural Studies* 13 (1): 77–95.

Galeano, Eduardo. 1971. *Open Veins of Latin America: Five Centuries of the Pillage of a Continent.* Translated by Cedric Belfrage. Monthly Review Press.

Garba, Tapji, and Sara-Maria Sorentino. 2020. "Slavery Is a Metaphor. A Critical Commentary on Eve Tuck and K. Wayne Yang's 'Decolonization Is Not a Metaphor.'" *Antipode* 52 (3): 764–82.

García, Maria Elena. 2005. *Making Indigenous Citizens: Identities, Education, and Multicultural Development in Peru.* Stanford, CA: Stanford University Press.

García Linera, Álvaro. 2009. *Forma Valor y Forma Comunidad.* La Muela del Diablo/CLASCO: La Paz.

Garcilaso de la Vega, Inca. 1609. Comentarios Reales de los Incas. https://archive .org/details/primerapartedelooovega. Accessed July 19, 2020.

Gill, Lesley. 1994. *Precarious Dependencies: Gender, Class, and Domestic Service in Bolivia.* New York: Columbia University Press.

———. 2004. *The School of the Americas: Military Training and Political Violence in the Americas.* Durham, NC: Duke University Press.

Ginsburg, Faye D., and Rayna Rapp. 1995. "Introduction: Conceiving the New World Order." In *Conceiving the New World Order.* Edited by Faye D. Ginsburg and Rayna Rapp, 1–18. Oakland: University of California Press.

Goldstein, Alyosha. 2018. "By Force of Expectation: Colonization, Public Lands, and the Property Relation." *UCLA Law Review Discourse* 65 (234): 125–39.

González Nuñez, E. 2014. "Luces y sombras en seis décadas de reforma agraria." *Página Siete* 4 (8): 2013.

Goodale, Mark. 2019. *A Revolution in Fragments: Traversing Scales of Justice, Ideology, and Practice in Bolivia.* Durham, NC: Duke University Press.

Gordillo, Gaston. 2014. *Rubble: The Afterlife of Destruction.* Durham, NC: Duke University Press.

Gordillo, José M. 1997. *Arando en la historia: La experiencia política campesina en Cochabamba*. Cochabamba: Plural Press.

———. 2000. *Campesinos revolucionarios en Bolivia: Identidad, territorio y sexualidad en el Valle Alto de Cochabamba, 1952–1964*. La Paz: Plural Press.

Gose, Peter. 1994. *Deathly Waters and Hungry Mountains: Agrarian Ritual and Class Formation in an Andean Town*. Toronto: University of Toronto Press.

Gotkowitz, L. 2007. *A Revolution for Our Rights: Indigenous Struggles for Land and Justice in Bolivia, 1880–1952*. Durham, NC: Duke University Press.

Gow, Peter. 1991. *Of Mixed Blood: Kinship and History in Peruvian Amazonia*. Oxford: Clarendon Press.

Graeber, David. 2001. *Toward an Anthropological Theory of Value: The False Coin of Our Own Dreams*. New York: Palgrave Macmillan.

———. 2011. *Debt: The First 5000 Years*. New York: Melville House.

Greene, Shane. 2009. *Customizing Indigeneity: Paths to a Visionary Politics in Peru*. Stanford, CA: Stanford University Press.

Greer, Allan. 2012. *Property and Dispossession: Natives, Empire, and Land in Early Modern North America*. Cambridge, UK: Cambridge University Press.

Grey, Thomas C. 1980. "Eros, Civilization, and the Burger Court." *Law and Contemporary Problems* 43 (3): 83–100.

Grieshaber, E. P. 1979. "Hacienda-Indian Community Relations and Indian Acculturation: An Historiographical Essay." *LARR* 14 (3): 107–28.

———. 1980. "Survival of Indian Communities in Nineteenth-Century Bolivia: A Regional Comparison." *Journal of Latin American Studies* 12 (2): 223–69.

Guerrero, Andrés. 1991 *La semántica de la dominación: El concertaje de indios*. Quito: Ediciones Libri Mundi, Enrique Grosse-Luemern.

Gustafson, Bret. 2010. "When States Act Like Movements: Dismantling Local Power and 'Seating' Sovereignty in Bolivia." *Latin American Perspectives* 37 (4): 48–66.

———. 2011. "Flashpoints of Sovereignty." In *Crude Domination*. Edited by Andrea Behrends, Stephen Reyna, and Günther Schlee, 220–40. London: Berghahn Books.

Guyer, Jane. 1993. "Wealth in People and Self-Realization in Africa." *Man* 28 (2): 243–65.

———. 2012. "Obligation, Binding, Debt, and Responsibility: Provocations about Temporality from Two New Sources." *Social Anthropology* 20 (4): 491–501.

———. 2016. "The Gift That Keeps on Giving." In *The Gift: Expanded Edition*, by Marcel Mauss, 1–25. Translated by Jane I. Guyer. Chicago: Hau Books.

Hale, Charles R. 1996. "Mestizaje, Hybridity, and the Cultural Politics of Difference in Post-Revolutionary Central America." *Journal of Latin American Anthropology* 2 (1): 34–61.

Haraway, Donna. 1988. "Situated Knowledges: The Science Question in Feminism and the Privilege of Partial Perspective." *Feminist Studies* 14 (3): 575–99.

———. 2016. *Staying with the Trouble*. Durham, NC: Duke University Press.

Hardt, Michael. 1999. "Affective Labor." *Boundary 2* 26 (2): 89–100.

Harris, Cheryl I. 1993. "Whiteness as Property." *Harvard Law Review* 106 (8): 1707–91.

Harris, John. 2016. "Circuits of Wealth, Circuits of Sorrow: Financing the Illegal Transatlantic Slave Trade in the Age of Suppression, 1850–66." *Journal of Global History* 11: 409–29.

Harris, Olivia. 1978. "Complementarity and Conflict: An Andean View of Women and Men." In *Sex and Age as Principles of Social Differentiation*. Edited by J. S. La Fontaine, 21–40. London: Academic Press.

———. 1980. "The Power of Signs: Gender, Culture, and the Wild in the Bolivian Andes." In *Nature, Culture, and Gender*. Edited by Carol MacCormack and Marilyn Strathern, 70–94. Cambridge: Cambridge University Press.

———. 1986. "From Asymmetry to Triangle: Symbolic Transformations in Northern Potosí." In *Anthropological History of Andean Politics*. Edited by John V. Murra, Nathan Wachtel, and Jacques Revel, 260–80. Cambridge: Cambridge University Press.

———. 1989. "The Earth and the State: The Sources and Meaning of Money in Northern Potosí." In *Money and the Morality of Exchange*. Edited by Jonathan Parry and Maurice Bloch, 232–68. New York: Cambridge University Press.

———. 2008. "Alterities: Kinship and Gender." *A Companion to Latin American Anthropology*. Edited by Deborah Poole, 276–302. Oxford: Blackwell Publishing.

Hartman, Saidiya. 1997. *Scenes of Subjection: Terror, Slavery, and Self-Making in Nineteenth-Century America*. New York: Oxford University Press.

———. 2008. *Lose Your Mother: A Journey along the Atlantic Slave Route*. New York: Farrar, Straus, and Giroux.

———. 2020. *Wayward Lives, Beautiful Experiments: Intimate Histories of Riotous Black Girls, Troublesome Women, and Queer Radicals*. New York: Norton.

Harvey, David. 1989. *The Condition of Postmodernity: An Enquiry into the Origins of Cultural Change*. Hoboken, NJ: Wiley-Blackwell.

Harvey, Penelope. 1998. "Los 'hechos naturales' de parentesco y género en un contexto andino." In *Gente de carne y hueso: Las tramas de parentesco en los Andes*. Edited by Denise Y. Arnold, 69–82. New York: Routledge.

Heck, Moritz. 2020. *Plurinational Afrobolivianity: Afro-Indigenous Articulations and Interethnic Relations in the Yungas of Bolivia*. Germany: Verlag.

Herzog, Tamar. 2015. *Frontiers of Possession: Spain and Portugal in Europe and the Americas*. Cambridge: Harvard University Press.

Hetland, Gabriel. 2019. "Many Wanted Morales Out: But What Happened in Bolivia Was a Military Coup." *The Guardian*. November 13. www.theguardian.com/commentisfree/2019/nov/13/morales-bolivia-military-coup.

Higgins, Eoin. 2020. "Study: Right-wing Coup in Bolivia Was Based on False Claims of Election Fraud." *Salon*. February 28. www.salon.com/2020/02/28/mit-study-right-wing-coup-in-bolivia-was-based-on-false-claims-of-election-fraud_partner/.

Hines, Sarah T. 2021. *Water for All: Community, Property, and Revolution in Modern Bolivia.* Oakland: University of California Press.

Hirschkind, Charles. 2016. "Granadan Reflections." *Material Religion* 12 (2): 209–32.

Humphrey, Caroline, and Katherine Verdery. 2004. *Property in Question: Value Transformation in the Global Economy.* New York: Routledge Press.

Hunt, Lynn. 1992. *The Family Romance of the French Revolution.* Oakland: University of California Press.

Hunter, Tera W. 2017. *Bound in Wedlock: Slave and Free Black Marriage in the Nineteenth Century.* Cambridge, MA: Harvard University Press.

Hurtado, Javier. 1986. *El Katarismo.* La Paz, Bolivia: HISBOL.

Hylton, Forrest, Félix Patzi Paco, Serio Serulnikov, and Sinclair Thomson. 2003. *Ya es otro tiempo el presente: cuatro momentos de insurgencia indígena.* La Paz: Muela del Diablo Editores.

Hylton, Forrest, Sinclair Thomson, and Adolfo Gilly. 2007. *Revolutionary Horizons: Past and Present in Bolivia Politics.* London: Verso Press.

Ingold, Tim. 2000. *The Perception of the Environment: Essays on Livelihood, Dwelling, and Skill.* London: Routledge.

Instituto Nacional de Reforma Agraria (INRA). 2008. "Breve historia del reparto de tierras en Bolivia." *De La Titulación Colonial a La Reconducción Comunitaria De La Reforma Agraria: Certezas y Proyecciones.* La Paz: INRA.

———. 2010. "La tierra vuelve a manos indígenas y campesinas." La Paz: Instituto Nacional de Reforma Agraria. www.inra.gob.bo/InraPb/upload/ LaTierraVuelveManosIndigenas.pdf. Accessed February 6, 2019.

Instituto Nacional de Estadistica (INE). 2012. "Resultados: Ficha Resumen Censo de Población y Vivienda 2012." http://censosbolivia.ine.gob.bo /censofichacomunidad/c_listadof/listar_comunidades.

International Human Rights Clinic (IHRC). 2020. "'They Shot Us Like Animals': Black November & Bolivia's Interim Government." http://hrp.law.harvard.edu /wp-content/uploads/2020/07/Black-November-English-Final_Accessible.pdf. Accessed February 1, 2022.

Isbell, Billie J. 1978. *To Defend Ourselves: Ritual and Ecology in an Andean Village.* Latin American Monographs. Austin: University of Texas Press.

Jackson, Marissa. 2009. "Neo-colonialism, Same Old Racism: A Critical Analysis of the United States' Shift Toward Colorblindness As a Tool for the Protection of the American Colonial Empire and White Supremacy." *Berkeley Journal of African American Literature and Policy* 11: 156.

Jackson, Robert H. 1994. *Regional Markets and Agrarian Transformation in Bolivia: Cochabamba 1539–1960.* Albuquerque: University of New Mexico Press.

Jackson, Robert H., and Gregory Maddox. 1993. "The Creation of Identity: Colonial Society in Bolivia and Tanzania." *Comparative Studies in Society and History* 35 (2): 263–84.

Jackson, Zakiyyah Iman. 2020. *Becoming Human: Matter and Meaning in an Antiblack World.* New York: NYU Press.

Johnson, Brian B. 2010. "Decolonization and Its Paradoxes: The (Re)envisioning of Health Policy in Bolivia." *Latin American Perspectives* 37 (3): 139–59.

Jones, Donna. 2017. *The Racial Discourses of Life Philosophy: Négritude, Vitalism, and Modernity*. New York: Columbia University Press.

Jordon, Caine, Guy Emerson Mount, and Kai Parker. 2018. "'A Disgrace to all slave-holders': The University of Chicago's Founding Ties to Slavery and the Path to Reparations." *Journal of African American History* 103 (1–2): 163–78.

Jørs, Erik, F. Konradsen, O. Huici, R. Morant, J. Volk, and F. Lander. 2016. "Impact of Training Bolivian Farmers on Integrated Pest Management and Diffusion of Knowledge to Neighboring Farmers." *Journal of Agromedicine* 21 (2): 200–208.

Kahn, Jeffrey S. 2018. *Islands of Sovereignty: Haitian Migration and the Borders of Empire*. Chicago: University of Chicago Press.

Kauanui, J. Kehaulani. 2016. "'A Structure, Not an Event': Settler Colonialism and Enduring Indigeneity." *Lateral: Journal of the Cultural Studies Association* 5 (1).

Keane, Webb. 2007. *Christian Moderns: Freedom and Fetish in the Mission Encounter*. Berkeley: University of California Press.

Keith, Robert G., ed. 1977. *Haciendas and Plantations in Latin American History*. Teaneck, NJ: Holmes and Meier Publishing.

Kirsch, Stuart. 2006. *Reverse Anthropology: Indigenous Analyses of Social and Environmental Relations in New Guinea*. Stanford, CA: Stanford University Press.

Klein, H. S. 1993 *Haciendas and Ayllus:. Rural Society in the Bolivian Andes in the Eighteenth and Nineteenth Centuries*. Stanford, CA: Stanford University Press.

Klein, Herbert S., and Ben Vinson. 2007. *African Slavery in Latin America and the Caribbean*. New York: Oxford University Press.

Koselleck, Reinhart. 2004. *Futures Past: On the Semantics of Historical Time*. Translated by Keith Tribe. New York: Columbia University Press.

Kosiba, Steve, and R. Alexander Hunter. 2017. "Fields of Conflict: A Political Ecology Approach To Land and Social Transformation in the Colonial Andes (Cuzco, Peru). *Journal of Archaeological Science* 84: 40–53.

Kovarik, Jacqulyn. 2019. "Bolivia's Anti-Indigenous Backlash Is Growing." *The Nation*. November 13. www.thenation.com/article/archive/bolivia-morales-whipala/.

Kurmanaev, Anatoly. 2019. "Evo Morales Is Like a Father to Us." *New York Times*. November 27. www.nytimes.com/2019/11/27/world/americas/evo-morales-boliviacoca.html.

La Patria. 2010. "Plagas destruyen cultivos de papa en cien comunidades de Ayopaya." *La Patria*. August 7, 2010. http://lapatriaenlinea.com/?nota=36828.

Lambek, Michael. 1993. *Knowledge and Practice in Mayotte: Local Discourses of Islam, Sorcery, and Spirit Possession*. Toronto: University of Toronto Press.

———. 2002. *The Weight of the Past: Living with History in Mahajanga, Madagascar*. New York: Palgrave Macmillan Press.

Langdon, Esther Jean. 2016. "The Revitalization of Yajé Shamanism among the

Siona: Strategies of Survival in Historical Context." *Anthropology of Consciousness* 27 (2): 180–203.

Langer, Erick D. 1985. "Labor Strikes and Reciprocity in Chuquisaca Haciendas." *Hispanic American Historical Review* 65: 255–77.

———. 1988. "El liberalismo y la abolición de la comunidad indígena en el siglo XIX." *Historia y Cultura* 14.

———. 1989. *Economic Change and Rural Resistance in Southern Bolivia, 1880–1930.* Stanford, CA: Stanford University Press.

Langer, Erick, and Robert Jackson. 1997. "Liberalism and the Land Question in Bolivia, 1825–1920." In *Liberals, the Church, and Indian Peasants: Corporate Lands and the Challenge of Reform in Nineteenth Century Spanish America.* Edited by Robert Jackson, 171–92. Albuquerque: University of New Mexico Press.

Larson, Brooke. 1998. *Cochabamba, 1550–1900.* Durham, NC: Duke University Press.

———. 2004. *Trials of Nation Making: Liberalism, Race, and Ethnicity in the Andes, 1810–1910.* Cambridge: Cambridge University Press.

———. 2014. "Indigeneity Unpacked: Politics, Civil Society, and Social Movements in the Andes." *Latin American Research Review* 49 (1): 223–41.

Larson, B., O. Harris, and E. Tandeter, eds. 1995. *Ethnicity, Markets, and Migration in the Andes: At the Crossroads of History and Anthropology.* Durham, NC: Duke University Press.

Lastarria-Cornhiel, Susana. 2007. "Who Benefits from Land Titling?: Lessons from Bolivia and Laos." *International Institute for Environment and Development (IIED).* Gatekeeper Series 132: 3–23.

Latour, Bruno. 1993. *We Have Never Been Modern.* Cambridge, MA: Harvard University Press.

Lau, George F. 2019. "An Inca Offering at Yayno (North Highlands, Peru): Objects, Subjects, and Gifts in the Ancient Andes." *Cambridge Archaeological Journal* 29 (1): 159–79.

Lazar, Sian. 2008. *El Alto, Rebel City: Self and Citizenship in Andean Bolivia.* Durham, NC: Duke University Press.

Lazzarato, Maurizio. 2012. *The Making of the Indebted Man: An Essay on the Neoliberal Condition.* Boston: MIT Press.

Leinaweaver, Jessica. 2008. *The Circulation of Children.* Durham, NC: Duke University Press.

Levi-Strauss, Claude. 1969. *The Elemental Structures of Kinship.* Boston: Beacon Press.

Li, Tania Murray. 2014. *Land's End: Capitalist Relations on an Indigenous Frontier.* Durham, NC: Duke University Press.

Locke, John. (1690) 1980. *Second Treatise on Government.* Project Gutenberg Ebook. www.gutenberg.org. Accessed November 2017.

———. (1689) 2001. *A Letter Concerning Toleration.* Project Gutenberg Ebook. www.gutenberg.org. Accessed July 2020.

Lopez Pila, Esther. 2014. "'We Don't Lie and Cheat Like the Collas Do': High-land-Lowland Regionalist Tensions and Indigenous Identity Politics in Amazonian Bolivia." *Critique of Anthropology* 34 (4): 429–49.

Los Tiempos. 2013. "Senape: De 16 mil ítems solo el 30% está saneada." *Los Tiempos*. June 30. www.lostiempos.com/actualidad/local/20130630/senape-16-mil-items-solo-30-esta-saneado.

Lyons, Barry. 2006. *Remembering the Hacienda: Religion, Authority, and Social Change in Highland Ecuador.* Austin: University of Texas Press.

MacCormack, Sabine. 1991. *Religion in the Andes: Vision and Imagination in Early Colonial Peru.* Princeton, NJ: Princeton University Press.

———. 2007. *On the Wings of Time: Rome, the Incas, Spain, and Peru.* Princeton, NJ: Princeton University Press.

Mahmood, Saba. 2015. *Religious Difference in a Secular Age: A Minority Report.* Princeton, NJ: Princeton University Press.

Malinowski, Bronislaw. 1922. *Argonauts of the Western Pacific: An Account of Native Enterprise and Adventure in the Archipelagoes of Melanesian New Guinea.* New York: Routledge.

Mallon, Florencia E. 1983. *The Defense of Community in Peru's Central Highlands: Peasant Struggle and Capitalist Transition, 1860–1940.* Princeton, NJ: Princeton University Press.

Malloy, James M. 1970. *Bolivia: The Uncompleted Revolution.* Pittsburgh: University of Pittsburgh Press.

Mamani Ramírez, Pablo. 2015. "¿Descolonización Real o Falsa Descolonización en Bolivia? Corrientes De Pensamiento." *Bolivian Studies Journal* 21.

Mannheim, Bruce. 1991. *The Language of the Inka since the European Invasion.* Austin: University of Texas Press.

Mannheim, Bruce, and Guillermo Salas Carreño. 2015. "Wak'a: Entifications of the Andean Sacred." In *The Archaealogy of W'akas: Explorations of the Sacred in the pre-Columbian Andes.* Edited by Tamara Bray, 46–72. Boulder: University Presses of Colorado.

Mariner, Kathryn. 2019. *Contingent Kinship: The Flows and Futures of Adoption in the United States.* Berkeley: University of California Press.

Martínez, María Elena. 2008. *Genealogical Fictions: Limpieza de Sangre, Religion, and Gender in Colonial Mexico.* Stanford, CA: Stanford University Press.

Marx, Karl. (1842) 1975. "Proceedings of the Sixth Rhine Province Assembly. Third Article. Debates on the Law of the Theft of Wood." In *Karl Marx and Frederick Engels, Collected Works, Vol. 1. Marx: 1835–1843.* Pp. 224–263. New York: International Publishers.

———. (1844) 1972. "Economic and Philosophical Manuscripts." In *The Marx–Engels Reader.* Second edition. Edited by Robert C. Tucker, 70–101. Translated by Ben Fowkes and David Fernbach. New York: Routledge.

———. (1852) 1972. "The Eighteenth Brumaire of Louis Bonaparte." In *The Marx–Engels Reader.* Second edition. Edited by Robert C. Tucker, 594–617. Translated by Ben Fowkes and David Fernbach. New York: Routledge.

———. (1867) 1972. "Capital: A Critique Of Political Economy, Vol. 1." In *The Marx–Engels Reader*. Second edition. Edited by Robert C. Tucker, 294–436. Translated by Ben Fowkes and David Fernbach. New York: Routledge.

Massumi, Brian. 2002. *Parables for the Virtual: Movement, Affect, Sensation*. Durham, NC: Duke University Press.

Mathews, Andrew S. 2011. *Instituting Nature: Authority, Expertise, and Power in Mexican Forests*. Boston: MIT Press.

Maurer, Bill. 2004. "Cyberspatial Properties: Taxing Questions about Propriatary Regimes." In *Property in Question: Value Transformation in the Global Economy*. Edited by Caroline Humphrey and Katherine Verdery, 297–318. Boston: Routledge.

———. 2016. "Foreword: Puzzles and pathways." In *The Gift: Expanded Edition*, by Marcel Mauss, ix–xvii. Translated by Jane I. Guyer. Chicago: Hau Books.

Mauss, Marcel. (1925) 2016. *The Gift: Expanded Edition*. Translated by Jane I. Guyer. Chicago: Hau Books.

Mayer, Enrique. 1974. *Reciprocity, Self-Sufficiency, and Market Relations in a Contemporary Community in the Central Andes of Peru*. Ithaca, NY: Cornell University Press.

———. 1977. "Beyond the Nuclear Family." In *Andean Kinship and Marriage*. Edited by Ralph Bolton and Enrique Mayer, 81–105. Washington, DC: American Anthropological Association.

———. 2007. *Ugly Stories of the Peruvian Agrarian Reform*. Durham, NC: Duke University Press.

McKeown, Maeve. 2021. "Backward-looking Reparations and Structural Injustice." *Contemporary Political Theory* 20: 771–94.

Medeiros, Carmen. 2005. "The Right 'To Know How To Understand': Coloniality and Contesting Visions of Development and Citizenship in the Times of Neo-Liberal Civility." PhD dissertation. City University of New York.

Miles, Tiya. 2015. *Ties That Bind: The Story of an Afro-Cherokee Family in Slavery and Freedom*. Berkeley: University of California Press.

Millones, Luis. 2007. "Mesianismo en América hispana: El taki onqoy." *Memoria americana* 15: 7–39.

Mintz, Sidney. 1974. "The Origins of Reconstituted Peasantries." In *Caribbean Transformations*, 146–56. New York :Columbia University Press.

Mintz, Sidney, and Eric Wolf. 1950. "An Analysis of Ritual Co-Parenthood (Compadrazgo)." *Southwestern Journal of Anthropology* 6: 341–68.

Mitchell, Timothy. 2002. *Rule of Experts: Egypt, Techno-Politics, Modernity*. Berkeley: University of California Press.

Mody, Perveez. 2008. *The Intimate State: Love-Marriage and the Law in Delhi*. New York: Routledge.

———. 2019. "Contemporary Intimacies." *Critical Themes in Indian Sociology*. Edited by S. Srivastava Y. Arif and J. Abraham, 257–66. New York: Sage.

Morgan, Lewis Henry. (1868) 1997. *Systems of Consanguinity and Affinity in the Human Family*. Lincoln: University of Nebraska Press.

Moreton-Robinson, Aileen. 2015. *The White Possessive: Property, Power, and Indigenous Sovereignty.* Minneapolis: University of Minnesota Press.

Moten, Fred. 2003. *In the Break: The Aesthetics of the Radical Black Tradition.* Minneapolis: University of Minnesota Press.

Mueggler, Erik. 2001. *The Age of Wild Ghosts: Memory, Violence, and Place in Southwest China.* Berkeley: University of California Press.

Mumford, Jeremy. 1998. "The Taki Onqoy and the Andean Nation: Sources and Interpretations." *Latin American Research Review* 33 (1): 150–65.

———. 2008. "Litigation as Ethnography In Sixteenth-Century Peru: Polo de Ondegardo and the Mitimaes." *Hispanic American Historical Review* 88 (1): 5–40.

Munn, Nancy. (1986) 1992. *The Fame of Gawa: A Symbolic Study of Value Transformation in a Massim (Papua New Guinea) Society.* Durham, NC: Duke University Press.

Murra, John V. 1968. "An Aymara Kingdom in 1567." *Ethnohistory* 15 (2): 115–51.

———. 2017. *Reciprocity and Redistribution in Andean Civilizations: The 1969 Lewis Henry Morgan Lectures.* Chicago: Hau Books.

Nash, June. (1980) 1993. *We Eat the Mines and the Mines Eat Us: Dependency and Exploitation in the Bolivian Tin Mines.* New York: Columbia University Press.

Nelson, Diane M. 1999. *A Finger in the Wound: Body Politics in Quincentennial Guatemala.* Berkeley: University of California Press.

———. 2009. *Reckoning: The Ends of War in Guatemala.* Durham, NC: Duke University Press.

———. 2015. *Who Counts? The Mathematics of Death and Life after Genocide.* Durham, NC: Duke University Press.

Niezen, Ronald. 2009. *The Rediscovered Self: Indigenous Identity and Cultural Justice.* Montreal: McGill University Press.

Oberem, Udo. 1978. "Contribución a la historia del trabajador rural en América Latina: 'Conciertos' y 'huasipungueros' en Ecuador." *Revista Sarance* 6: 49–78.

Oliva Oliva, María Elena. 2010. "La negritud, el indianismo y sus intelectuales: Aimé Césaire y Fausto Reinaga." Master's thesis, Estudios Latinoamericanos, Universidad de Chile.

Organization for Economic Co-operation and Development (OECD). 2003. "Aid Activities in Latin America and the Caribbean, 2001–2002." Published by the Organization for Economic Co-operation and Development (OECD). www.oecd-ilibrary.org/oecd/about.

Orlove, Benjamin S. 1974. "Reciprocidad, desigualidad y dominación." In *Reciprocidad e Intercambio en los Andes Peruanos.* Edited by Giorgio Alberti and Enrique Mayer, 290–321. Lima: Instituto de Estudios Peruanos.

Orta, Andrew. 2004. *Catechizing Culture: Missionaries, Aymara, and the "New Evangelization."* New York: Columbia University Press.

———. 2013. "Forged Communities and Vulgar Citizens: Autonomy and Its Límites in Semineoliberal Bolivia." *Journal of Latin American and Caribbean Anthropology* 18 (1): 108–33.

Ossio, Juan M. 1984. "Cultural Continuity, Structure, and Context: Some Peculiarities of the Andean Compadrazgo." In *Kinship Ideology and Practice in Latin America*. Edited by Raymond T. Smith, 118–46. Chapel Hill: University of North Carolina Press.

Ouweneel, Arij. 2005. *The Flight of the Shepherd: Microhistory and the Psychology of Cultural Resilience in Bourbon Central Mexico*. Amsterdam: Aksant Academic Publishers.

Pacheco, Diego. 1992. *El Indianismo y Los Indios Contemporaneos*. Movimeintos Sociales 7. La Paz, Bolivia: HISBOL.

Pacheco, Raquel. 2017. "The Promise of Gender Progress: The Civilizing Project of Biopolitical Citizenship." PhD dissertation, UC San Diego, https://escholarship.org/uc/item/2bn8591x.

Padron, Ricardo. 2004. *The Spacious Word: Cartography, Literature, and Empire in Early Modern Spain*. Chicago: University of Chicago Press.

Pagden, Anthony. 1995. *Lords of All the World: Ideologies of Empire in Spain, Britain, and France, c. 1500–1800*. New Haven, CT: Yale University Press.

Palmié, Stephan, and Charles Stewart. 2016. "Introduction: For an Anthropology of History." *HAU: Journal of Ethnographic Theory* 6 (1): 207–36.

Pandolfo, Stefania. 2018. *Knot of the Soul: Madness, Psychoanalysis, Islam*. Chicago: University of Chicago Press.

Parry, Jonathan. 1989. "On the Moral Perils of Exchange." In *Money and the Morality of Exchange*. Edited by Jonathan Parry and Maurice Bloch, 64–93. Cambridge: Cambridge University Press.

Parry, Jonathan, and Maurice Bloch. 1989. "Introduction: Money and the Morality of Exchange." In *Money and the Morality of Exchange*. Edited by Jonathan Parry and Maurice Bloch, 1–32. Cambridge: Cambridge University Press.

Pati Paco, Pelagio, Pablo Mamani Ramirez, and Norah Quise Chipana. 2009. *Sistematización de Experiencias de Movimientos Indígenas En Bolivia*. Temas Sociales 18. La Paz, Bolivia: Instituto de Investigaciones Sociológicas 'Mauricio Lefevbre'.

Patzi, Félix. 2004. *Sistema Comunal: Una propuesta alternative al sistema liberal*. La Paz: CEA.

Paulson, Susan. 2006. "Body, Nation, and Consubstantiation in Bolivian Ritual Meals." *American Ethnologist* 33 (4): 650–64.

Perrault, Tom. 2012. "Extracting Justice: Natural Gas, Indigenous Mobilization and the Bolivian State." In *Transnational Governmentality and Resource Extraction*. Edited by Terence Gomez and Suzana Sawyer, 75–102. New York: Palgrave Macmillan.

Piatote, Beth. 2013. *Domestic Subjects: Gender, Citizenship, and Law in Native American Literature*. New Haven, CT: Yale University Press.

Pictou, Sherry. 2020. "Decolonizing Decolonization: An Indigenous Feminist Perspective on the Recognition and Rights Framework." *South Atlantic Quarterly* 119 (2): 371–91.

Piliavsky, Anastasia. 2020. *Nobody's People: Hierarchy as Hope in a Society of Thieves.* Redwood City, CA: Stanford University Press.

Platt, Tristan. 1982. *Estado boliviano y ayllu andino: Tierra y tributo en el norte de Potosí.* Lima: Instituto de Estudios Peruanos.

———. 1984. "Liberalism and Ethnocide in the Southern Andes." *History Workshop Journal* 17 (1): 3–18.

———. 1987. "The Andean Experience of Bolivian Liberalism, 1825–1900: Roots of Rebellion in 19th-Century Chayanta (Potosí)." In *Resistance, Rebellion, and Consciousness in the Andean Peasant World, 18th to 20th Centuries.* Edited by Steve J. Stern, 280–324. Madison: University of Wisconsin Press.

Polanyi, Karl. (1944) 2001. *The Great Transformation: The Political And Economic Origins of Our Time.* Boston: Beacon Press.

Portugal Mollinedo, Pedro. 2020. "Por qué colapsó el MAS." *Pagina Siete.* July 29. www.paginasiete.bo/opinion/2020/7/29/por-que-colapso-el-mas-262729.html.

Portugal Mollinedo, Pedro, and Carlos Macusaya Cruz. 2016. "El Indianismo Katarista." https://library.fes.de/opus4/frontdoor/index/index/docId/44706.

Postero, Nancy. 2007. *Now We Are Citizens: Indigenous Politics in Postmulticultural Bolivia.* Stanford, CA: Stanford University Press.

———. 2017. *The Indigenous State: Race, Politics, and Performance in Andean Bolivia.* Berkeley: University of California Press.

Pottage, Alain. 2004. "Who Owns Academic Knowledge?" *Cambridge Anthropology* 1: 1–20.

Povinelli, Elizabeth. 2002. *The Cunning of Recognition: Indigenous Alterities and the Making of Australian Multiculturalism.* Durham, NC: Duke University Press.

———. 2006. *The Empire of Love: Toward a Theory of Intimacy, Genealogy, and Carnality.* Durham, NC: Duke University Press.

———. 2011. *Economies of Abandonment: Social Belonging and Endurance in Late Liberalism.* Durham, NC: Duke University Press.

———. 2016. *Geontologies.* Durham, NC: Duke University Press.

Proudhon, Pierre-Joseph. (1840) 1994. *Proudhon: What Is Property?* Edited by Donald R. Kelley and Bonnie G. Smith. Cambridge: Cambridge University Press.

Puar, Jasbir. 2007. *Terrorist Assemblages: Homonationalism in Queer Times.* Durham, NC: Duke University Press.

Quiggin, John. 2015. "John Locke against Freedom." *Jacobin* (June). www.jacobinmag.com/2015/06/locke-treatise-slavery-private-property/. Accessed July 17, 2020.

Raffles, Hugh. 2002. *In Amazonia: A Natural History.* Princeton, NJ: Princeton University Press.

Ramberg, Lucinda. 2014. *Given to the Goddess: South Indian Devadasis and the Sexuality of Religion.* Durham, NC: Duke University Press.

Ramírez, Susan Elizabeth. 1996. *The World Upside Down: Cross-Cultural Con-*

tact and Conflict in Sixteenth-century Peru. Stanford, CA: Stanford University Press.

———. 2002. *Tales of Two Cities: Race and Economic Culture in Early Republican North and South America: Guayaquil, Ecuador and Baltimore, Maryland*. Austin: University of Texas Press.

———. 2005. *To Feed and Be Fed: The Cosmological Bases of Authority and Identity in the Andes*. Stanford, CA: Stanford University Press.

Ramos, Alcida Rita. 1998. *Indigenism: Ethnic Movements in Brazil*. Madison: University of Wisconsin Press.

Rappaport, Joanne, and Thomas Cummins. 2011. *Beyond the Lettered City: Indigenous Literacies in the Andes*. Durham, NC: Duke University Press.

Ray, Raka, and Seemin Qayum. 2009. *Cultures of Servitude: Modernity, Domesticity, and Class in India*. Stanford, CA: Stanford University Press.

Reinaga, Fausto. (1970) 2007. *La Revolución India*. La Paz: Author and Hilda Reinaga.

Rifkin, Mark. 2017. *Beyond Settler Time: Temporal Sovereignty and Indigenous Self-Determination*. Durham, NC: Duke University Press.

Riles, Annelise. 2006. Introduction to *Documents: Artifacts of Modern Knowledge*. Edited by Annelise Riles, 1–40. Ann Arbor: University of Michigan Press.

Rivera Cusicanqui, Silvia. 1987. *Oppressed but Not Defeated: Peasant Struggles among the Aymara and Qhechwa in Bolivia, 1900–1980*. Geneva: United Nations Research Institute for Social Development.

———. 1989. "El potencial epistemológico de la historia oral: Algunas contribuciones de Silvia Rivera Cusicanqui." In *Estudios e outras practices intelectuales Latinamericanas en cultura e poder*. Edited by Daniel Mato, n.p. Caracas: CLASCO.

———. 2005. "Invisible Realities: Internal Markets and Subaltern Identities in Contemporary Bolivia." Amsterdam: SEPHIS-SEASREP.

———. 2012. "Ch'ixinakax utxiwa: A Reflection on the Practices and Discourses of Decolonization." *South Atlantic Quarterly* 111 (1): 95–109.

———. 2019. *Bolivia's Lesson in Triumphalism*. English transcription of Rivera Cusicanqui's Address at the Women's Parliament on November 12. https://towardfreedom.org/blog-blog/silviarivera-cusicanqui-bolivias-lesson-in-triumphalism/. Accessed January 5, 2020.

Robinson, Matthew. 2020. "Exiled Bolivian Former President Evo Morales Accused of Rape." *The Times*. www.thetimes.co.uk/article/exiled-bolivian-ex-president-evo-morales-accused-of-rape-xvmgl6d9d.

Rubbo, Anna, and Michael Taussig. 1983. "Up off Their Knees: Servanthood in Southwest Columbia." *Latin American Perspectives* 10 (4): 5–23.

Rubin, Gayle. 1975. "The Traffic in Women: Notes on the Political Economy of Sex." In *Toward an Anthropology of Women*. Edited by Wayne R. Reiter, 157–210. New York: Monthly Review Press.

Rutherford, Danilyn. 2016. "Affect Theory and the Empirical." *Annual Review of Anthropology* 45: 285–300.

Saavedra, José Luis. 2014. *Amuyt'apxañani: La Insurgencia de La Intelectualidad Aymara En Bolivia*. Cochabamba: Editorial Verbo Divino.

Safa, Helen I. 1990. "Women's Social Movements in Latin America." *Gender and Sexuality* 4 (3): 354–69.

———. 2005. "Challenging Mestizaje: A Gender Perspective on Indigenous and Afrodescendant Movements in Latin America." *Critique of Anthropology* 25 (3): 307–30.

Sahlins, Marshall. 1972a. "On the Sociology of Primitive Exchange." In *Stone Age Economics*, 185–230. London: Routledge.

———. 1972b. "The Spirit of the Gift." In *Stone Age Economics*, 149–84. Chicago: Aldine.

———. 2013. *What Kinship Is, and Is Not*. Chicago: University of Chicago Press.

Said, Edward. W. 1979. *Orientalism*. New York: Vintage Press.

Salas-Carreño, Guillermo. 2016. "Places Are Kin: Food, Cohabitation, and Sociality in the Andes." *Anthropological Quarterly* 89 (3): 813–40.

———. 2017. "Mining and the Living Materiality of Mountains in Andean Societies." *Journal of Material Culture* 22 (2): 133–50.

Salazar de la Torre, Cecillia, Juan Mirko Rodríquez Franco, and Evi Sulcata Guzmán. 2012. *Intelectuales Aymaras y Nuevas Mayorías Mestizas: Una Perspective Post 1952*. Informes de Investigación. La Paz: Programa de Investigacón Estratégica en Bolivia (PIEB).

Sallnow, Michael. 1989. "Precious Metals in the Andean Moral Economy." In *Money and the Morality of Exchange*. Edited by Jonathan Parry and Maurice Bloch, 209–231. New York: Cambridge University Press.

Salomon, Frank L. 1986. *Native Lords of Quito in the Age of the Incas: The Political Economy of North Andean Chiefdoms*. Cambridge: Cambridge University Press.

———. 2004. *The Cord Keepers: Khipus and Cultural Life in a Peruvian Village*. Durham, NC: Duke University Press.

Salomon, Frank, and George L. Urioste. 1991. *The Huarochirí Manuscript: A Testament of Ancient and Colonial Andean Religion*. Austin: University of Texas Press.

Sarmiento, Fausto, and Sarah Hitchner. 2017. *Indigeneity and the Sacred: Indigenous Revival and the Conservation of Sacred Natural Sites in the Americas*. New York: Berghahn Press.

Schavelzon, Salvador. 2016. "Cosmopolitica y yuxtaposición en la propuesta de Estado Plurinacional de Bolivia." *Revista Chilena de Antropología* 33: 87–101.

Scott, David. 2004. *Conscripts of Modernity: The Tragedy of Colonial Enlightenment*. Durham, NC: Duke University Press.

———. 2013. *Omens of Adversity: Tragedy, Time, Memory, Justice*. Durham, NC: Duke University Press.

Scott, James C. 1971. "Patron-Client Relations and Political Change in Southeast Asia." *American Political Science Review* 66 (1): 91–113.

———. 1976. *The Moral Economy of the Peasant: Rebellion and Resistance in Southeast Asia*. New Haven, CT: Yale University Press.

———. 1985. *Weapons of the Weak: Everyday Forms of Peasant Resistance*. New Haven, CT: Yale University Press.

Scott, Joan Wallach. (1988) 2018. *Gender and the Politics of History*. New York: Columbia University Press.

Seligmann, Linda J. 1993. "Between Worlds of Exchange: Ethnicity among Peruvian Market Women." *Cultural Anthropology* 8 (2):187–213.

Sexton, Jared. 2014. "The Vel of Slavery: Tracking the Figure of the Unsovereign." *Critical Sociology* 42 (4–5):1–15.

Sharpe, Christina. 2016. *In the Wake: On Blackness and Being*. Durham, NC: Duke University Press.

Shepherd, Verene A. 2018. "Past Imperfect, Future Perfect? Reparations, Rehabilitation, Reconciliation." *Journal of African American History* 103 (12): 19–43.

Shever, Elana. 2012. *Resources for Reform: Oil and Neoliberalism in Argentina*. Redwood City, CA: Stanford University Press.

Sigaud, Lygia. 2006. "Traps of Honor and Forgiveness: The Social Uses of Law in the Pernambuco Forest Region." *Mana* 10 (1): 131–63.

Simpson, Audra. 2014. *Mohawk Interruptus: Political Life across the Borders of Settler States*. Durham, NC: Duke University Press.

———. 2016. "Consent's Revenge." *Cultural Anthropology* 31 (3): 326–33.

Singer, Joseph W. 2000. "Property and Social Relations." *Property and Values: Alternatives to Public and Private Ownership*. Edited by Charles Geisler and Gail Daneker, 3–20. Washington, DC: Island Press.

Skinner, Quentin. 1998. *Liberty before Liberalism*. Cambridge: Cambridge University Press.

Smith, Adam. (1776) 1977. *An Inquiry into the Nature and Causes of the Wealth of Nations*. Chicago: University of Chicago Press.

Snelgrove, C., R. Dhamoon, and J. Corntassel. 2014. "Unsettling Settler Colonialism: The Discourse and Politics of Settlers, and Solidarity with Indigenous Nations." *Decolonization: Indigeneity, Education & Society* 3 (2): 1– 32.

Soliz, Carmen. 2017. "'Land to the Original Owners': Rethinking the Indigenous Politics of the Bolivian Agrarian Reform." *Hispanic American Historical Review* 97 (2): 259–96.

———. 2019. "Chaos in Bolivia after President Resigns." *The World*. Public Radio International. November 11. www.pri.org/file/2019-11-11/chaos-bolivia -afterpresident-resigns.

———. 2021. *Fields of Revolution: Agrarian Reform and Rural State Formation in Bolivia, 1935–1964*. Pittsburgh: University of Pittsburgh Press.

Soriano, Waldemar Espinoza. [1582] 1969. *El memorial de Charcas*. Unedited chronicle. Lima, Peru: Ediciones Universidad Nacional de Educacion.

Soruco Sologuren, Ximena. 2011. *La ciudad de los cholos: Mestizaje y colonialidad en Bolivia, siglos XIX y XX*. Lima: PIEB.

Soruco Sologuren, Ximena, Wilfredo Plata, and Gustavo Medieros. 2008. *Los barones del Oriente. El Poder de Santa Cruz Ayer y Hoy*. Cochabamba: Fundacion Tierra.

Spalding, Karen. 1970. "Social Climbers: Changing Patterns of Mobility among the Indians of *Peru*." *Hispanic American Historical Review* 50: 645–64.

———. 1980. "Class Structures in the Southern Peruvian Highlands, 1750–1920." In *Land and Power in Latin America*. Edited by Benjamin Orlove and Glenn Custred, 79–97. New York: Holmes and Meier.

Spedding, Alison. 1998. "Contra-afinidad: Algunos comentarios sobre el compadrazgo andino." In *Gente de carne y hueso: Las tarmas de parentesco en los Andes, Vol. 2, Parentesco y género en los Andes*. Edited by Denise Y. Arnold, 115–37. La Paz: Centre for Indigenous American Studies and Exchange.

Starn, Orin. 1991. "Missing the Revolution: Anthropologists and War in Peru." *Cultural Anthropology* 6 (1): 63–91.

Stephenson, Marcia. 1999. *Gender and Modernity in Andean Bolivia*. Austin: University of Texas Press.

———. 2002. "Forging an Indigenous Counterpublic Sphere: The Taller de Historia Oral Andina in Bolivia." *Latin American Research Review* 37 (2): 99–116.

Stern, Steve. 1982. *Peru's Indian Peoples and the Challenge of Spanish Conquest: Huamanga to 1640*. Madison: University of Wisconsin Press.

———, ed. 1987. *Resistance, Rebellion, and Consciousness in the Andean Peasant World, 18th to 20th Centuries*. Madison: University of Wisconsin Press.

Stevenson, Lisa. 2014. *Life Beside Itself: Imagining Care in the Canadian Arctic*. Oakland: University of California Press.

Stewart, Charles. 2016. "Historicity and Anthropology." *Annual Review of Anthropology* 45: 79–94.

Stewart, Kathleen. 2007. *Ordinary Affects*. Durham, NC: Duke University Press.

Stoler, Ann Laura. 2002. *Carnal Knowledge and Imperial Power: Race and the Intimate in Colonial Rule*. Berkeley: University of California Press.

———. 2008. "Imperial Debris: Reflections on Ruins and Ruination." *Cultural Anthropology* 23 (2): 191– 219.

———. 2016. *Duress: Imperial Durabilities in Our Times*. Durham, NC: Duke University Press.

Strathern, Marilyn. (1988) 2004. *The Gender of the Gift: Problems with Women and Problems with Society in Melanesia*. Berkeley: University of California Press.

———. 2005. *Kinship, Law, and the Unexpected: Relatives Are Always a Surprise*. Cambridge: Cambridge University Press.

Striffler, Steve. 2001. *In the Shadows of State and Capital: The United Fruit Company, Popular Struggle, and Agrarian Restructuring in Ecuador, 1900–1995*. Durham, NC: Duke University Press.

Sturtevant, Chuck. 2017. "Claiming Belonging, Constructing Social Spaces: Citizenship Practices in an Afro-Bolivian Town." *Critique of Anthropology* 37 (1): 3–26.

Swanson, Kate. 2007. "'Bad Mothers' and 'Delinquent Children': Unravelling Anti-Begging Rhetoric in the Ecuadorian Andes." *Gender, Place, and Culture* 14 (6): 703–20.

Swinehart, Karl. 2019. "Decolonial Time in Bolivia's *Pachakuti.*" *Signs and Society* 7 (1): 96–114.

TallBear, Kim. 2016. "The U.S.-Dakota War and Failed Settler Kinship." *Anthropology News* 57 (9): 92–95.

———. 2018. "Making Love and Relations Beyond Settler Sex and Family." In *Making Kin Not Population.* Edited by Adele E. Clark and Donna Haraway, 145–66. Chicago: Prickly Paradigm Press.

———. 2019. "Caretaking Relations, Not American Dreaming." *CALFOU* 6 (1): 24–41.

TallBear, Kim, and Angela Wiley. 2019. "Critical Relationality: Queer, Indigenous and Multispecies Belonging Beyond Settler Sex and Nature." *Imaginations* 10 (1): 5–16.

Tapia, Silvana Tapia. 2016. "Sumak Kawsay, Coloniality, and the Criminalization of Violence against Women in Ecuador." *Feminist Theory* 17 (2): 141–56.

Tarducci, Mónica. 2013. "Adopción y Parentesco desde la Antropología Feminista." *La Ventana* 37: 106–45.

Tassi, Nico. 2010. "The 'Postulate of Abundance': Cholo Market And Religion in La Paz, Bolivia." *Social Anthropology* 18 (2): 191–209.

Taussig, Michael. 1980. *The Devil and Commodity Fetishism in South America.* Chapel Hill: University of North Carolina Press.

———. 1991. *Shamanism, Colonialism, and the Wild Man: A Study in Terror and Healing.* Chicago: University of Chicago Press.

Tekelenburg, A. 2001. "Cactus Pear and Cochineal in Cochabamba: The Development of a Cross-Epistemological Toolkit for Interactive Design of Farm Innovation." PhD dissertation. Wageningen University, The Netherlands.

Thomas, Deborah A. 2019. *Life in the Wake of the Plantation: Sovereignty, Witnessing, Repair.* Durham, NC: Duke University Press.

Thomson, Sinclair. 2002. *We Alone Will Rule: Native Andean Politics in the Age of Insurgency.* Madison: University of Wisconsin Press.

Thurner, Mark. 1993. "Peasant Politics and Andean Haciendas in the Transition to Capitalism: An Ethnographic History." *Latin American Research Review* 28 (3): 41–82.

———. 1997. *From Two Republics to One Divided: Contradictions of Postcolonial Nationmaking in Andean Peru.* Durham, NC: Duke University Press.

Ticktin, Miriam. 2017. "A World Without Innocence." *American Ethnologist* 44: 577–90.

Ticona Alejo, Esteban. 2010. *Saberes, Conocimientos y Prácticas Anticoloniales del Pueblo Aymara-Quechua en Bolivia.* First edition. La Paz: AGRUCO, UMSS-FCAyP/COSUDE and Plural Editores.

Tockman, Jason, and John Cameron. 2014. "Indigenous Autonomy and the Contradictions of Plurinationalism in Bolivia." *Latin American Politics and Society* 56 (3): 46–69.

Tockman, Jason, John Cameron, and Wilfredo Plata. 2015. "New Institutions of

Indigenous Self-Governance in Bolivia: Between Autonomy and Self-Discipline." *Latin American and Caribbean Ethnic Studies* 10 (1): 37–59.

Todd, Zoe. 2018. "Refracting the State through Human-Fish Relations. Fishing, Indigenous Legal Orders and Colonialism in North/Western Canada." *Decolonization: Indigeneity, Education & Society* 7 (1): 60–75.

———. 2019. "An Indigenous Feminist's Take on the Ontological Turn: 'Ontology' Is Just Another Word for Colonialism." *Journal of Historical Sociology* 29 (1): 4–22.

Tomic, Patricia, Ricardo Trumper, and Rodrigo Hidalgo Dattwyler. "Manufacturing Modernity: Cleaning, Dirt, and Neoliberalism in Chile." *Antipode* 38 (3): 508–29.

Trouillot, Michel-Rolph. (1992) 2015. *Silencing the Past: Power and the Production of History.* Second edition. Boston: Beacon Press.

Tsing, Anna Lowenhaupt. 2005. *Friction: An Ethnography of Global Connection.* Princeton, NJ: Princeton University Press.

———. 2012. "Unruly Edges: Mushrooms as Companion Species: For Donna Haraway." *Environmental Humanities* 1 (1): 141–54.

Tuck, Richard. 1979. *Natural Rights Theories.* Cambridge: Cambridge University Press.

Tuhiwai Smith, Linda. (1999) 2012. *Decolonizing Methodologies: Research and Indigenous Peoples.* New York: Zed Books.

Twinam, Ann. 1999. *Public Lives, Private Secrets.* Stanford, CA: Stanford University Press.

Tylor, Edward Burnett. 1920 [1871]. *Primitive Culture: Researches into the Development of Mythology, Philosophy, Religion, Language, Art, and Custom.* London: G.P. Putnam's Sons.

Urioste, Miguel. 2001. *Bolivia: Reform and Resistance in the Countryside.* Occasional Papers. London: Institute of Latin American Studies.

———. 2005. *Bolivia: La Reforma Agraria abandonada. Valles y Altiplano.* La Paz: Fundación TIERRA – ILC – IDRC.

———. 2007. *La Revolución agraria de Evo Morales.* La Paz: Fundación TIERRA.

———. 2008. "La reforma agraria en la nueva constitución." *Pulso,* November 2–8, pp. 8–9.

———. 2009. *From INRA to Revolution: Bolivia post-constituyente.* 55-8. La Paz: Fundación TIERRA.

———. 2011. *Concentración y extranjerización de la tierra en Bolivia.* La Paz: Fundación TIERRA.

Urioste, Miguel, Rossana Barragán, and Gonzalo Colque, eds. 2007. "Los Nietos De La Reforma Agraria." *Tierra y Comunidad en el Altiplano de Bolivia.* La Paz: Fundación TIERRA - CIPCA.

Urton, Gary, and Alejandro Chu. 2018. "The Invention of Taxation in the Inka Empire." *Latin American Antiquity* 30 (1): 1–16.

Valdivia, Carmen. 2020. "Toward a Decolonial Feminist Research on Indigeneity in Contemporary Peru." *Transmodernity: Journal of Peripheral Cultural Production of the Luso-Hispanic World* 9 (5): 107–28.

Valdivia, G. 2010. "Agrarian Capitalism and Struggles over Hegemony in the Bolivian Lowlands." *Latin American Perspectives* 37 (4): 67–87.

Van Cott, Donna Lee. 2000. *The Friendly Liquidation of the Past: The Politics of Diversity in Latin America*. Pittsburgh: University of Pittsburgh Press.

Vanvalkenburg, Parker. 2017. "Unsettling Time: Persistence and Memory in Spanish Colonial Peru." *Journal of Archaeological Method and Theory* 24 (1): 117–48.

Van Vleet, Krista. 2008. *Performing Kinship: Narrative, Gender and the Intimacies of Power in the Andes*. Austin: University of Texas Press.

Vargas, Jessica. 2019. "Megaobras 'Bolivia cambia, Evo cumple' en el limbo del gasto público y el abandono." *Los Tiempos* July 15. www.lostiempos.com /especial-multimedia/20190715/megaobras-bolivia-cambia-evo-cumple-limbo -del-gasto-publico-abandono.

Venkat, Bharat. 2021. *At the Limits of Cure*. Durham, NC: Duke University Press.

Wachtel, Nathan. 1977. *The Vision of the Vanquished: The Spanish Conquest of Peru through Indian Eyes, 1530–1570*. New York: Barnes and Noble.

Wade, Peter. 2005. "Rethinking Mestizaje: Ideology and Lived Experience." *Journal of Latin American Studies* 37 (2): 239–57.

———. 2009. *Race and Sex in Latin America*. Berkeley: University of California Press.

Weaver, Brendan J. "Ghosts of the Haciendas: Memory, Architecture, and the Architecture of Memory in the Post-Hacienda Era of Southern Coastal Peru." *Ethnohistory* 67 (1): 149–73.

Weber, Max. (1922) 1968. *Economy and Society*. Berkeley: University of California Press.

Weeks, Jeffrey. 1998. "The Sexual Citizen." *Theory, Culture & Society* 15 (3–4): 35–52.

Weismantel, Mary. 1995. "Making Kin: Kinship Theory and Zumbagua Adoptions." *American Ethnologist* 22 (4): 685–709.

———. 2001. *Cholas and Pishtacos: Stories of Race and Sex in the Andes*. Chicago: University of Chicago Press.

———. 2006. "Ayllu: Real and Imagined Communities in the Andes." In *The Seductions of Community: Emancipations, Oppressions, Quandaries*. Edited by G. W. Creed, 77–100. Santa Fe, NM: School of American Research.

Weismantel, Mary, and Mary Elena Wilhoit. 2019. "Kinship in the Andes." *The Cambridge Handbook of Kinship*. Edited by Sandra Bamford, 179–210. Cambridge: Cambridge University Press.

Weiss, Brad. 2018. *Real Pigs: Shifting Values in the Field of Local Pork*. Durham, NC: Duke University Press.

Wernke, Steven A. 2013. *Negotiated Settlements: Andean Communities and Landscapes under Inka and Spanish Colonialism*. Gainesville: University Press of Florida.

West, Martha S. 1996. "The Historical Roots of Affirmative Action." *La Raza Law Journal* 10: 607–30.

Williams, Raymond. 1977. "Dominant, Residual, and Emergent." In *Marxism and Literature*, 121–35. Oxford: Oxford University Press.

Wilson, Ara. 2004. *The Intimate Economies of Bangkok: Tomboys, Tycoons, and Avon Ladies in the Global City*. Berkeley: University of California Press.

Winchell, Mareike. 2017. "Economies of Obligation: Patronage as Relational Wealth in Bolivian Gold Mining." *HAU: Journal of Ethnographic Theory* 7 (3): 159–83. DOI: http://dx.doi.org/10.14318/hau7.3.011.

———. 2018. "After Servitude: Bonded Histories and the Encumbrances of Exchange in Indigenizing Bolivia." *Journal of Peasant Studies* 45 (2): 453–73. DOI: 10.1080/03066150.2016.1229309.

———. 2020. "Liberty Time in Question: Historical Duration and Indigenous Refusal in Post–Revolutionary Bolivia." *Comparative Studies in Society and History* 62 (3): 551–87. DOI: 10.1017/S0010417520000171.

Wolf, Eric R. 1955. *The Mexican Bajio in the Eighteenth Century: An Analysis of Cultural Integration*. New Orleans: Tulane University Press.

———. 1999. *Envisioning Power: Ideologies of Dominance and Crisis*. Berkeley: University of California Press.

Wolf, Eric R., and Sidney Mintz. 1957. "Haciendas and Plantations." In *Haciendas and Plantations in Latin American History*. Edited by Robert G. Keith, 493–531. New York: Holmes & Meier.

Wolford, Wendy. 2010. *This Land Is Ours Now: Social Mobilization and the Meanings of Land in Brazil*. Durham, NC: Duke University Press.

Wood, Ellen M. (2002) 2017. *The Origins of Capitalism: A Longer View*. New York: Verso.

Wynter, Sylvia. 2003. "Unsettling the Coloniality of Being/Power/Truth/Freedom: Towards the Human, after Man, Its Overrepresentation—An Argument." *CR: The New Centennial Review* 3 (3): 257–337.

Yampara, Simón. 2011. "Andean Cosmovivencia. Living and Living Together in Integral Harmony—Suma Qamaña." *Bolivian Studies Journal/Revista de Estudios Bolivianos* 18: 1–22. https://doi.org/10.5195/bsj.2011.42.

Yanagisako, Sylvia. 2002. *Producing Culture and Capital: Family Firms in Italy*. Princeton, NJ: Princeton University Press.

———. 2013. "Transnational Family Capitalism: Producing 'Made in Italy' in China." In *Vital Relations: Modernity and the Persistent Life of Kinship*. Edited by Susan McKinnon and Fenella Canell, 63–84. Santa Fe: SAR Press.

Zambrana, Amílcar, ed. 2014. *El pueblo afroboliviano: Historia, cultura y economía*. Cochabamba: FUNPROEIB Andes.

Zibechi, Raúl. 2019. "Bolivia: Evo's Fall, the Fascist Right, and the Power of Memory." *New Politics*. November 18. https://newpol.org/bolivia-evos-fall-the-fascist-right-andthe-power-of-memory-by-Raul-Zibechi.

Zimmerer, Karl. 1996. *Changing Fortunes: Biodiversity and Peasant Livelihood in the Peruvian Andes*. Berkeley: University of California Press.

———. 2014. "Environmental Governance through 'Speaking Like an Indigenous State' and Respatializing Resources: Ethical Livelihood Concepts as Versatility or Verisimilitude?" *Geoforum* 64: 314–24.

Note: Page numbers in italics refer to figures. Those followed by n refer to notes, with note number.

antihacienda militancy (*continued*)
74; murder of "bad" *hacendados* in, 48;
outside influences and, 74–75, 77; peasant militias' and, 74–75; as "race war"
in *hacendados*' view, 75; union groups
and, 74
anti-Indigenous violence, after Morales' resignation, 234
Arce, Luis, election as president, 234;
and hope to fulfill Morales's unful-
filled promises, 235; as reaffirmation of
vibrancy of Bolivian Indigenous movements, 234–35
archipelago system, 70, 71
Arendt, Hannah, 255n24
Aristotle, 255n24
Arpasi, Ruben: on land titling program,
conflict created by, 101; and productivist
stance of land titling program, 112; recognition of jarring effect of land titling
program on rural laborers, 113; on regularization of property through titling,
99, 100; on rural dependency, 111; on
rural ignorance as obstacle to land
titling program, 109, 114
Arvin, M., 283n57
Asad, Talal, 261n72
asymmetrical exchange relations in
Ayopaya: Ayopaya's repurposing of, to
contest MAS political authority, 200;
as challenge to conception of modern
citizenship, 231; as challenge to idea of
timeless Indigeneity, 230; collapse of,
after Morales' resignation, 234; and
creative recasting of property in light
of regional history and violence, 243;
in *fiesta de promoción* in Rami, 217–18,
219–20; government view of as victimization, 94; and land gifting, 66, 67, 69,
95, 138–42, 231, 239; longevity of, 93–94;
and MAS efforts to co-opt Indigenous
ceremonies, 205–6; and meals, responsibility to host, 49–50, 178, 179, 203, 225,
281n16; as mutual dependence, in many
participants' view, 95; as problem for
land reform program, 94; as standard
for evaluating government officials and
programs, 200, 229, 237, 241, 284n8;

and telos of capital, 237; and transracial solidarity, 231–32. *See also* hacienda
owners' descendants, obligation to aid
former workers
asymmetrical exchange relations in
Ayopaya, creation of legitimate authority through: Flora Soliz and, 49–50,
51–52, 61–62, 74, 177, 178, 179, 225;
and modern politicians' dealings with
Indigenous people, 218–20, 225–26;
Morales' failure to understand, 203; and
Morales government, expectations for,
222–24, 225–27, 229–30, 241; Morales
government's failure to meet standard
for, 227–29, *228*; ongoing relevance in
Ayopaya, 220–23
authority, lessons on nature of, in Ayopayans' engagement with oppressive past
and inegalitarian present, 235–36
Ayala, Maria (former servant), support for
hacienda abolition, 78
ayllus, 11; activists' efforts to revive, 18; and
authentic Andean Indigeneity, 13; early
juridical recognition, 17; and Indigenous interface with political power, 108;
number of families in, in 1877 census,
17; politicization of, through Indigenous resistance, 18; and splitting of
haciendas into villages under agrarian
reform, 67
Aymara: activists' focus on collective landholding goals of, 26–27; and asymmetrical exchange system, 22, 167, 203;
and communal systems, 18, 22, 26, 107,
149, 209; and land reform, 104; and
land rights under Spanish, 71, 147; and
limited concept of Indigeneity, 26, 69;
opposition to property as means to create modern citizens, 22; pre-Incan, economic and political structures of, 70;
and Quechua, rarity of political alignment, 84; revivalism, 11, 160; views on
Criollo landlords, 83–84. *See also* ayllus
Ayopaya: agricultural plots in, *68*; as center of antihacienda militancy, 1, 6, 22,
25; descendants of *hacendados*, tenants,
and servants working side by side in, 26;
engagement with inegalitarian past and

present, lessons on nature of authority in, 235–36; eventual compliance with land titling program, 159; and governmental zones of rights-based remediation, alienation from, 146; labor subjection in, as ongoing issue, 4; as lawless and backward, in reformers' view, 6, 133, 186; and Morales, later ambivalence toward, 224–25, 241; ongoing anti-Mestizo violence in, 51–52; origin of author's interest in, 25–26; potential conversion to Native Community Land, controversy over, 27; preference for loose association with central government, 158; return of Mestizo elite in Banzer regime, 172; survey of (1550), 91. *See also* antihacienda militancy in Ayopaya; hacienda system in Ayopaya; Quechua

Ayopaya, and collective land titling: discussion of, in union meeting, 153–54; expansion of project to encompass all of Ayopaya, 148, 149; as government effort to integrate rural subjects into centralized rule, 156; INRA file on, 143, 144–45; insistence on local initiation of, 154; international funding for, 147–49, 277nn16–18

Ayopaya, and collective land titling, rejection of, 143–47, 148, 158; accusations of misleading information, 145, 276–77n11; characterization as new form of colonialism, 145; concerns about destruction of existing land use patterns and labor ties, 149; concerns about loss of individual land titles, 67, 146–47, 149, 153–54; and ejection of INRA from region, 147; as inconsistent with Indigenous self-determination, 146; and male tenant farmer as model, 146–47; objections to, 2, 67, 143–45; and positing of regional unity based on shared history of hacienda violence, 146; preference for system stressing former hacienda masters' obligation to aid former workers, 24, 61

Ayopaya, author as White foreigner in: and contingency of presence, 29; and implication in *hacendados'* obligation to help, 28–29, 267n141; and large number of White foreigners in regions, 27–28; and locals' views on research, 29, 148, 276n4

Ayopaya social system based in debt owed by former hacienda owners, 3–4; as "after servitude" condition, 4; as backward, in reformers' view, 6; and history as knotted threads of past and present, 4–5; vs. land title solution, 3–4, 7; and multiple lives of afterness, 4. *See also* asymmetrical exchange relations in Ayopaya; hacienda owners' descendants, obligation to aid former workers

Banzer, Hugo: anti-union stance of, 171–72; coup, violence in, 171–72, 278n33; and return of Mestizos to countryside, 172

Barrientos, René, 86, 171

Bastias Saavedra, Manuel, 133–35

Benjamin, Walter, 252n7

Bhandar, Brenna, 8–9, 160, 231

Bolivia Cambia. Evo Cumple program, *217*, 217–18, 226–27

bonded agrarian labor (*pongueaje*), and land use patterns, xii

Bonilla, Yarimar, 242, 261n79

Calle, Julio (MAS official), on childlike ignorance of rural laborers, 110–11, 114

Camacho, Adolfo (union representative), 80–81

Camacho, Pavel (descendant of Quechua hacienda manager): at *fiesta de promoción* in Rami, 215–16; land claim denied by peasant's union, 138–42, 160; and liminal space inhabited by descendants of hacienda overseers and managers, 141

capital: disembedded, Quechua laborers' rejection of, 193–97; reproduction of, Quechua rejection of distance as normative presumption of, 23; telos of, and asymmetrical exchange tradition, 168–69, 195–96, 237

Carter, Paul, 68

celebrations, sponsorship of, 216–17

CENDA. *See* Center for Communication and Andean Development

Center for Communication and Andean Development (CENDA): Ayopayan anger at underhanded tactics of, 153; cooperation with INRA, 143, 144–45; ejection from Ayopaya, 153; local suspicion about, 148–49

Central Obrera Boliviana (COB), 27; Ayopayan concerns about interference by, 151; Ayopayan preference for loose association with, 157–58; call for increased aid to women, 151; mass protests (April, 2011), 158–59; opposition to MAS government, 151; women's branch of, 151

Central Sindical Única de Trabajadores Campesinos Originarios de Ayopaya (Central Union of Campesino Workers of Ayopaya, CSUTCOA), 27, 144, 197, 267n140

Certeau, Michel de, 253–54n12

ch'alla ritual sacrifice: as annual rural ceremony, 49–50; employees' expectations for, shaped by debt owed by descendants of *hacendados*, 49–50, 178, 179; history of, 199–200; popularity in Ayopaya, 212; as sacrifice to Pachamama, 198, 199, 205; supplication of El Tio in, 200; uses of, 197

ch'alla ritual sacrifice, government-run, in Independencia (2012), 197–99, *199*; dubious authenticity of, 214; and MAS erasure of religious expressions of posthacienda Indigeneity, 215; and MAS revival of Indigenous traditions, 198, 200, 206, 215; participants' questioning of, 204–6, 210, 214, 215, 226; and positioning of government as benevolent *hacendado*, 225–26; and religious connotations of exchange, 199; and rewriting of boundaries between state and Indigenous traditions, 213

children of hacienda masters, servants' use of "my child" (*niñoy*) in referring to, 40

Choque, Angelo (Quechua union leader): arrest for threats and theft from *hacendado*, 181; on classes of workers, 87; family grudge against *hacendado*, 76; on *hacendados'* leadership of peasant

unions, 82; and hacienda abolishment, 78–79, 80; on hacienda abolishment, and conflict among villagers, 87–88; imprisonment for attempted homicide, 86; on land redistribution, 85, 86, 87–88; on local suspicion about NGOs, 148–49; on military junta of 1946, 77; and mob attacks on haciendas, 87; on opposition to land redistribution surveys, 91; and Quechua anger at ongoing Mestizo dominance, 169; on Socialist Revolution of 1952, 166–67

Choque, Eduardo, 143, 144, 146

Chullpani, land claim disputes in, 138–42

citizens, modern, created through property ownership, 10–11, 12, 16–17, 19–20; and antihacienda militancy, 74; Aymara opposition to, 22; and eradication of master's obligation to servant, 41–42; and erasure of expressions of posthacienda Indigeneity, 239; as goal of land reform, 94, 239–40; labor based land claims and, 68; land titling program of MAS and, 2, 100–101, 133–35, 136; and line between public and private, 258n48; and loss of traditional kinship obligations, 62; and potential loss of property, 241; Quechua opposition to, 22, 84, 237, 240; and settler/colonial ideas of agency, 242; and turn of attention from unjust present to hoped-for future, 240

COB. *See* Central Obrera Boliviana

Coca, José María, 76

Cochabamba city, author's residence in, xiii–xiv, xiv, 25–26

Cochabamba region: as center of anticolonial violence, 73; contesting of exchange systems and racialized abstraction, 21; and encomiendas, disbanding of, 72; and hacienda system, development of, 73; land conflicts of 16th century, 71–72; Spanish honoring of Inca land allotments, 16; tax rebellion (1730), 73

collective land titling: government restrictions on, 157; as key concern of Indigenous activism, 106; land reforms of 1953 and, 106; as less appealing in Ayopayan society shaped by hacienda bondage, 200; as means to constrain and domesticate Indigenous peoples, 230–31; Mestizo and settler concepts of Indigeneity in, 156; as only legitimate Indigenous politics, Ayopayan historical redress mechanisms as challenge to, 61; as rallying cry for Indigenous movements, 103; reformers' support for, 2; and reification of Indigeneity as community, 160; and reproduction of gendered and racialized hierarchies, 61; and subterranean resource rights, loss of, 2, 157, 241; and weakening of unions' ability to resolve land disputes, 155. *See also* Ayopaya, and collective land titling; socialist land collectives

colonialism: and limited capacity of colonial capitalism to supplant other exchange traditions, 259n59; in Peru, and women of Inca nobility as threat to colonial property regime, 257n38; and separation of economic sphere, 13

Colque, Ramón (former hacienda farmer): criticism of, for continued dependence, 36–37; and mutual dependency of *hacendados* and servants, 62; refusal to exit hacienda obligation, 35–39, 44, 56, 65

Communist Party of Bolivia. *See* El Partido Comunista de Bolivia

community: boundaries of, and land titling program, 108–9; as broad socio-spiritual space, 107; as concept in Indigenous activism, 106–7; Indigenous, as site of autonomous decision-making, in MAS view, 113; INRA insistence on, as unit of land titling negotiation, 130–32, 143–44; MAS land reform programs and, 106–7; as rubric in hacienda laborers' land claims, 108; as secular model of production in Morales government, 108; as Spanish-imposed concept, 106. *See also* collective land titling

Condorí, Gregorio: as agronomist, xv; author's first meeting with, xii; father's antihacienda activism, 77; land of, as inherited from parents, xii; and land

titles, opposition to, xi–xii, 20; Mestizo godfather, support from, xv; on Mestizo *hacendados'* sexual relationships with Quechua women, 57–58; peach orchards of, xi, xv, 4–5; as Quechua farmer, xi; on ties of obligation within community, 3; on workers' takeover of haciendas, 77

Condorí, Gregorio, parents of: abuse of, as hacienda workers, xi, xv; and elusiveness of property titles, xii, xiii; land received in land redistribution, xii

Condorí, Vitalio, 79

conservative anti-Indigenous faction, support for Añez regime, 234

constitutional convention of 1938, 74, 270n16

Constitution of 2009, and Indigenous revival movement, 213

contract, as tool of anticolonial justice, 261n79

contract law system, integration of Indigenous people into, 6; and colonial institutions, 14; and historical redress, 7, 13, 14–15; and Indigenous autonomy, 19; Indigenous contesting of, to address inequalities, 21–22; and loss of kinship-based idioms of care, 40, 103, 168; and Quechua opposition to loss of kinship-based idioms of care, 192, 194, 195, 236–37, 241; short duration of transaction in, 21, 265n120. *See also* citizens, modern, created through property ownership; property

Corntassel, J., 24

countryside, repopulation in twenty-first century, and pressure for land titling, 27

Cruz, Macasuya, 229

Cruz, René (son of hacienda master): background of, 173, 174; on *hacendados'* sex with servants, 57; imperious behavior by, 179; and respect given to Martín as *hacendado* descendant, inability to duplicate, 186–87; sexual aggression against maids, 190–91, 193; villagers' opinions of, 177–78

Cruz, René, gold mine owned by, *174*; consolidation as nominal collective, 177; and disembedded capital, workers'

Cruz, René *(continued)*
  rejection of, 193–96; effect on his personal life, 196; and hired driver's rape of local women, outrage at, 191; labor mobility in protest against, 189–94; legal efforts to blunt worker dissatisfaction, 175–76; number of workers employed at, 173; protests against, as reminder of contingency of wealth, 192; purchase of, 165, 173; René's flight from violent threats, 166; villagers' blocking of road to mine, 166, 176, 192; and villagers' demand for electricity and water supply, 165–66, 175; villagers hope to replace as mine owner, 176–77; and weight of *hacendados*' legacy, 196; workers' calls for René's expulsion from Ayopaya, 176, 188, 189–90; workers' housing at, 173
Cruz, René, and miners' expectations shaped by debt owed by descendants of *hacendados*, 167–69, 173–81, 192–93; and complication of narrative of capitalist progress, 195–96; and modern world of legal equality, workers' rejection of, 187–89, 192–93, 241; monthly *cha'lla* and, 178, 179; René's failure to socialize (*"compartir"*) with workers, offense caused by, 174, 178–79, 180–81; René's objections to, in new climate of equality, 179–81, 184; as source of labor unrest, 167, 175–76, 178, 193
CSUTCOA. *See* Central Sindical Única de Trabajadores Campesinos Originarios de Ayopaya
cultural assimilation programs, 6, 254–55n17; Indigenous kinship and, 10

Das, Veena, 266n129
deities, place-based, gift exchange with, 43. *See also* earth-beings
De la Cadena, Marisol, 282n32
Delgadillo, Carlos (INRA official), 127–32
Delgado, Huascar (INRA official), 114–15, 122–24, 125–26, 131
dependency of former servants: agentive dimension of positioning as, 63; and assertion of ethical claim on *hacendado*

families, 63, 64; and mutual dependence of *hacendados* and servants, 62
Dhamoon, R., 24
Dru Stanley, Amy, 261n79

earth-beings: farmers' reciprocal obligations to, 80; and obligations of *hacendados* descendants to former workers, 243; and ties of obligation within community, 3. *See also* Pachamama (earth mother)
ecological entities, environmental personhood for, 259n60
economic and political structures: of Incas, 70–71; in pre-Incan Aymara tribes, 70; in Spanish colonial rule, 71–73
Edelman, Marc, 42, 284n9
Edgar (godson of former hacienda owner): on family's children outside of marriage, 46; on family's original land grant, 47–48; on René Cruz's labor troubles, 175–76
El Partido Comunista de Bolivia (PCB), 78
Ellison, Susan, 44
Emiliano (former hacienda *colono*), on good and bad masters around Arani, 83
encomiendas: definition of, 251n5; disbanding of, 72; Inca systems as model for, 71
Engles, Friedrich, on alienable property and women, 260n61
Espada, Carlos, 138
Estatuto Organico de Ayopaya, 151–52
Estenssoro, Victor Paz, 78, 86, 225
ethnicity, reification of, in anticolonial projects, 112
exchange: in Ayopaya, resistance to telos of modern property, 70, 237–38; Ayopayans' resistance to alienability inherent in, 5; different obligations in different regimes of, 21; and former hacienda masters obligation to aid former workers, Quechua preference for system supporting, 22–24, 44–45, 61, 266n129; as knotted threads binding past and present, 5, 236; and mediation of value in economy and kinship spheres, 21; Polanyi on destructive dislocations of, 265n120; as privileged analytic in

hacienda owners (continued)
    inheritance, regulation of sexuality
    required for, 49, 64
hacienda owners, sexual relationships with
    Quechua women: and adoption of ille-
    gitimate children as godchildren, 38–39,
    49, 58, 63, 64; as assumed right, 190–91;
    as common, 57; and creation of kinship
    networks, 58; echoes of, in modern poli-
    ticians, 202–3; and hacendados descen-
    dants, guilt felt by, 58; and issue of rape
    vs. consensual sex, 57–58; land gifted to
    Quechua women bearing their children,
    66, 67, 231, 239; Mestizo vs. Quechua
    views on, 57; obligation to children
    from, 58; as perceived perversion of
    Mestizo masculinity, 47; as threat to
    Mestizo heteropatriarchy, 47–48, 49
hacienda owners' descendants: in Ayopaya,
    25; guilt about Quechua children
    fathered by hacendado, 58; Quechua still
    holding grudges against, 76; responses
    to violent past, 56; return to rural areas
    in twenty-first century, 26–27; ties to
    former workers, as both emotional and
    economic, 37
hacienda owners' descendants, obligation
    to aid former workers, 236–37; accep-
    tance of, by descendants, 181–84; affec-
    tive force of, 37; as complication of nar-
    rative of capitalist progress, 168–69,
    195–96; as debt owed for hacendados'
    misbehavior, 193; as double-edged,
    60–61; embarrassment of progressive
    descendants about, 184–86; ending of,
    as perceived social abandonment, 44;
    extension to any Mestizos filling role,
    236; as generally recognized, 35–39,
    44–45; hacendados' expectations of
    respect in return for, 52, 56; as idiom
    of historical obligation, 37; as inimi-
    cal to modern concept of citizen, 37;
    loss of, with turn to modern economic
    system, Quechua concern about, 2–3,
    22–23, 45–46, 62; Mestizos object-
    ing to, in new climate of legal equality,
    179–81; mutual vulnerability within
    kinship networks, 62, 64; periodic

feasts required by, 49–50, 178, 179, 203,
    225, 281n16; points of resistance sup-
    plied by, 43; Quechua preference for
    system maintaining, 22–24, 44–45, 61,
    266n129; and racial hierarchy, 23, 44;
    and redefinition of commodity system,
    23; redemptive force of, 49; as repur-
    posing of old obligations for histori-
    cal redress, 61, 64–65; as reworking of
    existing political forms, 195; shaping
    of miners' expectations of aid, 167–69,
    171–80; threat of violence underlying,
    48; as type of reparation, 180; types of
    aid traditionally provided, 167, 171. See
    also asymmetrical exchange relations in
    Ayopaya
hacienda owners' descendants, workers'
    insistence on obligation of, 35–38, 39,
    187–89, 192–93, 194–95, 236; and insuf-
    ficiency of reparations, 243; and mar-
    icón status, 36–37; as new growth from
    ruins of old system, 232; persistence
    of, as issue, 42–43, 44, 49, 53–54; and
    rejection of land titling and collectiv-
    ist solutions, 24, 240; and resistance to
    state bureaucratic norms, 236
haciendas: abolition of, xii, 77; as affective
    economies, 40–41; areas of hacienda
    persistence, 84; blurring of distinction
    between home and work, 41, 42; com-
    plex ties of kinship across groups in, 8;
    development of, 73–74; fusing of social
    and exchange relations in, 8, 256n27;
    harboring of mobile laborers, 73–74;
    land of, redistribution or abandon-
    ment after abolition, 25; as opportunity
    for servants to access land and escape
    state tribute burdens, 73; and racial-
    ized structures of coloniality, 256n26;
    ruins of, 44, 45; signs of decline by 1916,
    84; small size of, 25; violence, absence
    from pro-Indiginous activist accounts,
    26, 266–67n139; women's labor in, 25,
    266n138; women's labor in, and blurring
    of domestic service and sexual relations,
    25, 40
hacienda system in Ayopaya: and creation
    of ties inimical to modern land owner-

ship, 22, 265n125; ongoing influence of, xii; survival into mid-20th century, xii, 20, 22, 43, 84, 275–76n63; and unresolved legal disputes, xiii

hacienda system in Bolivia, development of, 25

Harris, Cheryl, 14, 160

Hartman, Saidiya, 261–62n80, 261n79

Herzog, Tamar, 262n90

historical epochs, linking specific institutions to, 69–70

historical redress, contract-based forms of: efficacy *vs.* Ayopaya system, 7; types of redress disallowed in, 7

historical redress mechanisms in Ayopaya: as challenge to standard view of legitimate Indigenous politics, 61; land redistribution and, xiii; and mutual vulnerability within kinship networks, 62, 64–65; repurposing of old hacienda obligations for, 61, 64–65

history in Ayopayan view, as knotted threads of past and present, 4–5, 253nn10–11, 254n13; exchange and, 5, 236; kinship and, 5, 46, 69, 236; property and, 5, 236; and reframing of scholarly debate, 5–6

Huarachi, Humberto (former servant): beating by antihacienda mob (1983), 86–87; on hacienda abolishment, violence during, 82–83

huérfano (orphan or illegitimate child), post-hacienda kinship ties of, 37

Hunter, Tera W., 261n79

illegitimate children, master's obligation to, and godchild relationship, 38–39, 49, 58, 63, 64

Incas: economic and political structures, 70–71; influence on Spanish colonial system, 16, 70, 71, 72, 94; and large-scale movement of migrant laborers, 71; and tradition of aid to Indigenous workers, 171

independence of Latin American countries, and production of modern citizens: Quechua opposition to, 22; through family interventions, 10–11. *See also* citizens, modern, created through property ownership

Independencia: author's research in, 24–26; Carnival in, 56; demographics and economy of, 24, 266n136; elder Mestizos' memories of 1947 uprising, 48; mayor of, accused of sexual exploitation, 202–3; pro-Indigenous activism in, 25–26. *See also* ch'alla ritual sacrifice, government-run, in Independencia (2012)

Indigeneity: government's abstract formulation of, Ayopayan critiques of, 142–43; negotiations with Spanish law, 157

Indigeneity, Ayopayan redefinition of: and challenging of reformers' view of Indigenous collectivity, 157, 160–61; and distinction between virtuous and nonvirtuous laborers, 160; in terms of shared hacienda legacy and not romantic Indigeneity (grounding Indigeneity), 156–58, 159–61

Indigenous autonomy: exchange relations in, similarity to private property regimes, 263n107; paradox of government's support for, within strict government guidelines, 150, 155–56

Indigenous communities in Bolivia: 1869 reform to destroy, backlash against, 17; Colonial debate on readiness for political rights, 6; and money and property-based reparations, 242–43; number of members, in 1880 census, 17

Indigenous Congress (1945), 76; and antihacienda militancy, 74; *hacendados'* efforts to suppress, 76

Indigenous feminism, insistence on viewing Indigenous sovereignty and gender violence together, 283n57

Indigenous identity: fragmented hierarchy of, based on past hacienda labor ties, 141–42; language as marker of, 251n1

Indigenous justice, ayllu-based forms of, 18–19

Indigenous land rights: Morales administration promises on, xiii. *See also* land titling program

Indigenous politics, legitimate, as outside modernity, Ayopayan challenge to, 61

Indigenous rebellion of 1780 (Túpaj Katari), 17, 25, 107

Indigenous rebellion of 1947: attacks on *hacendados* in, 48, 75–76; death of Villarroel and, 77

Indigenous rebellions, pro-Indigenous activists on, 25–26

Indigenous religious practices: and Indigenous revival movement, 198, 200, 206, 207; Spanish repurposing of, 214, 226; use to challenge Spanish colonial power, 213–14. *See also* earth-beings

Indigenous revival movement of MAS: and claimed inclusion of Indigenous people, 226; conflict with other anti-Indigenous government policies, 214, 241; effort to return to worship of precolonial deities, 198, 200, 206, 207; as effort to reverse Spanish influence, 207, 212; and erasure of expressions of posthacienda Indigeneity, 215, 230, 239; and government authority over Indigenous expression, 211–12; and government criticisms of Ayopayan villagers' entrenchment in Mestizo institutions, 214; Indigeneity in, as academic fabrication, 208, 212, 214; Indigeneity in, as practical impossibility, 210, 213–14, 229, 231; vs. Indigenous collectivity forged from existing traditions in rural areas, 208–10, 212; and injuries of redemptive property, 231; local attachment to Catholicism and, 207–8; as means to constrain and domesticate Indigenous peoples, 208, 210, 212, 214, 230–31; and positioning of government as benevolent *hacendado*, 225–26; Quechua skepticism about, 204–7, 214; recoverability of authentic Indigenous tradition as issue, 207, 208–9, 230; reified Indigeneity in, Ayopayans' objections to, 214–15; and rewriting of boundaries between state and Indigenous traditions, 213; as vexed, in Ayopayan society shaped by hacienda bondage, 200

Indigenous rights in Bolivia, movements to secure, 1

Indigenous ritual and ontology, impact on national political realities, 282n32

Indigenous traditions, authentic, rethinking criteria for, 70

Indio, as category, 17 47, 185

Ingold, Tim, 126–27

INRA. *See* Institúto Nacional de Reforma Agraria

Institúto Nacional de Reforma Agraria (National Institute for Agrarian Reform, INRA): and asymmetrical exchange tradition, expectations created by, 230; author's research at, xiv, 24; and author's research permission, 99–100; community as key concept in land reforms of, 107; complaints of corruption against field workers of, 129; concerns about MAS government authority over Indigenous expression, 211–12; and control over Indigenous terms of land ownership, 210; creation of, 104; and delays in breakup of *latifundios*, 106; and delays in land titling program, 109; ejection from Ayopaya, 153; and hacienda system as basis of Indigenous land claims, 19–20; imposition of Western land ownership norms, 19; and Indigeneity as racialized property and spatial enclosure, 159–61; and labor hierarchies among hacienda workers, failure to acknowledge, 132, 135; and land redistribution, 52, 53; and land titling project, 27; land titling teams in rural areas, 104, 114–15; opposition to clientism, 218; peasant union leaders' interface with, 108; political training for peasants, 111; process for contesting land titles, 130; Quechua mistrust of, xiii; regional office in Cochabamba, 114, 127; rigid processes for land titling imposed by, 131; secrecy surrounding files held by, 125; view of rural people as childlike, 109. *See also* land titling program; property, INRA production of

Institúto Nacional de Reforma Agraria, Archival Records office of, 127–31, *128*; author's research in, 128; file on Ayopaya rejection of collective titling, 143, 144–

45; as informal site of legal council and education, 130–31, 132; openness to rural laborers, vs. INRA view of them as children, 129–30; rural residents' research on land claims in, 128–31; types of files in, 128–29

itinerant Quechua labor, and land relations, 70

jallp'a sangres (attachment to land and soil): and Quechua anger at ongoing Mestizo dominance, 169; and Quechua claims to land, 82, 169

Jesuit missionaries, as mine owners, 171

Katari, Túpaj, 17, 25, 26, 107, 201, *202*

kinship: basis in circulation of women and gifts, 21; blood-based definitions of, and European inheritance systems, 9; blood-based definitions of, imposition in Latin America reforms, 10–12; blurring of lines between exchange and, 41–42; centrality in post-hacienda lines of accountability, 39, 44–45; colonial fragmentation of, 10; continuity in post-hacienda period, 37; creation of obligation in Ayopaya social system, 5; and domestic service, switch from family retainer model to wage-based model of, 40; as form of production, 41; and *hacendados* descendants' obligations to former servants, 60–61, 64; as historical ethics, 7–13; indeterminacy of, and broadness of *hacendados* descendants' obligations, 58, 61; as knotted threads binding past and present, 5, 46, 69; networks of, from Mestizo *hacendados*' sexual relationships with Quechua women, 58; and political collectivity, scholarship on, 43–44; and property, blurring of distinction between, 21; and Quechua claim to Mestizo accountability, 12–13, 55, 64, 69–70; remaking the creative duration of, 13; structures, and exchange relations, 259–60n61; and upholding of racial hierarchies, 13; Western social theory on, 255n24

labor mobility, in protest against mine owners, 189–94

La Gasca, Pedro de, 91

land: as living entity bearing kinship and religious significance for Andean farmers, 101; Quechua *jallp'a sangres* (attachment to land and soil) and, 82, 169. *See also* property

land boundaries, INRA determination of: and annulment of earlier property titles, 125; avoidance of past corrupt practices, 124, 126; contesting of, by citizens, 128–30; and establishment of property as empirical referent, 126; and geographic representation, assumptions underlying, 127; INRA office in charge of, 114–15; and Lockean ownership through land improvement, 127, 133, 142

land boundaries, INRA mapping of: and discrepancies between maps and actual land use, blaming of residents for, 132; hacienda boundaries as basis of, 115, 125–27, 132, 135–36, 237–38; mapping technologies used in, 115–24, *116–18*, *120–21*, *123*; resolution of inconsistencies in, 126–27; review by community representatives, 126, 131; use in settling competing claims, 125

land claims in Ayopaya: labor-based, as problematic for modernizing project, 68; labor-based, denial of, in favor of claim based on labor hierarchy status, 138–42; for land gifts from *hacendados*, denial of, in favor of claim based on labor hierarchy status, 138–42; by outsiders, violent Quechua response to, 51–54; shaping of, by historical forces, 69

land gifted by *hacendados*: asymmetrical exchange relations and, 95; denial of claims to, in favor of claim based on labor hierarchy status, 138–42; divided Quechua opinion on, 69; Quechua critics of, 67; to Quechua women bearing *hacendados*' children, 66, 67, 231, 239

land ownership norms, Western: creation of racialized benefits in, 20; imposition in Bolivia, 19; imposition in Latin

land ownership norms *(continued)*
American reforms, 10–11, 16–17; vs.
inalienable Indigenous attachment
to land, 12; Indigenous resistance to,
16–18, 20; integration of Indigenous
political systems into, 16, 17, 258nn48–
49, 263n95; and integration of land and
people into bureaucracy, 20, 264n114;
and Mestizo ability to avoid accountability, 24; Morales administration
reforms and, 19; as naturalized paradigm, 19–20; and new avenues of legal
contestation, 17; ongoing use in Bolivian reforms, 12; and property tax, Indigenous opposition to, 17; slow penetra-
tion in Ayopaya, 20. *See also* citizens,
modern, created through property
ownership
land redistribution: and association of land
types and labor positions, 87–88; asymmetrical exchange relations as problem
in, 94; backlash against, after 1964, 86;
and distinction between tenant farmers
and hacienda servants, 87–89; *hacendados'* leadership of peasant unions and,
82; historical repair component of, xiii;
identification activism for, 103; introduction of, 78; and "land for those who
worked it" vs. "land to original owners,"
18; and land grabbing by villagers, 85;
landowners' contesting of, 52; and *latifundio* breakups, delays in, 103, 106; lawsuits impeding, 85; local activism for, in
1960s, 86; necessity of land titling for,
100; and reproduction of existing hierarchies, 85; and reserve of 200 square
hectares of best land for *hacendado*,
85, 92, 135; shortage of lands available
for, 85; and some *colonos'* land added to
land lottery, 85; as tool against Bolivian
racial hierarchy, xiv
Land Regularization Committees, 131
land titling program, Quechua opposition
to, 6–7, 237; and association of surveying with state control, 90–91; and concerns about assimilation into national
bureaucracies, 2; and concerns about
assimilation into national paradigms of

ownership and repair, xiv; and concerns
about being constrained by government
definition of Indigeneity, 143, 144; and
concerns about state intrusion, 144; and
concerns about unjust distribution of
land, 90, 91; and demands for redress in
other ways, 20; for failure to dismantle
racial hierarchy, 3; and fear of ending
existing traditional land use, xi–xii, xiv,
xv, 90–91; and fear of land confiscations,
112, 143; and fears of violations of Indigenous sovereignty, 143; ineffectiveness of
past reforms and, xiii; officials' refusal to
acknowledge, 112; preference for system
stressing former hacienda masters' obligation to aid former workers, 24; range
of reasons for, 143–44; traditional fluid
land transfers and, 12. *See also* Ayopaya,
and collective land titling, rejection of
land titling program of MAS: autonomous
decision-making by rural communities
as goal of, 113; Ayopayans accusations
of misrepresentations by, 143; Ayopayans' eventual compliance with, 159; and
collective land rights, 106; and colonial ideas of justice, 242; community
as key concept in, 106–7; and community boundaries, 108–9; "community
renewal" as goal of, 143–44; conflict
created by, 101, 142, 143, 155; contesting of titles by citizens, 128–30; controversy surrounding, 27; and disruption
of existing aid networks, 133–34; and
division between hacienda-based and
community-based lands, 108; efficacy
vs. Ayopaya system based on debt owed
by former hacienda owners, 7; and elusiveness of property titles, xii, xiii, xv,
20, 22, 135; and entrenched servile labor
order, 90, 91, 93; and ethnic lines, 238–
39; and fixity of land use as precondition
for overcoming unjust past, 106; freedom from hacienda system as goal of,
104–9, 132, 135; goals of, 2, 104; and government power to confiscate and redistribute land, 101, 106, 112, 134, *134*, 143;
and government power to determine
deserving and undeserving owners, 102,

Malaysian peasant relations, persistence of feudal ties in, 43

Malinowski, Bronislaw, 260n61

Mallea Valencia, Giovana, 144

Mamani Ramírez, Pablo, 102

maps, and representational assumptions underlying geographic representation, 127

maricóns: expulsions from family, 46; Quechua's violent response to land claims of, 52–53; as term of derision for nonheteropatriarchal males, 36–37; as threat to Mestizo heteropatriarchy, 46–49; as type of post-hacienda kinship tie, 37

Marx, Karl: *Capital*, 196; denaturalizing of entities to focus on activity, 21, 264n118; on exchange as social construct, 265n120; "Law on the Theft of Wood," 275n59; and liberation through dispossession of property, 135; notes on Morgan, 260n61; on origin of capitalist exploitation, 195; on property as theft, 133, 263n96; on service labor, 41, 168n15; on social character of labor, 192; on telos from kinship to capital, 259n61; on veiling of force needed for capitalism to gain hegemony, 196

Marxist critics, on colonial ownership as universal, 262n90

MAS. *See* Movimiento al Socialismo (Movement toward Socialism Party, MAS)

Mauss, Marcel, 65, 168, 260n61, 265n120

Mela (god-daughter of Martín), 182–83, 191

Mercado, José, 76, 77–78

mestizaje, as cultural assimilation program, 10

Mestizo, as term, 252n12

Mestizo masculinity: military service and heterosexual marriage as defining features of, 47; and sexual relationships with Quechua women, 47

Mestizos in Ayopaya: and collective land rights, manipulation of, 2; contingency of authority on relations to Indigenous workers, 181; debt owed to former workers, as basis of social system, 3; and everpresent fear of Indigenous violence, 63; and racial hierarchy in Bolivia, xiv; sponsorship of religious events, legitimacy gained from, 52; violent unrest following ouster of Morales, 235. *See also* hacienda owners (*hacendados*)

migrant laborers: haciendas' harboring of, 73–74; origin in Inca policies, 71; under Spanish colonial rule, 72

Military-Campesino Pact, 86

military governments: land grants to supporters, 124; support of Mestizo interests, 171; and suppression of peasant unions, 171–72; violence against workers' movements, 158, 278n33

mines: limits on family inheritance under MAS, 177; limits on foreign ownership under MAS, 177; mercury runoff from, 212

mines, collectivization of: difficulty of, without Mestizo aid, 177; MAS policies on, 177, 180–81

mining in Ayopaya: and labor unrest, 221; by relatives of former hacienda owners, 25, 27; ties to agriculture, 171, 175; and women's domestic labor, 193; and workers' expectations of aid, owners' objections to, 179–81; and workers' expectations of aid, shaped by perceived debt owed to former hacienda workers, 23, 167–69, 173–81, 192–93, 238. *See also* Cruz, René (son of hacienda master); Rodriguez, Martín (relative of former hacienda owner)

mining in Ayopaya, workers' union activism: government suppression of, 168, 171, 172; history of strikes, 171

mining in Sarahuayto: and disembedded capital, workers' rejection of, 193–96; and local tensions based on former hacienda labor hierarchies, 166; and mine owners' claim to Indigenous respect as family of former *hacendado*, 165; and modern world of legal equality, workers' rejection of, 187–89, 192–93, 194–95; workers' expectations shaped by perceived debt owed to former hacienda workers, 167–69, 171–80; workers' union activism, as alternative

to MAS government support, 168, 172.
See also Cruz, René, gold mine owned
by; Rodriguez, Fabio (relative of former
hacendado); Rodriguez, Martín, mines
owned by
Ministry of Labor, abolition of *mitanaje*
and *pongueaje* (1940), 74
Mintz, Sidney, 41
MIR. *See* Movimiento de Izquierda
Revolucionaria
MNR. *See* Movimiento Nacionalista
Revolucionario
modernity, as evolution to property-based
exchange, 21. *See also* citizens, modern,
created through property ownership;
legal equality, modern
Mollinedo, Portugal, 229
Montero, Carmenia (former hacienda servant), 89–90
moral economy of hacienda system: points
of resistance supplied by, 43; as source of
its persistence, 43
Morales Ayma, Evo: Ayopayan reluctance
to rely on, 172–73; and civic movement,
241; claim to mineral rights on Indigenous lands, 19; and colonial logics of
self-possessed property, 19; dissatisfaction with (2011), 222; events leading to
presidency of, xiv, 252–53n3; and *fiesta
de promoción* in Rami, 217, 217–18, 219;
and *hacendado* descendants' return
to rural areas, 26–27, 49; Indigenous
activism for land reform and, 103; and
Indigenous justice, 18–19; Indigenous
people's sense of abandonment by, 235;
Indigenous policies, as insufficiently
strong, 242, 243; Indigenous support
for, 235; and land reform as plan to
bring Mestizo masters to their knees,
94, 103; and land titling program, 6, 94;
and national union association, combative relationship with, 172; and productivist stance of land titling program,
112; promises on Indigenous land rights,
xiii; protests against subsidy cuts, 222;
push for creating modern citizens, 38;
reputation for sexual exploitation, 201,
202; rights-based reform of, 63; and

term limits, 105–6; visits to Independencia, 24; visit to Cavari (February,
2012), 197, 198, 201–3, 210; waning of
support for, in Ayopaya, 224–25, 241;
"we are all Indigenous" declaration by,
141–42
Morales, Evo, and asymmetrical exchange
tradition: echoing of, in relations with
Indigenous population, 218, 219–20;
expectations created by, 222–24, 225–
27, 229–30, 241; failure to meet expectations created by, 227–29, *228*; failure to
understand, 203
Morales, Evo, as Indigenous person: 2008
film on, 224, *225*; and Indigenous people's assumed access to, 224; as key to
MAS appeal, 224
Morales, Evo, violent ouster of, 233–34; and
accusations of foreign influence, 234,
284n6; and collapse of asymmetrical
exchange relations in Ayopaya, 234; and
conflict between former friends, 233;
conflicting approaches to Indigenous
people as source of, 241–42; international forces leading to, in commentators' view, 241–42; and subsequent
denial of racial violence, 233–34; violent
unrest following, 234, 235
Moren, Fred, 231, 256n27
Morgan, Lewis Henry, 41, 113, 259–60n61
Morrill, A., 283n57
Moten, Fred, 264n118
mother (*mamitay, madrina*): assimilation of unruly relationships into family structure, 63, 64; Mestizo, displays
of generosity without demands by, and
Quechua tolerance, 49–50, 51–52; and
post-hacienda kinship ties, 39; and resolution of sexual and social transgression,
56; as term for mistress used by servants,
40; as type of post-hacienda kinship
tie, 37
Movimiento al Socialismo (Movement
toward Socialism Party, MAS): and
2020 election, 234; and agrarian reform,
78; Ayopayan preference for loose association with, 158; Bolivia Cambia. Evo
Cumple rural funding program,

Movimiento al Socialismo *(continued)*
217, 217–18, 226–27; COB opposition
to, 151; concerns about NGOs pushing foreign influence, 150; conflicting
approaches to Indigenous people, 214,
241–42; conversion of Indigenous subjects into peasants as goal of, 82; and
creation of modern Indigenous citizens
through property ownership, 239–40;
decolonizing agenda of, 2; dissatisfaction with (2002), 205; efforts to return
to power, 77, 78; El Proceso de Cambio
reform program, 2; expectations for,
asymmetrical exchange tradition and,
222–24; and Indigenous collective land
titles, 67; and Indigenous subterranean
resource rights, loss of, 2, 157, 241; and
Indigenous traditions in creation of
legitimate authority, failure to understand, 203; and land redistribution, 78,
94; and mines, policies favoring collectivization of, 177; mix of top-down
revivalism and bottom-up asymmetrical exchange tradition, 230; Morales's
identity as Indigenous person as key
to appeal of, 224; overthrown of government, 76; reforms of, and limits on
Indigenous autonomy, 260n62; return
to power (1952), 78; rural education, as
key policy of, 215; state violence against
peasant labor unions under, 167; suppression of Indigenous protests, 205;
tension between ideals of, and rural
Indigenous people, 100; view of *colonos*
as victims, 94; view of rural laborers as
ignorant children, 109–11; and violence
following Morales' resignation, 234. *See
also* Indigenous revival movement of
MAS; land titling program
Movimiento de Izquierda Revolucionaria
(Revolutionary Left Movement, MIR),
MAS views on, 110
Movimiento Nacionalista Revolucionario
(MNR): and agrarian reform, 104; land
titles under, 138; promise of land redis-
tribution and collective land rights, 18
Munn, Nancy, 192, 260n61
Murra, John, 11, 70

National Bartolina Sisa Campesino, Indig-
enous, and Native Women's Union, 151
Native Community Lands. *See* Tierras
Comunitarias de Orígen
Natusch Busch, Alberto, 278n33
Nelson, Diane M., 278n36

ontology, Indigenous, land as living entity
bearing kinship and religious significance in, 101. *See also* earth-beings
orphans (*waqcha*): adoption into *hacendado*
family, 48, 49, 53, 92–93; descendants of
hacendados felt responsibility for care of
half-siblings, 58–60; *hacendados'* obligations to, 56–63, 64; out-of-wedlock children of *hacendados* as, 10, 55; servants
outside hacienda system as, 44
Orta, Andrew, 260n62, 271n27

Pachamama (earth mother): farmers' sacrifices to, xv, 50, 80; government-sponsored *ch'alla* dedicated to, 198, 199,
205; pro-Indigenous activists' effort to
return to worship of, 207, *211*; role in
harvest, 80; sacrificial offerings to, 207
Padilla, Celso, 172, 222, 243
Parry, Jonathan, 219
Patiño, Simón Iturri, 220–22, 227
patron saints' day celebrations, hacienda
servants' forced participation in, 50
PCB. *See* El Partido Comunista de Bolivia
peasant insurrection of 1780–81, 17
peasant militias of 1940s: attacks on *hacendados*, 74–75; attacks on villagers, 75;
Quechua villagers' ambivalence about,
75; skirmishes with armed guards, 75
peasant union in Ayopaya: aspects of traditional Andean organization in, 108; and
community governance, support for,
82; conflicts within, 82; *hacendados* and
sons' control of, after 1952 revolution,
82; and Indigenous interface with political power, 108; and *jallp'a sangres*, 82;
oversight of hacienda abolishment, 78,
79, 80–81; reshaping of property debate,
159; reversal of collective land titling,
143; state violence against, under MAS,
167; vote to boycott local mine, 189–90

Quechua *(continued)*
activism, reworking of existing political forms by, 195; ties to Mestizo families, 1. *See also* asymmetrical exchange relations in Ayopaya; hacienda owners' descendants, obligation to aid former workers; land titling program, Quechua opposition to
Quechua language, government regularization of, 211–12
Quechua uprising (early 2000s): disruption of social order, 48–49; and obligation of former *hacendados*, persistence despite, 49
Quispe, Ricardo (INRA official), 211–12

race, reification of, with reification of property, 160
racial hierarchy: institutional solutions, Quechua's skepticism about, 22; and land claims in Ayopaya, 138–42; land redistribution as tool against, xiv; Mestizo objections to historical accounting in new climate of legal equality, 179–81; and obligation of hacienda owners' descendants to aid former workers, 23, 44
racial violence in Bolivia, denial of, after fall of Morales, 233–34
Rami. *See fiesta de promoción* in Rami
Ramirez, Alejo, embarrassment at deference given by Quechua, 184–85, 187
Ramírez, Susan, 258n49
Ramos, Alcida Rita, 278n36
Ray, Raka, 40, 41
regional unity of Ayopaya: basis in shared history of hacienda violence and not abstract Indigeneity, 156–57; emphasis on, 152, 156; and preference for loose association with central government, 158
Reinaga, Fausto, xiv
"Relations of Servitude and Verification of Their Existence" (2008), 104–5
René. *See* Cruz, René (son of hacienda master)
reparations for slavery, and money and property-based ideas of repayment, 15, 242–43

requierimiento, in Spanish legal tradition, 261n73
Revolutionary Left Movement. *See* Movimiento de Izquierda Revolucionaria
rights-based models of Indigenous sovereignty, problems with, 242
Robinson, Cedric J., 283n61
Roca, Enrique (union leader), 204–6, 210
Rocha, Felix (union official), 74–75
Rodriguez, Carlos (former *hacendado*), adoption of servant's children, 91–93; antihacienda mob attacks on, 83, 87; as "good" *hacendado*, 83; and land redistribution activism, 86
Rodriguez, Fabio (relative of former *hacendado*): advice to Cruz on relations with Indigenous residents, 165, 174–75; claim to respect of Indigenous residents as family of former *hacendado*, 165, 175, 178; friendship with god-brother, 35, 36–37; obligation to aid former workers, 35–39; and Rodriguez families' relatively good relations with locals, 166–67; sale of gold mine to René Cruz, 165; sale of hacienda house to nephew, 35; villagers' hope to form mining collective with, 176–77
Rodriguez, Martín (relative of former hacienda owner): background of, 181; childhood on hacienda, 181; and deference still given to descendants of *hacendados*, 178, 185–89; demeanor of, as mixture of generosity and force, 181, 186–87; on family's children outside of marriage, 46–47; on family's original land grant, 47–48; as godfather to local children, 182–83, 186; hacienda land parcels retained by, 170; land inherited by, 91; lands and gold mine in Sarahuayto, 66–67; obligation of *hacendado* families to aid workers, acceptance of, 35–39, 171, 181–84, 225; as owner of land near René's gold mine, 165–66; popularity with villagers, 181–82, 183–84, 189–90; on René's labor unrest, 175–76; sale of mine to René Cruz, 170; sense of racialized superiority in, 181; sexual impropriety rumors, 191; as uncle of Fabio, 165

Snelgrove, C., 24

socialist land collectives: Ayopayans' opposition to, 18; focus on land rights, 18; MNR promise of, 18. *See also* collective land titling

Socialist Revolution of 1952: and murder of all "bad" *hacendados*, 166–67; and replacement of "Indigenous people" with "peasants," 108

socializing ("*compartir*") with workers, necessity of, for Mestizo elite in Ayopaya, 174, 178–79, 180–81, 188

Soliz, Flora: on anti-hacienda uprisings, 51; on *campesinos'* lack of tenderness toward former masters, 51–52; as daughter of former *hacendado*, 49; family history of, 56–57; generosity to former servants without corresponding demands, 49–50, 51–52, 178, 179; on her responsibility to help former dependents, 54–55; and kinship attachments, endurance of, 53, 62; legitimate authority of, through ethical aid relationships, 61–62, 74, 177, 225; and lost hacienda lands, lack of interest in return of, 54, 60; as mother figure, 55, 59, 62, 64; and muddying racial categories, 61; on ongoing anti-Mestizo violence, 51–52; and precarity of family status, 60

Soliz, Flora, and half-siblings: felt responsibility for care of, 58–60; generosity toward, 55; half sister as child of unwed servant in father's hacienda, 50; ingratitude of one sibling, 55; racialized superiority over, 56

Soliz, Hasintu (Quechua godchild): lack of gratitude to adopted mother, 55, 56, 59; refusal of interview, 269n38

Soliz, Raul (descendant of hacienda master): on debt owed to Quechua former servants, 61; and family history, willingness to discuss, 60; on his family, 56–57; on his family's humble origins, 59; on his mother's acceptance of half-siblings, 58–60; on his mother's Quechua half-siblings, 57, 58

Sorentino, Sara-Maria, 254n15

Spanish colonialism: denial of Indigenous land rights based on unfamiliarity with Western property concepts, 147; economic and political structures in, 71–73; forced resettlement program, 71, 72–73; forms of ownership in, 15, 262nn89–90; and gender normativity, 9–10; imposition of blood-based inheritance systems, 9–10; and imposition of modern landholding regime, 16; and Incan land gifts, disputes over, 71–72; influence of Inca systems on, 16, 70, 71, 72, 94; and *mitayo* labor in mines, 72; and money tribute, introduction of, 71; negotiations with Indigeneity in, 157; ongoing influence of, xii–xiii; principles of land ownership in, and *dominio*, 15–16; seizure of Indigenous lands through imposed modern landholding regime, 16; and theories of property, 9

Spanish language, and loss of authentic Indigeneity, 251n1

spatial history (Carter), 68

Stephenson, Marcia, 40

Stoler, Ann, 41

Strathern, Marilyn, 62, 260n61

Sylvia (research assistant), 91, 92

Taki Onqoy rebellions, 107

TallBear, Kim, 13

Tapia, Elvira (municipal worker), 203–6, 210

TCOs. *See* Tierras Comunitarias de Orígen

Tekelenburg, A., 28

Territorio Indígena Parque Nacional Isiboro Sécure (TIPNIS): effectiveness of autonomy of, as issue for Ayopayans, 152; highway through, police repression of mass mobilizations against, 172, 214, 235, 241

Tesis India (Reinaga), xiv

"Theses on the Philosophy of History" (Benjamin), 252n7

Thomas, Deborah, 254n14

Thomson, E. P., 43

Tierras Comunitarias de Orígen (Native Community Lands, TCOs): titling of, in MAS land reform programs, 106. *See also* collective land titling

Founded in 1893,
UNIVERSITY OF CALIFORNIA PRESS
publishes bold, progressive books and journals
on topics in the arts, humanities, social sciences,
and natural sciences—with a focus on social
justice issues—that inspire thought and action
among readers worldwide.

The UC PRESS FOUNDATION
raises funds to uphold the press's vital role
as an independent, nonprofit publisher, and
receives philanthropic support from a wide
range of individuals and institutions—and from
committed readers like you. To learn more, visit
ucpress.edu/supportus.